BARRON'S BUSINESS TRAVELERS

JAPANESE FOR THE BUSINESS TRAVELER

Nobuo Akiyama

Professorial Lecturer in Japanese
The Paul H. Nitze
School of Advanced International Studies
The Johns Hopkins University
Washington, D.C.

and

Carol Akiyama

Language Training Consultant
Washington, D.C.

BARRON'S

Peta

Portions of Part I of this book are reprinted with permission from *Japanese at a Glance*, by Nobuo Akiyama and Carol Akiyama, published by Barron's Educational Series, Inc.

All inquiries should be addressed to:
Barron's Educational Series, Inc.
250 Wireless Boulevard
Hauppauge, New York 11788

Library of Congress Catalog Card No. 94-18090

International Standard Book No. 0-8120-1770-6

Library of Congress Cataloging-in-Publication Data
Akiyama, Nobuo.
Japanese for the business traveler : dictionary and reference for international business : phrases and words you need to know / by Nobuo Akiyama and Carol Akiyama.
p. cm. — (Barron's business travelers)
Rev. ed. of: Talking business in Japanese. 1988.
ISBN 0-8120-1770-6
1. Business—Dictionaries. 2. English language—Dictionaries—Japanese. 3. Business—Dictionaries—Japanese. 4. Japanese language—Dictionaries—English. I. Akiyama, Carol. II. Akiyama, Nobuo. Talking business in Japanese. III. Title. IV. Series.
HF1002.A34 1994
650'.03—dc20

94-18090
CIP

PRINTED IN THE UNITED STATES OF AMERICA

4567 8800 987654321

CONTENTS

Preface v

I. **PRONUNCIATION GUIDE** 1

II. **INTRODUCTION** 3
Doing Business in Japan 3

Before You Go... 5

III. **BASIC WORDS AND PHRASES** 8
General words and phrases for getting by, including amenities, answers to standard questions, and other essential expressions.

IV. **BUSINESS DICTIONARY** 51
English to Japanese 51
Japanese to English 144
Key Words for Key Industries 233

V. **GENERAL INFORMATION** 300
Abbreviations 300
Weights and Measures 308
Temperature and Climate 308
Communications 309
Postal Services 311
Major Holidays 312
Time Zones 313
Currency Information 313
Major Periodicals 315
Annual Trade Fairs 316
Travel Times 318
Travel Tips 321
Major Hotels 323
Major Restaurants 326
Useful Addresses 327
Road Signs in Japanese 329
Maps 335
Travel Diary 340

PREFACE

It is the nature of business to seek out new markets for its products, to find more efficient ways to bring its goods to more people. In the global marketplace, this often means travel to foreign countries, where languages and customs are different. Even when a businessperson knows the language of the host country, the specific and often idiosyncratic terminology of the business world can be an obstacle to successful negotiations in a second language. Pocket phrase books barely scratch the surface of these problems, while standard business dictionaries prove too cumbersome.

Now there is a solution—*Barron's Japanese for the Business Traveler*. Here is the essential pocket reference for all those who are traveling to Japan on business. Whether your business is manufacturing or finance, communications or sales, this three-part guide will put the right words in your mouth and the best expressions in your correspondence. It is a book you'll carry with you on every trip and take to every meeting. But it is also the reference you'll keep on your desk in the office. This is the business dictionary for people who do business with the Japanese.

Barron's Japanese for the Business Traveler offers you the following features:

- a 6,000-entry list of basic business terms, dealing with accounting, advertising and sales, banking, computers, export/import, finance and investment, labor relations, management, manufacturing, marketing, retail and wholesale sales, and more;
- a quick guide to basic terms and expressions for getting by when you don't know the language;
- a pronunciation guide for speaking the language;
- a comprehensive list of common business abbreviations;
- reference words for numbers and amounts, days of the week, months of the year, and seasons;
- converstion tables for metric and customary measurements;
- lists of major holidays, annual trade fairs, travel times between cities, average temperatures throughout the year;
- information on international currencies, country and city telephone codes, useful addresses in Japan.

This book is one of a new series of business dictionaries. We welcome your comments on additional phrases that could be included in future editions.

I. PRONUNCIATION GUIDE

This book assumes that you are already somewhat familiar with the basic pronunciation rules of Japanese, but for those who need a little help, here are some guidelines.

Writing Conventions

For each Japanese phrase or vocabulary item used in this book, both the Japanese writing and the Hepburn spelling are given. The latter is the most common system of Romanization of Japanese words; it's called *romaji.*

Vowels

Japanese vowels are more like those of Spanish than English.

The following vowels are short and pure, with no glide—that is, they are not diphthongs.

JAPANESE VOWEL	SOUND IN ENGLISH	EXAMPLE	
a	as in f**a**ther	*akai*	ah-kah-ee
e	as in m**e**n	*ebi*	eh-bee
i	as in s**ee**	*imi*	ee-mee
o	as in b**oa**t	*otoko*	oh-toh-koh
u	as in f**oo**d	*uma*	oo-mah

The following vowels are like the ones above, but lengthened.

JAPANESE VOWEL	SOUND IN ENGLISH	EXAMPLE	
ā	as in f**a**ther, but lengthened	*batā*	bah-$\overline{\text{tah}}$
ei	as in m**e**n, but lengthened	*eigo*	$\overline{\text{eh}}$-goh
ii	as in s**ee**, but lengthened	*iiharu*	$\overline{\text{ee}}$-hah-roo
ō	as in b**oa**t, but lengthened	*ōsama*	$\overline{\text{oh}}$-sah-mah
ū	as in f**oo**d, but lengthened	*yūbin*	y$\overline{\text{oo}}$-been

And keep in mind:

1. Long vowels are important: pronouncing a long vowel incorrectly can result in a different word or even an unintelligible one. For instance, *obasan* (oh-bah-sahn) means aunt; *obāsan* (oh-$\overline{\text{bah}}$-sahn) means grandmother. *Ojisan* (oh-jee-sahn) means uncle; *ojiisan* (oh-$\overline{\text{jee}}$-sahn) means grandfather. *Seki* (seh-kee) means seat; *seiki* ($\overline{\text{seh}}$-kee) means century.
2. Sometimes the **i** and the **u** are not pronounced. This usually occurs between voiceless consonants (p, t, k, ch, f, h, s, sh), or at the end of a word following a

voiceless consonant. An example you may already know is *sukiyaki* (skee-yah-kee). This word for a popular Japanese dish begins not with *soo*, but with *skee*. You omit the **u** entirely. In *tabemashita* (tah-beh-mahsh-tah), which means "I ate," the last **i** is omitted.

Consonants

With a few exceptions, Japanese consonants are similar to those of English. Note the differences:

- **f** The English **f** is pronounced by a passage of air between the upper teeth and the lower lip. To make the Japanese **f**, blow air lightly between your lips as if you were just beginning a whistle.
- **g** As in **g**o. You may also hear it pronounced as the **ng** sound in ri**ng**, although not at the beginning of a word.
- **r** This is different from the English **r**. The Japanese **r** is made by lightly touching the tip of the tongue to the bony ridge behind the upper teeth, almost in the English **d** position. It's more like the Spanish **r**, but it's not flapped or trilled.
- **s** It's always hissed, as in **s**o; it's *never* pronounced as in hi**s** or plea**s**ure.

Please note:

1. If you have trouble making these consonants the Japanese way, your English pronunciation will be intelligible and will not be considered incorrect.
2. Some Japanese consonants are doubled. In English, this is just a feature of spelling and often doesn't affect pronunciation. In Japanese, the doubling is important and may change the meaning of a word. For example, *kite kudasai* (kee-teh koo-dah-sah-ee) means "please put it on (clothing)." *Kitte kudasai* (keet-teh koo-dah-sah-ee) means "please cut it." In a word with a doubled consonant, don't say the consonant twice—just hold the sound longer.

Loan Words

If you know English, you may already know more Japanese than you think. There are thousands of English loan words in everday use in Japan. Most of these common words have been borrowed with no change in meaning. But there is a change in pronunciation. This can be tricky. On the one hand, you're secure with the familiar words; on the other, if you pronounce them as you're used to doing, you won't be understood, and you won't understand the words when Japanese use them. For example, **baseball** won't work; *bēsubōru* (beh-soo-boh-roo) will! If you order a **beer**, you might not get one; say *bīru* (bee-roo) and you will. (Note the long vowel: *biru* with a short vowel means **building**.)

Here are a few more examples of familiar words with somewhat different pronunciations in Japanese:

gasoline	*gasorin*	gah-soh-reen
pocket	*poketto*	poh-keht-toh
pink	*pinku*	peen-koo
ballpoint pen	*bōru pen*	boh-roo pehn
supermarket	*sūpā*	soo-pah
yacht	*yotto*	yoht-toh
handkerchief	*hankachi*	hahn-kah-chee

II. INTRODUCTION

DOING BUSINESS IN JAPAN

Doing business with another culture and in another language can be a difficult and mystifying experience. Customs and procedures may be quite different from what is perceived as the "normal" way of conducting oneself in a business circumstance.

In this introduction, some of the customs and economic aspects of Japan are outlined to help you conduct business there effectively. Some basic knowledge of these factors will help you become more accustomed to the business situation of Japan.

Usual Hours of Operation

	Weekdays	**Saturdays**	**Sundays & Holidays**
Banks	9:00–3:00	Closed	Closed
Post Offices*	9:00–5:00	Closed	Closed
Department Stores**	10:00–7:00	10:00–7:00	10:00–7:00
Stores	10:00–7:00	10:00–7:00	10:00–7:00
Government Offices	9:00–5:00	Closed	Closed
Large Companies	9(9:30)–5:00	9(9:30)–12:00 or Closed	Closed

*Main post office branches are open on Saturdays. Check the business hours with the individual branch.

**Closed once a week.

Business Customs

Because so many Japanese customs differ from Western ones to begin with, conducting business there presents a special challenge. No foreigner is expected to behave exactly as the Japanese do. But these guidelines should prove useful.

- Use personal contacts whenever possible. Face-to-face meetings, especially initial ones, are far more effective than letters.
- Arrange for a personal introduction to the Japanese businessperson or government official you want to meet. The importance of proper introductions in Japan cannot be overestimated. Finding a suitable friend or acquaintance to perform this function for you may take some effort, but it will pay off in how you are received initially. It may even affect whether the relationship will continue.
- When important issues are at stake in your business dealings, a high official in your company should make a courtesy visit to his or her counterpart in the Japanese company. This is not to discuss business, but to pay respects and establish a personal relationship.
- Present your business card whenever you meet someone new in the business context. Your airline or hotel desk staff can help you have the cards printed. They should have English on one side and Japanese on the other. When handing your card to the new

acquaintance, do it with some care, making sure it's facing so the recipient can read it. The Japanese card-exchanging ritual has a practical function: It establishes who you are and where you rank in your company, and it relieves both parties of the need to rely on memory for names and addresses. A file of these business cards is a valuable asset to anyone doing business in Japan.

- In business situations, conservative dress and behavior are more appropriate than informality.
- Don't use first names with Japanese businesspersons. Use the English *Mr.*, *Mrs.*, *Miss*, or *Ms.* with the last name, or use the last name followed by the Japanese word *san*. For high-level company or government officials, learn the person's title in Japanese beforehand, and use it when speaking to or referring to him or her.
- When negotiations appear to be going slowly, be patient. Decisions are based on a process of consensus, which can take time. Once the decision is made, however, things can move quickly.
- If your Japanese colleagues take you out for an evening of dining and drinking, although there probably won't be any negotiating, consider it part of the process of doing business. It's a chance for you to get to know each other in a less formal situation than in the office, specifically, for the Japanese to see how comfortable they feel with you. Relax and enjoy yourself, but at the same time, take it seriously. Important bonds of trust are built during these informal sessions.

General Government Policy and Economic Situation

From World War II defeat in 1945 to world superpower status today, Japan's economic achievement has been called a modern miracle. Indeed, Japan has become the free world's second greatest economic power despite two serious obstacles to development: First, only 20 percent of the land is usable—the rest is too mountainous—and more than half of that is farmed. Most of the 124 million people live on just 2 percent of the land, making Japan one of the world's most densely populated nations. Second, the lack of coal, oil, gas, and other natural resources makes Japan dependent on imports for energy and most raw materials.

With limited natural resources, Japan rapidly became an export-oriented economy, importing raw materials and exporting high-quality finished goods. The 1960s saw big gains, with the government initiating economic policies that would protect domestic industries and engender cooperation between the public and private sectors for the common good. Until the early 1970s, the economy expanded at an average of about 10 percent each year. After the first oil crisis in 1973, that rate slowed down somewhat to a 5 percent yearly average, still high in comparison with growth rates in other industrialized countries. This pace continued through the mid-1980s.

Since the latter half of the 1980s, Japan has faced new successes, some setbacks, and new challenges. The newly industrialized countries such as South Korea, Taiwan, Thailand, and Singapore, with cheaper labor costs and improving technology, are competing in industries where Japan has dominated, such as iron and steel, shipbuilding, automobiles, electronics, and textiles. Many Japanese companies are now going overseas, establishing plants in the United States, Asia, and elsewhere. This trend toward internationalization of Japanese industry continues.

The appreciating value of the yen has caused problems, especially for small and medium-sized export-oriented industries. And Japan's huge trade surpluses have evoked "get tough" responses from some other countries, especially its largest trading partner, the United States. Japan has been criticized for tariff and nontariff barriers to free trade.

The Japanese government is responding to those charges. They are reorganizing Japan's domestic economic structure, trying to open their markets to foreign goods and services. Lower interest rates and new tax reforms make more money available for domestic consumer spending. In addition to increasing foreign access to Japanese markets and encouraging the Japanese to buy foreign products, the government is trying to reduce its own role in the market. Part of the strategy is privatization of three huge public corporations: Nippon Telegraph and Telephone (NTT), Japan Tobacco and Salt (JTS), and the Japanese National Railways (JNR). The divestiture has been proceeding in phases.

For the future, two trends emerge. One is the growth of advanced technology. Both the government and the private sector are devoting significant resources to research and development in this area. Another is the growth of service industries. Japan is moving from an industry-oriented to a service-oriented economy. For example, Japanese banks and securities companies are already key players in world financial markets. Japan is now one of the most liquid nations and the Tokyo Stock Exchange is one of the biggest markets in the world.

Statistics given in this section are generally accurate for the early 1990s.

Main imports: petroleum, coal, liquified natural gas, machinery and equipment, metal ores, other raw materials, foodstuffs, chemicals, textiles, textile materials.

Main exports: machinery and equipment, motor vehicles, scientific/optical equipment, video cassette recorders, vessels, TV and radio receivers, metals, iron and steel products, chemicals, textiles, foodstuffs, other manufactured goods.

Inflation rate: 2.1%

Principal trading partners: United States, Canada, European Community, Australia, South Korea, Indonesia, Saudi Arabia, China, Malaysia, Taiwan, Thailand.

Population: 124 million

Language: Japanese

Religion: Buddhism, Shintoism

GDP: $3,346 billion

Per capita GNP: $27,005

Unemployment rate: 2.2%

BEFORE YOU GO

Passports

All permanent U.S. citizens must carry a valid passport in order to travel to Japan. Application should be made by mail or in person several months in advance to either (1) a U.S. Passport Agency office (located in 12 major cities and Washington, D.C.), (2) designated U.S. Post Offices throughout the country, or (3) state and federal courthouses.

Visas

U.S. citizens who hold transit or return-trip tickets may visit Japan either on business or for pleasure for up to 90 days without a visa. For longer trips, application can be made through your travel agent or directly to the Japanese consulate in the following cities: Anchorage, Chicago, Honolulu, Houston, Los Angeles, New Orleans, New York City, Portland (Oregon), San Francisco, and Seattle; also the Japanese embassy in Washington, D.C.

Immunizations

There are no immunization requirements (against smallpox or other diseases) for entry into Japan or upon return to the United States. If you plan to include travel in Southeast Asia, consult your doctor or the nearest U.S. Public Health Service office for recommended inoculations.

Customs and Currency Regulations

In general, travelers to Japan from the United States are allowed to bring in fairly generous amounts of duty-free items for their own *personal* use. These items include tobacco, alcohol, perfume, and other items in the following amounts:

200 cigarettes *or* 50 cigars *or* 250 grams of tobacco (about 1/2 lb.)
3 bottles (about 1/5 of a gallon each) of alcoholic beverages
2 ounces of perfume
Other articles altogether worth less than 200,000 yen

If you are not carrying items well in excess of these amounts, a simple statement of "nothing to declare" will be respected by Japanese customs officials.

For personal valuables like jewelry or furs and foreign-made items like watches, cameras, typewriters, or tape recorders (acquired before your trip) you should have proof of prior possession or register them with U.S. customs before departure. This will ensure that they are not subject to duty by the United States upon return.

Upon return to the United States each person (including children) has a duty-free allowance of $400, including 100 cigars and 1 carton of cigarettes. Each adult may bring in only 1 liter of wine *or* other liquor duty-free. Gifts worth $50 or less may be sent home subject to certain restrictions. For further up-to-date details, ask your travel agent or airline to provide a copy of U.S. customs regulations or write: U.S. Customs Service, P.O. Box 7407, Washington, D.C. 20044, and ask for a copy of the booklet, "Know Before You Go."

There is no restriction on the amounts of foreign currency (or traveler's checks) that foreign nationals may bring into or take out of Japan, subject to a customs declaration. Up to 5 million yen may be taken out and any amount brought in.

Traveler's Checks, Credit Cards, Foreign Exchange

Although all major international traveler's checks and credit cards are accepted by large travel agencies and most of the better (more expensive) hotels, restaurants, and shops in Japan, it is always best to check at each establishment beforehand. The checks most recognized are: American Express, Visa, and Thomas Cook & Sons. The cards most acceptable are: American Express, MasterCard, Visa, and Diners Club.

For record-keeping, when charging, make sure that the following information appears on the original and all copies of your bill: the correct date; the type of currency being charged (yen); the official exchange rate for that date (if possible); and the total amount of the bill.

The airport where you arrive in Japan is a good place to buy yen. The exchange rates are current and fair.

Driving in Japan

An American (state) license is *not* valid for driving in Japan. You will need to obtain an international driver's document through the AAA or a local automobile club. Also, despite local rules, car rental agencies may restrict rentals to people 21 years old or over. AND REMEMBER, in Japan, drive on the *left*!

Electrical Appliances

Japan's system of electric current and voltage is basically the same as ours. In some places, including Tokyo, a difference in frequency (cycles) will only affect those appliances with precise timing requirements like record players, CD players, and (electric) clocks.

III. BASIC WORDS AND PHRASES

Greetings

Good morning.	おはようございます。 *Ohayō gozaimasu.*
Good afternoon.	こんにちは。 *Konnichiwa.*
Good evening.	こんばんは。 *Konbanwa.*
Good night.	おやすみなさい。 *Oyasuminasai.*
My name is ______________ .	私の名前は、_________です。 *Watakushi no namae wa, _________ desu.*
What's your name?	あなたのお名前は。 *Anata no onamae wa.*
How are you?	お元気ですか。 *Ogenki desu ka.*
Fine, thank you.	はい、おかげさまで。 *Hai, okagesama de.*
Goodbye.	さようなら。 *Sayōnara.*

Common Expressions

Yes.	はい。／ええ。 *Hai./Ee.*
No.	いいえ。 *Iie.*
Mr./Mrs./Miss/Ms.	さん *san*
Thank you.	どうもありがとう。 *Dōmo arigatō.*
Pleased to meet you.	はじめて、おめにかかります。 *Hajimete, ome ni kakarimasu.*
You're welcome.	いいえ、どういたしまして。 *Iie, dō itashimashite.*
I'm sorry.	ごめんなさい。／すみません。 *Gomennasai./Sumimasen.*
Excuse me.	ごめんなさい。／失礼します。 *Gomennasai./Shitsurei shimasu.*
Please.	どうぞ。／お願いします。 *Dōzo./Onegai shimasu.*
Hello (for telephone calls, for getting someone's attention).	もしもし。 *Moshi moshi.*
Of course.	もちろん。 *Mochiron.*
Maybe.	多分。 *Tabun.*

Pardon me, but ___________ .	すみませんが。 *Sumimasen ga.*
It's all right.	だいじょうぶです。 *Daijōbu desu.*
It doesn't matter.	かまいません。 *Kamaimasen.*
With pleasure.	喜んで。 *Yorokonde.*
I don't mind.	いいですよ。／かまいません。 *Ii desu yo./Kamaimasen.*
Oh, I see.	ああ、そうですか。 *Aa, sō desu ka.*
Is that so?	そうですか。 *Sō desu ka.*
Really?	そうですか。 *Sō desu ka.*
Let's go.	行きましょう。 *Ikimashō.*
Shall we go?	行きましょうか。 *Ikimashō ka.*
Let's (go/eat/etc.)	さあ。 *Saa.*
No thank you.	いいえ、けっこうです。 *Iie, kekkō desu.*
I don't want it.	いりません。／けっこうです。 *Irimasen./Kekkō desu.*
I think so.	そうだと、思います。 *So dā to, omoimasu.*
I don't think so.	そう思いません。 *Sō omoimasen.*
It's interesting/fun.	おもしろいです。 *Omoshiroi desu.*
It's over/I'm finished.	終わました。 *Owarimashita.*
Yes, it is.	はい、そうです。 *Hai, sō desu.*
No, it isn't.	いいえ、ちがいます。 *Iie, chigaimasu.*
Just a moment, please.	ちょっと待って下さい。 *Chotto, matte kudasai.*
Not yet.	まだです。 *Mada desu.*
Soon.	もうすぐです。 *Mō sugu desu.*
Right away (request).	すぐ、お願いします。 *Sugu, onegai shimasu.*
Right away (response).	ただいま。 *Tadaima.*

Now.	今。 *Ima.*
Later.	あとで。 *Ato de.*

Some Questions and Question Words

What's the matter?	どうか、しましたか。 *Dō ka, shimashita ka.*
What's this?	これは、何ですか。 *Kore wa, nan desu ka.*
Where's the ________ ?	________は、どこですか。 ________*wa, doko desu ka.*
• bathroom	お手洗／トイレ／お便所 *otearai/toire/obenjo*
• dining room	食堂 *shokudō*
• entrance	入口 *iriguchi*
• exit	出口 *deguchi*
• telephone	電話 *denwa*
When?	いつ。 *Itsu.*
Where?	どこ。 *Doko.*
Why?	なぜ。／どうして。 *Naze./Dōshite.*
Who?	だれ。／どなた。 *Dare./Donata.*
Which?	どれ。／どちら。 *Dore./Dochira.*
What?	何。 *Nani.*
How?	どうやって。 *Dōyatte.*
How much?	どのくらい。 *Dono kurai.*
How much (money)?	いくら。 *Ikura.*

Needs

Could you tell me where the ________ is?	________がどこか、教えて下さい。 ________ *ga doko ka, oshiete kudasai.*
Could you give me ________ ?	________を下さい。 ________ *o kudasai.*
I need ________ .	________がいります。 ________ *ga irimasu.*

I want ________ .	________が欲しいです。 ________ *ga hoshii desu.*
I want to go to ________ .	________に、行きたいです。 ________ *ni, ikitai desu.*
I want to see ________ .	________を見たいです。 ________ *o mitai desu.*
I want to buy ________ .	________を買いたいです。 ________ *o kaitai desu.*
I want to eat ________ .	________を食べたいです。 ________ *o tabetai desu.*
I want to drink ________ .	________を飲みたいです。 ________ *o nomitai desu.*

Your Personal Condition

I'm thirsty.	のどが、かわいています。 *Nodo ga, kawaite imasu.*
I'm hungry.	おなかが、すいています。 *Onaka ga, suite imasu.*
I'm full.	おなかが、いっぱいです。 *Onaka ga, ippai desu.*
I'm tired.	つかれています。 *Tsukarete imasu.*
I'm sleepy.	ねむいです。 *Nemui desu.*
I'm sick.	病気です。 *Byōki desu.*
I'm fine.	元気です。 *Genki desu.*
I'm all right.	だいじょうぶです。 *Daijōbu desu.*

Some Adjectives

It's cold.	寒いです。 *Samui desu.*
It's hot.	暑いです。 *Atsui desu.*
It's hot and humid.	蒸し暑いです。 *Mushiatsui desu.*
pretty, beautiful/ugly	きれい／みにくい *kirei/minikui*
delicious/awful-tasting	おいしい／まずい *oishii/mazui*
good, fine/bad	いい／悪い *ii/warui*
fast, quick/slow	速い／おそい *hayai/osoi*
high/low	高い／低い *takai/hikui*

expensive/cheap	高い／安い *takai/yasui*
hot/cold	熱い／冷たい *atsui/tsumetai*
same	同じ *onaji*
warm/cool	暖かい／涼しい *atatakai/suzushii*
big/small	大きい／小さい *ōkii/chiisai*
long/short	長い／短い *nagai/mijikai*
strong/weak	強い／弱い *tsuyoi/yowai*
far/near	遠い／近い *tōi/chikai*
wide/narrow	広い／せまい *hiroi/semai*
heavy/light	重い／軽い *omoi/karui*
new/old	新しい／古い *atarashii/furui*
young	若い *wakai*
dark/light	暗い／明るい *kurai/akarui*
quiet/noisy	静か／やかましい *shizuka/yakamashii*
a lot, many/a little, few	たくさん／すこし *takusan/sukoshi*
intelligent/stupid	利口／ばか *rikō/baka*
right/wrong	正しい／悪い *tadashii/warui*
easy/difficult	易しい／難しい *yasashii/muzukashii*
early/late	早い／おそい *hayai/osoi*

Pronouns

I	私 *watakushi*
you (singular)	あなた *anata*
he/she	彼／彼女 *kare/kanojo*
we	私たち *watakushi tachi*

you (plural)	あなたたち *anata tachi*
they	彼ら *karera*

Note: To form the possessive, simply add the particle no to the above pronouns:

my	私の *watakushi no*

More Basic Words

here/there/over there	ここ／そこ／あそこ *koko/soko/asoko*
this/that/that over there (nouns)	これ／それ／あれ *kore/sore/are*
this/that/that over there (adjectives)	この／その／あの *kono/sono/ano*
and (between nouns)	と *to*
and (between sentences)	そして *soshite*
but	けれども／でも *keredomo/demo*
or	それとも／または／あるいは *soretomo/matawa/aruiwa*
also	も／また *mo/mata*
before	________の前に ________ *no mae ni*
during	________の間に ________ *no aida ni*
after	________のあとで ________ *no ato de*
to	________へ ________ *e*
from	________から ________ *kara*
at	________で ________ *de*
in	________に ________ *ni*
up	________の上に ________ *no ue ni*
down	________の下に ________ *no shita ni*
inside	________の中に ________ *no naka ni*
outside	________の外に ________ *no soto ni*

on	________の上に ________ *no ue ni*
near	________の近くに ________ *no chikaku ni*

Communicating

Do you understand?	わかりますか。 *Wakarimasu ka.*
Yes, I understand.	はい、わかります。 *Hai, wakarimasu.*
No, I don't understand.	いいえ、わかりません。 *Iie, wakarimasen.*
Do you understand English?	英語がわかりますか。 *Eigo ga wakarimasu ka.*
I speak a little Japanese.	日本語が、少し話せます。 *Nihon go ga, sukoshi hanasemasu.*
I know very little Japanese.	日本語は、ほんの少ししか知りません。 *Nihon go wa, hon no sukoshi shika shirimasen.*
I don't understand Japanese.	日本語は、わかりません。 *Nihon go wa, wakarimasen.*
Could you repeat it, please?	もう一度、お願いします。 *Mō ichido, onegai shimasu.*
Please speak slowly.	もう少し、ゆっくり話して下さい。 *Mō sukoshi, yukkuri hanashite kudasai.*
Write it down on the paper, please.	紙に書いて下さい。 *Kami ni kaite kudasai.*
Is there anyone who understands English?	だれか、英語がわかる人がいますか。 *Dare ka, eigo ga wakaru hito ga imasu ka.*
Do you speak English?	英語を話しますか。 *Eigo o hanashimasu ka.*
What's this called in Japanese?	これは、日本語で何といいますか。 *Kore wa, Nihon go de nan to iimasu ka.*
What do you call this?	これは、何といいますか。 *Kore wa, nan to iimasu ka.*
Excuse me, could you help me, please?	すみませんが、助けていただけませんか。 *Sumimasen ga, tasukete itadakemasen ka.*
Please point to the phrase in this book.	この本から、適当な文を選んで、示してください。 *Kono hon kara, tekitō na bun o erande shimeshite kudasai.*

Introductions

Who is that?	あの方は、どなたですか。 *Ano kata wa, donata desu ka.*
Do you know who that is?	あの方は、どなたかごぞんじですか。 *Ano kata wa, donata ka gozonji desu ka.*
I would like to meet him/her (literally, *that person*).	あの方に、おめにかかりたいのですが。 *Ano kata ni, ome ni kakaritai no desu ga.*

Would you introduce me to him/her (that person)?	あの方に、紹介していただけませんか。 *Ano kata ni, shōkai shite itadakemasen ka.*
Pardon me, may I introduce myself?	突然失礼ですが、自己紹介してもよろしいですか。 *Totsuzen shitsurei desu ga, jiko shōkai shitemo yoroshii desu ka.*
My name is Jean Brown.	私の名前は、ジーン・ブラウンです。 *Watakushi no namae wa, Jīn Buraun desu.*
What's your name?	あなたのお名前は。 *Anata no onamae wa.*
How do you do?	初めまして、どうぞよろしく。 *Hajimemashite. Dōzo yoroshiku.*
How do you do? (reply)	初めまして、こちらこそよろしく。 *Hajimemashite. Kochira koso yoroshiku.*
I'm honored to meet you.	おめにかかれて、光栄です。 *Ome ni kakarete, kōei desu.*
I'm glad to meet you.	よろしくお願いします。 *Yoroshiku onegai shimasu.*

Cards

card	名刺 *meishi*
Here's my card.	名刺をどうぞ。 *Meishi o dōzo.*
Thank you very much.	ありがとうございます。 *Arigatō gozaimasu.*
Here's mine.	私のもどうぞ。 *Watakushi no mo dōzo.*
May I have your card?	名刺をちょうだいできますか。 *Meishi o chōdai dekimasu ka.*

Useful Sentences

Where are you from?	お国は、どちらですか。 *Okuni wa, dochira desu ka.*
How long will you be staying?	どの位、滞在の予定ですか。 *Dono kurai, taizai no yotei desu ka.*
Where are you staying?	どちらにお泊りですか *Dochira ni otomari desu ka.*
Where can I reach you?	連絡先は、どこですか。 *Renraku saki wa, doko desu ka.*
Here's my address and phone number.	これが私の住所と電話番号です。 *Kore ga, watakushi no jūsho to denwa bangō desu.*
Could you pick me up at my hotel this evening?	今晩私のホテルへむかえに来ていただけますか。 *Konban, watakushi no hoteru e mukae ni kite itadakemasu ka.*

See you later.	それでは、のちほど。 *Soredewa nochi hodo.*
See you tomorrow.	それでは、また明日。 *Soredewa mata ashita.*

Useful Nouns

address	住所 *jūsho*
amount	量 *ryō*
appointment	面会の約束 *menkai no yakusoku*
bill (payment)	請求書 *seikyū sho*
business	ビジネス *bijinesu*
car	自動車 *jidōsha*
cashier	会計所 *kaikei sho*
check (payment)	勘定 *kanjō*
city	市 *shi*
customs	税関 *zeikan*
date	日付け *hizuke*
document	書類 *shorui*
elevator	エレベーター *erebētā*
friend	友人 *yūjin*
hanger	ハンガー *hangā*
key	鍵 *kagi*
list	リスト *risuto*
magazine	雑誌 *zasshi*
maid	メイド *meido*
mail	郵便 *yūbin*
manager	マネージャー *manējā*

map	地図 *chizu*
mistake	間違い *machigai*
money	お金 *okane*
name	名前 *namae*
newspaper	新聞 *shinbun*
office	オフィス *ofisu*
package	小包 *kozutsumi*
paper	紙 *kami*
passport	パスポート *pasupōto*
pen	ペン *pen*
pencil	鉛筆 *enpitsu*
porter	ポーター *pōtā*
post office	郵便局 *yūbin kyoku*
postage	郵便料金 *yūbin ryōkin*
price	値段 *nedan*
raincoat	レインコート *reinkōto*
reservation	予約 *yoyaku*
restroom	お手洗い *otearai*
restaurant	レストラン *resutoran*
road	道 *michi*
room	部屋 *heya*
shirt	シャツ *shatsu*
shoes	くつ *kutsu*
shower	シャワー *shawā*
store	店 *mise*

street	通り／道 *tōri/michi*
suit	スーツ *sūtsu*
suitcase	スーツケース *sūtsukēsu*
taxi	タクシー *takushī*
telegram	電報 *denpō*
telephone	電話 *denwa*
ticket	切符 *kippu*
time	時間 *jikan*
tip	チップ *chippu*
train	列車 *ressha*
train station	駅 *eki*
trip	旅行 *ryokō*
umbrella	かさ *kasa*
waiter	ウェイター *weitā*
watch	時計 *tokei*
water	水 *mizu*

Useful Verbs

accept	引受ける *hikiukeru*
answer	答える *kotaeru*
arrive	着く *tsuku*
ask	尋ねる *tazuneru*
begin (transitive)	始める *hajimeru*
(intransitive)	始まる *hajimaru*
bring	持って来る *motte kuru*

buy	買う *kau*
call (telephone)	電話する *denwa suru*
carry	運ぶ *hakobu*
change	かえる *kaeru*
close (transitive)	閉める *shimeru*
(intransitive)	閉まる *shimaru*
come	来る *kuru*
confirm	確認する *kakunin suru*
continue	続ける *tsuzukeru*
cost	かかる *kakaru*
deliver	届ける *todokeru*
direct	道を教える *michi o oshieru*
do	する *suru*
eat	食べる *taberu*
end	終わる *owaru*
enter	入る *hairu*
examine	確かめる *tashikameru*
exchange	交換する *kōkan suru*
feel	感じる *kanjiru*
finish	終える *oeru*
fix	直す *naosu*
follow	あとをついていく *ato o tsuite iku*
forget	忘れる *wasureru*
forward	転送する *tensō suru*
get	手に入れる *te ni ireru*

give	あげる *ageru*
go	行く *iku*
hear	聞く *kiku*
help	助ける *tasukeru*
keep	とっておく *totte oku*
know	知る *shiru*
learn	習う *narau*
leave	出発する *shuppatsu suru*
like	好む *konomu*
listen	聞く *kiku*
look	見る *miru*
lose	なくす *nakusu*
make	作る *tsukuru*
mean	意味する *imi suru*
meet	会う *au*
miss (transportation)	乗りそこなう *norisokonau*
need	いる *iru*
open (transitive)	開ける *akeru*
(intransitive)	開く *aku*
order	注文する *chūmon suru*
pay	払う *harau*
prefer	むしろ________を好む *mushiro ________ o konomu*
prepare	準備する *junbi suru*
present	あげる *ageru*
prove	証明する *shōmei suru*

put	置く *oku*
read	読む *yomu*
receive	受取る *uketoru*
recommend	推薦する *suisen suru*
register	登録する *tōroku suru*
repair	修理する *shūri suru*
repeat	繰り返す *kurikaesu*
rest	休む *yasumu*
return	帰る *kaeru*
run	走る *hashiru*
say	言う *iu*
see	見る *miru*
send	送る *okuru*
show	示す *shimesu*
sit	座る *suwaru*
speak	話す *hanasu*
stand	立つ *tatsu*
start	出発する *shuppatsu suru*
stay	滞在する *taizai suru*
stop (transitive)	止める *tomeru*
(intransitive)	止まる *tomaru*
take	取る *toru*
talk	話す *hanasu*
tell	話す *hanasu*
think	思う *omou*

try	試す *tamesu*
turn	曲がる *magaru*
use	使う *tsukau*
visit	訪問する *hōmon suru*
wait	待つ *matsu*
walk	歩く *aruku*
want	欲しい *hoshii*
wear	着る *kiru*
work	働く *hataraku*
write	書く *kaku*

Directions

north	北 *kita*
south	南 *minami*
east	東 *higashi*
west	西 *nishi*
at the corner	角で *kado de*
on the corner	角に *kado ni*
straight ahead	まっすぐ先に *massugu saki ni*
left	左 *hidari*
right	右 *migi*
middle	中間 *chūkan*

Days of the Week

Sunday	日曜日 *nichiyōbi*
Monday	月曜日 *getsuyōbi*

Tuesday	火曜日 *kayōbi*
Wednesday	水曜日 *suiyōbi*
Thursday	木曜日 *mokuyōbi*
Friday	金曜日 *kinyōbi*
Saturday	土曜日 *doyōbi*
day	一日 *ichi nichi*
today	今日 *kyō*
yesterday	昨日 *kinō*
the day before yesterday	おととい *ototoi*
tomorrow	明日 *ashita*
the day after tomorrow	あさって *asatte*
week	週 *shū*
this week	今週 *konshū*
last week	先週 *senshū*
next week	来週 *raishū*
for one week	一週間 *isshūkan*
for two weeks	二週間 *nishūkan*
in one week	一週間で *isshūkan de*
in two weeks	二週間で *nishūkan de*
for two days	二日間 *futsuka kan*
in one day	一日で *ichi nichi de*
in two days	二日で *futsuka de*
three days ago	三日前 *mikka mae*
this morning	けさ *kesa*
this afternoon	今日の午後 *kyō no gogo*

tonight	今晩 *konban*
tomorrow night	明日の晩 *ashita no ban*
in the morning	午前中 *gozen chū*
in the afternoon	午後 *gogo*
in the early evening	夕方 *yūgata*
in the evening	夜 *yoru*
by morning	朝までに *asa made ni*
by Tuesday	火曜日までに *kayōbi made ni*
What day is today?	今日は、何曜日ですか。 *Kyō wa, nani yōbi desu ka.*
It's ________ .	今日は、________です。 *Kyō wa, ________ desu.*
weekday	平日 *heijitsu*
weekend	週末 *shūmatsu*
every day	毎日 *mainichi*
a week from today	今日から一週間後 *kyō kara isshukan go*
from today on	今日から *kyō kara*
day off	休み *yasumi*
holiday	休日 *kyūjitsu*
work day	仕事日 *shigoto bi*
per day	一日につき *ichinichi ni tsuki*
during the day	今日中に *kyō jū ni*
during the week	今週中に *konshū jū ni*

Counting Days

one day	一日 *ichi nichi*
two days	二日 *futsuka*

three days	三日 *mikka*
four days	四日 *yokka*
five days	五日 *itsuka*
six days	六日 *muika*
seven days	七日 *nanoka*
eight days	八日 *yōka*
nine days	九日 *kokonoka*
ten days	十日 *tōka*
eleven days	十一日 *jūichi nichi*
twelve days	十二日 *jūni nichi*

Months of the Year

January	一月 *ichi gatsu*
February	二月 *ni gatsu*
March	三月 *san gatsu*
April	四月 *shi gatsu*
May	五月 *go gatsu*
June	六月 *roku gatsu*
July	七月 *shichi gatsu*
August	八月 *hachi gatsu*
September	九月 *ku gatsu*
October	十月 *jū gatsu*
November	十一月 *jūichi gatsu*
December	十二月 *jūni gatsu*

Days of the Month

1st	一日	*tsuitachi*
2nd	二日	*futsuka*
3rd	三日	*mikka*
4th	四日	*yokka*
5th	五日	*itsuka*
6th	六日	*muika*
7th	七日	*nanoka*
8th	八日	*yōka*
9th	九日	*kokonoka*
10th	十日	*tōka*
11th	十一日	*jūichi nichi*
12th	十二日	*jūni nichi*
13th	十三日	*jūsan nichi*
14th	十四日	*jūyokka*
15th	十五日	*jūgo nichi*
16th	十六日	*jūroku nichi*
17th	十七日	*jūshichi nichi*
18th	十八日	*jūhachi nichi*
19th	十九日	*jūku nichi*
20th	二十日	*hatsuka*
21st	二十一日	*nijūichi nichi*
22nd	二十二日	*nujūni nichi*
23rd	二十三日	*nijūsan nichi*
24th	二十四日	*nijūyokka*

25th	二十五日 *nijūgo nichi*
26th	二十六日 *nijūroku nichi*
27th	二十七日 *nijūshichi nichi*
28th	二十八日 *nijūhachi nichi*
29th	二十九日 *nijūku nichi*
30th	三十日 *sanjū nichi*
31st	三十一日 *sanjūichi nichi*
2 months ago	二か月前 *nikagetsu mae*
last month	先月 *sen getsu*
this month	今月 *kon getsu*
next month	来月 *rai getsu*
during the month of ________	________月中に ________ *gatsu chū ni*
since the month of ________	________月以来 ________ *gatsu irai*
for the month of ________	________月に ________ *gatsu ni*
every month	毎月 *mai tsuki*
per month	一か月につき *ikkagetsu ni tsuki*
one month	一か月 *ikkagetsu*
a few months	数か月 *sūkagetsu*
What is today's date?	今日は、何日ですか。 *Kyō wa, nan nichi desu ka.*
Today is ________ .	今日は、________です。 *Kyō wa,* ________ *desu.*
Monday, May 1	五月一日、月曜日 *go gatsu tsuitachi, getsuyōbi*
Tuesday, June 2	六月二日、火曜日 *roku gatsu futsuka, kayōbi*

(*Note:* for these expressions, be sure to use the days of the month listed above.)

year	年 *toshi*
per year	一年につき *ichi nen ni tsuki*

all year	一年中 *ichi nen jū*
every year	毎年 *mai toshi*
last year	去年 *kyo nen*
this year	今年 *kotoshi*
next year	来年 *rai nen*
for two years	二年間 *ni nen kan*

The Four Seasons

spring	春 *haru*
summer	夏 *natsu*
fall	秋 *aki*
winter	冬 *fuyu*

Telling Time

A.M.	午前 *gozen*
P.M.	午後 *gogo*
noon	正午 *shōgo*
midnight	真夜中／午前零時 *ma yonaka/gozen rei ji*
o'clock	時 *ji*

First, a list of hours, then a list of minutes, then we'll put them together!

Hours

1 o'clock	一時 *ichi ji*
2 o'clock	二時 *ni ji*
3 o'clock	三時 *san ji*
4 o'clock	四時 *yo ji*
5 o'clock	五時 *go ji*

6 o'clock	六時 *roku ji*
7 o'clock	七時 *shichi ji*
8 o'clock	八時 *hachi ji*
9 o'clock	九時 *ku ji*
10 o'clock	十時 *jū ji*
11 o clock	十一時 *jūichi ji*
12 o'clock	十二時 *jūni ji*

Minutes

1 minute	一分 *ippun*
2 minutes	二分 *ni fun*
3 minutes	三分 *san pun*
4 minutes	四分 *yon pun*
5 minutes	五分 *go fun*
6 minutes	六分 *roppun*
7 minutes	七分 *nana fun*
8 minutes	八分 *happun*
9 minutes	九分 *kyū fun*
10 minutes	十分 *juppun*
11 minutes	十一分 *jū ippun*
12 minutes	十二分 *jū ni fun*
13 minutes	十三分 *jū san pun*
14 minutes	十四分 *jū yon pun*
15 minutes	十五分 *jū go fun*
16 minutes	十六分 *jū roppun*

17 minutes	十七分 *jū nana fun*
18 minutes	十八分 *jū happun*
19 minutes	十九分 *jū kyū fun*
20 minutes	二十分 *ni juppun*
21 minutes	二十一分 *ni jū ippun*
22 minutes	二十二分 *ni jū ni fun*
23 minutes	二十三分 *ni jū san pun*
24 minutes	二十四分 *ni jū yon pun*
25 minutes	二十五分 *ni jū go fun*
26 minutes	二十六分 *ni jū roppun*
27 minutes	二十七分 *ni jū nana fun*
28 minutes	二十八分 *ni jū happun*
29 minutes	二十九分 *ni jū kyū fun*
30 minutes	三十分 *san juppun*
31 minutes	三十一分 *san jū ippun*
32 minutes	三十二分 *san jū ni fun*
33 minutes	三十三分 *san jū san pun*
34 minutes	三十四分 *san jū yon pun*
35 minutes	三十五分 *san jū go fun*
36 minutes	三十六分 *san jū roppun*
37 minutes	三十七分 *san jū nana fun*
38 minutes	三十八分 *san jū happun*
39 minutes	三十九分 *san jū kyū fun*
40 minutes	四十分 *yon juppun*
41 minutes	四十一分 *yon jū ippun*

42 minutes	四十二分 *yon jū ni fun*
43 minutes	四十三分 *yon jū san pun*
44 minutes	四十四分 *yon jū yon pun*
45 minutes	四十五分 *yon jū go fun*
46 minutes	四十六分 *yon jū roppun*
47 minutes	四十七分 *yon jū nana fun*
48 minutes	四十八分 *yon jū happun*
49 minutes	四十九分 *yon jū kyū fun*
50 minutes	五十分 *go juppun*
51 minutes	五十一分 *go jū ippun*
52 minutes	五十二分 *go jū ni fun*
53 minutes	五十三分 *go jū san pun*
54 minutes	五十四分 *go jū yon pun*
55 minutes	五十五分 *go jū go fun*
56 minutes	五十六分 *go jū roppun*
57 minutes	五十七分 *go jū nana fun*
58 minutes	五十八分 *go jū happun*
59 minutes	五十九分 *go jū kyū fun*

a quarter after ten — *jūji jūgo fun* or *jūji jūgo fun sugi*

(*Note:* using *sugi*, which means "past" or "after," is optional.)

a quarter to ten — *jūji jūgo fun mae*

(*Note:* start using *mae*, which means "to" or "before," at 15 minutes before the hour.)

half past ten — *jūji han*

(*Note: han* means "half.")

What time is it?	何時ですか。 *Nanji desu ka.*
It's <u>5:00 o'clock</u>.	五時です。 *<u>Go ji</u> desu.*

5:05	五時五分 *go ji go fun*
5:10	五時十分 *go ji juppun*
5:15	五時十五分 *go ji jū go fun*
5:20	五時二十分 *go ji ni juppun*
5:25	五時二十五分 *go ji ni jū go fun*
5:30	五時三十分 *go ji han*
5:35	五時三十五分 *go ji san jū go fun*
5:40	五時四十分 *go ji yon juppun*
5:45/a quarter to six	五時四十五分／六時十五分前 *go ji yon jū go fun/roku ji jū go fun mae*
5:50 (ten to six)	六時十分前 *roku ji juppun mae*
5:55 (five to six)	六時五分前 *roku ji go fun mae*

For time schedules, as in railway and airline timetables, numbers 1 to 59 are used for minutes, *not* "a quarter to," or "ten to" the hour.

My train leaves at 1:48 pm	私の汽車は、午後一時四十八分に出ます。 *Watakushi no kisha wa, gogo ichi ji yon jū happun ni demasu.*
My plane arrives at 10:53 am	私の飛行機は、午前十時五十三分に着きます。 *Watakushi no hikōki wa, gozen jū ji go jū san pun ni tsukimasu.*

Note: that transportation timetables are based on the 24-hour clock. Airline and train schedules are expressed in terms of a point within a 24-hour sequence.

per hour	一時間につき *ichi jikan ni tsuki*
three hours ago	三時間前 *san jikan mae*
early (adj)	早い *hayai*
(adv)	早く *hayaku*
late (adj)	遅い *osoi*
(adv)	遅く *osoku*
late (in arriving) (adv)	遅れて *okurete*

on time	時間通りに *jikan dōri ni*
in the morning	午前中 *gozen chū*
in the afternoon	午後 *gogo*
in the evening	夕方 *yūgata*
at night	夜 *yoru*
second	秒 *byō*
minute	分 *fun*
hour	時 *ji*

Arrival/Hotel

My name is ________ .	私の名前は________です。 *Watakushi no namae wa ________ desu.*
I'm American.	アメリカ人です。 *Amerika jin desu.*
I'm staying at ________ .	________に、泊まります。 *________ ni, tomarimasu*
Here's my <u>passport</u>.	これが、私の<u>パスポート</u>です。 *Kore ga, watakushi no <u>pasupōto</u> desu.*
• business card	• 名刺 *meishi*
I'm on a business trip.	仕事の旅行です。 *Shigoto no ryokō desu.*
I'm just passing through.	ちょっと、立ち寄るだけです。 *Chotto, tachiyoru dake desu.*
I'll be staying here <u>a few days</u>.	<u>数日</u>滞在の予定です。 *<u>Sūjitsu</u> taizai no yotei desu.*
• a week	• 一週間 *isshūkan*
• a few weeks	• 二、三週間 *ni, san shūkan*
• a month	• 一か月 *ikkagetsu*
I have nothing to declare.	申告するものは、何もありません。 *Shinkoku suru mono wa, nani mo arimasen.*
I'd like to go to the ________ hotel.	________ホテルへ、行きたいのですが。 *________ hoteru e, ikitai no desu ga.*
Where can I get a taxi?	どこで、タクシーに乗れますか。 *Doko de, takushī ni noremasu ka.*
I have a reservation.	予約がしてあります。 *Yoyaku ga shite arimasu.*

I need a room for one night.	一晩泊りたいのですが、部屋がありますか。 *Hitoban tomaritai no desu ga, heya ga arimasu ka.*
I want a double room with a bath.	バスルーム付きの、ダブルの部屋をください。 *Basurūmu tsuki no, daburu no heya o kudasai.*
What is the rate for the room?	その部屋の料金は、いくらですか。 *Sono heya no ryōkin wa, ikura desu ka.*
Where is the elevator?	エレベーターは、どこですか。 *Erebētā wa, doko desu ka.*
Please send up some mineral water.	ミネラル・ウォーターを、部屋に届けて下さい。 *Mineraru wōtā o, heya ni todokete kudasai.*
Please wake me tomorrow at ________ .	明日、________時に起こして下さい。 *Ashita, ________ ji ni okoshite kudasai.*
Did anyone call for me?	私に電話がありましたか。 *Watakushi ni, denwa ga arimashita ka.*
I'd like to put this in the hotel safe.	これを、貴重品の金庫に預けたいのですが。 *Kore o, kichō hin no kinko ni azuketai no desu ga.*
Can you please make this call for me?	この番号に、電話してもらえますか。 *Kono bangō ni, denwa shite moraemasu ka.*
Please send someone up for the bags.	荷物を取りに、誰かよこして下さい。 *Nimotsu o torini, dare ka yokoshite kudasai.*
I'd like the bill, please.	お勘定を、お願いします。 *Okanjō o, onegai shimasu.*

Transportation

Note: For short-term visitors to Japan, driving is not recommended. Business-persons will find using taxis and public transportation more convenient than renting cars. Hiring a car with driver, either by the hour or the half-day or day, is another option. Your hotel staff or the company you're doing business with may help you arrange for this.

taxi	タクシー *takushī*
car with driver	ハイヤー *haiyā*
bus	バス *basu*
subway	地下鉄 *chikatetsu*
train	汽車／電車 *kisha/densha*
plane	飛行機 *hikōki*

Car with Driver

This is the Japanese equivalent of limousine service, but don't expect a limousine! What you can expect is a standard size, immaculate car, with a polite, efficient driver. The Japanese call this "Hire." Be sure to pronounce it in the Japanese way, HAH-ee-yah.

Where can I get a car with driver?	ハイヤーは、どこでやとえますか。 *Haiyā wa, doko de yatoemasu ka.*
How much will it cost to (place) in Tokyo?	東京の________まで、いくらかかりますか。 *Tōkyō no ________ made, ikura kakarimasu ka.*
Is the rate by the hour?	料金は、時間制ですか。 *Ryōkin wa, jikan sei desu ka.*
• by the half-day	• 半日 *han nichi*
• by the day	• 一日 *ichi nichi*
I'd like to get one.	一台お願いします。 *Ichi dai onegai shimasu.*

Taxis

Where can I get a taxi?	タクシーは、どこでひろえますか。 *Takushī wa, doko de hiroemasu ka.*
Please take me to ________ .	________まで行って下さい。 ________ *made itte kudasai.*
Please take me to this address.	この住所まで、行って下さい。 *Kono jūsho made, itte kudasai.*
Stop here, at the corner, please.	その角で、止まって下さい。 *Sono kado de, tomatte kudasai.*
How much is it?	いくらですか。 *Ikura desu ka.*
Please wait for me. I'll be right back.	待っていて下さい。すぐ戻ってきます。 *Matte ite kudasai. Sugu modotte kimasu.*

Buses

If you travel by bus, it's a good idea to have someone write down your destination so you can show it to the driver, who may not understand English.

Where is the bus stop?	バス停は、どこですか。 *Basu tei wa, doko desu ka.*
Does this bus go to ________ ?	このバスは、________へ行きますか。 *Kono basu wa, ________ e ikimasu ka.*

Subways and Commuter Trains

subway	地下鉄 *chikatetsu*
commuter train	電車 *densha*
Is there a subway in this city?	この市には、地下鉄がありますか。 *Kono shi niwa, chikatetsu ga arimasu ka.*
Is there a subway map in English?	英語の地下鉄の地図がありますか。 *Eigo no, chikatetsu no chizu ga arimasu ka.*
Is there a commuter train map in English?	英語の電車の地図がありますか。 *Eigo no, densha no chizu ga arimasu ka.*

Where is the subway station?	地下鉄の駅は、どこですか。 *Chikatetsu no eki wa, doko desu ka.*
Which line goes to _______ ?	_______に行くには、何線に乗ったらいいですか。 _______ *ni iku niwa, nani sen ni nottara ii desu ka.*
Does this train go to _______ ?	この電車は、_______に行きますか。 *Kono densha wa,* _______ *ni ikimasu ka.*
Do I have to change trains?	乗り換えがありますか。 *Norikae ga arimasu ka.*
Is this seat taken?	この席は、ふさがっていますか。 *Kono seki wa, fusagatte imasu ka.*
When we're about to arrive at _______ , please let me know.	_______に着くちょっと前に、教えて下さい。 _______ *ni tsuku chotto mae ni, oshiete kudasai.*

Intercity Trains

Is there a timetable in English?	英語の時刻表がありますか。 *Eigo no jikoku hyō ga, arimasu ka.*
I'd like a <u>one-way ticket</u> to Kyoto.	京都への<u>片道</u>を一枚下さい。 *Kyōto e no, <u>katamichi</u> o ichimai kudasai.*
• round-trip ticket	• 往復 *ōfuku*
• ticket for a reserved seat	• 座席指定券 *zaseki shitei ken*
• first-class ticket	• グリーン車の券／一等の券 *gurīn sha no ken/ittō no ken*
Where is the track for the Shinkansen?	新幹線の乗り場は、どこですか。 *Shinkansen no noriba wa, doko desu ka.*
Where is the dining car?	食堂車は、何号車ですか。 *Shokudō sha wa, nan gō sha desu ka.*

Air Travel

When is there a flight to _______ ?	_______行きの便は、いつありますか。 _______ *iki no bin wa, itsu arimasu ka.*
I'd like a <u>round-trip ticket</u>.	<u>往復</u>券を買いたいのですが。 *<u>Ōfuku</u> ken o, kaitai no desu ga.*
• an economy class	• エコノミー・クラスの *ekonomī kurasu no*
• a first class	• ファースト・クラスの *fāsuto kurasu no*
I'd like a seat <u>in the nonsmoking section</u>.	<u>禁煙</u>席を下さい。 *<u>Kin-en</u> seki o, kudasai.*
• near the window	• 窓際の *mado giwa no*
• on the aisle	• 通路側の *tsūro gawa no*
What time does the plane leave?	何時発ですか。 *Nanji hatsu desu ka.*

What's my flight number?	何便ですか。 *Nanbin desu ka.*
What's the gate number?	出発ゲートは、何番ですか。 *Shuppatsu gēto wa, nanban desu ka.*
I'd like to confirm my flight reservation.	予約確認をしたいのですが。 *Yoyaku kakunin o shitai no desu ga.*

Leisure Time

Where can I buy an English-language newspaper?	英語の新聞は、どこで売っていますか。 *Eigo no shinbun wa, doko de utte imasu ka.*
I'd like to see a baseball game.	野球を、見たいのですが。 *Yakyū o, mitai no desu ga.*
• a sumo match	• 相撲 *sumō*
• a kabuki performance	• 歌舞伎 *kabuki*
• an ikebana demonstration	• 生け花のデモンストレーション *ikebana no demonsutorēshon*
• a tea ceremony	• 茶道の儀式 *sadō no gishiki*
Where can I buy the tickets?	どこで、券が買えますか。 *Doko de, ken ga kaemasu ka.*
Is there a pool near the hotel?	ホテルの近くに、プールがありますか。 *Hoteru no chikaku ni, pūru ga arimasu ka.*

Restaurants

breakfast	朝食／ブレックファースト *chōshoku/burekku fāsuto*
lunch	昼食／ランチ *chūshoku/ranchi*
dinner	夕食／ディナー *yūshoku/dinā*
Japanese food	和食／日本料理 *washoku/Nihon ryōri*
Western food	洋食／西洋料理 *yōshoku/seiyō ryōri*
Japanese restaurant	和食／日本料理のレストラン *washoku/Nihon ryōri no resutoran*
Western restaurant	レストラン *resutoran*
Do you know a good restaurant?	いいレストランを知っていますか。 *Ii resutoran o, shitte imasu ka.*
Is it very expensive?	とても高いですか。 *Totemo takai desu ka.*
Waiter!/Waitress!	ちょっと、すみませんが。 *Chotto, sumimasen ga.*
We'd like to have lunch.	ランチをお願いします。 *Ranchi o, onegai shimasu.*

The menu, please.	メニューを下さい。 *Menyū o kudasai.*
What's today's special?	今日のスペシャルは、何ですか。 *Kyō no supesharu wa, nan desu ka.*
What do you recommend?	おすすめ品がありますか。 *Osusume hin ga, arimasu ka.*
To begin, please bring us a cocktail.	始めに、カクテルを下さい。 *Hajime ni, kakuteru o kudasai.*
• a bottle of mineral water	• ミネラル・ウォーターを一本 *mineraru wōtā o ippon*
• a beer	• ビール *bīru*
Do you have a house wine?	ハウス・ワインがありますか。 *Hausu wain ga arimasu ka.*
I'd like to order now.	注文したいのですが。 *Chūmon shitai no desu ga.*
Could you bring me a knife?	ナイフを持って来て下さい。 *Naifu o, motte kite kudasai.*
• a fork	• フォーク *fōku*
• a spoon	• スプーン *supūn*
• a teaspoon	• 小さじ *kosaji*
• a tablespoon	• 大さじ *ōsaji*
• a glass	• コップ *koppu*
• a cup	• コーヒー茶わん *kōhī jawan*
• a saucer	• 受け皿 *ukezara*
• a plate	• お皿 *osara*
• a bowl	• ボール *bōru*
• a napkin	• ナプキン *napukin*
• some toothpicks	• ようじ *yōji*
• an ashtray	• 灰皿 *haizara*
Show me the menu again, please.	メニューをもう一度見せて下さい。 *Menyū o, mō ichido misete kudasai.*
I'd like some coffee, please.	コーヒーを下さい。 *Kōhī o kudasai.*
I'd like some decaffeinated coffee, please.	カフェイン抜きのコーヒーを下さい。 *Kafein nuki no kōhī o kudasai.*
Do you mind if I smoke?	たばこを吸ってもかまいませんか。 *Tabako o suttemo kamaimasen ka.*

Check, please.	チェック／（お）勘定をお願いします。 *Chekku/(o)kanjō o, onegai shimasu.*
Do you take <u>credit cards</u>?	クレジット・カードが使えますか。 *<u>Kurejitto</u> kādo ga, tsukaemasu ka.*
• traveler's checks	• トラベラー・チェック *toraberā chekku*
Which credit cards do you take?	どのクレジット・カードが使えますか。 *Dono kurejitto kādo ga, tsukaemasu ka.*
Are the tax and service charge included?	税金とサービス料が入っていますか。 *Zeikin to sābisu ryō ga, haitte imasu ka.*
Is this correct?	これは、あっていますか。 *Kore wa, atte imasu ka.*
May I have a receipt, please?	領収書をお願いします。 *Ryōshūsho o, onegai shimasu.*
We don't have much time.	時間があまりありません。 *Jikan ga, amari arimasen.*
Where are the restrooms?	トイレは、どこですか。 *Toire wa, doko desu ka.*

Shopping

How much is it?	いくらですか。 *Ikura desu ka.*
Where can I find _______ ?	_______は、どこにありますか。 _______ *wa, doko ni arimasu ka.*
Can you help me?	ちょっと、お願いします。 *Chotto, onegai shimasu.*
I need _______ .	_______が欲しいのですが。 _______ *ga, hoshii no desu ga.*
Do you have any others?	ほかに、何かありますか。 *Hoka ni, nani ka arimasu ka.*
Do you have anything <u>smaller</u>?	もう少し、<u>小さい</u>のがありますか。 *Mō sukoshi <u>chiisai</u> no ga, arimasu ka.*
• larger	• 大きい *ōkii*
Can I pay with a traveler's check?	トラベラー・チェックで払えますか。 *Toraberā chekku de haraemasu ka.*

Medical Care

Where is the nearest pharmacy?	一番近い薬屋は、どこにありますか。 *Ichiban chikai kusuri ya wa, doko ni arimasu ka.*
Is there a pharmacy that carries American/European products?	アメリカ／ヨーロッパ製品を売っている薬屋がありますか。 *Amerika/Yōroppa seihin o utteiru, kusuri ya ga arimasu ka.*
I need something for <u>a cold</u>.	<u>風邪</u>の薬を下さい。 *<u>Kaze</u> no kusuri o kudasai.*
• constipation	• 便秘 *benpi*

• a cough	• せき *seki*
• diarrhea	• 下痢 *geri*
• a headache	• 頭痛 *zutsū*
• indigestion	• 消化不良 *shōka furyō*
• insomnia	不眠症 *fumin shō*
• a toothache	• 歯痛／歯いた *shitsū/haita*
• an upset stomach	• 胃の調子がおかしいとき *i no chōshi ga okashii toki*
I don't feel well. I need a doctor who speaks English.	気分がすぐれません。英語が話せる医者が必要です。 *Kibun ga suguremasen. Eigo ga hanaseru isha ga, hitsuyō desu.*
I'm dizzy.	めまいがします。 *Memai ga shimasu.*
I feel weak.	体に、力が入りません。 *Karada ni, chikara ga hairimasen.*
I have a pain in my chest around my heart.	心臓の近くに、痛みがあります。 *Shinzō no chikaku ni, itami ga arimasu.*
I had a heart attack some years ago.	数年前、心臓麻痺の発作がありました。 *Sūnen mae, shinzō mahi no hossa ga arimashita.*
I'm taking this medicine.	今、この薬を使っています。 *Ima, kono kusuri o tsukatte imasu.*
Do I have to be hospitalized?	入院しなければなりませんか。 *Nyūin shinakereba narimasen ka.*
I have a toothache. Could you recommend a dentist?	歯が痛みます。歯医者を紹介してもらえますか。 *Ha ga, itamimasu. Ha isha o shōkai shite moraemasu ka.*
I just broke my glasses. Can you repair them while I wait?	眼鏡をこわしてしまいました。待っている間に、直してもらえますか。 *Megane o, kowashite shimaimashita. Matte iru aida ni, naoshite moraemasu ka.*

Telephones

Where is a public telephone?	公衆電話は、どこにありますか。 *Kōshū denwa wa, doko ni arimasu ka.*
Is there an English telephone directory?	英語の電話帳がありますか。 *Eigo no denwa chō ga, arimasu ka.*
I'd like to make a phone call. Could you give me some change?	電話をかけるのに、こまかくしてもらえますか。 *Denwa o kakeru no ni, komakaku shite moraemasu ka.*

May I use your phone?	電話をはいしゃくできますか。 *Denwa o haishaku dekimasu ka.*
I want to make a person-to-person call.	パーソナル・コールをかけたいのですが。 *Pāsonaru kōru o, kaketai no desu ga.*
How do you call the United States?	アメリカへは、どうやって電話しますか。 *Amerika e wa, dō yatte denwa shimasu ka.*
I'd like to talk to the operator.	交換手と、話したいのですが。 *Kōkanshu to, hanashitai no desu ga.*
May I speak to ______ ?	______をお願いします。 ______ *o, onegai shimasu.*
Who's calling?	どちら様でしょうか。 *Dochira sama deshō ka.*
Speak slowly, please.	もう少し、ゆっくり話して下さい。 *Mō sukoshi, yukkuri hanashite kudasai.*
Speak louder, please.	もう少し、大きい声で話して下さい。 *Mō sukoshi, ōkii koe de hanashite kudasai.*
Don't hang up.	どうぞ、切らないで下さい。 *Dōzo, kiranaide kudasai.*
I got a wrong number.	間違い電話でした。 *Machigai denwa deshita.*
I was disconncted.	電話が切れてしまいました。 *Denwa ga, kirete shimaimashita.*
I'd like to leave a message.	伝言を残したいのですが。 *Dengon o, nokoshitai no desu ga.*

Postal Service

post office	郵便局 *yūbin kyoku*
post card	葉書 *hagaki*
letter	手紙 *tegami*
telegram	電報 *denpō*
air mail letter	航空便 *kōkū bin*
registered letter	書留 *kakitome*
special delivery letter	速達 *sokutatsu*
package	小包 *kozutsumi*
Where is a mailbox?	ポストは、どこにありますか。 *Posuto wa, doko ni arimasu ka.*
Where is a post office?	郵便局は、どこにありますか。 *Yūbin kyoku wa, doko ni arimasu ka.*
I'd like to buy some stamps.	切手を買いたいのですが。 *Kitte o kaitai no desu ga.*

Which window is it?	どの窓口ですか。 *Dono mado guchi desu ka.*
What's the postage to the United States?	アメリカへの郵便料金は、いくらですか。 *Amerika e no yūbin ryōkin wa, ikura desu ka.*
I'd like to send a telex.	テレックスを送りたいのですが。 *Terekkusu o, okuritai no desu ga.*
How late are you open?	何時まで、開いていますか。 *Nan ji made, aite imasu ka.*
How much is it per minute?	一分あたり、いくらですか。 *Ippun atari, ikura desu ka.*
• per word	• 一語あたり *ichi go atari*

Signs

Most signs are in Japanese characters. With this list, you can recognize the characters and understand the meaning.

Entrance	入口 *iriguchi*
Exit	出口 *deguchi*
East Exit	東口 *higashi guchi*
West Exit	西口 *nishi guchi*
South Exit	南口 *minami guchi*
North Exit	北口 *kita guchi*
Lavatory	便所 *benjo*
Lavatory	お手洗 *ote arai*
Men	男 *otoko*
Women	女 *onna*
Adult	大人 *otona*
Child	小人 *kodomo*
Danger	危険 *kiken*
Keep Out	立入禁止 *tachiiri kinshi*
Fire Extinguisher	消火器 *shōka ki*
No Matches	火気厳禁 *kaki genkin*

Fee Required	有料 *yūryō*
Free Admission	無料 *muryō*
Closed Today	本日休業 *honjitsu kyūgyō*
Temporarily Closed	準備中 *junbi chū*
No Smoking	禁煙 *kin-en*
No Shoes (no street shoes allowed on the floor)	土足禁止 *dosoku kinshi*
Full	満席 *manseki*
Parking Place	駐車場 *chūsha jō*
Hospital	病院 *byōin*
Vacant	空き *aki*
Occupied	使用中 *shiyō chū*
Please Ring	ベルを押して下さい。 *Beru o oshite kudasai.*
Pull	引く *hiku*
Push	押す *osu*
Caution	注意 *chūi*
Emergency Exit	非常口 *hijōguchi*
Don't Touch	触れるな *fureru na*
Information	案内所 *annai sho*
Beware of Dog	猛犬に注意 *mōken ni chūi*
Cashier	会計 *kaikei*
For Rent, For Hire	貸し出し／貸します *kashidashi/kashimasu*
Enter Without Knocking	ノックせずにお入り下さい。 *Nokku sezu ni ohairi kudasai.*
No Entry	入場禁止 *nyūjō kinshi*
No Admittance	入場お断り *nyūjō okotowari*
Private Property	私有地 *shiyū chi*

Warning
警告
keikoku

Stop
止まれ
tomare

Sold Out
売れきれ
urikire

Numbers

Cardinal Numbers

0
ゼロ／零
zero/rei

1
一
ichi

2
二
ni

3
三
san

4
四
shi/yon

5
五
go

6
六
roku

7
七
shichi/nana

8
八
hachi

9
九
kyū/ku

10
十
jū

11
十一
jū ichi

12
十二
jū ni

13
十三
jū san

14
十四
jū shi/jū yon

15
十五
jū go

16
十六
jū roku

17
十七
jū shichi/jū nana

18
十八
jū hachi

19
十九
jū ku

20	二十 *ni jū*
30	三十 *san jū*
40	四十 *yon jū*
50	五十 *go jū*
60	六十 *roku jū*
70	七十 *nana jū*
80	八十 *hachi jū*
90	九十 *kyū jū*
100	百 *hyaku*
200	二百 *ni hyaku*
300	三百 *san byaku*
400	四百 *yon hyaku*
500	五百 *go hyaku*
600	六百 *roppyaku*
700	七百 *nana hyaku*
800	八百 *happyaku*
900	九百 *kyū hyaku*
1,000	千 *sen*
2,000	二千 *ni sen*
3,000	三千 *san zen*
4,000	四千 *yon sen*
5,000	五千 *go sen*
6,000	六千 *roku sen*
7,000	七千 *nana sen*
8,000	八千 *hassen*

9,000	九千 *kyū sen*
10,000	一万 *ichi man*
20,000	二万 *ni man*
30,000	三万 *san man*
40,000	四万 *yon man*
50,000	五万 *go man*
60,000	六万 *roku man*
70,000	七万 *nana man*
80,000	八万 *hachi man*
90,000	九万 *kyū man*
100,000	十万 *jū man*
200,000	二十万 *ni jū man*
300,000	三十万 *san jū man*
400,000	四十万 *yon jū man*
500,000	五十万 *go jū man*
600,000	六十万 *roku jū man*
700,000	七十万 *nana jū man*
800,000	八十万 *hachi jū man*
900,000	九十万 *kyū jū man*
1,000,000	百万 *hyaku man*
2,000,000	二百万 *ni hyaku man*
3,000,000	三百万 *san byaku man*
4,000,000	四百万 *yon hyaku man*
5,000,000	五百万 *go hyaku man*
6,000,000	六百万 *roppyaku man*

7,000,000	七百万 *nana hyaku man*
8,000,000	八百万 *happyaku man*
9,000,000	九百万 *kyū hyaku man*
10,000,000	千万 *sen man*
20,000,000	二千万 *ni sen man*
100,000,000	一億 *ichi oku*
1,000,000,000	十億 *jū oku*
10,000,000,000	百億 *hyaku oku*
100,000,000,000	千億 *sen oku*
1,000,000,000,000	一兆 *itchō*
10,000,000,000,000	十兆 *jutchō*
100,000,000,000,000	百兆 *hyaku chō*
1,000,000,000,000,000	千兆 *sen chō*

Examples

540	五百四十 *go hyaku yon jū*
1,540	千五百四十 *sen go hyaku yon jū*
11,540	一万千五百四十 *ichi man sen go hyaku yon jū*
1,611,540	百六十一万千五百四十 *hyaku roku jū ichi man sen go hyaku yon jū*

Note: When dealing with very large numbers, be aware that while the concepts are the same, the ways of counting are different. The Japanese count units of 10,000, units of 100,000,000, and units of 1 trillion. It's a good idea to back up your verbal understanding by writing the numbers (Western-style) on a piece of paper and checking them with your Japanese colleagues.

Cardinal Numbers (Another system)

1	一つ *hitotsu*
2	二つ *futatsu*
3	三つ *mittsu*

4	四つ *yottsu*
5	五つ *itsutsu*
6	六つ *muttsu*
7	七つ *nanatsu*
8	八つ *yattsu*
9	九つ *kokonotsu*
10	十 *tō*
11	十一 *jū ichi*
12	十二 *jū ni*

Ordinal Numbers

first	一番目／第一 *ichi ban me/dai ichi*
second	二番目／第二 *ni ban me/dai ni*
third	三番目／第三 *san ban me/dai san*
fourth	四番目／第四 *yon ban me/dai yon*
fifth	五番目／第五 *go ban me/dai go*
sixth	六番目／第六 *roku ban me/dai roku*
seventh	七番目／第七 *nana ban me/dai nana*
eighth	八番目／第八 *hachi ban me/dai hachi*
ninth	九番目／第九 *kyū ban me/dai ku*
tenth	十番目／第十 *jū ban me/dai jū*

Quantities

a half	半分 *han bun*
a quarter	四分の一 *yon bun no ichi*
three quarters	四分の三 *yon bun no san*
a third	三分の一 *san bun no ichi*

two thirds	三分の二 *san bun no ni*
a cup	カップ一杯 *kappu ippai*
a dozen	一ダース *ichi dāsu*
a kilo	一キロ *ikkiro*
a liter	一リットル *ichi rittoru*
a little	少し *sukoshi*
a lot	たくさん *takusan*
a pair	一対 *ittsui*
enough	十分な *jūbun na*

Counting Different Kinds of Things

1 (one)	2 (two)	3 (three)	4 (four)	5 (five)
people				
一人 *hitori*	二人 *futari*	三人 *san nin*	四人 *yo nin*	五人 *go nin*
long, skinny objects (pencils, sticks, bottles, and so forth)				
一本 ippon	二本 *ni hon*	三本 *san bon*	四本 *yon hon*	五本 *go hon*
thin, flat objects (paper, bills, cloth, dishes, tickets, and so forth)				
一枚 *ichi mai*	二枚 *ni mai*	三枚 *san mai*	四枚 *yon mai*	五枚 *go mai*
bound objects (books, magazines, notebooks, and so forth)				
一冊 *issatsu*	二冊 *ni satsu*	三冊 *san satsu*	四冊 *yon satsu*	五冊 *go satsu*
liquid or dry measures (glasses or cups of water, coffee, tea, sugar, and so forth)				
一杯 *ippai*	二杯 *ni hai*	三杯 *san bai*	四杯 *yon hai*	五杯 *go hai*
vehicles, machines				
一台 *ichi dai*	二台 *ni dai*	三台 *san dai*	四台 *yon dai*	五台 *go dai*
things to wear (jackets, sweaters, shirts, coats, and so forth)				
一着 *itchaku*	二着 *ni chaku*	三着 *san chaku*	四着 *yon chaku*	五着 *go chaku*

1 (one)	2 (two)	3 (three)	4 (four)	5 (five)
pairs of things to wear on feet or legs (socks, shoes, slippers, and so forth)				
一足 *issoku*	二足 *ni soku*	三足 *san zoku*	四足 *yon soku*	五足 *go soku*
sets of dishes, pairs of people, and so forth				
一組 *hito kumi*	二組 *futa kumi*	三組 *mi kumi*	四組 *yo kumi*	五組 *itsu kumi*
boxes, cases, and so forth				
一箱 *hito hako*	二箱 *futa hako*	三箱 *mi hako*	四箱 *yo hako*	五箱 *itsu hako*
floors of buildings				
一階 *ikkai*	二階 *ni kai*	三階 *san gai*	四階 *yon kai*	五階 *go kai*
houses, buildings				
一軒 *ikken*	二軒 *ni ken*	三軒 *san gen*	四軒 *yon ken*	五軒 *go ken*
copies (newspapers, documents, books, and so forth)				
一部 *ichi bu*	二部 *ni bu*	三部 *san bu*	四部 *yon bu*	五部 *go bu*
portions, servings				
一人前 *ichi nin mae*	二人前 *ni nin mae*	三人前 *san nin mae*	四人前 *yo nin mae*	五人前 *go nin mae*
slices				
一切れ *hito kire*	二切れ *futa kire*	三切れ *mi kire*	四切れ *yo kire*	五切れ *itsu kire*
small objects not in the categories listed above				
一個／一つ *ikko/ hitotsu*	二個／二つ *niko/ futatsu*	三個／三つ *san ko/ mittsu*	四個／四つ *yon ko/ yottsu*	五個／五つ *go ko/ itsutsu*

Years

1994	千九百九十四年 *sen kyū hyaku kyū jū yo nen*
1995	千九百九十五年 *sen kyū hyaku kyū jū go nen*
1996	千九百九十六年 *sen kyū hyaku kyū jū roku nen*
1997	千九百九十七年 *sen kyū hyaku kyū jū nana nen*
2000	二千年 *ni sen nen*

IV. BUSINESS DICTIONARY

ENGLISH TO JAPANESE/ROMAJI

A

abandon (v)	放棄する	*hōki suru*
abandon (insurance) (v)	委付する	*ifu suru*
abandonment	放棄	*hōki*
abandonment (insurance)	委付	*ifu*
abatement	割戻し	*warimodoshi*
ability-to-pay concept	支払能力概念	*shiharai nōryoku gainen*
above par	額面以上の価格	*gakumen ijō no kakaku*
above par (adv)	額面以上で	*gakumen ijō de*
above-mentioned (adj)	上記の	*jōki no*
above-the-line item	画線上の項目	*kakusen jō no kōmoku*
absentee ownership	不在地主権	*fuzai jinushi ken*
absenteeism	常習欠勤	*jōshū kekkin*
absolute temperature	絶対温度	*zettai ondo*
absorb (v)	吸収する	*kyūshū suru*
absorb the loss (v)	損失を吸収する	*sonshitsu o kyūshū suru*
absorption costing (accounting)	全部原価計算	*zenbu genka keisan*
abstract of title	権利証明要約書	*kenri shōmei yōyaku sho*
accelerated depreciation	加速減価償却	*kasoku genka shōkyaku*
acceleration clause	債務の即時返済条項	*saimu no sokuji hensai jōkō*
accelerator (computer)	アクセラレータ	*akuserarēta*
accelerator (car)	アクセル	*akuseru*
accept (v)	引き受ける	*hikiukeru*
acceptable quality level	合格品質水準	*gōkaku hinshitsu suijun*
acceptance	引受け	*hikiuke*
acceptance agreement	引受承諾書	*hikiuke shōdaku sho*
acceptance bill	引受手形	*hikiuke tegata*
acceptance credit	期限付為替手形信用状	*kigen tsuki kawase tegata shin-yō jō*
acceptance house	手形引受業者	*tegata hikiuke gyōsha*
acceptance sampling	受入見本抜取検査	*ukeire mihon nukitori kensa*
acceptance test	受入れ検査	*ukeire kensa*
acceptor	引受人	*hikiuke nin*
access time	アクセス時間	*akusesu jikan*
accession rate	入職率	*nyūshoku ritsu*
accessory	アクセサリー、付属品	*akusesarī, fuzoku hin*
accidental damage	偶発的損害	*gūhatsu teki songai*
accommodation bill	融通手形	*yūzū tegata*
accommodation credit	融通手形信用状	*yūzū tegata shin-yō jō*
accommodation endorsement	融通手形の裏書	*yūzū tegata no uragaki*

accommodation paper	融通手形	*yūzū tegata*
accommodation party	融通手形当事者	*yūzū tegata tōji sha*
accompanied goods	同行の品	*dōkō no shina*
accord and satisfaction	代物弁済	*daibutsu bensai*
account	勘定	*kanjō*
account (banking)	口座	*kōza*
account balance	取引勘定残高	*torihiki kanjō zandaka*
account day	勘定決済日	*kanjō kessai bi*
account executive (advertising)	アカウント エグゼクティブ	*akaunto eguzekutibu*
account executive (securities)	証券会社営業部員	*shōken gaisha eigyō buin*
account for (v)	明細報告する	*meisai hōkoku suru*
account number	口座番号	*kōza bangō*
account period	会計期間	*kaikei kikan*
account statement	勘定書	*kanjōsho*
account, current	当座勘定	*tōza kanjō*
accountability (accounting)	会計責任	*kaikei sekinin*
accountability (management)	経営責任	*keiei sekinin*
accountant	会計係	*kaikei gakari*
accountant, chief	会計主任	*kaikei shunin*
accounting department	会計部	*kaikei bu*
accounting method	会計方式	*kaikei hōshiki*
accounting period	会計期間	*kaikei kikan*
accounting, cost	原価計算	*genka keisan*
accounting, management	管理会計	*kanri kaikei*
accounts payable	支払勘定	*shiharai kanjō*
accounts receivable	受取勘定	*uketori kanjō*
accounts, group	グループ勘定	*gurūpu kanjō*
accounts, secured	担保付勘定	*tanpo tsuki kanjō*
accretion	自然増加	*shizen zōka*
accrual	経過利子	*keika rishi*
accrual method	発生主義法	*hassei shugi hō*
accrue (v)	利子を生ずる	*rishi o shōzuru*
accrued assets	見越資産	*mikoshi shisan*
accrued depreciation	減価償却累計額	*genka shōkyaku ruikei gaku*
accrued expenses	未払費用	*miharai hiyō*
accrued interest	経過利子	*keika rishi*
accrued revenue	未収収益	*mishū shūeki*
accrued taxes	未払税金	*miharai zeikin*
accumulated depreciation	累積減価償却引当金	*ruisekigenka shōkyaku hikiate kin*
acetaldehyde	アセト アルデヒド	*aseto arudehido*
acetate	アセテート	*asetēto*
acetic acid	酢酸	*sakusan*
acetone	アセトン	*aseton*
acid (adj)	酸性の	*san sei no*
acknowledge (v)	認める	*mitomeru*
acknowledge receipt of (v)	の受取りを認める	*no uketori o mitomeru*

acoustic coupler	音響カプラ	*onkyō kapura*
acquire (v)	取得する	*shutoku suru*
acquired rights	既得権	*kitoku ken*
acquisition	取得	*shutoku*
acquisition cost	取得原価	*shutoku genka*
acreage allotment	作付け面積割当て	*sakuzuke menseki wariate*
acronym	頭文字語	*kashira moji go*
across-the-board settlement	全面的決着	*zenmen teki ketchaku*
across-the-board tariff negotiation	全面的関税交渉	*zenmen teki kanzei kōshō*
acrylamide	アクリルアミド	*akuriru amido*
acrylonitrile	アクリロニトル	*akuriro nitoru*
act of God	不可抗力	*fuka kōryoku*
action plan	実行計画	*jikkō keikaku*
action research	実行調査	*jikkō chōsa*
active account	活動勘定	*katsudō kanjō*
active assets	生産資産	*seisan shisan*
active debt	活動負債	*katsudō fusai*
active matrix	アクテイブマトリックス	*akutibu matorikkusu*
active trust	積極信託	*sekkyoku shintaku*
activity chart	活動調査表	*katsudō chōsa hyō*
actual (adj)	実際の	*jissai no*
actual cash value	現金換価価値	*genkin kanka kachi*
actual costs	実際原価	*jissai genka*
actual income	実収入	*jisshūnyū*
actual liability	実質債務	*jisshitsu saimu*
actual market volume	実質市場取引高	*jisshitsu shijō torihiki daka*
actual total loss	現実全損	*genjitsu zenson*
actuary	保険経理人	*hoken keiri nin*
adaptor	アダプタ	*adaputa*
add-on sales	割賦販売	*kappu hanbai*
addendum	補追	*hotsui*
addendum (insurance)	追加特約	*tsuika tokuyaku*
address commission	積荷周旋料	*tsumini shūsen ryō*
adjudge (v)	判定する	*hantei suru*
adjudication	判決	*hanketsu*
adjust (v)	調整する	*chōsei suru*
adjustable peg	調整可能な釘づけ相場	*chōsei kanō na kugizuke sōba*
adjusted CIF price	調整済保険料運賃込値段	*chōsei zumi hoken ryō unchin komi nedan*
adjusted earned income	調整済勤労所得	*chōsei zumi kinrō shotoku*
adjusted rate	調整率	*chōsei ritsu*
adjusting entry	調整記入	*chōsei kinyū*
adjustment process	調整過程	*chōsei katei*
adjustment trigger	調整基準点	*chōsei kijun ten*
administration	経営管理	*keiei kanri*
administrative (adj)	管理の	*kanri no*

administrative expense	（一般）管理費	*(ippan) kanri hi*
administrative guidance	行政指導	*gyōsei shidō*
administrator	経営者	*keiei sha*
administratrix	女性経営者	*josei keiei sha*
advance (finance)	前がし金	*maegashikin*
advance (v)	前払いする	*mae barai suru*
advance freight	前払い運賃	*mae barai unchin*
advance notice	予告	*yokoku*
advance payments	前払い	*mae barai*
advance refunding	公債事前借り換え	*kōsai jizen karikae*
advanced technology	先端技術	*sentan gijutsu*
advantage, competitive	競争上の利点	*kyōsō jō no riten*
adverse balance	輸入超過	*yunyū chōka*
advertisement (request) for bid	入札広告	*nyūsatsu kōkoku*
advertising agency	広告代理店	*kōkoku dairi ten*
advertising budget	広告費予算	*kōkoku hi yosan*
advertising campaign	宣伝活動	*senden katsudo*
advertising drive	宣伝売り込み	*senden urikomi*
advertising expenses	広告費	*kōkoku hi*
advertising	広告	*kōkoku*
advertising manager	広告部長	*kōkoku buchō*
advertising media	広告媒体	*kōkoku baitai*
advertising research	広告調査	*kōkoku chōsa*
advice note	通知状	*tsūchi jō*
advise (v)	忠告する	*chūkoku suru*
advisor's fee	顧問料	*komon ryō*
advisory council	諮問会議	*shimon kaigi*
aerial photographic camera	航空カメラ	*kōkū kamera*
affidavit	供述書／宣誓供述書	*kyōjutsu sho/sensei kyōjutsu sho*
affiliate	系列会社	*keiretsu gaisha*
affiliation	提携	*teikei*
affirmative action	女性、少数民族積極雇用	*josei shōsū minzoku sekkyoku koyō*
affreightment	船荷運送傭船契約	*funani unsō yōsen keiyaku*
afloat (finance)	流通している	*ryūtsū shite iru*
after-hours trading	時間外取引き	*jikan gai torihiki*
after-sales service	アフターサービス	*afutā sābisu*
after-tax real rate of return	税引き利益率	*zei biki rieki ritsu*
afterdate (v)	日付後払いにする	*hizuke go barai ni suru*
against all risks (insurance)	全危険担保で	*zen kiken tanpo de*
agency	代理店	*dairi ten*
agency bank	業務代行銀行	*gyōmu daikō ginkō*
agency fee	代理店手数料	*dairi ten tesū ryō*
agenda	協議事項	*kyōgi jikō*
agent	代理人	*dairi nin*
agent bank	業務代行銀行	*gyōmu daikō ginkō*
aggregate demand	総需要	*sō juyō*
aggregate risk	総リスク	*sō risuku*
aggregate supply	総供給	*sō kyōkyū*

agreement	合意	*gōi*
agricultural paper	農業証券	*nōgyō shōken*
agricultural products	農産物	*nō sanbutsu*
agriculture	農業	*nōgyō*
air conditioner (car)	カー・クーラー	*kā kūrā*
air express	航空速達便	*kōkū sokutatsu bin*
air freight	航空貨物輸送	*kōkū kamotsu yusō*
air shipment	空輸	*kūyu*
algorithm	アルゴリズム	*arugorizumu*
algorithmic language	アルゴル	*arugoru*
alien corporation	外国会社	*gaikoku gaisha*
alkaline (adj)	アルカリ性の	*arukari sei no*
alkylbenzene	アルキルベンゼン	*arukiru benzen*
all in cost	総原価	*sō genka*
all or none	全部引受け一部不可	*zenbu hikiuke ichibu fuka*
all-weather camera	全天候カメラ	*zen tenkō kamera*
allocation of costs	経費割当て	*keihi wariate*
allocation of costs (accounting)	原価配分	*genka haibun*
allocation of responsibilities	責任分担	*sekinin buntan*
allocation, resources	資源配分	*shigen haibun*
allonge (of a draft)	附箋	*fusen*
allot (v)	割当てる	*wariateru*
allotment	割当て	*wariate*
allotment letter	株式割当通知書	*kabushiki wariate tsūchi sho*
allow (v)	差し引く	*sashihiku*
allowance (finance)	引当金	*hikiate kin*
allowance (sales)	割引き	*waribiki*
allowance, depreciation	減価償却引当金	*genka shōkyaku hikiate kin*
alloy	合金	*gōkin*
alloy steel	合金鋼	*gōkin kō*
alongside (adv)	船側に	*sensoku ni*
alteration	変更	*henkō*
alternating current	交流	*kōryū*
alternative order	代品選択注文	*daihin sentaku chūmon*
alternator	オルタネーター	*orutanētā*
alumina	アルミナ	*arumina*
aluminum	アルミニュウム	*aruminyūmu*
amalgamation	合併	*gappei*
amend (v)	修正する	*shūsei suru*
amendment	修正	*shūsei*
amicable settlement	和解	*wakai*
amine	アミン	*amin*
ammonia	アンモニア	*anmonia*
amorphous semiconductor	アモルファス半導体	*amorufasu handōtai*
amorphous silicon	アモルファス・シリコン	*amorufasu shirikon*
amortization	年賦償還	*nenpu shōkan*
amount	総額	*sōgaku*

amount due	満期支払い高	*manki shiharai daka*
amplifier	増幅器／アンプ	*zōfuku ki/anpu*
amplitude modulation	エーエム	*ē emu*
analgesic	鎮痛薬	*chintsū yaku*
analog computer	アナログ・コンピュータ	*anarogu konpūta*
analysis	分析	*bunseki*
analysis, break-even	損益分岐点分析	*soneki bunki ten bunseki*
analysis, competitor	競合者分析	*kyōgō sha bunseki*
analysis, cost	原価分析	*genka bunseki*
analysis, cost-benefit	費用効果分析	*hiyō kōka bunseki*
analysis, critical path	最長経路分析	*saichō keiro bunseki*
analysis, financial	財務分析	*zaimu bunseki*
analysis, functional	機能分析	*kinō bunseki*
analysis, input-output	投入産出分析	*tōnyū sanshutsu bunseki*
analysis, investment	投資分析	*tōshi bunseki*
analysis, job	職務分析	*shokumu bunseki*
analysis, needs	必需品分析	*hitsuju hin bunseki*
analysis, product	製品分析	*seihin bunseki*
analysis, profitability	収益率分析	*shūeki ritsu bunseki*
analysis, risk	危険分析	*kiken bunseki*
analysis, sales	販売分析	*hanbai bunseki*
analysis, systems	システム分析	*shisutemu bunseki*
analyst	分析者	*bunseki sha*
anchorage (dues)	碇泊料	*teihaku ryō*
ancillary expenses	付随費用	*fuzui hiyō*
anesthetic	麻酔薬	*masui yaku*
angora	アンゴラ	*angora*
angular cutter	山形フライス	*yamagata furaisu*
annealing	焼なまし	*yaki namashi*
annual (adj)	毎年の	*mainen no*
annual accounts	年次決算報告	*nenji kessan hōkoku*
annual audit	年次会計検査	*nenji kaikei kensa*
annual report	年次営業報告	*nenji eigyō hōkoku*
annuitant	年金受取人	*nenkin uketori nin*
annuity	年金	*nenkin*
antacid	制酸薬	*seisan yaku*
antenna	アンテナ	*antena*
anti-inflammatory (adj)	抗炎症用の	*kō enshō yō no*
anti-monopoly law	独占禁止法	*dokusen kinshi hō*
antibiotic	抗生物質	*kōsei busshitsu*
anticholinergic	副交感神経抑制剤	*fuku kōkan shinkei yokusei zai*
anticoagulant	血液凝固阻止薬	*ketsueki gyōko soshi yaku*
antidumping duty	ダンピング防止関税	*danpingu bōshi kanzei*
antique authenticity certificate	骨董品認定書	*kottō hin nintei sho*
antiseptic	消毒剤	*shōdoku zai*
antitrust laws	独占禁止法	*dokusen kinshi hō*

aperture	絞り	*shibori*
apparel	衣服	*ifuku*
appeal (v)	上告する	*jōkoku suru*
application	アプリケーション、申請	*apurikēshon, shinsei*
application form	申請書	*shinsei sho*
appointment	任命	*ninmei*
appraisal	評価	*hyōka*
appraisal, capital expenditure	資本支出査定	*shihon shishutsu satei*
appraisal, financial	財務査定	*zaimu satei*
appraisal, investment	投資査定	*tōshi satei*
appraisal, market	市場査定	*shijō satei*
appreciation	価格騰貴	*kakaku tōki*
apprentice	見習い	*minarai*
appropriation	支払い充当金	*shiharai jūtō kin*
approval	認可	*ninka*
approve (v)	認可する	*ninka suru*
approved delivery facility	認可済引渡し施設	*ninka zumi hikiwatashi shisetsu*
approved securities	確実な証券	*kakujitsu na shōken*
arbitrage	裁定取引	*saitei torihiki*
arbitrage (securities)	鞘取り	*sayatori*
arbitration	仲裁／調停	*chūsai/chōtei*
arbitration agreement	仲裁協定	*chūsai kyōtei*
arbitrator	仲裁人／調停者	*chūsainin/chōteisha*
area manager	地域担当支配人	*chiiki tantō shihai nin*
arithmetic mean	単純算術平均	*tanjun sanjutsu heikin*
armaments	武器	*buki*
arm's length	相対取引	*aitai torihiki*
around (exchange term) (adv)	がらみ	*garami*
arrears	滞納金	*tainō kin*
articulated robot	多関節ロボット	*takansetsu robotto*
artificial intelligence	人工知能	*jinkō chinō*
as is goods	無保証品	*mu hoshō hin*
as per advice	通知の通り	*tsūchi no tōri*
as soon as possible	すぐに	*sugu ni*
ASA speed	ASA感度	*ē esu ē kando*
asking price	言い値	*iine*
aspirin	アスピリン	*asupirin*
assay	分析	*bunseki*
assemble (v)	組立てる	*kumitateru*
assembly	組立て	*kumitate*
assembly factory	組立て工場	*kumitate kōjō*
assembly line	流れ作業列	*nagare sagyō retsu*
assess (v)	査定する	*satei suru*
assessed valuation	査定価格	*satei kakaku*
assessment	査定	*satei*
asset (sing./pl.)	資産	*shisan*
asset turnover	資産回転率	*shisan kaiten ritsu*

asset value	資産価格	*shisan kakaku*
assets, accrued	増殖資産	*zōshoku shisan*
assets, current	流動資産	*ryūdō shisan*
assets, deferred	繰延べ資産	*kurinobe shisan*
assets, fixed	固定資産	*kotei shisan*
assets, intangible	無形資産	*mukei shisan*
assets, liquid	流動資産	*ryūdō shisan*
assets, net	純資産	*jun shisan*
assets, tangible	有形資産	*yūkei shisan*
assign (v)	指定する	*shitei suru*
assign (v) (business law)	譲渡する	*jōto suru*
assignee	被譲渡人	*hi jōto nin*
assignor	譲渡人	*jōto nin*
assistant	助手	*joshu*
assistant general manager	副総支配人	*fuku sō shihai nin*
assistant manager	副支配人	*fuku shihai nin*
associate company	関連会社	*kanren gaisha*
assumed liability	継承債務	*keishō saimu*
at and from (adv)	その地において	*sono chi ni oite*
at best (adv)	最も有利な値段で	*mottomo yūri na nedan de*
at call (adv)	短期融資で	*tanki yūshi de*
at or better (adv)	指値又はそれより良い価格で	*sashine mata wa sore yori yoi kakaku de*
at par (adv)	平価で	*heika de*
at sight (adv)	一覧払いで	*ichiran barai de*
at the close (adv)	大引け相場注文で	*ōbike sōba chūmon de*
at the market (adv)	成行注文で	*nariyuki chūmon de*
at the opening (adv)	寄付き相場注文で	*yoritsuki sōba chūmon de*
attach (v)	添付する	*tenpu suru*
attache case	アタシェケース	*atashe kēsu*
attachment	差し押さえ	*sashiosae*
attended time	出勤時間数	*shukkin jikan sū*
attestation	署名の認証	*shomei no ninshō*
attorney	弁護士	*bengoshi*
attorney, power of	委任権	*ininken*
attrition	人員削減	*jin-in sakugen*
audio component system	オーディオ・コンポ	*ōdio konpo*
audio response equipment	音声応答装置	*onsei ōtō sōchi*
audit (v)	会計監査する	*kaikei kansa suru*
audit trail	監査証跡	*kansa shōseki*
audit, internal	内部監査	*naibu kansa*
auditing balance sheet	監査貸借対照表	*kansa taishaku taishō hyō*
auditor	会計監査人	*kaikei kansa nin*
autarky	自給自足	*jikyū jisoku*
authority, to have (v)	権威を所有する	*ken-i o shoyū suru*
authorize (v)	権限を与える	*kengen o ataeru*
authorized dealer	公認取扱業者	*kōnin toriatsukai gyōsha*
authorized shares	認定株	*nintei kabu*
authorized signature	正式の署名	*seishiki no shomei*

auto parts	自動車部品	*jidōsha buhin*
auto-loading	自動装填	*jidō sōten*
autochecker	オートチェッカー	*ōto chekkā*
automatic (adj)	自動的な	*jidō teki na*
automatic aperture control device	自動絞り	*jidō shibori*
automatic collection service	自動集金サービス	*jidō shūkin sābisu*
automatic developing machine	自動現像機	*jidō genzō ki*
automatic exposure	自動露出機構	*jidō roshutsu kikō*
automatic focusing	自動焦点	*jidō shōten*
automatic gearshift	オートクラッチ	*ōto kuratchi*
automatic pallet changer	パレット チェンジャー	*paretto chenjā*
automatic printing machine	オートプリンター	*ōto purintā*
automatic rewinding	自動巻上げ	*jidō makiage*
automatic screw machine	自動ねじ切り盤	*jidō nejikiri ban*
automatic teller machine	自動預金受け払い機	*jidō yokin ukebarai ki*
automatic tool changer	自動工具交換装置	*jidō kōgu kōkan sōchi*
automatic transfer service	自動振替サービス	*jidō furikae sābisu*
automatic transmission	自動変速機	*jidō hensoku ki*
automatically (adv)	自動的に	*jidō teki ni*
automation	オートメーション	*ōtomēshon*
automobile	自動車	*jidōsha*
autonomous (adj)	自主的な	*jishu teki na*
autonomously (adv)	自主的に	*jishu teki ni*
autoreverse	オートリバース	*ōto ribāsu*
auxiliary lens	アッタチメント レンズ	*atatchimento renzu*
availability, subject to	入手可能性を条件 として	*nyūshu kanō sei o jōken to shite*
average	平均	*heikin*
average (shipping)	海損	*kaison*
average cost	平均原価	*heikin genka*
average life	平均寿命	*heikin jumyō*
average price	平均値段	*heikin nedan*
average unit cost	平均単価	*heikin tanka*
average unit cost (accounting)	平均単位原価	*heikin tan-i genka*
average yield	平均利回り	*heikin rimawari*
averaging	平均法	*heikin hō*
averaging (securities)	なんぴん売買	*nanpin baibai*
avoidable costs	回避可能原価	*kaihi kanō genka*
axle	車軸	*shajiku*

B

back date (v)	前日付けにする	*mae hizuke ni suru*
back haul	逆航	*gyakkō*
back order	未調達注文	*mi chōtatsu chūmon*

B

back taxes	遡及課税	*sokyū kazei*
back-to-back credit	同時開設信用状	*dōji kaisetsu shin-yō jō*
backed note (shipping)	裏書貨物受取証	*uragaki kamotsu uketori shō*
backlog	注文残高	*chūmon zandaka*
backwardation	受渡し猶予	*ukewatashi yūyo*
backwash effect	逆流効果	*gyakuryū kōka*
bad debt	不良債権	*furyō saiken*
balance	残高	*zandaka*
balance of payments	国際収支	*kokusai shūshi*
balance of trade	貿易収支	*bōeki shūshi*
balance ratios	収支比率	*shūshi hiritsu*
balance sheet	貸借対照表	*taishaku taishō hyō*
balance, bank	銀行預金残高	*ginkō yokin zandaka*
balance, credit	貸方残高	*kashigata zandaka*
bale capacity	包装能力	*hōsō nōryoku*
bale cargo	俵貨物	*tawara kamotsu*
balloon (payment)	残額期日一括返済	*zangaku kijitsu ikkatsu hensai*
bank	銀行	*ginkō*
bank acceptance	銀行引受手形	*ginkō hikiuke tegata*
bank account	銀行預金口座	*ginkō yokin kōza*
bank balance	銀行預金残高	*ginkō yokin zandaka*
bank bill	銀行手形	*ginkō tegata*
bank charges	銀行手数料	*ginkō tesū ryō*
bank check	銀行小切手	*ginkō kogitte*
bank deposit	銀行預金	*ginkō yokin*
bank draft	銀行手形	*ginkō tegata*
bank examiner	銀行検査官	*ginkō kensa kan*
bank exchange	銀行為替手形	*ginkō kawase tegata*
bank holiday	銀行休日	*ginkō kyūjitsu*
bank letter of credit	銀行信用状	*ginkō shin-yō jō*
bank loan	銀行貸付	*ginkō kashitsuke*
bank money order	銀行送金手形	*ginkō sōkin tegata*
bank note	銀行券	*ginkō ken*
bank rate	公定歩合	*kōtei buai*
bank statement	銀行勘定報告書	*ginkō kanjō hōkoku sho*
bankruptcy	破産	*hasan*
bar chart	棒グラフ	*bō gurafu*
barbiturate	バルビツール酸系催眠薬	*barubitsūru san kei saimin yaku*
bareboat charter	裸傭船	*hadaka yōsen*
bargain	格安品	*kakuyasu hin*
bargain (securities)	売買約定	*baibai yakutei*
bargaining power	交渉権	*kōshō ken*
bargaining, collective	団体交渉	*dantai kōshō*
barratry (business law)	訴訟教唆	*soshō kyōsa*
barratry (transportation)	船長又は船員の不法行為	*senchō mata wa sen-in no fuhō kōi*
barrier, nontariff	非関税障壁	*hi kanzei shōheki*
bars	棒	*bō*

barter (v)	現物取引きする	*genbutsu torihiki suru*
base (chemicals)	塩基	*enki*
base currency	基準通貨	*kijun tsūka*
base price	基準値段	*kijun nedan*
base rate (transportation)	一般運賃率	*ippan unchin ritsu*
base rate (wage)	ベース・レート	*bēsu rēto*
base year	基準年次	*kijun nenji*
basis point (1/100%)	ベーシス・ポイント	*bēshisu pointo*
basket	バスケット	*basuketto*
batch processing	一括処理	*ikkatsu shori*
batch production	連続生産	*renzoku seisan*
battery	バッテリー	*batterī*
battery life	バッテリー連続使用時間	*batterī renzoku shiyō jikan*
battery recharger	充電池	*jūdenchi*
baud	ボー	*bō*
bear market	売相場	*uri sōba*
bearer	持参人	*jisan nin*
bearer bond	無記名債券	*mukimei saiken*
bearer security	無記名証券	*mukimei shōken*
bearer stock	無記名株	*mukimei kabu*
bell-shaped curve	鐘形曲線	*shōkei kyokusen*
bellwether issue	指標銘柄	*shihyō meigara*
below par (adv)	額面以下で	*gakumen ika de*
below-the-line item	画線下の項目	*kakusen ka no kōmoku*
belt	ベルト	*beruto*
beneficiary	受取人	*uketori nin*
benzene	ベンゼン	*benzen*
bequest	遺贈	*izō*
berth terms	船内人夫賃船主負担	*sennai ninpu chin senshu futan*
bid	入札	*nyūsatsu*
bid (takeover)	株式買取り公開申込み	*kabushiki kaitori kōkai mōshikomi*
bid and asked	呼び値	*yobine*
bill (banknote)	紙幣	*shihei*
bill (sales)	請求書	*seikyū sho*
bill broker	手形仲買人	*tegata nakagai nin*
bill of exchange	為替手形	*kawase tegata*
bill of lading	船荷証券	*funani shōken*
bill of sale	売渡し証書	*uriwatashi shōsho*
bill of sight	仮輸入願い	*kari yunyū negai*
billboard	掲示版	*keiji ban*
billets	小鋼片	*shō kōhen*
binary notation	二進法	*nishin hō*
binder	仮契約	*kari keiyaku*
bio-ceramics	バイオセラミックス	*baio seramikkusu*
bio-computer	バイオコンピュータ	*baio konpyūta*
biochemistry	生化学	*sei kagaku*
bisphenol	ビスフェノール	*bisu fenōru*

B

bit	ビット	*bitto*
black and white (adj)	単色の	*tanshoku no*
black and white film	白黒フィルム	*shiro kuro firumu*
black and white TV	白黒テレビ	*shiro kuro terebi*
black market	闇市場	*yami ichiba*
blanket bond	総括抵当権付債券	*sōkatsu teitō ken tsuki saiken*
blanket order	総括注文	*sōkatsu chūmon*
blanket order (production)	継続製造指図書	*keizoku seizō sashizu sho*
blast furnace	高炉	*kō ro*
blazer	ブレザー	*burezā*
bleed (printing)	断ち切り	*tachikiri*
bleed (v)	出血する	*shukketsu suru*
blockage of funds	資金封鎖	*shikin fūsa*
blocked currency	封鎖通貨	*fūsa tsūka*
blood	血液	*ketsueki*
blouse	ブラウス	*burausu*
blowup	引伸ばし	*hikinobashi*
blue chip stock	優良株	*yūryō kabu*
blue-collar worker	ブルーカラー労働者	*burū karā rōdō sha*
blueprint	青写真	*ao jashin*
board	ボード	*bōdo*
board meeting	取締役会議	*torishimariyaku kaigi*
board of directors	取締役会	*torishimariyaku kai*
board of supervisors	管理職員会	*kanri shokuin kai*
board, executive	理事会	*riji kai*
boardroom	会議室	*kaigi shitsu*
boardroom (securities)	立会場	*tachiai jō*
body	車体	*shatai*
boilerplate (contract)	（契約書に含まれる）標準条項	*(keiyaku sho ni fukumareru) hyōjun jōkō*
boilerplate (metal)	ボイラー板	*boirā ban*
boldface	肉太活字	*nikubuto katsuji*
bond	債券	*saiken*
bond areas	保税地域	*hozei chiiki*
bond credit rating	債券格付け	*saiken kakuzuke*
bond issue	社債発行	*shasai hakkō*
bond rating	債券格付け	*saiken kakuzuke*
bonded carrier	保税貨物運搬人	*hozei kamotsu unpan nin*
bonded goods	保税貨物	*hozei kamotsu*
bonded warehouse	保税倉庫	*hozei sōko*
bone china	ボーンチャイナ	*bōn chaina*
bonus (premium)	利益配当	*rieki haitō*
book	本	*hon*
book inventory	帳簿棚卸し	*chōbo tanaoroshi*
book value	帳簿価格	*chōbo kakaku*
book value per share	一株当たりの帳簿価格	*hitokabu atari no chōbo kakaku*
bookkeeping	簿記	*boki*
boom	好況	*kōkyō*

boots	ブーツ	*būtsu*
border	国境	*kokkyō*
border tax adjustment	国境税調整	*kokkyō zei chōsei*
boring machine	中刳盤	*nakaguri ban*
borrow (v)	借金する	*shakkin suru*
borrowing cost	借入コスト	*shakunyū kosuto*
botanic	植物性薬品	*shokubutsu sei yakuhin*
bow tie	蝶ネクタイ	*chō nekutai*
bowl	ボール	*bōru*
boycott (v)	ボイコットする	*boikotto suru*
brainstorming	ブレイン・ストーミング	*burein sutōmingu*
brake	ブレーキ	*burēki*
branch	支店	*shiten*
branch office	支店	*shiten*
brand	銘柄	*meigara*
brand acceptance	銘柄承認	*meigara shōnin*
brand image	銘柄イメージ	*meigara imēji*
brand loyalty	銘柄忠実性	*meigara chūjitsu sei*
brand manager	ブランド・マネージャー	*burando manējā*
brand recognition	銘柄認識	*meigara ninshiki*
Braun tube	ブラウン管	*buraun kan*
breach of contract	契約違反	*keiyaku ihan*
breadbasket	パンかご	*pan kago*
break even (v)	損益なしにやる	*son-eki nashi ni yaru*
break-even analysis	損益分岐点分析	*son-eki bunki ten bunseki*
break-even point	損益分岐点	*son-eki bunki ten*
briefcase	ブリーフケース	*burīfu kēsu*
broaching machine	ブローチ盤	*burōchi ban*
broken lot	端株	*ha kabu*
broken stowage	埋め荷	*umeni*
broker	仲買人	*nakagai nin*
broker, software	ソフトウェア・ブローカー	*sofutowea burōkā*
budget	予算	*yosan*
budget appropriation	予算割当て	*yosan wariate*
budget forecast	予算予測	*yosan yosoku*
budget, advertising	宣伝広告費	*senden kōkoku hi*
budget, capital	固定支出予算	*kotei shishutsu yosan*
budget, cash	現金収支予算	*genkin shūshi yosan*
budget, investment	投資予算	*tōshi yosan*
budget, marketing	市場開拓費	*shijō kaitaku hi*
budget, sales	販売予算	*hanbai yosan*
buffer memory	バッファ・メモリ	*baffa memori*
bug (defect in computer program)	バグ	*bagu*
built-in	内蔵	*naizō*
bull market	買相場	*kai sōba*

B

bumper	バンパー	*banpā*
bundle (computer)	セット	*setto*
burden rate (production)	製造間接費配賦率	*seizō kansetsu hi haifu ritsu*
bureaucrat	官僚	*kanryō*
business activity	景気	*keiki*
business card	名刺	*meishi*
business cycle	景気循環	*keiki junkan*
business management	経営管理	*keiei kanri*
business plan	経営管理計画	*keiei kanri keikaku*
business policy	経営方針	*keiei hōshin*
business practice	商慣行	*shō kankō*
business strategy	経営戦略	*keiei senryaku*
butanol	ブタノール	*butanōru*
butter dish	バター皿	*batā zara*
butter knife	バターナイフ	*batā naifu*
buy at best (v)	最も有利な値段で買う	*mottomo yūri na nedan de kau*
buy back (v)	買い戻す	*kaimodosu*
buy on close (v)	大引けで買う	*ōbike de kau*
buy on opening (v)	寄付きで買う	*yoritsuki de kau*
buyer	買手	*kaite*
buyer, chief	購買主任	*kōbai shunin*
buyer, credit	掛け買い人	*kake gai nin*
buyer, potential	見込み客	*mikomi kyaku*
buyer's market	買手市場	*kaite shijō*
buyer's option	買手の選択権	*kaite no sentaku ken*
buyer's responsibility	買手側責任	*kaite gawa sekinin*
buyout	買収	*baishū*
by-product	副産物	*fuku sanbutsu*
bylaws	定款	*teikan*
byte	バイト	*baito*

C

cable	電信	*denshin*
cable release	ケーブル・リリース	*kēburu rerīsu*
cable transfer	電信送金	*denshin sōkin*
calcium	カルシュウム	*karushūmu*
calculator	計算機	*keisan ki*
call loan	コール・ローン	*kōru rōn*
call money	コール・マネー	*kōru manē*
call option	株式買付け選択権	*kabushiki kaitsuke sentaku ken*
call price (securities)	買い戻し値段	*kaimodohi nedan*
call rate	コール・レート	*kōru rēto*
call rule	コール・ルール	*kōru rūru*
callback	回収	*kaishū*
camel's hair	ラクダ	*rakuda*
camera	カメラ	*kamera*

camera body	ボディー	*bodī*
campaign, advertising	宣伝活動	*senden katsudō*
campaign, productivity	生産性向上運動	*seisan sei kōjō undō*
camshaft	カムシャフト	*kamushafuto*
cancel (v)	取消す	*torikesu*
canceled check	抹消小切手	*masshō kogitte*
cancellation	解約	*kaiyaku*
cancellation money	解約金	*kaiyaku kin*
candlestick	ろうそく立て	*rōsoku tate*
capacity	能力	*nōryoku*
capacity, manufacturing	製造能力	*seizō nōryoku*
capacity, plant	工場生産能力	*kōjō seisan nōryoku*
capacity, utilization	利用能力	*riyō nōryoku*
capital	頭文字／資本	*kashira moji/shihon*
capital account	資本勘定	*shihon kanjō*
capital allowance	資本引当て	*shihon hikiate*
capital asset	固定資産	*kotei shisan*
capital budget	固定支出予算	*kotei shishutsu yosan*
capital expenditure	資本支出	*shihon shishutsu*
capital expenditure appraisal	資本支出査定	*shihon shishutsu satei*
capital exports	資本輸出	*shihon yushutsu*
capital formation	資本形成	*shihon keisei*
capital gain	資産売買益	*shisan baibai eki*
capital gain tax	キャピタルゲイン税	*kyapitaru gein zei*
capital gain/loss	資本利得及び損失	*shihon ritoku oyobi sonshitsu*
capital goods	資本財	*shihon zai*
capital increase	資本増加	*shihon zōka*
capital market	資本市場	*shihon shijō*
capital spending	資本支出	*shihon shishutsu*
capital stock	株式資本金	*kabushiki shihon kin*
capital structure	資本構成	*shihon kōsei*
capital surplus	資本剰余金	*shihon jōyo kin*
capital, raising	資金調達	*shikin chōtatsu*
capital, return on	資本利益率	*shihon rieki ritsu*
capital, risk	危険資本	*kiken shihon*
capital, working	運転資本	*unten shihon*
capital-intensive (adj)	資本集約の	*shihon shūyaku no*
capital-output ratio	資本産出量比率	*shihon sanshutsu ryō hiritsu*
capitalism	資本主義	*shihon shugi*
capitalization	資本化	*shihon ka*
capsule	カプセル	*kapuseru*
car	自動車	*jidōsha*
car telephone	自動車電話	*jidōsha denwa*
carbon dioxide laser	炭酸ガス・レーザー	*tansan gasu rēzā*
carbon fiber	炭素繊維	*tanso sen-i*
carbon steel	炭酸鋼	*tansan kō*
carburetor	キャブレター	*kyaburetā*
card	カード	*kādo*
cargo	積荷	*tsumi ni*

C

carload	一車貸切り貨物	*issha kashikiri kamotsu*
carnet	仮輸入免許	*kari yunyū menkyo*
carrier	運送業者	*unsō gyōsha*
carrier's risk	運送業者危険担保	*unsō gyōsha kiken tanpo*
carry forward (v)	進める	*susumeru*
carry forward (accounting) (v)	繰越す	*kurikosu*
carry-forward	繰越し	*kurikoshi*
carryback	繰戻し	*kurimodoshi*
carrying charges	諸掛かり	*shogakari*
carrying charges (securities)	繰延べ手数料	*kurinobe tesū ryō*
carryover (accounting)	繰越し	*kurikoshi*
carryover (merchandising)	残品	*zanpin*
cartel	カルテル、企業連合	*karuteru, kigyō rengō*
cartesian coordinates robot	直角座標ロボット	*chokkaku zahyō robotto*
cartridge	カートリッジ	*kātorijji*
carving knife	切り盛り用ナイフ	*kiri mori yō naifu*
cash	現金	*genkin*
cash and carry (trade)	現金自国船主義の	*genkin jikokusen shugi no*
cash balance	現金残高	*genkin zandaka*
cash basis	現金ベース	*genkin bēsu*
cash basis (accounting)	現金主義	*genkin shugi*
cash before delivery	引渡し前の現金払い	*hikiwatashi mae no genkin barai*
cash book	現金出納簿	*genkin suitō bo*
cash budget	現金収支予算	*genkin shūshi yosan*
cash delivery	当日決済取引き	*tōjitsu kessai torihiki*
cash discount	現金割引き	*genkin waribiki*
cash dividend	現金配当	*genkin haitō*
cash entry	普通輸入申告	*futsū yunyū shinkoku*
cash flow	資金繰り	*shikinguri*
cash flow statement	現金収支一覧表	*genkin shūshi ichiran hyō*
cash in advance	前払い	*mae barai*
cash management	資金管理	*shikin kanri*
cash on delivery	現金引換え払い	*genkin hikikae barai*
cash register	レジスター	*rejisutā*
cash surrender value	解約戻し金	*kaiyaku modoshikin*
cash-and-carry (adj)	現金店頭渡しの	*genkin tentō watashi no*
cashier's check	銀行小切手／支払人小切手	*ginkō kogitte/shiharainin kogitte*
cashmere	カシミヤ	*kashimiya*
cassette	カセット	*kasetto*
cast iron	鋳鉄	*chūtetsu*
cast steel	鋳鋼	*chūkō*
casualty insurance	災害保険	*saigai hoken*
catalog	カタログ	*katarogu*
catalyst	触媒	*shokubai*
CB	市民ラジオ	*shimin rajio*
CD-ROM disk	シーディーロムディスク	*shīdīromu disuku*

CD-ROM drive	シーディーロム ドライブ	*shīdīromu doraibu*
ceiling	最高限度	*saikō gendo*
centerless grinder	心無し研削盤	*kokoro nashi kensaku ban*
central bank	中央銀行	*chūō ginkō*
central processing unit (CPU)	中央処理装置	*chūō shori sōchi*
central rate	セントラル・レート	*sentoraru rēto*
centralization	集中化	*shūchū ka*
ceramic condenser	セラミック コンデンサー	*seramikku kondensa*
ceramic engine	セラミックエンジン	*seramikku enjin*
ceramic fiber	セラミック ファイバー	*seramikku faibā*
ceramic filter	セラミック フィルター	*seramikku firutā*
ceramic sensor	セラミックセンサー	*seramikku sensā*
cermet	サーメット	*sāmetto*
certificate	証明書	*shōmei sho*
certificate (securities)	証券	*shōken*
certificate of deposit	預金証書	*yokin shōsho*
certificate of incorporation	会社設立許可証	*kaisha setsuritsu kyoka shō*
certificate of origin	原産地証明書	*gensanchi shōmei sho*
certification	認証	*ninshō*
certified check	支払保証小切手	*shiharai hoshō kogitte*
certified public accountant	公認会計士	*kōnin kaikeishi*
chain of command	指揮系統	*shiki keitō*
chain store	チェーン・ストア	*chēn sutoa*
chain store group	チェーン・ストア 組織	*chēn sutoa soshiki*
chairman of the board	取締役会長	*torishimariyaku kaichō*
chamber of commerce	商工会議所	*shōkō kaigisho*
champagne glass	シャンペン・グラス	*shanpen gurasu*
channel of distribution	流通経路	*ryūtsū keiro*
chapter (publishing)	章	*shō*
charge account	売掛け金勘定	*urigake kin kanjō*
charge off (v)	損失扱いにする	*sonshitsu atsukai ni suru*
charges (finance)	料金	*ryōkin*
charges (sales)	諸掛かり	*shogakari*
chart, activity	活動調査表	*katsudō chōsa hyō*
chart, bar	棒グラフ	*bō gurafu*
chart, flow	業務運行表	*gyōmu unkō hyō*
chart, flow (production)	生産工程順序一覧表	*seisan kōtei junjo ichiran hyō*
chart, management	管理活動表	*kanri katsudō hyō*
charter (shipping)	傭船	*yōsen*
chartered accountant	公認会計士	*kōnin kaikeishi*
charterparty agent	傭船契約代理店	*yōsen keiyaku dairiten*
chassis	シャーシー	*shāshī*
chattel	動産	*dōsan*
chattel mortgage	動産抵当	*dōsan teitō*

C

cheap (adj)	安い	*yasui*
check (banking)	小切手	*kogitte*
check, counter	預金引出し票	*yokin hikidashi hyō*
checking account	当座預金口座	*tōza yokin kōza*
checklist	照合表	*shōgō hyō*
cheese tray	チーズの盛り皿	*chīzu no mori zara*
chemical (n)	化学製品	*kagaku seihin*
chemical fertilizer	化学肥料	*kagaku hiryō*
chief accountant	会計主任	*kaikei shunin*
chief buyer	購買主任	*kōbai shunin*
chief executive	最高経営責任者	*saikō keiei sekininsha*
china	磁器	*jiki*
chip	チップ	*chippu*
chip condenser	チップ・コンデンサ	*chippu kondensa*
chloride	塩化物	*enka butsu*
chloroform	クロロホルム	*kurorohorumu*
chromium	クローム	*kurōmu*
circuit breaker	回路遮断機	*kairo shadan ki*
civil action	民事訴訟	*minji soshō*
civil engineering	土木工学	*doboku kōgaku*
civil law	民法	*minpō*
civil suit	民事訴訟	*minji soshō*
claim (business law)	損害賠償請求	*songai baishō seikyū*
claim (insurance)	支払い請求	*shiharai seikyū*
class action	クラス・アクション	*kurasuakushon*
classified ad	項目別広告	*kōmoku betsu kōkoku*
clearinghouse	手形交換所	*tegata kōkansho*
client	依頼人	*irainin*
close-up lens	クローズ・アップ・レンズ	*kurōzu appu renzu*
closed account	封鎖勘定	*fūsa kanjō*
closely held corporation	非公開会社	*hi kōkai gaisha*
closing entry	決算記入	*kessan kinyū*
closing price	大引け値段	*ōbike nedan*
clutch	クラッチ	*kuratchi*
co-ownership	共同所有権	*kyōdō shoyū ken*
coal	石炭	*sekitan*
coaster	コップ敷き	*koppu shiki*
coat	コート	*kōto*
coated paper	アート紙	*āto shi*
codicil	追加条項	*tsuika jōkō*
coffee break	休憩時間	*kyūkei jikan*
coffeepot	コーヒーポット	*kōhī potto*
coil	コイル	*koiru*
coinsurance	共同保険	*kyōdō hoken*
cold rolling	冷間圧延	*reikan atsuen*
collar	衿	*eri*
collateral	見返り担保、担保	*mikaeri tanpo, tanpo*
colleague	同僚	*dōryō*

collect on delivery	代金引換え払い	*daikin hikikae barai*
collection period	取立て期間	*toritate kikan*
collections	コレクション	*korekushon*
collective agreement	団体協約	*dantai kyōyaku*
collective bargaining	団体交渉	*dantai kōshō*
collector of customs	税関長	*zeikan chō*
colloquium	共同討議	*kyōdō tōgi*
collusion	談合	*dangō*
color	色、カラー	*iro, karā*
color film	カラーフィルム	*karā firumu*
color liquid crystal	カラー液晶	*karā ekishō*
color print	カラープリント	*karā purinto*
color separation	カラー分解	*karā bunkai*
color slide	カラースライド	*karā suraido*
color TV	カラーテレビ	*karā terebi*
combination (industry)	企業結合	*kigyō ketsugō*
commerce	通商	*tsūshō*
commercial (advertisement)	コマーシャル	*komāsharu*
commercial bank	市中銀行、商業銀行	*shichū ginkō, shōgyō ginkō*
commercial grade	商業格付け	*shōgyō kakuzuke*
commercial invoice	商業送り状	*shōgyō okurijō*
commercial law	商法	*shōhō*
commission (agency)	取次	*toritsugi*
commission (fee)	手数料	*tesūryō*
commitment	約定	*yakutei*
commitment (securities)	委託売買契約	*itaku baibai keiyaku*
commodity	商品	*shōhin*
commodity exchange	商品取引所	*shōhin torihikisho*
commodity market	商品市場	*shōhin shijō*
common carrier	一般運送業者	*ippan unsō gyōsha*
common market	共同市場	*kyōdō shijō*
common stock	普通株	*futsū kabu*
compact disc	コンパクト・ディスク	*konpakuto disuku*
compact disc player	コンパクト・ディスク・プレーヤー	*konpakuto disuku purēyā*
company	会社	*kaisha*
company goal	企業目的	*kigyō mokuteki*
company policy	企業政策	*kigyō seisaku*
company, holding	持株会社	*mochikabu gaisha*
company, parent	親会社	*oya gaisha*
compatibility	互換性	*gokansei*
compensating balance	補償預金	*hoshō yokin*
compensation	賠償、報酬	*baishō, hōshū*
compensation (business law)	補償	*hoshō*
compensation trade	求償貿易	*kyūshō bōeki*
competition	競争	*kyōsō*
competitive advantage	競争上の利点	*kyōsō jō no riten*
competitive edge	競争上の優越性	*kyōsō jō no yūetsu sei*

C

competitive price	競争値段	*kyōsō nedan*
competitive strategy	競争戦略	*kyōsō senryaku*
competitor	競争相手	*kyōsō aite*
competitor analysis	競合者分析	*kyōgō sha bunseki*
complimentary copy	贈呈本	*zōtei bon*
component	構成要素	*kōsei yōso*
component (stereo)	コンポ	*konpo*
compound (sing./pl.)	化合物	*kagō butsu*
composite index	総合指数	*sōgō shisū*
composite materials	複合材料	*fukugō zairyō*
compound interest	複利	*fukuri*
compound semiconductor	化合物半導体	*kagō butsu handōtai*
comptroller	会計監査役	*kaikei kansa yaku*
computer	コンピュータ	*konpyūta*
computer bank	コンピュータ・バンク	*konpyūta banku*
computer center	コンピュータ・センタ	*konpyūta senta*
computer input	コンピュータ入力	*konpyūta nyūryoku*
computer language	コンピュータ言語	*konpyūta gengo*
computer memory	コンピュータ・メモリ	*konpyūta memori*
computer output	コンピュータ出力	*konpyūta shutsuryoku*
computer program	コンピュータ・プログラム	*konpyūta puroguramu*
computer storage	コンピュータ・ストレージ	*konpyūta sutorēji*
computer terminal	コンピュータ・ターミナル	*konpyūta tāminaru*
computer, analog	アナログ・コンピュータ	*anarogu konpyūta*
computer, digital	デジタル・コンピュータ	*dejitaru konpyūta*
computerized numerical control (CNC)	コンピュータ内蔵数値制御装置	*konpyūta naizō sūchi seigyo sōchi*
condenser	コンデンサ	*kondensa*
condenser lens	集光レンズ	*shūkō renzu*
conditional acceptance	条件付き引受け	*jōken tsuki hikiuke*
conditional sales contract	条件付き売買契約	*jōken tsuki baibai keiyaku*
conductivity	電導率	*dendō ritsu*
conference room	会議室	*kaigi shitsu*
confidential (adj)	機密の	*kimitsu no*
confirmation of order	注文確認	*chūmon kakunin*
conflict of interest	利害の衝突	*rigai no shōtotsu*
conglomerate	複合企業	*fukugō kigyō*
connecting rod	連接棒	*rensetsu bō*
connector	コネクター	*konekutā*
connector cable	接続ケーブル	*setsuzoku kēburu*
consideration (bus. law)	代償	*daishō*

consignee	受託者	*jutaku sha*
consignee (shipping)	荷受人	*niuke nin*
consignment	販売委託	*hanbai itaku*
consignment note	委託貨物運送状	*itaku kamotsu unsō jō*
consolidated financial statement	連結財務諸表	*renketsu zaimu shohyō*
consolidation	合併	*gappei*
consortium	借款団	*shakkan dan*
consular invoice	領事証明送り状	*ryōji shōmei okurijō*
consultant	コンサルタント	*konsarutanto*
consultant, management	経営顧問	*keiei komon*
consumer	消費者	*shōhi sha*
consumer acceptance	消費者承認	*shōhi sha shōnin*
consumer credit	消費者信用	*shōhi sha shin-yō*
consumer credit company	信販会社	*shinpan gaisha*
consumer goods	消費財	*shōhi zai*
consumer loan	消費者ローン	*shōhisha rōn*
consumer price index	消費者物価指数	*shōhi sha bukka shisū*
consumer research	消費者調査	*shōhi sha chōsa*
consumer satisfaction	消費者満足	*shōhi sha manzoku*
contact	接点	*setten*
container	コンテナー	*kontenā*
content (pharmaceuticals)	容量	*yōryō*
contingencies	不測事態	*fusoku jitai*
contingent fund	緊急用積立て金	*kinkyū yō tsumitate kin*
contingent liability	偶発債務	*gūhatsu saimu*
continuous caster	連続鋳造	*renzoku chūzō*
contract	契約	*keiyaku*
contract carrier	請負運送業者	*ukeoi unsō gyōsha*
contract month	契約月	*keiyaku zuki*
control, cost	原価管理	*genka kanri*
control, financial	財務統制	*zaimu tōsei*
control, inventory	在庫品管理	*zaiko hin kanri*
control, manufacturing	製造管理	*seizō kanri*
control, production	生産管理	*seisan kanri*
control, quality	品質管理	*hinshitsu kanri*
control, stock	在庫品管理	*zaiko hin kanri*
controllable costs	管理可能費	*kanri kanō hi*
controller	会計監査役	*kaikei kansa yaku*
controller (computer)	コﾝﾄローラ	*kontorōra*
controlling interest	支配権	*shihai ken*
converter	変換機	*henkan ki*
convertible bond	転換社債	*tenkan shasai*
convertible debentures	転換社債	*tenkan shasai*
convertible preferred stock	転換優先株	*tenkan yūsen kabu*
convertible securities	転換証券	*tenkan shōken*
cooperation agreement	協業協約	*kyōgyō kyōyaku*
cooperative	協同組合	*kyōdō kumiai*
cooperative advertising	協同広告	*kyōdō kōkoku*

C

copper	銅	*dō*
coprocessor	コプロセッサ	*kopurosessa*
copy	原稿	*genkō*
copy (text) (advertising)	広告文案	*kōkoku bun-an*
copy testing	原稿調査	*genkō chōsa*
copyright	著作権／版権	*chosaku ken/hanken*
copyright law	著作権法	*chosakuken hō*
cordless phone	コードレスホン	*kōdoresu hon*
corporate bonds	社債	*shasai*
corporate growth	企業成長	*kigyō seichō*
corporate image	企業イメージ	*kigyō imēji*
corporate income tax	法人税	*hōjin zei*
corporate planning	企業計画	*kigyō keikaku*
corporate structure	事業形態	*jigyō keitai*
corporate tax	法人税	*hōjinzei*
corporation	社団法人	*shadan hōjin*
corporation tax	法人税	*hōjin zei*
corpus	元金	*gankin*
correlator	相関器	*sōkan ki*
correspondence	通信	*tsūshin*
correspondent bank	取引先銀行	*torihiki saki ginkō*
cortisone	コーチゾン	*kōchizon*
cost	原価	*genka*
cost (v)	費用がかかる	*hiyō ga kakaru*
cost accounting	原価計算	*genka keisan*
cost analysis	原価分析	*genka bunseki*
cost and freight	運賃込み値段	*unchin komi nedan*
cost control	原価管理	*genka kanri*
cost effectiveness	原価能率	*genka nōritsu*
cost factor	原価要素	*genka yōso*
cost of capital	資本コスト	*shihon kosuto*
cost of goods sold	売上げ原価	*uriage genka*
cost of living	生活費	*seikatsu hi*
cost reduction	原価切下げ	*genka kirisage*
cost, average	平均原価	*heikin genka*
cost, direct	直接費	*chokusetsu hi*
cost, indirect	間接費	*kansetsu hi*
cost, replacement	取替え原価	*torikae genka*
cost-benefit analysis	費用便益分析	*hiyō ben-eki bunseki*
cost-plus contract	原価加算契約	*genka kasan keiyaku*
cost-price squeeze	原価引締め	*genka hikishime*
costs, allocation of (accounting)	原価配分	*genka haibun*
costs, allocation of	経費割当て	*keihi wariate*
costs, fixed	固定費	*kotei hi*
costs, managed	マネージド・コスト	*manējido kosuto*
costs, production	生産費	*seisan hi*
costs, set-up	段取り費	*dandori hi*
costs, standard	標準原価	*hyōjun genka*
costs, variable	変動費	*hendō hi*

cotton	綿	*men*
cough drop	咳止めドロップ	*seki dome doroppu*
cough syrup	咳止めシロップ	*seki dome shiroppu*
counter check	預金引出票	*yokin hikidashi hyō*
counterfeit	偽造品	*gizō hin*
countervailing duty	相殺関税	*sōsai kanzei*
country of origin	原産国	*gensan koku*
country risk	国別信用度	*kuni betsu shin-yō do*
coupon (bond interest)	利札	*rifuda*
courier service	宅配便	*takuhai bin*
court	裁判所、法廷	*saibansho, hōtei*
covenant	誓約	*seiyaku*
cover (publishing)	表紙	*hyōshi*
cover charge	サービス料	*sābisu ryō*
cover charge (finance)	保証金	*hoshō kin*
cover letter	添え状	*soejō*
coverage (insurance)	信用保険制限高	*shin-yō hoken seigen daka*
crankshaft	クランクシャフト	*kurankushafuto*
crawling peg	平価の小刻み調整	*heika no kokizami chōsei*
credit	信用	*shin-yō*
credit (accounting)	貸方	*kashigata*
credit (finance)	信用	*shin-yō*
credit (v)	信用する	*shin-yō suru*
credit account	掛け勘定	*kakekanjō*
credit balance	貸方残高	*kashigata zandaka*
credit bank	信用銀行	*shin-yō ginkō*
credit bureau	商業興信所	*shōgyō kōshin sho*
credit card	クレジット・カード	*kurejittokādo*
credit check	信用調査	*shin-yō chōsa*
credit control	信用統制	*shin-yō tōsei*
credit insurance	信用保険	*shin-yō hoken*
credit line	貸出し限度額／信用限度額	*kashidashi gendo gaku/shin-yō gendo gaku*
credit management	得意先管理	*tokui saki kanri*
credit note	貸方票	*kashigata hyō*
credit rating	信用格付け	*shin-yō kakuzuke*
credit reference	信用紹介	*shin-yō shōkai*
credit terms	信用支払い条件	*shin-yō shiharai jōken*
credit union	信用組合	*shin-yō kumiai*
creditor	債権者	*saiken sha*
criminal action	刑事訴訟	*keiji soshō*
criminal law	刑法	*keihō*
critical path analysis	最長経路分析	*saichō keiro bunseki*
crop (v)	余白を切落とす	*yohaku o kiriotosu*
cross examination	反対尋問	*hantai jinmon*
cross-licensing	特許権交換	*tokkyo ken kōkan*
crucible	るつぼ	*rutsubo*
crystal glass	カット・グラス	*katto gurasu*
cufflink	カフス・ボタン	*kafusu botan*

cultural export permit	文化財輸出許可書	*bunka zai yushutsu kyoka sho*
cultural property	文化財	*bunka zai*
cum dividend	配当付き	*haitō tsuki*
cumulative (adj)	累積的	*ruiseki teki*
cumulative preferred stock	累積優先株	*ruiseki yūsen kabu*
cup	茶碗	*chawan*
cupola	キューポラ	*kyūpora*
currency	通貨	*tsūka*
currency band	通貨帯	*tsūka tai*
currency clause	通貨約款	*tsūka yakkan*
currency conversion	通貨切替え	*tsūka kirikae*
current account	当座勘定	*tōza kanjō*
current assets	流動資産	*ryūdō shisan*
current liabilities	流動負債	*ryūdō fusai*
current ratio	流動比率	*ryūdō hiritsu*
current yield	現在利回り	*genzai rimawari*
customer	顧客	*kokyaku*
customer service	顧客サービス	*kokyaku sābisu*
customs	税関	*zeikan*
customs broker	税関貨物取扱い人	*zeikan kamotsu toriatsukai nin*
customs duty	関税	*kanzei*
customs entry	税関手続き	*zeikan tetsuzuki*
customs invoice	税関送り状	*zeikan okuri jō*
customs regulations	通関規制	*tsūkan kisei*
customs union	関税同盟	*kanzei dōmei*
cut (fashion) (v)	裁断する	*saidan suru*
cutback	削減	*sakugen*
cutlery	刃物類	*hamono rui*
cutting tool	バイト	*baito*
cycle billing	請求書の分割発行	*seikyū sho no bunkatsu hakkō*
cycle, business	景気循環	*keiki junkan*
cylinder	シリンダー	*shirindā*
cylinder boring machine	シリンダー中剥盤	*shirindā nakaguri ban*
cylindrical coordinates robot	円筒座標ロボット	*entō zahyō robotto*
cylindrical grinder	円筒研削盤	*entō kensaku ban*

D

D-RAM	ダイナミック・ラム	*dainamikku ramu*
daily (adj)	毎日の	*mainichi no*
daily (adv)	毎日	*mainichi*
dairy products	酪農製品	*rakunō seihin*
damage	損害	*songai*
data	資料	*shiryō*
data acquisition	データ収集	*dēta shūshū*
data bank	データ・バンク	*dēta banku*
data base	データ・ベース	*dēta bēsu*
data compression	データ圧縮	*dēta asshuku*

data file	データ・ファイル	*dēta fairu*
data processing	データ処理	*dēta shori*
data transmission	データ転送	*dēta tensō*
date of delivery	受渡し日	*ukewatashi bi*
day loan	当日限り貸付け	*tōjitsu kagiri kashitsuke*
day order	当日限り有効注文	*tōjitsu kagiri yūkō chūmon*
DC machine	直流機	*chokuryū ki*
dead freight	空荷運賃	*karani unchin*
deadline	最終期限	*saishū kigen*
deadlock	行詰まり	*ikizumari*
deal	取引き	*torihiki*
deal, package	一括取り引き	*ikkatsu torihiki*
dealer	ディーラー	*dīrā*
dealership	販売権	*hanbai ken*
debentures	社債	*shasai*
debit entry	借方記入	*karigata kinyū*
debit	負債、借方	*fusai, karigata*
debit note	借方票	*karigata hyō*
debt	負債	*fusai*
debug (v)	デバッグする	*debaggu suru*
decanter	デカンター	*dekantā*
declaration of bankruptcy	破産宣告	*hasan senkoku*
deductible (adj)	控除できる	*kōjo dekiru*
deduction	控除	*kōjo*
deed	証書	*shōsho*
deed of contract	約定書	*yakutei sho*
deed of sale	売渡し証書	*uriwatashi shōsho*
deed of transfer	名義書換え証書	*meigi kakikae shōsho*
deed of trust	信託証書	*shintaku shōsho*
default	支払い不能	*shiharai funō*
default (v)	債務履行を怠る	*saimu rikō o okotaru*
defective (adj)	欠陥がある	*kekkan ga aru*
defend	弁護する	*bengosuru*
defense, the	弁護側	*bengo gawa*
deferred annuities	据置き年金	*sueoki nenkin*
deferred assets	繰延べ資産	*kurinobe shisan*
deferred charges	繰延べ費用	*kurinobe hiyō*
deferred delivery	延べ渡し	*nobe watashi*
deferred income	繰延べ収益	*kurinobe shūeki*
deferred liabilities	据置き負債	*sueoki fusai*
deferred tax	据置き税	*sueoki zei*
deficit	赤字	*akaji*
deficit financing	赤字財政	*akaji zaisei*
deficit spending	超過支出	*chōka shishutsu*
deflation	通貨収縮	*tsūka shūshuku*
defroster	デフロスター	*defurosutā*
delay	延滞	*entai*
delinquent account	支払い延滞勘定	*shiharai entai kanjō*
delivered price	引渡し値段	*hikiwatashi nedan*

D

D

delivery	引渡し	*hikiwatashi*
delivery date	納期	*nōki*
delivery notice	引渡し通知書	*hikiwatashi tsūchi sho*
delivery points	受渡し場所	*ukewatashi basho*
delivery price (securities)	受渡し標準値段	*ukewatashi hyōjun nedan*
delivery price (shipping)	運賃込み値段	*unchin komi nedan*
demand (business)	需要	*juyō*
demand (finance)	請求	*seikyū*
demand (v)	要求する	*yōkyū suru*
demand deposit	要求払い預金	*yōkyū barai yokin*
demographic (adj)	人口統計学上の	*jinkō tōkei gaku jō no*
demotion	格下げ	*kakusage*
demurrage	停滞料	*teitai ryō*
density	濃度	*nōdo*
department	部門	*bumon*
Department of Commerce (U.S.)	商務省	*shōmushō*
Department of Justice (U.S.)	司法省	*shihōshō*
department (U.S. Government)	省	*shō*
department store	デパート	*depāto*
deposit	預金	*yokin*
deposit (banking)	銀行預金	*ginkō yokin*
deposit (securities)	供託金	*kyōtaku kin*
deposit account	預金勘定	*yokin kanjō*
deposit, bank	銀行預金	*ginkō yokin*
deposition	宣誓供述書	*sensei kyōjutsusho*
depository	受託所	*jutaku sho*
depreciation	価値下落	*kachi geraku*
depreciation (accounting)	減価償却	*genka shōkyaku*
depreciation allowance	減価償却引当て金	*genka shōkyaku hikiate kin*
depreciation of currency	通貨低落	*tsūka teiraku*
depreciation, accelerated	加速減価償却	*kasoku genka shōkyaku*
depreciation, accrued	減価償却累計額	*genka shōkyaku ruikei gaku*
depression	不況／不景気	*fukyō/fukeiki*
deputy chairman	副会長	*fuku kaichō*
deputy manager	副支配人	*fuku shihai nin*
design (v)	デザインする	*dezain suru*
design engineering	デザイン工学	*dezain kōgaku*
designer	デザイナー	*dezainā*
desk-top calculator	電卓	*dentaku*
desktop computer	デスク型コンピュータ	*desukugata konpyūta*
desktop presentation (DTPR)	デスクトップ・プレゼンテーション	*desukutoppu purezentēshon*
desktop publishing	卓上電子出版	*takujō denshi shuppan*
dessert plate	デザート皿	*dezāto zara*
devaluation	平価切下げ	*heika kirisage*
develop (photography) (v)	現像する	*genzō suru*
diabetes	糖尿病	*tōnyō byō*
die	ねじ切りダイス	*nejikiri daisu*

die casting	ダイカスト	*daikasuto*
diesel	ディーゼル	*dīzeru*
differential, price	価格格差	*kakaku kakusa*
differential, tariff	関税率格差	*kanzei ritsu kakusa*
differential, wage	賃金格差	*chingin kakusa*
digital (adj)	デジタル	*dejitaru*
digital audio disc	デジタル・オーディオ・デスク	*dejitaru ōdio disuku*
digital audio tape recorder	デジタル・オーディオ・レコーダー	*dejitaru ōdio tēpu rekōdā*
digital computer	デジタル・コンピュータ	*dejitaru konpyuta*
dilution of equity	持株比率の低下	*mochikabu hiritsu no teika*
dilution of labor	労働希釈	*rōdō kishaku*
diode	ダイオード	*daiōdo*
direct access storage	直接アクセス・ストレージ	*chokusetsu akusesu sutorēji*
direct cost	直接費	*chokusetsu hi*
direct expenses	直接経費	*chokusetsu keihi*
direct investment	直接投資	*chokusetsu tōshi*
direct labor	直接労働	*chokusetsu rōdō*
direct mail	ダイレクト・メール	*dairekuto mēru*
direct papers	直接為替手形	*chokusetsu kawase tegata*
direct quotation	直接相場	*chokusetsu sōba*
direct reduction process	直接製鉄法	*chokusetsu seitetsu hō*
direct selling	直接販売	*chokusetsu hanbai*
director	取締役	*torishimari yaku*
disbursement	支払い	*shiharai*
disc brake	ディスク・ブレーキ	*disuku burēki*
discharge (business law) (v)	責任解除する	*sekinin kaijo suru*
discharge (personnel) (v)	解雇する	*kaiko suru*
discount	割引き	*waribiki*
discount (v)	割引きする	*waribiki suru*
discount rate	手形割引き歩合	*tegata waribiki buai*
discount securities	割引き債券	*waribiki saiken*
discounted cash flow	現金収支割引法	*genkin shūshi waribiki hō*
discretion	自由裁量権	*jiyū sairyō ken*
discretionary account	一任勘定	*ichinin kanjō*
discretionary order	成行き注文	*nariyuki chūmon*
dish	皿	*sara*
dishonored check	不渡り小切手	*fuwatari kogitte*
disincentive	行動抑制要素	*kōdō yokusei yōso*
disk	ディスク	*disuku*
dispatch	発送	*hassō*
display	ディスプレイ	*disupurei*
display unit	ディスプレイ装置	*disupurei sōchi*
disposable income	処分可能所得	*shobun kanō shotoku*
dispute	争議	*sōgi*
dispute (v)	論争する	*ronsō suru*

D

dispute, labor	労働争議	*rōdō sōgi*
distillation	蒸留	*jōryū*
distribution	分配	*bunpai*
distribution costs	流通コスト	*ryūtsū kosuto*
distribution costs (advertising)	販売原価	*hanbai genka*
distribution network	流通網	*ryūtsū mō*
distribution policy (merchandising)	流通政策	*ryūtsū seisaku*
distribution policy (securities)	分配法	*bunpai hō*
distribution, channel of	流通経路	*ryūtsū keiro*
distributor (car)	デストリビューター	*desutoribūtā*
distributor (sales)	販売元	*hanbai moto*
district court	地方裁判所	*chihō saibansho*
diuretic	利尿薬	*rinyō yaku*
diversification (business)	多角経営化	*takaku keiei ka*
diversification (securities)	多角投資	*takaku tōshi*
divestment	権利喪失	*kenri sōshitsu*
dividend	配当	*haitō*
dividend reinvestment plan	配当再投資	*haitō saitōshi*
dividend yield	配当利回り	*haitō rimawari*
division of labor	分業	*bungyō*
dock (ship's receipt)	ドック受取り証	*dokku uketori shō*
dock handling charges	船渠貨物取扱い費	*senkyo kamotsu toriatsukai hi*
document	書類	*shorui*
dollar cost averaging	ドル平均法	*doru heikin hō*
domestic bill	国内手形	*kokunai tegata*
domestic corporation	国内会社	*kokunai gaisha*
door-to-door (sales)	戸別訪問販売	*kobetsu hōmon hanbai*
dose	服用量	*fukuyō ryō*
double dealing	両天秤取引き	*ryō tenbin torihiki*
double pricing	二重価格	*nijū kakaku*
double taxation	二重課税	*nijū kazei*
double time	賃金倍額払い	*chingin baigaku barai*
double-entry bookkeeping	複式簿記	*fukushiki boki*
Dow Jones Average	ダウ・ジョーンズ平均	*Dau Jōnzu heikin*
down payment	頭金／前渡し金	*atamakin/maewatashikin*
down period	工場閉鎖期間	*kōjō heisa kikan*
down the line (adv)	全面的に	*zenmen teki ni*
down-the-line (adj)	全面的な	*zenmen teki na*
download	ダウンロード	*daunrōdo*
downswing	下降	*kakō*
downtime	作業一時中止時間	*sagyō ichiji chūshi jikan*
downturn	沈滞	*chintai*
draft	手形	*tegata*
draft (banking)	手形振出し	*tegata furidashi*
draft (document)	下書き	*shita gaki*
draw down (v)	引下ろす	*hikiorosu*

drawback	戻し税	*modoshi zei*
drawee	手形名当人	*tegata naate nin*
drawer	手形振出人	*tegata furidashi nin*
drayage	運搬賃	*unpan chin*
dress	ドレス	*doresu*
drilling machine	ボール盤	*bōru ban*
drive	ドライブ	*doraibu*
drop (pharmaceuticals)	点滴薬	*tenteki yaku*
drop shipment	生産者直送	*seisan sha chokusō*
drug	薬	*kusuri*
dry cargo	乾荷	*kan ni*
dry goods (grain)	穀類	*kokurui*
dry goods (textile)	織物	*orimono*
due date	満期日	*mankibi*
dummy	体裁見本	*teisai mihon*
dumping (goods in foreign market)	ダンピング	*danpingu*
dun (v)	厳しく催促する	*kibishiku saisoku suru*
dunnage	荷敷	*ni shiki*
duopoly	複占	*fukusen*
durable goods	耐久財	*taikyū zai*
duress	強迫	*kyōhaku*
duty	義務	*gimu*
duty (customs)	関税	*kanzei*
duty, ad valorem	従価関税	*jūka kanzei*
duty, anti-dumping	ダンピング防止関税	*danpingu bōshi kanzei*
duty, countervailing	相殺関税	*sōsai kanzei*
duty, export	輸出税	*yushutsu zei*
duty, specific	従量税	*jūryō zei*
duty-free (adj)	免税の	*menzei no*
dynamic memory	ダイナミック・メモリ	*dainamikku memori*
dynamics, group	集団力学	*shūdan rikigaku*
dynamo	ダイナモ	*dainamo*

E

earmark (v)	別勘定にする	*betsu kanjō ni suru*
earnest money	手付け金	*tetsuke kin*
earnings on assets	資産所得	*shisan shotoku*
earnings per share	一株当りの利益	*hitokabu atari no rieki*
earnings performance	利益獲得業績	*rieki kakutoku gyōseki*
earnings report	収益報告	*shueki hōkoku*
earnings	利益、収益	*rieki, shūeki*
earnings yield	収益利回り	*shūeki rimawari*
earnings, retained	保留利益	*horyū rieki*
earnings/price ratio	収益株価率	*shūeki kabuka ritsu*
earthenware	陶器	*tōki*

econometrics	計量経済学	*keiryō keizaigaku*
economic (adj)	経済の	*keizai no*
economic barometer	経済観測指数	*keizai kansoku shisū*
economic indicators	経済指標	*keizai shihyō*
economic life	経済的機能的耐用年数	*keizai teki kinō teki taiyō nen sū*
economic order quantity	経済発注量	*keizai teki hatchū ryō*
economics	経済学	*keizaigaku*
economy of scale	規模の経済	*kibo no keizai*
edit (v)	編集する	*henshū suru*
edition	版	*han*
editor	編集者	*henshū sha*
EE camera	電子カメラ	*denshi kamera*
effective yield	実効利回り	*jikkō rimawari*
efficiency	効率	*kōritsu*
egg cup	ゆで卵立て	*yude tamago tate*
elasticity (of supply or demand)	弾力性	*danryoku sei*
electric arc furnace	弧光式炉	*kokō shiki ro*
electric circuit	電気回路	*denki kairo*
electric furnace	電気炉	*denki ro*
electric heater	電気暖房器	*denki danbō ki*
electric interlocking machine	電気連動機	*denki rendō ki*
electric resistance	電気抵抗	*denki teikō*
electric shaver	電気剃刀	*denki kamisori*
electric tools	電気工具	*denki kōgu*
electrical engineering	電気工学	*denki kōgaku*
electrical resistance	電気抵抗	*denki teikō*
electrically conductive rubber	電導性ゴム	*dendō sei gomu*
electro-magnetic shielding	電磁波シールド	*denji ha shīrudo*
electroconductive glass	電導性ガラス	*dendō sei garasu*
electroconductive polymer	電導性高分子	*dendō sei kōbunshi*
electrode	電極	*denkyoku*
electrolysis	電気分解	*denki bunkai*
electrolytic process	電解法	*denkai hō*
electromagnet	電磁石	*denjishaku*
electron beam	電子ビーム	*denshi bīmu*
electron gun	電子銃	*denshi jū*
electron microscope	電子顕微鏡	*denshi kenbikyō*
electronic bulletin board	電子掲示板	*denshi keijiban*
electronic cash register	電子レジスター	*denshi rejisutā*
electronic desk calculator	卓上電子計算機	*takujō denshi keisan ki*
electronic mail	電子メール	*denshi mēru*
electronic musical instruments	電子楽器	*denshi gakki*
electronic organ	電子オルガン	*denshi orugan*
electronic sewing machine	電子ミシン	*denshi mishin*
electronic typewriter	電子タイプライター	*denshi taipuraitā*
electronics	電子工学	*denshi kōgaku*
embargo	通商停止	*tsūshō teishi*
embezzlement	横領	*ōryō*

employee	従業員	*jūgyō in*
employee counseling	従業員相談制度	*jūgyō in sōdan seido*
employee relations	従業員関係	*jūgyō in kankei*
employment agency	職業紹介所	*shokugyō shōkai sho*
encumbrances (liens, liabilities)	負担	*futan*
end mill	エンド・ミル	*endo miru*
end of period	期末	*kimatsu*
end product	最終生産物	*saishū seisan butsu*
end-use certificate	最終用途証明書	*saishū yōto shōmei sho*
endorsee	被裏書き人	*hi uragaki nin*
endorsement	裏書き	*uragaki*
endorser	裏書き人	*uragaki nin*
endowment	財産寄贈	*zaisan kizō*
engine	エンジン	*enjin*
engineering	工学	*kōgaku*
engineering and design department	技術設計部門	*gijutsu sekkei bumon*
engineering plastic	エンジニアリング・プラスチック	*enjiniaringu purasuchikku*
engineering, design	デザイン工学	*dezain kōgaku*
engineering, industrial	インダストリアル・エンジニアリング	*indasutoriaru enjiniaringu*
engineering, systems	システム・エンジニアリング	*shisutemu enjiniaringu*
engineering, value	価値工学	*kachi kōgaku*
engrave (v)	彫る	*horu*
enlarge (v)	拡大する	*kakudai suru*
enlargement	引伸し	*hikinobashi*
enlarger	引伸し機	*hikinobashi ki*
enterprise	企業	*kigyō*
entrepreneur	企業家	*kigyō ka*
entry permit	通関免許	*tsūkan menkyo*
entry, cash	普通輸入申告	*futsū yunyū shinkoku*
entry, debit	借方記入	*karigata kinyū*
entry, ledger	元帳記入	*motochō kinyū*
enzyme	酵素	*kōso*
EP-ROM	消去可能読み出し専用メモリ	*shōkyo kanō yomidashi senyō memori*
equal pay for equal work	同一労働同一賃金	*dōitsu rōdō dōitsu chingin*
equalizer	イコライザー	*ikoraizā*
equipment	設備	*setsubi*
equipment leasing	設備品のリース	*setsubi hin no rīsu*
equity	持分	*mochibun*
equity (capital)	自己資本	*jiko shihon*
equity (stock)	株式	*kabushiki*
equity investments	直接出資	*chokusetsu shusshi*
equity, dilution of	持株比率の低下	*mochikabu hiritsu no teika*
equity, return on	持分利益率	*mochibun rieki ritsu*
ergonomics	人間工学	*ningen kōgaku*

error	エラー	*erā*
escalator clause	エスカレーター条項	*esukarētā jōkō*
escape clause	免責条項	*menseki jōkō*
escheat	没収	*bosshū*
escrow	条件付き譲渡証書	*jōken tsuki jōto shōsho*
escrow account	エスクロー・アカウント	*esukurō akaunto*
espresso cup	エスプレッソコーヒー用茶碗	*esupuresso kōhī yō chawan*
estate	資産	*shisan*
estate (business law)	遺産	*isan*
estate agent	財産管理人	*zaisan kanri nin*
estate tax	遺産相続税	*isan sōzoku zei*
estimate	見積り	*mitsumori*
estimate (v)	見積る	*mitsumoru*
estimate, sales	予想売上げ高	*yosō uriage daka*
estimated price	見積り価格	*mitsumori kakaku*
estimated time of arrival	到着予定時刻	*tōchaku yotei jikoku*
estimated time of departure	出発予定時刻	*shuppatsu yotei jikoku*
ethane	エタン	*etan*
ether	エーテル	*ēteru*
ethylene dichloride	二塩化エチレン	*ni enka echiren*
ethylene	エチレン	*echiren*
ethylene glycol	エチレン・グリコール	*echiren gurikōru*
ethylene oxide	エチレン・オキサイド	*echiren okisaido*
Eurobond	ユーロ・ボンド	*yūro bondo*
Eurocurrency	ユーロ通貨	*yūro tsūka*
Eurodollar	ユーロ・ダラー	*yūro darā*
evaluation	評価	*hyōka*
evaluation, job	職務評価	*shokumu hyōka*
evidence	証拠	*shōko*
ex dividend	配当落ち	*haitō ochi*
ex dock	埠頭渡し	*futō watashi*
ex factory	工場渡し	*kōjō watashi*
ex mill	工場渡し	*kōjō watashi*
ex mine	鉱業所渡し	*kōgyō sho watashi*
ex rights	権利落ち	*kenri ochi*
ex ship	着船渡し	*chakusen watashi*
ex warehouse	倉庫渡し	*sōko watashi*
ex works	工場渡し	*kōjō watashi*
excess demand	超過需要	*chōka juyō*
exchange (stock, commodity)	取引所	*torihiki sho*
exchange (v)	交換する	*kōkan suru*
exchange control	外国為替管理	*gaikoku kawase kanri*
exchange discount	為替割引き	*kawase waribiki*
exchange loss	為替差損	*kawase sason*
exchange market	外国為替市場	*gaikoku kawase shijō*

exchange rate	外国為替相場	*gaikoku kawase sōba*
exchange risk	為替リスク	*kawase risuku*
exchange value	交換価値	*kōkan kachi*
excise duty	消費税	*shōhi zei*
excise license	免許税	*menkyo zei*
excise tax	国内消費税	*kokunai shōhi zei*
exclusive agent	一手代理店	*itte dairi ten*
execution	執行	*shikkō*
executive	経営幹部	*keiei kanbu*
executive board	常任理事会	*jōnin riji kai*
executive committee	常務執行委員会	*jōmu shikkō iinkai*
executive compensation	幹部役員報酬	*kanbu yakuin hōshū*
executive director	専務取締役	*senmu torishimari yaku*
executive secretary	事務局長	*jimu kyokuchō*
executive, chief	最高経営責任者	*saikō keiei sekinin sha*
executive, line	ライン部門幹部職員	*rain bumon kanbu shokuin*
executor	指定遺言執行者	*shitei yuigon shikkō sha*
exempt	免除	*menjo*
exemption	免除	*menjo*
expandable	拡張可能	*kakuchō kanō*
expansion slot	拡張スロット	*kakuchō surotto*
expected results	期待利益	*kitai rieki*
expenditure	支出	*shishutsu*
expense account	接待費	*settai hi*
expenses	経費	*keihi*
expenses, direct	直接経費	*chokusetsu keihi*
expenses, indirect	間接経費	*kansetsu keihi*
expenses, running	運転費	*unten hi*
expenses, shipping	船積み費	*funazumi hi*
expiry date (securities)	手形買い取り最終日	*tegata kaitori saishū bi*
export (v)	輸出する	*yushutsu suru*
export agent	輸出代理店	*yushutsu dairi ten*
export ban	輸出禁止	*yushutsu kinshi*
export credit	輸出信用状	*yushutsu shin-yō jō*
export duty	輸出関税	*yushutsu kanzei*
export entry	輸出申告書	*yushutsu shinkoku sho*
export house	輸出業者	*yushutsu gyōsha*
export manager	輸出課長	*yushutsu kachō*
export middleman	輸出ブローカー	*yushutsu burōkā*
export permit	輸出許可	*yushutsu kyoka*
export quota	輸出割当て	*yushutsu wariate*
export regulations	輸出規制	*yushutsu kisei*
export sales contract	輸出販売契約	*yushutsu hanbai keiyaku*
export tax	輸出品税	*yushutsu hin zei*
export, for	輸出用	*yushutsu yō*
export-import bank	輸出入銀行	*yushutsunyū ginkō*
exposure	露出	*roshutsu*
exposure meter	露出計	*roshutsu kei*
expropriation	徴収	*chōshū*

external	外部	*gaibu*
extra dividend	特別配当金	*tokubetsu haitō kin*

F

fabric	ファブリック	*faburikku*
face value	額面価格	*gakumen kakaku*
facilities	設備	*setsubi*
facsimile	ファクシミリ	*fakushimiri*
factor	要素	*yōso*
factor (sales)	代理業者	*dairi gyōsha*
factor analysis	要素分析	*yōso bunseki*
factor, cost	原価要素	*genka yōso*
factor, load	負荷率	*fuka ritsu*
factor, profit	利益要素	*rieki yōso*
factory	工場	*kōjō*
factory overhead	製造間接費	*seizō kansetsu hi*
fail (v)	失敗する	*shippai suru*
fail (business) (v)	倒産する	*tōsan suru*
failure	失敗	*shippai*
failure (business)	倒産	*tōsan*
Fair Trade Commission	公正取引き委員会	*kōsei torihiki iinkai*
fair market value	公正市場価格	*kōsei shijō kakaku*
fair return	適正利益	*tekisei rieki*
fair trade	公正貿易	*kōsei bōeki*
farm out (v)	外注する	*gaichū suru*
fashion	ファッション	*fasshon*
fax	ファックス	*fakkusu*
fee	手数料	*tesūryō*
feedback	フィードバック	*fīdo bakku*
fender	フェンダー	*fendā*
ferrite	フェライト	*feraito*
ferroalloys	合金鉄	*gōkin tetsu*
ferrochromium	フェロクローム	*ferokurōmu*
ferromanganese	フェロマンガン	*feromangan*
ferronickel	フェロニッケル	*feronikkeru*
ferrosilicon	フェロシリコン	*feroshirikon*
fiber-optic communication	光通信	*hikari tsūshin*
fiber-reinforced plastics	ガラス繊維強化プラスチック	*garasu sen-i kyōka purasuchikku*
fidelity insurance	身元保証保険	*mimoto hoshō hoken*
fiduciary	受託者	*jutaku sha*
fiduciary issue	信用発行	*shin-yō hakkō*
fiduciary loan	信用貸付け	*shin-yō kashitsuke*
field warehousing	委託倉庫業務	*itaku sōko gyōmu*
fifth-generation computer	第五世代コンピュータ	*dai go sedai konpyūta*
file	ファイル	*fairu*

film	フィルム	*firumu*
filter	フィルター	*firutā*
finalize (v)	最終化する	*saishū ka suru*
finance (v)	融資する	*yūshi suru*
finance company	金融会社	*kin-yū gaisha*
financial analysis	財務分析	*zaimu bunseki*
financial appraisal	財務査定	*zaimu satei*
financial control	財務統制	*zaimu tōsei*
financial director	財務管理者	*zaimu kanri sha*
financial highlights	財務最重要点	*zaimu sai jūyō ten*
financial incentive	財務誘因	*zaimu yūin*
financial instrument	金融商品	*kin-yū shōhin*
financial leverage	ファイナンシャル・レバレッジ	*fainansharu rebarejji*
financial management	財務管理	*zaimu kanri*
financial market	金融市場	*kin-yū shijō*
financial period	会計期間	*kaikei kikan*
financial planning	財務計画	*zaimu keikaku*
financial product	金融商品	*kin-yū shōhin*
financial services	ファイナンシャル・サービス	*fainansharu sābisu*
financial statement	財務諸表	*zaimu shohyō*
financial year	会計年度	*kaikei nendo*
fine (penalty)	罰金	*bakkin*
fine ceramics	ファイン セラミックス	*fain seramikkusu*
fine polymer	ファイン ポリマー	*fain porimā*
finished goods inventory	在庫製品目録	*zaiko seihin mokuroku*
fire (v)	解雇する	*kaiko suru*
firm	会社	*kaisha*
firm (securities) (adj)	堅調な	*kenchō na*
first in-first out	先入先出法	*saki ire saki dashi hō*
first preferred stock	第一優先株	*daiichi yūsen kabu*
fiscal agent	財務代理店	*zaimu dairi ten*
fiscal year	会計年度	*kaikei nendo*
fish-eye lens	魚眼レンズ	*gyogan renzu*
fix the price (v)	価格操作をする	*kakaku sōsa o suru*
fixed assets	固定資産	*kotei shisan*
fixed capital	固定資本	*kotei shihon*
fixed charges (business)	確定費	*kakutei hi*
fixed charges	固定費	*kotei hi*
fixed costs	固定費	*kotei hi*
fixed expenses	固定費	*kotei hi*
fixed focus camera	固定焦点カメラ	*kotei shōten kamera*
fixed investment	固定資本投資	*hotei shihon tōshi*
fixed liability	固定負債	*kotei fusai*
fixed price	定価	*teika*
fixed rate	固定金利	*kotei kinri*

fixed rate of exchange	為替定率	*kawase teiritsu*
fixed resistor	固定抵抗器	*kotei teikō ki*
fixed sequence robot	固定シーケンス・ロボット	*kotei shīkensu robotto*
fixed term	定期	*teiki*
fixed terms	確定条件	*kakutei jōken*
fixtures (on balance sheet)	備品	*bihin*
flannel	フランネル	*furanneru*
flashbulb	フラッシュ・バルブ	*furasshu barubu*
flashcube	フラッシュ・キューブ	*furasshu kyūbu*
flat bond	無利息公債	*murisoku kōsai*
flat rate	均一料金	*kin-itsu ryōkin*
flat yield	均一利回り	*kin-itsu rimawari*
flatcar	平台貨車	*hiradai kasha*
fleet policy	フリート保険証券	*furīto hoken shōken*
flexible tariff	伸縮関税	*shinshuku kanzei*
float (issue stock) (v)	起債する	*kisai suru*
float (outstanding checks, stock)	フロート	*furōto*
floater (insurance policy)	包括保険契約	*hōkatsu hoken keiyaku*
floating asset	流動資産	*ryūdō shisan*
floating charge	浮動担保	*fudō tanpo*
floating debt (government)	短期公債	*tanki kōsai*
floating debt	一時借入れ金	*ichiji kariire kin*
floating exchange rate	変動為替相場	*hendō kawase sōba*
floating point unit (FPU)	浮動小数点ユニット	*fudō shōsūten yunitto*
floating rate	自由変動相場	*jiyū hendō sōba*
floor (of exchange)	立会場	*tachiai jō*
floppy disk	フロッピー・ディスク	*furoppī disuku*
flow chart	業務運行表	*gyōmu unkō hyō*
flow chart (production)	生産行程順序一覧表	*seisan kōtei junjo ichiran hyō*
flute	細長いシャンペン・グラス	*hosonagai shanpen gurasu*
focus	焦点	*shōten*
follow up (v)	追跡調査する	*tsuiseki chōsa suru*
follow-up order	追掛け注文	*oikake chūmon*
font (computer)	フォント	*fonto*
font (printing and publishing)	フォント／字体	*fonto/jitai*
food processor	フード・プロセッサ	*fūdo purosessa*
foodstuffs	食料	*shokuryō*
footing (accounting)	しめ高	*shimedaka*
for export	輸出用	*yushutsu yō*
forecast	予測	*yosoku*
forecast (v)	予測する	*yosoku suru*
forecast, budget	予算見積り	*yosan mitsumori*
forecast, market	市場見通し	*shijō mitōshi*
forecast, sales	販売予測	*hanbai yosoku*

foreclosure	没収	*bosshū*
foreign agent	外国代理店	*gaikoku dairi ten*
foreign bill of exchange	外国為替手形	*gaikoku kawase tegata*
foreign bond	外国債券	*gaikoku saiken*
foreign corporation	外国会社	*gaikoku gaisha*
foreign correspondent bank	コルレス先銀行	*koruresu saki ginkō*
foreign currency	外貨	*gaika*
foreign currency bond	外貨債	*gaika sai*
foreign debt	外債	*gaisai*
foreign demand	外需	*gaiju*
foreign exchange	外国為替	*gaikoku kawase*
foreign exchange rate	外国為替相場	*gaikoku kawase sōba*
foreign investment	海外投資	*kaigai tōshi*
foreign securities	外国証券	*gaikoku shōken*
foreign tax credit	外国税額控除	*gaikoku zeigaku kōjo*
foreign trade	外国貿易	*gaikoku bōeki*
foreman	職長	*shoku chō*
forgery	偽造	*gizō*
fork	フォーク	*fōku*
form (printing)	組版	*kumiban*
form letter	ひな形書簡	*hina gata shokan*
formaline	ホルマリン	*horumarin*
format	体裁	*teisai*
forward contract	先物契約	*sakimono keiyaku*
forward margin	先物マージン	*sakimono mājin*
forward market	先物市場	*sakimono shijō*
forward purchase	先物買付け	*saikimono kaitsuke*
forward shipment	先積出し	*saki tsumidashi*
forwarding agent	運送業者	*unsō gyōsha*
foul bill of lading	故障付船荷証券	*koshō tsuki funani shōken*
foundry	鋳造工場	*chūzō kōjō*
four colors	四色刷り	*yonshoku zuri*
four-wheel drive	四輪駆動	*yonrin kudō*
franchise (insurance)	免責歩合	*menseki buai*
franchise (sales)	一手販売権	*itte hanbai ken*
fraud	詐欺	*sagi*
fraud action	詐欺訴訟	*sagi soshō*
free alongside ship	船側渡し	*sensoku watashi*
free and clear	抵当に入っていない	*teitō ni haitte inai*
free enterprise	自由企業	*jiyū kigyō*
free time	自由時間	*jiyū jikan*
free list (commodities without duty)	免税品目録	*menzei hin mokuroku*
free market	自由市場	*jiyū shijō*
free market industry	自由市場企業	*jiyū shijō kigyō*
free of particular average	単独海損不担保	*tandoku kaison futanpo*
free on board (FOB)	本船渡し	*honsen watashi*
free on rail	貨車渡し	*kasha watashi*
free port	自由貿易港	*jiyū bōeki kō*

free trade	自由貿易	*jiyū bōeki*
free trade zone	自由貿易圏	*jiyū bōeki ken*
freeboard	乾舷標	*kangen hyō*
freelancer	自由業者	*jiyūgyō sha*
freight	貨物	*kamotsu*
freight all kinds	エフ・エー・ケー・レート	*efu ē kē rēto*
freight allowed	運賃立替払い協約	*unchin tatekae barai kyōyaku*
freight collect	運賃到着地払い	*unchin tōchaku chi barai*
freight forwarder	貨物運送業者	*kamotsu unsō gyōsha*
freight included	運賃込み	*unchin komi*
freight prepaid	運賃前払い	*unchin mae barai*
french cuff	フレンチ・カフス	*furenchi kafusu*
frequency curve	頻度曲線	*hindo kyokusen*
frequency modulation	エフ・エム	*efu emu*
friction press	摩擦プレス	*masatsu puresu*
fringe benefits	付加給付	*fuka kyūfu*
fringe market	二次的市場	*niji teki shijō*
front-end fee	シンジケート組成費	*shinjikēto sosei hi*
front end processor (FEP)	フロントエンド・プロセッサ	*furontoendo purosessa*
front-wheel drive	前輪駆動	*zenrin kudō*
frozen assets	凍結資産	*tōketsu shisan*
fuel consumption	燃料消費量	*nenryō shōhi ryō*
fuel injection system	燃料噴射装置	*nenryō funsha sōchi*
full settlement	総決算	*sō kessan*
functional analysis	機能分析	*kinō bunseki*
fund	資金	*shikin*
fund, contingent	臨時資金	*rinji shikin*
fund, sinking	減債資金	*gensai shikin*
fund, trust	信託金	*shintaku kin*
funded debt	長期債	*chōki sai*
funding	資金調達	*shikin chōtatsu*
funds, public	公共基金	*kōkyō kikin*
funds, working	運転資金	*unten shikin*
fungible goods	代替え可能物	*daigae kanō butsu*
furnace	炉	*ro*
futures	先物契約	*sakimono keiyaku*
futures (finance)	先物取引き	*sakimono torihiki*
futures (securities)	先物契約	*sakimono keiyaku*
futures option	先物オプション	*sakimono opushon*

G

galley proof	ゲラ刷り	*gera zuri*
garnishment	差押え	*sashiosae*
gas laser	気体レーザー	*kitai rēzā*

gas pedal	アクセル	*akuseru*
gasoline	ガソリン	*gasorin*
gasoline tank	ガソリン・タンク	*gasorin tanku*
gear cutting machine	歯切り盤	*hagiri ban*
gearing	ギアリング	*giaringu*
gearless	ギアのない	*gia no nai*
gearshift	ギア転換装置	*gia tenkan sōchi*
general acceptance	普通引受け	*futsū hikiuke*
general average loss	共同海損損失	*kyōdō kaison sonshitsu*
general manager	総支配人	*sō shihai nin*
general meeting	総会	*sōkai*
general meeting (securities)	株主総会	*kabunushi sōkai*
general partnership	合名会社	*gōmei gaisha*
general strike	ゼネスト	*zenesuto*
generator	発電機／ジェネレーター	*hatsuden ki, jenerētā*
gentleman's agreement	紳士協定	*shinshi kyōtei*
gilt (Brit. govt. security)	金縁証券	*kinbuchi shōken*
glass fiber	ガラス繊維	*garasu sen-i*
glass	コップ	*koppu*
glass laser	ガラスレーザー	*garasu rēzā*
glass-reinforced cement	ガラス強化セメント	*garasu kyōka semento*
glassy semiconductor	ガラス半導体	*garasu handōtai*
glossy (adj)	艶だしの	*tsuya dashi no*
glut	供給過剰	*kyōkyū kajō*
go around (v)	行き渡る	*ikiwataru*
go public (v)	株式公開する	*kabushiki kōkai suru*
go-go fund	思惑投資	*omowaku tōshi*
godown	倉庫	*sōko*
going concern value	継続企業価値	*keizoku kigyō kachi*
going rate (or price)	現行歩合	*genkō buai*
gold clause	金約款	*kin yakkan*
gold price	金価格	*kin kakaku*
gold reserves	金準備	*kin junbi*
goldplated (adj)	金めっきの	*kin mekki no*
good delivery (securities)	適法受渡し	*tekihō ukewatashi*
goods	商品	*shōhin*
goods, capital	資本財	*shihon zai*
goods, consumer	消費財	*shōhi zai*
goods, durable	耐久財	*taikyū zai*
goods, industrial	生産資材	*seisan shizai*
goodwill	営業権	*eigyō ken*
government	政府	*seifu*
government agency	政府機関	*seifu kikan*
government bank	中央銀行	*chūō ginkō*
government bond	国債	*kokusai*
government securities	政府証券	*seifu shōken*
grace period	支払い猶予期間／猶予期間	*shiharai yūyo kikan, yūyo kikan*

grade, commercial	商業格付け	*shōgyō kakuzuke*
graft	収賄	*shūwai*
grain (printing)	きめ	*kime*
grant an overdraft (v)	当座借越を認める	*tōza karikoshi o mitomeru*
graph	グラフ	*gurafu*
graphic equalizer	グラフィック・イコライザー	*gurafikku ikoraizā*
graphics	グラフィックス	*gurafikkusu*
gratuity	ギフト	*gifuto*
gravy boat	肉汁ソース入れ	*niku jū sōsu ire*
gray market	グレー・マーケット	*gurē māketto*
gray scale	グレー・スケール	*gurēsukēru*
grid	碁盤目	*goban me*
grievance procedure	苦情処理手続き	*kujō shori tetsuzuki*
grinder	研削盤	*kensaku ban*
gross domestic product (GDP)	国内総生産	*kokunai sō seisan*
gross income	総所得	*sō shotoku*
gross investment	総投資	*sō tōshi*
gross loss	総損失	*sō sonshitsu*
gross margin	総利益	*sō rieki*
gross national product (GNP)	国民総生産	*kokumin sō seisan*
gross price	諸掛込み値段	*shogakari komi nedan*
gross profit	総利益	*sō rieki*
gross sales	総売上げ高	*sō uriage daka*
gross spread	値ざや	*ne zaya*
gross weight	総重量	*sō jūryō*
gross yield	総利回り	*sō rimawari*
group (pharmaceuticals) (adj)	粉末状の	*funmatsu jō no*
group accounts	グループ勘定	*gurūpu kanjō*
group dynamics	グループ・ダイナミクッス	*gurūpu dainamikkusu*
group insurance	団体保険	*dantai hoken*
group training	集団訓練	*shūdan kunren*
group, product	製品グループ	*seihin gurūpu*
growth	成長	*seichō*
growth index	成長指数	*seichō shisū*
growth industry	成長産業	*seichō sangyō*
growth potential	成長の可能性	*seichō no kanōsei*
growth rate	成長率	*seichō ritsu*
growth stock	成長株	*seichō kabu*
growth, corporate	企業成長	*kigyō seichō*
guarantee	保証	*hoshō*
guaranty bond	保証書	*hoshō sho*
guaranty company	保証会社	*hoshō gaisha*
guesstimate	当て推量	*ate zuiryō*
guidelines	ガイドライン	*gaidorain*
guilty	有罪	*yūzai*

H

hand scanner	ハンド・スキャナ	*handosukyana*
hand-knit (adj)	手編みの	*teami no*
hand-sewn (adj)	手縫いの	*te-nui no*
handbag	ハンドバッグ	*handobaggu*
handblown glass	口吹きグラス	*kuchi buki gurasu*
handicap	ハンデキャップ	*handekyappu*
handler (computer)	ハンドラ	*handora*
handmade (adj)	手作りの	*tezukuri no*
handpainted (adj)	手塗りの	*tenuri no*
handwoven (adj)	手織りの	*teori no*
harbor dues	入港税	*nyūkō zei*
hard copy (computer)	ハード・コピー	*hādo kopī*
hard currency	交換可能通貨	*kōkan kanō tsūka*
hard disk	ハード・ディスク	*hādo disuku*
hard sell	ハード・セル	*hādo seru*
hardcover	堅表紙本	*kata byōshi bon*
hardware	ハードウェア	*hādo wea*
head office	本社	*honsha*
headhunter	人材スカウト	*jinzai sukauto*
headline	ヘッドライン	*heddo rain*
headquarters	本部	*honbu*
hearsay evidence	伝聞証拠	*denbun shōko*
heat-resistant ceramics	耐熱セラミックス	*tainetsu seramikkusu*
heavy industry	重工業	*jū kōgyō*
heavy lift charges	重量貨物揚荷料	*jūryō kamotsu ageni ryō*
hedge	掛けつなぎ売買	*kaketsunagi baibai*
hedge (v)	掛けつなぐ	*kake tsunagu*
hedge-buying	買いつなぎ	*kaitsunagi*
hedge-selling	売りつなぎ	*uritsunagi*
hem	縁	*heri*
hertz	ヘルツ	*herutsu*
hexachlorophene	ヘキサクロロフェン	*hekisakurorofen*
hidden assets	隠匿資産	*intoku shisan*
hidden assets (securities)	含み資産	*fukumi shisan*
high court	高等裁判所	*kōtō saibansho*
high density	高密度	*kō mitsudo*
high fidelity	ハイファイ	*haifai*
high resolution	高解像度	*kō kaizōdo*
high technology	ハイテク	*haiteku*
high yield	高利回り	*kō rimawari*
highest bidder	最高入札人	*saikō nyūsatsu nin*
hoard (v)	退蔵する	*taizō suru*
holder (negotiable instruments)	所持人	*shoji nin*
holder in due course	正当な所持人	*seitō na shoji nin*
holding company	持ち株会社	*mochikabu gaisha*
holding period	保留期間	*horyū kikan*

holographic memory	ホログラフィックメモリ	*horogurafikku memori*
home equity loan	ホームエクイティローン	*hōmuekuiti rōn*
home market	国内市場	*kokunai shijō*
home mortgage	住宅モーゲージ	*jūtaku mōgēji*
hormone	ホルモン	*horumon*
horsepower	馬力	*bariki*
host computer	ホスト・コンピュータ	*hosuto konpyūta*
hot money	ホット・マネー	*hotto manē*
hot rolling	熱間圧延	*nekkan atsuen*
hot strip coil	熱延広幅帯鋼	*netsuen hirohaba obikō*
hourly earnings	時間収	*jikan shū*
housing authority	公共住宅機関	*kōkyō jūtaku kikan*
housing loan	住宅ローン	*jūtaku rōn*
hub	ハブ	*habu*
human resources	人的資源	*jin-teki shigen*
hybrid computer	ハイブリッド・コンピュータ	*haiburiddo konpyūta*
hybrid materials	ハイブリッド材料	*haiburiddo zairyō*
hydrocarbon	炭化水素	*tanka suiso*
hydrochloric acid	塩酸	*ensan*
hydrolysis	加水分解	*kasui bunkai*
hypothecation	担保契約	*tanpo keiyaku*

H

I

ice bucket	氷入れ	*kōri ire*
idle capacity	遊休設備	*yūkyū setsubi*
ignition	イグニッション	*igunisshon*
illegal	違法の／不法の	*ihō no/fuhō no*
illegal shipments	違法の船積み	*ihō no funazumi*
illustration	イラスト	*irasuto*
image	イメージ	*imēji*
imitation	模造品	*mozō hin*
impact, have an . . . on (v)	影響を与える	*eikyō o ataeru*
impending changes	差し迫った変化	*sashisematta henka*
implication	連座	*renza*
implied agreement	黙諾	*moku daku*
import (n)	輸入	*yunyū*
import (v)	輸入する	*yunyū suru*
import declaration	輸入申告	*yunyū shinkoku*
import deposits	輸入担保	*yunyū tanpo*
import duty	輸入関税	*yunyū kanzei*
import entry	輸入手続き	*yunyū tetsuzuki*
import license	輸入許可	*yunyū kyoka*
import quota	輸入割当て	*yunyū wariate*

import regulation	輸入規制、輸入規則	*yunyū kisei, yunyū kisoku*
import restriction	輸入制限	*yunyū seigen*
import surcharge	輸入加徴金	*yunyū kachōkin*
import tariff	輸入税率	*yunyū zeiritsu*
import tax	輸入税	*yunyū zei*
impound (v)	差し押える	*sashi osaeru*
improve upon (v)	改良を加える	*kairyō o kuwaeru*
improvements	改善	*kaizen*
impulse buying	衝動買い	*shōdō gai*
imputed (adj)	帰属した	*kizoku shita*
in the red (adv)	赤字で	*akaji de*
in transit (adv)	運送中	*unsō chū*
inadequate (adj)	不適切な	*futekisetsu na*
incentive	誘因	*yūin*
incidental expenses	臨時費	*rinji hi*
income	収入／所得	*shūnyū/shotoku*
income account	収入勘定	*shūnyū kanjō*
income bonds	収益債券	*shūeki saiken*
income bracket	所得階層	*shotoku kaisō*
income return	所得申告	*shotoku shinkoku*
income statement	所得計算書	*shotoku keisan sho*
income tax rate	所得税率	*shotoku zeiritsu*
income tax, corporate	法人税	*hōjin zei*
income tax, personal	個人所得税	*kojin shotoku zei*
income yield	収益利回り	*shūeki rimawari*
income, gross	総所得	*sō shotoku*
income, net	純所得	*jun shotoku*
incorporate (v)	株式会社にする	*kabushiki gaisha ni suru*
incorporation	法人設立	*hōjin setsuritsu*
increase	増加	*zōka*
increase (v)	増加する	*zōka suru*
increased costs	増加費用	*zōka hiyō*
incremental cash flow	増加キャッシュ・フロー	*zōka kyasshu furō*
incremental costs	増分原価	*zōbun genka*
indebtedness	負債	*fusai*
indemnity	補償損害賠償	*hoshō songai baishō*
indenture	契約書	*keiyaku sho*
independent suspension	独立懸架	*dokuritsu kenka*
index	指数	*shisū*
index (indicator)	指数	*shisū*
index, growth	成長指数	*seichō shisū*
indexing	物価スライド	*bukka suraido sei*
indicator	指標	*shihyō*
indirect claim	間接要求	*kansetsu yōkyū*
indirect cost	間接費	*kansetsu hi*
indirect expenses	間接経費	*kansetsu keihi*
indirect labor	間接労働	*kansetsu rōdō*
indirect tax	間接税	*kansetsu zei*

individual retirement account	個人退職年金勘定	*kojin taishoku nenkin kanjō*
induction furnace	誘導炉	*yūdō ro*
industrial accident	労務災害	*rōmu saigai*
industrial arbitration	労働調停	*rōdō chōtei*
industrial engineering	インダストリアル・エンジニアリング	*indasutoriaru enjiniaringu*
industrial goods	生産資材	*seisan shizai*
industrial insurance	簡易保険	*kan-i hoken*
industrial planning	産業計画	*sangyō keikaku*
industrial relations	労使関係	*rōshi kankei*
industrial robot	産業ロボット	*sangyō robotto*
industrial union	産業別労働組合	*sangyō betsu rōdō kumiai*
industry	産業	*sangyō*
industrywide (adj)	産業全体の	*sangyō zentai no*
inefficient (adj)	非能率的な	*hi nōritsu-teki na*
inelastic demand or supply	非弾性需要／供給	*hi dansei juyō/kyōkyū*
infant industry	幼稚産業	*yōchi sangyō*
inflation	インフレ	*infure*
inflationary (adj)	インフレの	*infure no*
infrared film	赤外写真フィルム	*sekigai shashin firumu*
infrastructure (economy)	経済基盤	*keizai kiban*
infrastructure (industry)	下部構造	*kabu kōzō*
infringement	侵害	*shingai*
ingot	インゴット	*ingotto*
inheritance tax	遺産相続税	*isan sōzoku zei*
initial public offering	新規公募	*shinki kōbo*
injection	注射	*chūsha*
injection molding machine	射出成形機	*shashutsu seikei ki*
injection pump	インジェクション・ポンプ	*injekushon ponpu*
injunction	強制命令	*kyōsei meirei*
injury	被害	*higai*
ink	インク	*inku*
inland bill of lading	国内船荷証券	*kokunai funani shōken*
innocence	無罪	*muzai*
innovation	技術革新	*gijutsu kakushin*
input	インプット	*inputto*
input-output analysis	投入産出分析	*tōnyū sanshutsu bunseki*
insert	挿入	*sōnyū*
insert machine	自動挿入機	*jidō sōnyū ki*
insider trading	インサイダー取引き	*insaidā torihiki*
insolvent (adj)	支払い不能の	*shiharai funō no*
insolvent	支払い不能者	*shiharai funō sha*
inspection	検査	*kensa*
inspector	検査官	*kensa kan*
instability	不安定	*fuantei*
installment credit	賦払い信用	*fubarai shin-yō*
installment plan	分割支払い方式	*bunkatsu shiharai hōshiki*

I

institutional advertising	企業広告	*kigyō kōkoku*
institutional investor	機関投資家	*kikan tōshi ka*
instruct (v)	指図する	*sashizu suru*
instrument (finance)	証書	*shōsho*
instrumental capital	製造資本	*seizō shihon*
insulin	インシュリン	*inshurin*
insurance	保険	*hoken*
insurance broker	保険仲立ち人	*hoken nakadachi nin*
insurance company	保険会社	*hoken gaisha*
insurance fund	保険積立て金	*hoken tsumitate kin*
insurance policy	保険証書	*hoken shōsho*
insurance premium	保険料	*hoken ryō*
insurance underwriter	保険業者	*hoken gyōsha*
intangible assets	無形資産	*mukei shisan*
integrated circuit	集積回路	*shūseki kairo*
integrated management system	統合的経営管理方式	*tōgō-teki keiei kanri hōshiki*
intellectual property	知的所有権	*chiteki shoyūken*
intelligent robot	知能ロボット	*chinō robotto*
interact (v)	相互作用する	*sōgo sayō suru*
interactive	インターアクティブ	*intā akutibu*
interbank (adj)	銀行間の	*ginkō kan no*
interchangeable lens	交換レンズ	*kōkan renzu*
interest	利子	*rishi*
interest arbitrage	金利裁定取引き	*kinri saitei torihiki*
interest expenses	支払い利息	*shiharai risoku*
interest income	利子所得	*rishi shotoku*
interest parity	金利平価	*kinri heika*
interest period	金利期間	*kinri kikan*
interest rate	金利／利率	*kinri, riritsu*
interest, compound	複利	*fukuri*
interface	インターフェース	*intā fēsu*
interim (adj)	仮の	*kari no*
interim budget	暫定予算	*zantei yosan*
interim statement	仮計算書	*kari keisan sho*
interlocking directorate	兼任重役	*kennin jūyaku*
intermediary	仲介者	*chūkai sha*
intermediary goods	中間財	*chūkan zai*
internal (adj)	内部の	*naibu no*
internal audit	内部監査	*naibu kansa*
internal finance	自己金融	*jiko kin-yū*
internal rate of return	内部収益率	*naibu shūeki ritsu*
internal revenue tax	内国収入税	*naikoku shūnyū zei*
International Date Line	国際日付け変更線	*kokusai hizuke henkō sen*
international investment trust	国際投資信託	*kokusai tōshi shintaku*
international law	国際法	*kokusaihō*
interstate commerce	州間通商	*shū kan tsūshō*
intervene (v)	介入する	*kainyū suru*
interview	インタビュー	*intabyū*
intestate (adj)	遺言のない	*yuigon no nai*

intestate	無遺言死亡者	*mu yuigon shibō sha*
intrinsic value	本質価値	*honshitsu kachi*
introduction (publishing)	序	*jo*
invalidate (v)	無効にする	*mukō ni suru*
invalidation	失効	*shikkō*
inventory	在庫品	*zaiko hin*
inventory control	在庫品管理	*zaiko hin kanri*
inventory turnover	棚卸し資産回転率	*tana oroshi shisan kaiten ritsu*
inventory, perpetual	継続棚卸し表	*keizoku tana oroshi hyō*
inventory, physical	実地棚卸し	*jitchi tana oroshi*
inverter	インバーター	*inbāta*
invest (v)	投資する	*tōshi suru*
invested capital	投下資本	*tōka shihon*
investment	投資	*tōshi*
investment adviser	投資顧問	*tōshi komon*
investment analysis	投資分析	*tōshi bunseki*
investment appraisal	投資査定	*tōshi satei*
investment bank	投資銀行	*tōshi ginkō*
investment budget	投資予算	*tōshi yosan*
investment company	投資信託会社	*tōshi shintaku gaisha*
investment credit	投資信用	*tōshi shin-yō*
investment criteria	投資基準	*tōshi kijun*
investment management company	投資顧問会社	*tōshi komon gaisha*
investment policy	投資政策	*tōshi seisaku*
investment program	投資計画	*tōshi keikaku*
investment strategy	投資戦略	*tōshi senryaku*
investment trust	投資信託	*tōshi shintaku*
investment trust bank	投資信託銀行	*tōshi shintaku ginkō*
investment, return on	投資利回り	*tōshi rimawari*
invisibles	貿易外収支	*bōeki gai shūshi*
invitation to bid	入札勧誘	*nyūsatsu kan-yū*
invoice	送り状	*okurijō*
invoice cost	送り状金額	*okurijō kingaku*
invoice, commercial	商業送り状	*shōgyō okurijō*
invoice, consular	領事証明送り状	*ryōji shōmei okurijō*
invoice, pro forma	見積り送り状	*mitsumori okuirjō*
iodine	ヨード	*yōdo*
ionomer resin	アイオノマー樹脂	*aionomā jushi*
IOU	借用証書	*shakuyō shōsho*
iron (pharmaceuticals)	鉄剤	*tetsu zai*
iron ore	鉄鉱	*tekkō*
issue (stock)	発行	*hakkō*
issue (v)	発行する	*hakkō suru*
issue price	発行価格	*hakkō kakaku*
issued stocks	発行済み株式	*hakkō zumi kabushiki*
italic	イタリック体	*itarikku tai*
item	項目	*kōmoku*
itemize (v)	明細化する	*meisaika suru*
itemized account	明細精算書	*meisai seisan sho*

J

jack	ジャック	*jakku*
jacket (publishing)	カバー	*kabā*
Japan Federation of Bar Associations	日弁連（日本弁護士連合会）	*Nichibenren (Nippon bengoshi rengōkai)*
Jason clause	ジェーソン条項	*Jēson jōkō*
jawbone (v)	強引に説得する	*gōin ni settoku suru*
jet condenser	ジェット・コンデンサ	*jetto kondensa*
jet lag	時差ぼけ	*jisa boke*
jewel	宝石類	*hōseki rui*
jig (production)	ジグ	*jigu*
job	仕事	*shigoto*
job analysis	職務分析	*shokumu bunseki*
job description	職務記述書	*shokumu kijutsu sho*
job evaluation	職務評定	*shokumu hyōtei*
job hopper	常習転職者	*jōshū tenshoku sha*
job lot (merchandising)	込み売りの廉売品	*komi uri no renbai hin*
job performance	職務遂行	*shokumu suikō*
job security	仕事の保障	*shigoto no hoshō*
jobber (merchandising)	卸し屋	*oroshiya*
jobber (securities)	場内仲買人	*jōnai nakagai nin*
joint account	共同預金口座	*kyōdō yokin kōza*
joint cost	結合原価	*ketsugō genka*
joint estate	共有財産	*kyōyū zaisan*
joint liability	連帯責任	*rentai sekinin*
joint owner	共有者	*kyōyū sha*
joint stock company	株式会社	*kabushiki gaisha*
joint venture	合弁	*gōben*
Josephson device	ジョセフソン装置	*Josefuson sōchi*
journal (accounting)	仕訳帳	*shiwake chō*
journeyman	職工	*shokkō*
joystick	ジョイ・スティック	*joi sutikku*
judge	裁判官／判事	*saibankan/hanji*
judicial decision	判決	*hanketsu*
junior partner	一般社員	*ippan shain*
junior security	後次ぎ担保証券	*atotsugi tanpo shōken*
junk bond	ジャンク・ボンド	*janku bondo*
jurisdiction	管轄／司法権	*kankatsu/shihō ken*
justify (publishing) (v)	行間を揃える	*gyōkan o soroeru*

K

key exports	主要輸出品	*shuyō yushutsu hin*
key man insurance	事業家保険	*jigyōka hoken*
keyboard	キーボード	*kī bōdo*
Keynesian economics	ケインズ経済学	*Keinzu keizaigaku*

keypuncher	キーパンチャー	*kī panchā*
kickback	リベート	*ribēto*
kiting (banking)	融通手形の振出し	*yūzū tegata no furidashi*
knife	ナイフ	*naifu*
knot (nautical)	ノット	*notto*
know-how	ノウハウ	*nou hau*
knurling tool	ローレット	*rōretto*

L

labor	労働	*rōdō*
labor code	労働規約	*rōdō kiyaku*
labor dispute	労働争議	*rōdō sōgi*
labor force	労働力	*rōdō ryoku*
labor law	労働法	*rōdō hō*
labor leader	労働組合幹部	*rōdō kumiai kanbu*
labor market	労働市場	*rōdō shijō*
labor relations	労使関係	*rōshi kankei*
labor turnover	労働移動	*rōdō idō*
labor union	労働組合	*rōdō kumiai*
labor-intensive industry	労働集約産業	*rōdō shūyaku sangyō*
labor-saving (adj)	労働節約的	*rōdō setsuyaku teki*
laborer	労働者	*rōdō sha*
lace	レース	*rēsu*
ladle	柄杓	*hishaku*
lagging indicator	遅行指標	*chikō shihyō*
laissez-faire	無干渉主義	*mukanshō shugi*
land	土地	*tochi*
land grant	無償土地払い下げ	*mushō tochi haraisage*
land reform	農地改革	*nōchi kaikaku*
land tax	地租	*chiso*
landed cost	陸揚げ費込み値段	*rikuage hi komi nedan*
landing certificate	陸揚げ証明書	*rikuage shōmei sho*
landing charges	陸揚げ費	*rikuage hi*
landing costs	陸揚げ費	*rikuage hi*
landowner	地主	*jinushi*
lapping machine	ラップ盤	*rappu ban*
laptop computer	ラップ型コンピユータ	*rappugata konpyūta*
large-scale (adj)	大規模の	*daikibo no*
large-scale integrated circuit	大規模集積回路	*daikibo shūseki kairo*
laser	レーザー	*rēzā*
laser beam printer	レーザー・ビームプリンタ	*rēzā bīmu purinta*
laser fusion	レーザー核融合	*rēzā kaku yūgō*
laser printer	レーザー・プリンタ	*rēzā purinta*
laser processing	レーザー加工	*rēzā kakō*

K

last in-first out	後入先出法	*ato ire saki dashi hō*
latex	ラテックス	*ratekkusu*
lathe	旋盤	*senban*
law	法律	*hōritsu*
law firm	法律事務所	*hōritsu jimusho*
law of diminishing returns	収益逓減の法則	*shūeki teigen no hōsoku*
lawsuit	訴訟	*soshō*
lawyer	弁護士	*bengoshi*
lay time	停泊期間	*teihaku kikan*
lay up (shipping) (v)	係船する	*keisen suru*
lay up (v)	貯蔵する	*chozō suru*
lay-off	一時解雇	*ichiji kaiko*
laydays	碇泊期間	*teihaku kikan*
layout	割付け	*waritsuke*
layout (advertising)	広告割付け	*kōkoku waritsuke*
layout (computer)	レイアウト	*rei auto*
lead time	先行期間	*senkō kikan*
lead time (computer)	リード・タイム	*rīdo taimu*
leader	指導者	*shidō sha*
leading indicator	先行指標	*senkō shihyō*
leads and lags	リーズ・アンド・ラグス	*rīzu ando ragusu*
leakage	漏損	*rōson*
learning curve	学習曲線	*gakushū kyokusen*
lease	リース	*rīsu*
lease (to grant) (v)	賃貸しする	*chingashi suru*
lease (to hold) (v)	賃借りする	*chingari suru*
leased department	賃借りデパート	*chingari depāto*
leave of absence	休暇	*kyūka*
ledger	元帳	*motochō*
ledger account	元帳勘定	*motochō kanjō*
ledger entry	元帳金融	*motochō kin-yū*
legacy	遺贈財産	*izō zaisan*
legal	法律の	*hōritsu no*
legal adviser	顧問弁護士	*komon bengoshi*
legal capital	法定資本	*hōtei shihon*
legal entity	法的実体	*hō-teki jittai*
legal holiday	公休日	*kōkyū bi*
legal monopoly	法定独占	*hōtei dokusen*
legal tender	法定通貨	*hōtei tsūka*
lending	貸付け	*kashitsuke*
length (fashion)	丈	*take*
lens	レンズ	*renzu*
less-than-carload	小口扱い鉄道貨物	*koguchi atsukai tetsudō kamotsu*
less-than-truckload	小口扱いトラック貨物	*koguchi atsukai torakku kamotsu*
lessee	賃借り人	*chingari nin*
lessor	賃貸し人	*chingashi nin*

letter (certificate)	証書	*shōsho*
letter of credit	信用状	*shin-yō jō*
letter of guaranty	保証状	*hoshō jō*
letter of guaranty (transportation)	荷物引取り保証状	*nimotsu hikitori hoshō jō*
letter of indemnity	念書	*nensho*
letter of indemnity (transportation)	毀損荷物保証状	*kison nimotsu hoshō jō*
letter of introduction	紹介状	*shōkai jō*
letterpress	活字印刷	*katsuji insatsu*
level out (v)	横ばいになる	*yokobai ni naru*
leverage, financial	ファイナンシャル・レバレッジ	*fainansharu rebarejji*
levy taxes (v)	課税する	*kazei suru*
liability	債務	*saimu*
liability insurance	責任保険	*sekinin hoken*
liability, actual	実質債務	*jisshitsu saimu*
liability, assumed	継承債務	*keishō saimu*
liability, contingent	偶発債務	*gūhatsu saimu*
liability, current	流動負債	*ryūdō fusai*
liability, fixed	固定負債	*kotei fusai*
liability, secured	担保付負債	*tanpo tsuki fusai*
liability, unsecured	無担保負債	*mutanpo fusai*
liable for tax	税金支払いの義務がある	*zeikin shiharai no gimu ga aru*
liable to (adj)	しがちの	*shigachi no*
liaison	連絡	*renraku*
libel	名誉毀損	*meiyo kison*
license	免許／ライセンス	*menkyo, raisensu*
license fees	特許権使用料	*tokkyo ken shiyō ryō*
licensed warehouse	保税倉庫	*hozei sōko*
lien	差押え権	*sashiosae ken*
lien (securities)	先取り特権	*sakidori tokken*
life cycle of a product	製品寿命	*seihin jumyō*
life insurance policy	生命保険証券	*seimei hoken shōken*
life member	終身会員	*shūshin kaiin*
life of a patent	特許権の存続期間	*tokkyo ken no sonzoku kikan*
lifetime employment	終身雇用	*shūshin koyō*
lighterage	艀賃	*hashike chin*
light-emitting diode	発光ダイオード	*hakkō daiōdo*
limestone	石灰岩	*sekkai gan*
limit order (stock market)	指値注文	*sashine chūmon*
limited liability	有限責任	*yūgen sekinin*
limited partnership	合資会社	*gōshi gaisha*
line (publishing)	行	*gyō*
line drawing	線画	*senga*
line executive	ライン部門幹部職員	*rain bumon kanbu shokuin*
line management	ライン部門管理	*rain bumon kanri*
line of business	営業品目	*eigyō hinmoku*

line printer	ライン・プリンタ	*rain purinta*
line, product	製品種目	*seihin shumoku*
linear (adj)	直線の	*chokusen no*
linear estimation	線形推定	*senkei suitei*
linear programming	リニアー・プログラミング	*riniā puroguramingu*
linen	麻	*asa*
linen (adj)	麻性の	*asa sei no*
lining	裏地	*uraji*
liquid assets	流動資産	*ryūdō shisan*
liquid crystal	液晶	*ekishō*
liquid helium	液体ヘリウム	*ekitai heriumu*
liquid-crystal display (LCD)	液晶ディスプレイ	*ekishō disupurei*
liquidation	精算	*seisan*
liquidation value	精算価値	*seisan kachi*
liquidity	流動性	*ryūdō sei*
liquidity preference (economics)	流動性選り好み	*ryūdō sei erigonomi*
liquidity ratio	流動比率	*ryūdō hiritsu*
list (v)	目録に記入する	*mokuroku ni kinyū suru*
list price	表示価格	*hyōji kakaku*
listed securities	上場証券	*jōjō shōken*
listed stock	上場株	*jōjō kabu*
litigation	訴訟	*soshō*
living trust	生存信託	*seizon shintaku*
load (sales charge)	付加料	*fuka ryō*
load factor	負荷率	*fuka ritsu*
loan	ローン／融資／貸付け	*rōn/yūshi/kashitsuke*
loan stock	転換社債	*tenkan shasai*
lobbying	陳情	*chinjō*
local area network (LAN)	ローカル・エリア・ネットワーク	*rōkaru eria nettowāku*
local bank	地方銀行	*chihō ginkō*
local customs	地方税関	*chihō zeikan*
local taxes	地方税	*chihō zei*
lock in (rate of interest) (v)	固定させる	*kotei saseru*
lock out	ロック・アウト	*rokku auto*
logistics	ロジスティックス	*rojisutikkusu*
logo	シンボル・マーク	*shinboru māku*
long interest (securities)	強気	*tsuyoki*
long sleeves	長袖	*naga sode*
long ton	英トン	*ei ton*
long-focus lens	長焦点レンズ	*chō shōten renzu*
long-range planning	長期計画	*chōki keikaku*
long-term	長期	*chōki*
long-term capital account	長期資本勘定	*chōki shihon kanjō*
long-term credit bank	長期信用銀行	*chōki shin-yō ginkō*
long-term debt	長期借入れ金	*chōki kariire kin*

lose a suit	敗訴する	*haisosuru*
loss	損失	*sonshitsu*
loss leader	目玉商品	*medama shōhin*
loss, gross	総損失	*sō sonshitsu*
loss, net	純損失	*jun sonshitsu*
lot	一口	*hitokuchi*
lot (securities)	単位	*tan-i*
low income	低所得	*tei shotoku*
low-interest loans	低金利ローン	*tei kinri rōn*
low-yield bonds	低利回り債券	*tei rimawari saiken*
lower case	小文字	*komoji*
lump sum	総額	*sōgaku*
luxury goods	贅沢品	*zeitaku hin*
luxury tax	奢侈税	*shashi zei*

M

machine tools	工作機械	*kōsaku kikai*
machinery	機械	*kikai*
machining center	マシニング・センター	*mashiningu sentā*
macro lens	接写レンズ	*sessha renzu*
macroeconomics	マクロ経済学	*makuro keizai gaku*
magnet optical disk (MO)	光磁気ディスク	*hikari jiki disuku*
magnetic bubble memory	磁気バブルメモリ	*jiki baburu memori*
magnetic disc unit	磁気ディスク装置	*jiki disuku sōchi*
magnetic fluid	磁性液体、磁性流体	*jisei ekitai, jisei ryūtai*
magnetic memory	磁気メモリ	*jiki memori*
magnetic tape	磁気テープ	*jiki tēpu*
magnetic tape unit	磁気テープ装置	*jiki tēpu sōchi*
mail order	メール・オーダー	*mēru ōdā*
mailing list	郵便先名簿	*yūbin saki meibo*
mainframe	メインフレーム	*mein furēmu*
mainframe computer	メインフレーム・コンピュータ	*mein furēmu konpyūta*
maintenance	維持	*iji*
maintenance contract	保守契約	*hoshu keiyaku*
maintenance margin (securities)	維持証拠金	*iji shōko kin*
maize (grain)	とうもろこし	*tōmorokoshi*
majority interest	過半数株式持分	*kahansū kabushiki mochibun*
make available (v)	利用できるようにする	*riyō dekiru yō ni suru*
make-or-buy decision	作るか買うかの決定	*tsukuru ka kau ka no kettei*
maker (of a check, draft, etc.)	手形振出し人	*tegata furidashi nin*
makeshift	当座しのぎの手段	*tōza shinogi no shudan*
makeshift (adj)	当座しのぎの	*tōza shinogi no*
man (gal) Friday	忠実で有能なアシスタント	*chūjitsu de yūnō na ashisutanto*

man hours	延べ時間	*nobe jikan*
man-made fibers	合成繊維	*gōsei sen-i*
manage (v)	経営する	*keiei suru*
managed costs	マネージド・コスト	*manējido kosuto*
managed economy	管理経済	*kanri keizai*
managed float	管理変動相場制	*kanri hendō sōba sei*
management	経営管理	*keiei kanri*
management accounting	管理会計	*kanri kaikei*
management business	経営管理	*keiei kanri*
management by objectives	目標管理	*mokuhyō kanri*
management chart	管理活動表	*kanri katsudō hyō*
management consultant	経営コンサルタント	*keiei konsarutanto*
management fee (securities)	幹事手数料	*kanji tesū ryō*
management group	マネジメント・グループ	*manejimento gurūpu*
management team	マネジメント・チーム	*manejimento chīmu*
management, credit	得意先管理	*tokui saki kanri*
management, financial	財務管理	*zaimu kanri*
management, line	ライン部門管理	*rain bumon kanri*
management, market	市場管理	*shijō kanri*
management, middle	ミドル・マネジメント	*midoru manejimento*
management, office	事務管理	*jimu kanri*
management, personnel	人事管理	*jinji kanri*
management, product	製品管理	*seihin kanri*
management, sales	販売管理	*hanbai kanri*
management, top	トップ・マネジメント	*toppu manejimento*
manager	支配人	*shihai nin*
mandate	委任	*inin*
mandatory redemption	定時償還	*teiji shōkan*
manganese ore	マンガン鉱	*mangan kō*
manganese steel	マンガン鋼	*mangan kō*
manifest	積荷目録	*tsumini mokuroku*
manipulator	マニピュレータ	*manipyurēta*
manpower	人的資源	*jinteki shigen*
manual workers	肉体労働者	*nikutai rōdō sha*
manufacturer	製造業者	*seizō gyōsha*
manufacturer's agent	製造業者代理店	*seizō gyōsha dairi ten*
manufacturer's representative	製造業者代理店	*seizō gyōsha dairi ten*
manufacturing capacity	製造能力	*seizō nōryoku*
manufacturing control	製造管理	*seizō kanri*
margin (difference)	売買価格差	*baibai kakaku sa*
margin (money)	証拠金	*shōkokin*
margin call	追加証拠金	*tsuika shōko kin*
margin of safety	安全余裕率	*anzen yoyū ritsu*
margin requirements	委託証拠金	*itaku shōko kin*

margin trading	信用取引き	*shin-yō torihiki*
margin, gross	粗利益	*so rieki*
margin, net	純利益	*jun rieki*
margin, profit	利ざや	*ri zaya*
marginal account	限界勘定	*genkai kanjō*
marginal cost	限界費用	*genkai hiyō*
marginal pricing	限界価格決定	*genkai kakaku kettei*
marginal productivity	限界生産性	*genkai seisan sei*
marginal revenue	限界収入	*genkai shūnyū*
marine cargo insurance	貨物海上保険	*kamotsu kaijō hoken*
marine underwriter	海上保険業者	*kaijō hoken gyōsha*
maritime contract	海事契約	*kaiji keiyaku*
mark down (v)	値下げする	*nesage suru*
market	市場	*shijō*
market (v)	市場に出す	*shijō ni dasu*
market access	市場への接近	*shijō e no sekkin*
market appraisal	市場評価	*shijō hyōka*
market concentration	市場集中	*shijō shūchū*
market forces	市場の実勢	*shijō no jissei*
market forecast	市場見通し	*shijō mitōshi*
market index	市場指数	*shijō shisū*
market management	市場管理	*shijō kanri*
market penetration	市場浸透	*shijō shintō*
market plan	市場計画	*shijō keikaku*
market position	市況	*shikyō*
market potential	販売可能量	*hanbai kanō ryō*
market price	市価	*shika*
market rating	市場格付け	*shijō kakuzuke*
market report	市況報告	*shikyō hōkoku*
market research	市場調査	*shijō chōsa*
market saturation	市場飽和	*shijō hōwa*
market share	市場占有率	*shijō sen-yū ritsu*
market survey	市場調査	*shijō chōsa*
market trends	市場動向	*shijō dōkō*
market value	市場価格	*shijō kakaku*
market, buyer's	買手市場	*kaite shijō*
market, fringe	二次的市場	*niji-teki shijō*
market-leader (securities)	主導株	*shudō kabu*
marketable securities	換金可能証券	*kankin kanō shōken*
marketing	マーケティング	*māketingu*
marketing budget	市場開拓費	*shijō kaitaku hi*
marketing concept	マーケティング・コンセプト	*māketingu konseputo*
marketing plan	マーケティング計画	*māketingu keikaku*
marketplace	市場	*shijō*
markup	値上げ	*neage*
mass communications	マスコミ	*masukomi*
mass marketing	大量マーケティング	*tairyō māketingu*

mass media	マスメディア	*masumedia*
mass production	大量生産	*tairyō seisan*
material handling robot	マテハン・ロボット	*matehan robotto*
materials	材料	*zairyō*
maternity leave	出産休暇	*shussan kyūka*
math coprocessor	数値演算コプロセッサ	*sūchi enzan kopurosessa*
mathematical model	数学的モデル	*sūgaku-teki moderu*
matrix (printing)	母型	*bokei*
matrix management	マトリックス・マネジメント	*matorikkusu manejimento*
matt (adj)	つや消しの	*tsuya keshi no*
maturity	満期／償還期間	*manki/shōkan kikan*
maturity date	支払い期日	*shiharai kijitsu*
maximize (v)	最大限に活用する	*saidaigen ni katsuyō suru*
mean (average) (adj)	平均の	*heikin no*
measure (v)	測る	*hakaru*
mechanical (publishing)	割付け用台紙	*waritsuke yō daishi*
mechanical engineering	機械工学	*kikai kōgaku*
mechanical press	メカニカル・プレス	*mekanikaru puresu*
mechanics' lien	建築工事の留置権	*kenchiku kōji no ryūchi ken*
median	中位数	*chūi sū*
mediation	調停／仲介	*chōtei/chūkai*
medication	薬物治療	*yakubutsu chiryō*
medicine	薬	*kusuri*
medium of exchange	交換手段	*kōkan shudan*
medium term (adj)	中期の	*chūki no*
medium-term	中期	*chūki*
meet the price (v)	値段に応じる	*nedan ni ōjiru*
meeting	会合	*kaigō*
meeting, board	取締役会議	*torishimari yaku kaigi*
megabyte (MB)	メガバイト	*megabaito*
megahertz (MHz)	メガヘルツ	*megaherutsu*
member firm	加盟会社	*kamei gaisha*
member of firm	社員	*shain*
memorandum	覚書	*oboegaki*
memory	メモリ	*memori*
mercantile (adj)	商業の	*shōgyō no*
mercantile agency	商業興信所	*shōgyō kōshin sho*
mercantile law	商法	*shōhō*
merchandise	商品	*shōhin*
merchandising (manufacturing)	商品化計画	*shōhin ka keikaku*
merchandising (retailing)	販売増進策	*hanbai zōshin saku*
merchant	商人	*shōnin*
merchant bank	商業銀行	*shōgyō ginkō*
merchant guild	商人ギルド	*shōnin girudo*
merger	吸収合併	*kyūshū gappei*

merger and acquisition (M & A)	合併・買収	*gappei • baishū*
metal alloys for hydrogen storage	水素吸蔵合金	*suiso kyūzō gōkin*
metal hydride	金属水素化物	*kinzoku suiso ka butsu*
metallic fiber	金属繊維	*kinzoku sen-i*
metals	金属	*kinzoku*
methane	メタン	*metan*
methanol	メタノール	*metanōru*
method	方法	*hōhō*
metrication	メートル法に換算	*mētoru hō ni kansan*
micro camera	マイクロカメラ	*maikuro kamera*
micro cassette recorder	マイクロカセットレコーダー	*maikuro kasetto rekōdā*
microchip	マイクロチップ	*maikuro chippu*
microcomputer	マイクロコンピュータ	*maikuro konpyūta*
microfiche	マイクロフィッシュ	*maikuro fisshu*
microfilm	マイクロフィルム	*maikuro firumu*
microprocessor	マイクロプロセッサ	*maikuro purosessa*
microwave	極超短波	*gokuchō tanpa*
microwave oven	電子レンジ	*denshi renji*
middle management	ミドル・マネジメント	*midoru manejimento*
middleman	中間業者	*chūkan gyōsha*
mileage	走行マイル数	*sōkō mairu sū*
milling	製粉	*seifun*
milling machine	フライス盤	*furaisu ban*
mini component system	ミニコンポ	*mini konpo*
minicomputer	ミニコンピュータ	*mini konpyūta*
minimum margin requirement	最低証拠金率	*saitei shōkokin ritsu*
minimum reserves	最低準備制度	*saitei junbi seido*
minimum wage	最低賃金	*saitei chingin*
Ministry of International Trade and Industry (MITI)	通商産業省／通産省	*tsūshō sangyō shō/tsūsanshō*
Ministry of Justice	法務省	*hōmushō*
minority interest	少数株主持分	*shōsū kabunushi mochibun*
mint	造幣局	*zōhei kyoku*
miscalculation	計算違い	*keisan chigai*
miscellaneous (adj)	雑多な	*zatta na*
misleading	誤解させやすい	*gokai saseyasui*
misunderstanding	誤解	*gokai*
mixed cost	混合費	*kongō hi*
mobility of labor	労働力の移動性	*rōdō ryoku no idō sei*
mock-up	実物大の模型	*jitsubutsu dai no mokei*
mode	モード	*mōdo*
model	モデル	*moderu*
modem	モデム	*modemu*
modular production	モジュラー生産	*mojurā seisan*
moire	モアレ	*moare*

molding machine	造形機	*zōkei ki*
molybdenum	モリブデン	*moribuden*
monetary base	財政基盤	*zaisei kiban*
monetary policy	金融政策	*kin-yū seisaku*
money	通貨	*tsūka*
money broker	金融業者	*kin-yū gyōsha*
money market	金融市場	*kin-yū shijō*
money market account	短期金融口座	*tanki kin-yū kōza*
money market fund	短期金融商品投資信託	*tanki kin-yū shōhin tōshi shintaku*
money order	郵便為替	*yūbin gawase*
money shop	マネーショップ	*manē shoppu*
money supply	通貨供給量	*tsūka kyōkyu ryō*
monitor	モニター	*monitā*
monochrome	モノクローム	*monokurōmu*
monopoly	独占	*dokusen*
monopsony	需要独占	*juyō dokusen*
Monte Carlo technique	モンテカルロ法	*Monte Karuro hō*
moonlighting	副業	*fuku gyō*
morale	勤労意欲	*kinrō iyoku*
moratorium	支払い停止	*shiharai teishi*
morphine	モルヒネ	*moruhine*
mortgage	モーゲジ／抵当権	*mōgeji/teitō ken*
mortgage bank	担保貸し銀行／抵当銀行	*tanpo gashi ginkō/teitō ginkō*
mortgage bond	担保付き債券	*tanpo tsuki saiken*
mortgage certificate	抵当証券	*teitō shōken*
mortgage debenture	担保付き社債券	*tanpo tsuki shasai ken*
most-favored nation	最恵国	*saikei koku*
motherboard	マザーボード	*mazābōdo*
motion	動作	*dōsa*
motivation study	動機調査	*dōki chōsa*
motor drive	モータードライブ	*mōtā doraibu*
mouse	マウス	*mausu*
movement of goods	商品の出入	*shōhin no deiri*
moving average	移動平均法	*idō heikin hō*
moving expenses	引越し費用	*hikkoshi hiyō*
mug	マグカップ	*magu kappu*
multicurrency	複数通貨	*fukusū tsūka*
multicut lathe	多刃旋盤	*tajin senban*
multilateral agreement	多国間協定	*takoku kan kyōtei*
multilateral trade	多角貿易	*takaku bōeki*
multimedia	マルチメディア	*maruchimedia*
multinational corporation	多国籍企業	*takokuseki kigyō*
multiple exchange rate	複数為替相場	*fukusū kawase sōba*
multiple taxation	複税	*fuku zei*
multiples	倍数	*baisū*
multiplier	乗数	*jōsū*
multiprogramming	マルチプログラミング	*maruchi puroguramingu*

multispindle drilling machine	多軸ボール盤	*tajiku bōru ban*
multitask operation	マルチタスク・オペレーション	*maruchitasuku operēshon*
municipal bond	地方公共団体債券／市債券	*chihō kōkyō dantai saiken/shi saiken*
muslin	モスリン	*mosurin*
mutual fund	ミューチュアル・ファンド	*myūchuaru fando*
mutual savings bank	相互貯蓄銀行	*sōgo chochiku ginkō*
mutually exclusive classes	相互排他的階級	*sōgo haita-teki kaikyū*

N

named inland point in country of origin	原産国内指定地点	*gensankoku nai shitei chiten*
named point of destination	指定仕向い地点	*shitei shimukai chiten*
named point of exportation	指定輸出地点	*shitei yushutsu chiten*
named point of origin	指定原産地点	*shitei gensan chiten*
named port of importation	指定輸入港	*shitei yunyū kō*
named port of shipment	指定積出し港	*shitei tsumidashi kō*
naphtha	ナフサ	*nafusa*
napkin	ナプキン	*napukin*
narcotic	麻酔薬	*masui yaku*
national bank	国立銀行	*kokuritsu ginkō*
national debt	国家債務	*kokka saimu*
nationalism	ナショナリズム	*nashonarizumu*
nationalization	国有化	*kokuyū ka*
native produce	現地農産物	*genchi nōsanbutsu*
natural resources	天然資源	*tennen shigen*
near money	準通貨	*jun tsūka*
needs analysis	必需品分析	*hitsuju hin bunseki*
negative (photography)	ネガ	*nega*
negative cash flow	現金流出	*genkin ryūshutsu*
negligent (adj)	怠慢な	*taiman na*
negotiable (adj)	譲渡できる	*jōto dekiru*
negotiable securities	有価証券	*yūka shōken*
negotiate (securities) (v)	買取る	*kaitoru*
negotiate (v)	交渉する	*kōshō suru*
negotiated sale	商談による販売	*shōdan ni yoru hanbai*
negotiation	交渉／商談	*kōshō/shōdan*
negotiation (securities)	流通	*ryūtsū*
net (adj)	純	*jun*
net asset value (securities)	純資産価値	*jun shisan kachi*
net asset worth	正味資産価値	*shōmi shisan kachi*
net assets	純資産	*jun shisan*
net borrowed reserves	正味借入れ準備金	*shōmi kariire junbi kin*
net cash flow	ネット・キャッシュ・フロー	*netto kyasshu furō*

net change	前日比	*zenjitsu hi*
net equity assets	正味持分資産	*shōmi mochibun shisan*
net income	純所得	*jun shotoku*
net investment	純投資	*jun tōshi*
net loss	純損失	*jun sonshitsu*
net margin	正味利益	*shōmi rieki*
net present value	正味現在価値	*shōmi genzai kachi*
net profit	純益	*jun eki*
net sales	純売上げ高	*jun uriage daka*
net working capital	純運転資本	*jun unten shihon*
net worth	正味資産	*shōmi shisan*
network (v)	販売網を広げる	*hanbai mō o hirogeru*
neutral (adj)	中性の	*chūsei no*
New York Stock Exchange	ニューヨーク証券取引所	*Nyūyōku shōken torihiki jo*
new ceramics	ニューセラミックス	*nyū seramikkusu*
new issue	新規発行債券	*shinki hakkō saiken*
new materials	新素材	*shin sozai*
new money	新通貨	*shin tsūka*
new product development	新製品開発	*shin seihin kaihatsu*
new stock issue	増資	*zōshi*
newsprint	新聞用紙	*shinbun yō shi*
nickel-cadmium battery	ニッカド電池	*nikkado denchi*
night depository	夜間預金保管所	*yakan yokin hokan sho*
Nikkei Dow Jones Average	日経ダウ	*Nikkei Dau*
Nikkei Stock Average	日経平均株価	*Nikkei heikin kabuka*
nitrate	硝酸塩	*shōsan en*
nitric acid	硝酸	*shōsan*
nitrite	亜硝酸塩	*a shōsan en*
nitrogen	窒素	*chisso*
no par value (adj)	無額面の	*mugakumen no*
no problem	問題無し	*mondai nashi*
no-load fund	ノーロード・ファンド	*nōrōdo fando*
nominal price	名目価格	*meimoku kakaku*
nominal yield	名目利回り	*meimoku rimawari*
non-performance of contract	契約不履行	*keiyaku furikō*
noncumulative preferred stock	非累積優先株	*hi ruiseki yūsen kabu*
nondurable goods	非耐久財	*hi taikyū zai*
nonfeasance	義務不履行	*gimu furikō*
nonmember	非会員	*hi kaiin*
nonmember bank	非加盟銀行	*hi kamei ginkō*
nonprofit (adj)	非営利の	*hi eiri no*
nonresident	非居住者	*hi kyojū sha*
nonvoting stock	無議決権株式	*mu giketsu ken kabushiki*
norm	基準	*kijun*
not guilty	無罪	*muzai*
not otherwise indexed by name	別に名前の明記がない限り	*betsu ni namae no meiki ga nai kagiri*

notary	公証人	*kōshōnin*
note, credit	貸方票	*kashigata hyō*
note, debit	借方票	*karikata hyō*
note, promissory	約束手形	*yakusoku tegata*
notebook computer	ノートブック・コンピュータ	*nōtobukku knopyūta*
notes receivable	受取り約束手形	*uketori yakusoku tegata*
novation	更改	*kōkai*
null and void (adj)	無効な	*mukō na*
nullify (v)	取消す	*torikesu*
numerical control	数値制御	*sūchi seigyo*
numerical control machine	NC工作機械	*enu shī kōsaku kikai*
numerical control robot	NCロボット	*enu shī robotto*
nylon	ナイロン	*nairon*

O

objective lens	対物レンズ	*taibutsu renzu*
obligation	債務	*saimu*
obsolescence	陳腐化	*chinpu ka*
occupation	職業	*shokugyō*
occupational hazard	職業上の危険	*shokugyō jō no kiken*
odd lot	端株	*ha kabu*
odd lot broker	端株のブローカー	*ha kabu no burōkā*
odometer	走行距離計	*sōkō kyori kei*
off board (stock market) (adj)	立会場外の	*tachiai jō gai no*
off-line (computer)	オフライン	*ofu rain*
off-the-books (adj)	帳簿外の	*chōbo gai no*
offer (v)	提供する	*teikyō suru*
offer for sale (v)	売りに出す	*uri ni dasu*
offered price	呼び値	*yobine*
offered rate	オファード・レート	*ofādo rēto*
office	オフィス	*ofisu*
office management	事務管理	*jimu kanri*
office, branch	支店	*shiten*
office, head	本社	*honsha*
official discount rate	公定歩合	*kōtei buai*
offset printing	オフセット印刷	*ofusetto insatsu*
offshore company	オフショア・カンパニー	*ofushoa kanpanī*
offshore fund	海外ファンド	*kaigai fando*
ohm	オーム	*ōmu*
oil pump	オイル・ポンプ	*oiru ponpu*
ointment	軟膏	*nankō*
oligopoly	寡占	*kasen*
oligopsony	少数購買独占	*shōsū kōbai dokusen*
omit (v)	省略する	*shōryaku suru*

on account (adv)	掛け売りで	*kakeuri de*
on consignment (adv)	委託販売で	*itaku hanbai de*
on cost (n)	間接費	*kansetsu hi*
on demand (adv)	要求払いで	*yōkyū barai de*
on line (computer) (adv)	オンラインで	*on rain de*
on-the-job training	職場訓練	*shokuba kunren*
onboard	オンボード	*onbōdo*
online	オンライン	*onrain*
open account	オープン勘定	*ōpun kanjō*
open cover	予定保険	*yotei hoken*
open door policy	門戸開放政策	*monko kaihō seisaku*
open market	公開市場	*kokai shijō*
open market operations	公開市場操作	*kōkai shijō sōsa*
open order	保留注文	*horyū chūmon*
open shop	オープン・ショップ	*ōpun shoppu*
opening balance	期首残高	*kishu zandaka*
opening price	寄付き値段	*yoritsuki nedan*
operating budget	営業予算	*eigyō yosan*
operating expenses	営業費	*eigyō hi*
operating income	営業収益	*eigyō shūeki*
operating profit	営業利潤	*eigyō rijun*
operating statement	営業損益計算書	*eigyō son-eki keisan sho*
operations audit	業務監査	*gyōmu kansa*
operations headquarters	運営本部	*un-ei honbu*
operations management	業務管理	*gyōmu kanri*
operator (computer)	オペレータ	*operēta*
operator (securities)	相場師	*sōba shi*
opium	アヘン	*ahen*
opportunity costs	機会費用	*kikai hiyō*
optical cable	光ケーブル	*hikari kēburu*
optical character reader (OCR)	光学式文字読み取り装置	*kōgakushiki moji yomitori sōchi*
optical computer	光コンピュータ	*hikari konpyūta*
optical disc	光ディスク	*hikari disuku*
optical fiber	光ファイバー	*hikari faibā*
optical integrated circuit	光半導体	*hikari handōtai*
optical magnetic memory	光磁気メモリ	*hikan jiki memori*
optical mark reader	光学式マーク読み取り装置	*kōgari shiki māku yomitori sōchi*
optical memory	光メモリ	*hikari memori*
optical transmission	光伝送	*hikari densō*
option	オプション	*opushon*
option trading	オプション取引き	*opushon torihiki*
option, stock	ストック・オプション	*sutokku opushon*
optional (adj)	選択自由の	*sentaku jiyū no*
optional equipment	オプション部品	*opushon buhin*

opto-electronics	光技術	*hikari gijutsu*
opto-electronics industry	光産業	*hikari sangyō*
oral bid	口頭入札	*kōtō nyūsatsu*
order	注文	*chūmon*
order (v)	注文する	*chūmon suru*
order form	注文書式	*chūmon shoshiki*
order number	注文番号	*chūmon bangō*
order of the day	日程	*nittei*
order, to place an (v)	発注する	*hatchū suru*
ordinary capital	経常資本	*keijō shihon*
organization	組織	*soshiki*
organization chart	会社機構図	*kaisha kikō zu*
original cost	取得原価	*shutoku genka*
original entry	初記入	*sho kinyū*
Osaka Stock Exchange	大証	*Daishō*
other assets (and liabilities)	他の資産（及び負債）	*ta no shisan (oyobi fusai)*
out-of-court settlement	示談	*jidan*
out-of-pocket expenses	経費の一時立て替え	*keihi no ichiji tatekae*
outbid (v)	競り落とす	*seriotosu*
outlay	支出	*shishutsu*
outlet	販路	*hanro*
outlook	見通し	*mitōshi*
output (computer)	アウトプット	*auto putto*
output (manufacturing)	生産高	*seisan daka*
outsized articles	特大品	*tokudai hin*
outstanding contract	未完の契約	*mikan no keiyaku*
outstanding debt	未払い債務	*miharai saimu*
outstanding stock	発行済株式	*hakkō zumi kabushiki*
outturn	産出額	*sanshutsu gaku*
over-the-counter quotation	店頭取引き相場	*tentō torihiki sōba*
overage	供給過剰	*kyōkyū kajō*
overage (shipping)	過多量	*kata ryō*
overbuy (v)	買いすぎる	*kaisugiru*
overcapitalized (adj)	過大資本の	*kadai shihon no*
overcharge (shipping)	積荷過重	*tsumini kajū*
overcharge	法外な代金請求	*hōgai na daikin seikyū*
overdraft	貸方勘定／当座貸越し	*kashigata kanjō/tōza kashi koshi*
overdue (adj)	支払い期限が過ぎた	*shiharai kigen ga sugita*
overhang	張出し	*haridashi*
overhead (adj)	諸掛込みの	*shogakari komi no*
overhead (n)	間接費	*kansetsu hi*
overlap	重複	*jūfuku*
overnight (adj)	宵越しの	*yoi goshi no*
overnight (securities)	翌日物	*yokujitsu mono*
overnight transaction	オーバーナイト取引き	*ōbānaito torihiki*
overpaid (adj)	払い過ぎの	*haraisugi no*

overseas affiliated firm	現地法人	*genchi hōjin*
overseas investment	海外投資	*kaigai tōshi*
overseas private investment corporation	海外民間投資会社	*kaigai minkan tōshi gaisha*
oversell (securities) (v)	から売りする	*karauri suru*
oversell (v)	売りすぎる	*urisugiru*
overstock	在庫過剰	*zaiko kajō*
oversubscribed (adj)	申込み超過の	*mōshikomi chōka no*
oversupply	供給過剰	*kyōkyū kajō*
overtime	超過勤務	*chōka kinmu*
overvalued (adj)	過大評価された	*kadai hyōka sareta*
owner	所有者	*shoyū sha*
owner's equity	所有者持分	*shoyū sha mochibun*
ownership	所有権	*shoyū ken*
ownership, absentee	不在地主権	*fuzai jinushi ken*
oxidation	酸化	*sanka*

P

(price) ticker	株式相場表示器	*kabushiki sōba hyōji ki*
p/e ratio	株価収益率	*kabuka shūeki ritsu*
package deal	一括取り引き	*ikkatsu torihiki*
packaging	包装	*hōsō*
packing case	輸送用包装箱	*yusō yō hōsō bako*
packing list	包装明細書	*hōsō meisai sho*
page	ページ	*pēji*
page makeup	ページ組	*pēji kumi*
pagination	ページ付け	*pēji zuke*
paid holiday	有給休暇	*yūkyū kyūka*
paid in full	全額支払い済み	*zengaku shiharaizumi*
paid up capital	払い込み済み資本金	*haraikomizumi shihonkin*
paid up shares	払い込み済み株	*haraikomizumi kabu*
paid-in surplus	払い込み剰余金	*haraikomi jōyokin*
paint	塗装	*tosō*
pallet	パレット	*paretto*
palletized freight	パレット輸送	*paretto yusō*
palm-size computer	ポケット型コンピュータ	*pokettogata konpyūta*
pamphlet	パンフレット	*panfuretto*
paper	紙	*kami*
paper (document)	書類	*shorui*
paper (securities)	手形	*tegata*
paper profit	紙上利益	*shijō rieki*
paper tape	紙テープ	*kami tēpu*
paperback	紙表紙版	*kami byōshi ban*
par	平価	*heika*
par value	額面価格	*gakumen kakaku*
par value stock	額面株	*gakumen kabu*

par, above (adv)	額面以上で	*gakumen ijō de*
par, above	額面以上の価格	*gakumen ijō no kakaku*
par, below (adv)	額面以下で	*gakumen ika de*
par, below (n)	額面以下の価格	*gakumen ika no kakaku*
parallel port	パラレルポート	*parareru pōto*
parallel processing	並列処理	*heiretsu shori*
parcel post	小包郵便	*kozutsumi yūbin*
parent company	親会社	*oya gaisha*
parity	等価	*tōka*
parity income ratio	パリティー収入比率	*paritī shūnyū hiritsu*
parity price	パリティー価格	*paritī kakaku*
part cargo	半端荷物	*hanpa nimotsu*
partial payment	分割払い込み	*bunkatsu haraikomi*
participating preferred stock	利益配当優先株	*rieki haitō yūsen kabu*
participation fee	参加料	*sanka ryō*
participation loan	共同融資	*kyōdō yūshi*
particular average loss	単独海損損失	*tandoku kaison sonshitsu*
partner	パートナー	*pātonā*
partnership	合名会社	*gōmei gaisha*
parts	部品	*buhin*
passbook	預金通帳	*yokin tsūchō*
passbook savings account	通帳貯金口座	*tsūchō chokin kōza*
passed dividend	保留配当	*horyū haitō*
past due	支払い期限経過	*shiharai kigen keika*
pastry server	菓子の切り盛りナイフ	*kashi no kiri mori naifu*
patent	特許	*tokkyo*
patent application	特許権申請	*tokkyo ken shinsei*
patent law	特許法	*tokkyo hō*
patent pending	特許出願中	*tokkyo shutsugan chū*
patent right	特許権	*tokkyoken*
patent royalty	特許権使用料	*tokkyo ken shiyō ryō*
patented process	特許権を持つ生産方法	*tokkyo ken o motsu seisan hōhō*
pattern	型／見本／模様	*kata/mihon/moyō*
pattern recognition	パターン認識	*patān ninshiki*
pay (v)	支払う	*shiharau*
pay up (v)	全額支払う	*zengaku shiharau*
pay-as-you-go basis	現金払い主義	*genkinbarai shugi*
payable on demand	要求払い	*yōkyū barai*
payable to bearer	持参人払い	*jisan nin barai*
payable to order	指図人払い	*sashizu nin barai*
payback period	回収期間	*kaishū kikan*
payee	受取り人	*uketori nin*
payer	支払い人	*shiharai nin*
payload (administration)	給料負担	*kyūryō futan*
payload (transportation)	有料荷重	*yūryō kajū*
paymaster	会計部長	*kaikei buchō*
payment	支払い	*shiharai*

payment in full	全額支払い	*zengaku shiharai*
payment in kind	現物払い	*genbutsu barai*
payment refused	支払い拒絶	*shiharai kyozetsu*
payment terms	支払い条件	*shiharai jōken*
payoff (administration)	支払い日	*shiharai bi*
payoff (illegal finance)	贈賄	*zōwai*
payout period	回収期間	*kaishū kikan*
payroll	給料支払い簿	*kyūryō shiharai bo*
payroll tax	給与税	*kyūyo zei*
peak load	ピーク・ロード	*pīku rōdo*
peg (v)	釘付けにする	*kugizuke ni suru*
pegged price	釘付け価格	*kugizuke kakaku*
pellet	ペレット	*peretto*
penalty	違約金	*iyakukin*
penalty clause	違約条項	*iyaku jōkō*
penalty action	違約金訴訟	*iyaku kin soshō*
penicillin	ペニシリン	*penishirin*
penny stock	ペニー株	*penī kabu*
pension fund	年金基金	*nenkin kikin*
pentaerythritol	ペンタエリスリトール	*penta erisuritōru*
pepper mill	胡椒挽	*koshō hiki*
pepper shaker	胡椒入	*koshō ire*
per annum rate	年利	*nenri*
per capita (adj)	一人当りの	*hitori atari no*
per diem	旅費日当	*ryohi nittō*
per diem (adj)	一日当りの	*ichinichi atari no*
per share (adj)	一株当りの	*hitokabu atari no*
percentage earnings	歩合収入	*buai shūnyū*
percentage of profits	利益率	*rieki ritsu*
perfect crystal device technology	完全結晶技術	*kanzen kesshō gijutsu*
performance	運用実績	*un-yō jisseki*
performance bond	契約履行保証	*keiyaku rikō hoshō*
periodic inventory	定期棚卸し	*teiki tanaoroshi*
peripheral equipment	周辺機器	*shūhen kiki*
peripherals	周辺機器／周辺装置	*shūhen kiki/shūhen sōchi*
perks	臨時手当て	*rinji teate*
permission	認可	*ninka*
permit	許可	*kyoka*
perpetual inventory	継続棚卸し	*keizoku tanaoroshi*
personal cassette player	パーソナル・カセット・プレーヤー	*pāsonaru kasetto purēyā*
personal check	個人当座小切手	*kojin tōza kogitte*
personal computer	パーソナル・コンピュータ	*pāsonaru konpyūta*
personal computer	パソコン	*pasokon*
personal deduction	個人所得税の控除（額）	*kojin shotoku zei no kōjo (gaku)*

P

personal exemption	基礎控除	*kiso kōjo*
personal income	個人所得	*kojin shotoku*
personal income tax	個人所得税	*kojin shotoku zei*
personal income tax rate	個人所得税率	*kojin shotoku zeiritsu*
personal liability	個人損害賠償責任	*kojin songai baishō sekinin*
personal property	動産	*dōsan*
personal stereo radio	パーソナル・ステレオ・ラジオ	*pāsonaru sutereo rajio*
personal TV	パーソナル・テレビ	*pāsonaru terebi*
personality test	性格検査	*seikaku kensa*
personnel administration	人事管理	*jinji kanri*
personnel department	人事部	*jinji bu*
personnel management	人事管理	*jinji kanri*
petrochemical (sing./pl.)	石油化学製品	*sekiyu kagaku seihin*
petrodollars	オイル・ダラー	*oiru darā*
petroleum	石油	*sekiyu*
pharmaceutical	薬品	*yakuhin*
pharmacist	薬剤師	*yakuzai shi*
phase in (v)	段階的に組入れる	*dankai-teki ni kumiireru*
phase out (v)	段階的に取除く	*dankai-teki ni torinozoku*
phenol	フェノール／石炭酸	*fenōru/sekitan san*
phone answering machine	留守番電話	*rusuban denwa*
phosphate	燐酸塩	*rinsan en*
photo conductive materials	光伝導物質	*hikari dendō busshitsu*
photo conductivity	光伝導	*hikari dendō*
photo electromagnetic effect	光電磁効果	*hikari denji kōka*
physical inventory	実地棚卸し	*jitchi tanaoroshi*
physician	医者	*isha*
picket line	ピケット・ライン	*piketto rain*
pickling	酸洗い	*san arai*
pickup and delivery	集配サービス	*shūhai sābisu*
pie chart	円グラフ	*en gurafu*
piecework	賃仕事	*chin shigoto*
pig iron	銑鉄	*sentetsu*
piggyback service	ピギーバック・サービス	*pigī bakku sābisu*
pigment	顔料	*ganryō*
pilferage	抜荷	*nukini*
pill	丸薬	*gan yaku*
pilotage	水先案内料	*mizusaki annai ryō*
pinion	ピニオン	*pinion*
pipage	パイプ輸送	*paipu yusō*
piston	ピストン	*pisuton*
pitcher	水差し	*mizu sashi*
pixel	ピクセル	*pikuseru*
place an order (v)	発注する	*hatchū suru*
place mat	テーブル・マット	*tēburu matto*
place of business	営業所	*eigyō sho*
place setting	一人前の食卓用食器具	*ichinin mae no shokutaku yō shokkigu*

placement (personnel)	配置	*haichi*
plaintiff	原告	*genkoku*
plan	計画	*keikaku*
plan (v)	計画する	*keikaku suru*
plan, action	実行計画	*jikkō keikaku*
plan, market	市場計画	*shijō keikaku*
planetary gear train	遊星歯車装置	*yūsei haguruma sōchi*
planned obsolescence	計画的老朽化	*keikaku-teki rōkyū ka*
plant capacity	工場生産能力	*kōjō seisan nōryoku*
plant export	プラント輸出	*puranto yushutsu*
plant location	工場の位置	*kōjō no ichi*
plant manager	工場長	*kōjō chō*
plasma cutting machine	プラズマ切断装置	*purazuma setsudan sōchi*
plasma etching	プラズマ・エッチング	*purazuma etchingu*
plate	板／プレート／皿	*ita/purēto/sara*
platter	大皿	*ōzara*
playback robot	プレイバック・ロボット	*pureibakku robotto*
plead	嘆願する	*tangansuru*
pleat	プリーツ	*purītsu*
pledge	抵当	*teitō*
plenary meeting	本会議	*hon kaigi*
plow back (earnings) (v)	再投資する	*saitōshi suru*
pocket-size TV	ポケット・テレビ	*poketto terebi*
point	ポイント	*pointo*
point (percentage, mortgage term)	ポイント	*pointo*
point of order	議事進行に関する件	*giji shinkō ni kansuru ken*
point of sale	販売時点	*hanbai jiten*
point, break-even	損益分岐点	*son-eki bunki ten*
polar coordinates robot	極座標ロボット	*kyoku zahyō robotto*
policy (administration)	方針	*hōshin*
policy (insurance)	保険証券	*hoken shōken*
policyholder	保険契約者	*hoken keiyaku sha*
poly-crystal silicon	多結晶シリコン	*takesshō shirikon*
polyester	ポリエステル	*poriesuteru*
polymer	重合体	*jūgō tai*
polystyrene	ポリスチレン	*porisuchiren*
polyurethane	ポリウレタン	*poriuretan*
pool (funds) (n)	共同出資	*kyōdō shusshi*
pool (funds) (v)	共同出資する	*kyōdō shusshi suru*
pool (organization) (v)	カルテルを作る	*karuteru o tsukuru*
pooling of interests	持分プーリング	*mochibun pūringu*
poplin	ポプリン	*popurin*
port	ポート	*pōto*
portable TV	ポータブル・テレビ	*pōtaburu terebi*

P

portfolio	所有有価証券／金融資産／有価証券明細書	*shoyū yūka shōken/kin-yū shisan/yūka shōken meisai sho*
portfolio management	投資管理	*tōshi kanri*
portfolio theory	資産選択の理論	*shisan sentaku no riron*
portfolio, stock	株式投資配分表	*kabushiki tōshi haibun hyō*
position limit	持高制限	*mochidaka seigen*
positive (photography)	陽画	*yōga*
positive cash flow	現金流入	*genkin ryūnyū*
post (bookkeeping) (v)	転記する	*tenki suru*
postdated (adj)	事後日付の	*jigo hizuke no*
postpone (v)	延期する	*enki suru*
potential buyer	見込み客	*mikomi kyaku*
potential sales	販売可能性	*hanbai kanō sei*
pottery	陶器類	*tōki rui*
powder metallurgy	粉末冶金	*funmatsu yakin*
power of attorney	委任権	*inin ken*
power steering	パワー・ステアリング	*pawā sutearingu*
practical (adj)	実用的な	*jitsuyō-teki na*
precision machinery	精密機械	*seimitsu kikai*
preemptive right	新株引受け権	*shinkabu hikiuke ken*
prefabrication	プレハブ	*purehabu*
preface	前書き	*maegaki*
preferential debts	優先債務	*yūsen saimu*
preferred stock	優先株	*yūsen kabu*
preferred tariff	特恵関税	*tokkei kanzei*
preliminary prospectus	仮趣意書	*kari shui sho*
premises (location)	構内	*kōnai*
premium payment	保険料払い込み	*hoken ryō haraikomi*
premium, insurance	保険料	*hoken ryō*
prepaid expenses (balance sheet)	前払い費用	*maebarai hiyō*
prepay (v)	前払いする	*maebarai suru*
prepayment	前払い	*maebarai*
prescription	処方箋	*shohō sen*
president	社長	*shachō*
preventive maintenance	予防保全	*yobō hozen*
price	価格	*kakau*
price (v)	値段を付ける	*nedan o tsukeru*
price cutting	値下げ	*ne sage*
price differential	価格格差	*kakaku kakusa*
price elasticity	価格弾力性	*kakaku danryoku sei*
price index	物価指数	*bukka shisū*
price limit	指値	*sashine*
price list	価格表	*kakaku hyō*
price range	価格帯	*kakaku tai*
price support	価格支持	*kakaku shiji*

(price) ticker	株式相場表示器	*kabushiki sōba hyōjiki*
price war	値下げ競争	*ne sage kyōsō*
price, competitive	競争価格	*kyōsō kakaku*
price, fix the (v)	価格操作をする	*kakaku sōsa o suru*
price, market	市場価格	*shijō kakaku*
price-earnings ratio	株価収益率	*kabuka shūeki ritsu*
primary market	主要市場	*shuyō shijō*
primary reserves	第一支払い準備金	*dai ichi shiharai junbi kin*
prime cost (economics)	主要費用	*shuyō hiyō*
prime cost (manufacturing)	素価	*soka*
prime rate	プライム・レート	*puraimurēto*
prime time	最高潮期	*sai kōchō ki*
principal	元金／元本	*gankin/ganpon*
principal (finance)	元金	*gankin*
principal (legal)	本人	*hon nin*
principal and interest	元利	*ganri*
principal guaranteed	元本保証	*ganpon hoshō*
print	プリント	*purinto*
printed matter	印刷物	*insatsu butsu*
printer	プリンタ	*purinta*
printing (printing)	印刷	*insatsu*
printing (photography)	焼き付け	*yakitsuke*
printing shop	印刷所	*insatsu sho*
printout	プリントアウト	*purinto auto*
priority	優先権	*yūsen ken*
private fleet	プライベート・フリート	*puraibēto furīto*
private label (or brand)	自家商標	*jika shōhyō*
private placement (finance)	私募	*shibo*
pro forma invoice	見積送り状	*mitsumori okurijō*
pro forma statement	見積書	*mitsumori sho*
probate	遺言検認権	*yuigon kennin ken*
probation	執行猶予	*shikkō yūyo*
problem	問題	*mondai*
problem analysis	問題分析	*mondai bunseki*
problem solving	問題解決	*mondai kaiketsu*
proceeds	売上高	*uriage daka*
process (v)	加工処理する	*kakō shori suru*
process, production	生産工程	*seisan kōtei*
processing error	処理過程での誤差	*shori katei de no gosa*
processor	プロセッサ	*purosessa*
procurement	調達	*chōtatsu*
product	製品	*seihin*
product analysis	製品分析	*seihin bunseki*
product design	製品設計	*seihin sekkei*
product development	製品開発	*seihin kaihatsu*
product group	製品グループ	*seihin gurūpu*
product life	製品寿命	*seihin jumyō*
product line	製品種目	*seihin shumoku*

product management	製品管理	*seihin kanri*
product profitability	製品の収益性	*seihin no shūeki sei*
production	生産	*seisan*
production control	生産管理	*seisan kanri*
production costs	生産費	*seisan hi*
production line	流れ作業	*nagare sagyō*
production process	生産工程	*seisan kōtei*
production schedule	製造予定表	*seizō yotei hyō*
productivity	生産性	*seisan sei*
productivity campaign	生産性向上運動	*seisan sei kōjō undō*
profession	専門職	*senmon shoku*
profiler	プロファイラー	*purofairā*
profit	利潤	*rijun*
profit and loss statement	損益計算書	*son-eki keisan sho*
profit factor	利益要素	*rieki yōso*
profit margin	利ざや／収益率	*rizaya/shūeki ritsu*
profit projection	利益予測	*rieki yosoku*
profit sharing	利潤分配	*rijun bunpai*
profit taking	利食い	*rigui*
profit, gross	総利益	*sō rieki*
profit, net	純益	*jun-eki*
profitability	収益性	*shūeki sei*
profitability analysis	収益率分析	*shūeki ritsu bunseki*
program (computer) (v)	プログラムを組む	*puroguramu o kumu*
program (computer)	プログラム	*puroguramu*
program	計画	*keikaku*
program (v)	計画を立てる	*keikaku o tateru*
programming	プログラミング	*puroguramingu*
prohibited goods	禁制品	*kinsei hin*
project	企画	*kikaku*
project (v)	企画する	*kikaku suru*
project planning	プロジェクト・プランニング	*purojekuto puranningu*
projector	映写機	*eisha ki*
promissory note	約束手形	*yakusoku tegata*
promotion (personnel)	昇進	*shōshin*
promotion (retailing)	促進	*sokushin*
promotion, sales	販売促進	*hanbai sokushin*
prompt (adj)	即座の	*sokuza no*
proof of loss	損害証明書	*songai shōmei sho*
proofreading	校正	*kōsei*
property	財産	*zaisan*
proposal	申し込み	*mōshikomi*
proprietary (adj)	所有主の	*shoyū nushi no*
proprietor	所有者	*shoyū sha*
propylene	プロピレン	*puropiren*
prosecute	起訴する	*kisosuru*
prosecution, the	検察当局	*kensatsu tōkyoku*
prospectus	趣意書	*shui sho*

protectionism	保護貿易主義	*hogo bōeki shugi*
protective duties	保護関税	*hogo kanzei*
protest (banking law) (v)	異議を申し立てる	*igi o mōshitateru*
proxy	代理	*dairi*
proxy (document)	委任状	*ininjō*
proxy (right)	代理権	*dairiken*
proxy statement	委任状	*inin jō*
prudent man rule	プルーデント・マン・ルール	*purūdento man rūru*
public auction	競売	*kyōbai*
public company (finance)	株式公開会社	*kabushiki kōkai gaisha*
public company (government)	公共企業体	*kōkyō kigyō tai*
public domain (government)	公有地	*kōyū chi*
public domain (patent)	権利消滅状態	*kenri shōmetsu jōtai*
public funds	公金	*kōkin*
public hearing	公聴会	*kōchōkai*
public offering	公募	*kōbo*
public opinion poll	世論調査	*yoron chōsa*
public property	公有財産	*kōyū zaisan*
public prosecutor	検事	*kenji*
public relations	ピーアール	*pī āru*
public sale	公売	*kōbai*
public sector	公共部門	*kōkyō bumon*
public utilities	公益事業	*kōeki jigyō*
public works	公共事業	*kōkyō jigyō*
publicity	宣伝	*senden*
publisher	出版社	*shuppan sha*
pulse	パルス	*parusu*
pump priming	呼び水政策	*yobi mizu seisaku*
punch card	パンチ・カード	*panchi kādo*
punch press	パンチ・プレス	*panchi puresu*
purchase (v)	購入する	*kōnyū suru*
purchase money mortgage	購買代金抵当	*kōbai daikin teitō*
purchase order (securities)	買い注文	*kai chūmon*
purchase order	購入指図書	*kōnyū sashizu sho*
purchase price	買入価格／仕入れ価格	*kaiire kakaku/shiire kakaku*
purchasing agent	購買係	*kōbai gakari*
purchasing manager	購買主任	*kōbai shunin*
purchasing power	購買力	*kōbai ryoku*
pure risk	純危険	*jun kiken*
purgative	下剤	*gezai*
put and call	特権付き売買	*tokken tsuki baibai*
put in a bid (v)	入札する	*nyūsatsu suru*
put option	売りオプション	*uri opushon*
pyramid selling	マルチ商法	*maruchi shōhō*

Q

qualifications	資格	*shikaku*
qualified acceptance endorsement	手形制限引受け裏書き	*tegata seigen hikiuke uragaki*
quality control	品質管理	*hinshitsu kanri*
quality goods	優良品	*yūryō hin*
quantity	数量	*sūryō*
quantity discount	数量割引き	*sūryō waribiki*
quarter	四半期	*shihanki*
quasi-public company	準公共企業体	*jun kōkyō kigyō tai*
quench (v)	焼き入れする	*yakiire suru*
quick assets	流動資産	*ryūdō shisan*
quick assets (finance)	急速換価資産	*kyūsoku kanka shisan*
quitclaim deed	権利放棄証書	*kenri hōki shōsho*
quorum	定数	*teisū*
quota	割当て額	*wariate gaku*
quota system	割当て制	*wariate sei*
quota, export	輸出割当て	*yushutsu wariate*
quota, sales	販売割当て	*hanbai wariate*
quotation	相場	*sōba*

R

rack jobber	ラック・ジョバー	*rakku jobā*
radar	レーダー	*rēdā*
radial drilling machine	ラジアル・ボール盤	*rajiaru bōru ban*
radial tire	ラジアル・タイヤ	*rajiaru taiya*
radiator	ラジエーター	*rajiētā*
radio	ラジオ	*rajio*
radio cassette player	ラジカセ	*rajikase*
rail shipment	鉄道輸送	*testudō yusō*
rain check	引換え券	*hikikae ken*
raincoat	レインコート	*reinkōto*
raising capital	資金調達	*shikin chōtatsu*
rally	反騰	*hantō*
RAM	随時書き込み読出しメモリ	*zuiji kakikomi yomidashi memori*
random access memory	ランダム・アクセス・メモリ	*randamu akusesu memori*
random sample	無作為抽出見本	*musakui chūshutsu mihon*
rangefinder	距離計	*kyori kei*
rate	割合	*wariai*
rate (finance)	料金	*ryōkin*
rate of growth	成長率	*seichō ritsu*
rate of increase	増加率	*zōka ritsu*
rate of interest	利率	*ri ritsu*

rate of return	収益率	*shūeki ritsu*
rate, base (transportation)	一般運賃率	*ippan unchin ritsu*
rate, base (wage)	ベース・レート	*bēsu rēto*
rating, credit	信用格付け	*shin-yō kakuzuke*
rating, market	市場格付け	*shijō kakuzuke*
ratio	比率	*hiritsu*
ration (v)	配給する	*haikyū suru*
raw materials	原材料	*gen zairyō*
rayon	レーヨン	*rēyon*
re-export	再輸出	*sai yushutsu*
read-only memory (ROM)	リード・オンリメモリ	*rīdo onri memori*
ready cash	即金払い	*sokkin barai*
ready-to-wear	既製服	*kisei fuku*
real estate	不動産	*fudōsan*
real estate investment trust	不動産投資信託	*fudōsan tōshi shintaku*
real estate tax	固定資産税	*kotei shisan zei*
real income	実質所得	*jisshitsu shotoku*
real interest rate	実質金利	*jisshitsu kinri*
real investment	実物投資	*jitsubutsu tōshi*
real investment return	実質投資収益率	*jisshitsu tōshi shūeki ritsu*
real price	実質価格	*jisshitsu kakaku*
real wages	実質賃金	*jisshitsu chingin*
real yield	実質利回り	*jisshitsu rimawari*
ream	連	*ren*
reamer	リーマ	*rīma*
rear axle	後車軸	*kōshajiku*
reasonable care	当然の注意	*tōzen no chūi*
rebate (finance)	割り戻し	*wari modoshi*
rebate (sales)	払い戻し	*harai modoshi*
recapitalization	資本再構成	*shihon saikōsei*
receipt	受取り証	*uketori shō*
recession	景気後退	*keiki kōtai*
rechargeable (adj)	再充電可能の	*sai jūden kanō no*
reciprocal trade	互恵貿易	*gokei bōeki*
reconciliation	和解	*wakai*
record date	登録期日	*tōroku kijitsu*
record player	レコード・プレーヤー	*rekōdo purēyā*
recourse	償還請求権	*shōkan seikyū ken*
recovery	回復	*kaifuku*
recovery (insurance)	回収	*kaishū*
recovery of expenses	費用の取り戻し	*hiyō no tori modoshi*
rectifier	整流器	*seiryū ki*
red tape	御役所仕事	*o-yakusho shigoto*
redeemable bonds	随時償還公債	*zuiji shōkan kōsai*
redemption	償還	*shōkan*
redemption fund	償還積立て金	*shōkan tsumitate kin*
redemption with a premium	割増し金付き償還	*warimashi kin tsuki shōkan*

R

rediscount rate	再割引き率	*sai waribiki ritsu*
reduction (chemicals)	還元	*kangen*
reference number	照合番号	*shōgō bangō*
reference, credit	信用照会先	*shin-yō shōkai saki*
refinancing	リファイナンス	*rifainansu*
reflation	リフレーション	*rifurēshon*
reflex camera	リフレックス・カメラ	*refurekkusu kamera*
refractories	耐火煉瓦	*taika renga*
refund	払い戻し	*harai modoshi*
refuse acceptance (v)	引受けを拒絶する	*hikiuke o kyozetsu suru*
refuse payment (v)	支払いを拒絶する	*shiharai o kyozetsu suru*
regarding (with regard to)	に関しては	*ni kanshite wa*
register (printing)	レジスター	*rejisutā*
registered check	レジスタード・チェック	*rejisutādo chekku*
registered mail	書留郵便	*kakitome yūbin*
registered representative	顧客係	*kokyaku gakari*
registered security	記名証券	*kimei shōken*
registered trademark	登録商標	*tōroku shōhyō*
regression analysis	回帰分析	*kaiki bunseki*
regressive tax	逆進税	*gyakushin zei*
regular warehouse	普通倉庫	*futsū sōko*
regulation	規則	*kisoku*
reimburse (v)	払い戻す	*harai modosu*
reinsurer	再保険者	*sai hoken sha*
reinvestment	再投資	*sai tōshi*
reliable source	信頼筋	*shinrai suji*
remainder (v)	催促する	*saisoku suru*
remedies	治療法	*chiryō hō*
remedy (law)	救済手続き	*kyūsai tetsuzuki*
remission of a tax	税免除	*zei menjo*
remittance check	送金小切手	*sōkin kogitte*
remote control	リモート・コントロール	*rimōto kontorōru*
removable hard disk	着脱型ハード・ディスク	*chakudatsugata hādodisuku*
remuneration	報酬	*hōshū*
renegotiate (v)	再交渉する	*sai kōshō suru*
renew (securities) (v)	書替える	*kakikaeru*
renew (v)	更新する	*kōshin suru*
renewal	更新	*kōshin*
rent	賃借料	*chin gari ryō*
reorder (v)	再注文する	*sai chūmon suru*
reorganize (v)	再編成する	*sai hensei suru*
repay (v)	返済する	*hensai suru*
repayment	返済	*hensai*
repeat order	再注文	*sai chūmon*
repeatable robot	繰り返しロボット	*kurikaeshi robotto*

replacement cost	新品取替え費	*shinpin torikae hi*
replacement parts	交換部品	*kōkan buhin*
reply (in . . . to)	の答えとして	*no kotae to shite*
reply (v)	答える	*kotaeru*
report	報告	*hōkoku*
repossession	商品取り戻し	*shōhin torimodoshi*
representative	代理	*dairi*
reproduction costs	再生産費	*sai seisan hi*
request for bid	入札請求	*nyūsatsu seikyū*
requirements	必要条件	*hitsuyō jōken*
resale	転売	*tenbai*
research	研究	*kenkyū*
research and development	研究開発	*kenkyū kaihatsu*
reserve	準備金	*junbi kin*
resident buyer	在住仕入れ人	*zaijū shiire nin*
resolution (photography)	解像度	*kaizōdo*
resolution (legal document)	決議	*ketsugi*
resources allocation	資源配分	*shigen haibun*
restrictions on export	輸出制限	*yushutsu seigen*
restrictive labor practices	制限的労働慣習	*seigen-teki rōdō kanshū*
restructure (v)	再構成する	*sai kōsei suru*
restructuring	リストラ	*risutora*
résumé	履歴書	*rireki sho*
retail	小売り	*kouri*
retail merchandise	小売り商品	*kouri shōhin*
retail outlet	小売店	*kouri ten*
retail price	小売り値段	*kouri nedan*
retail sales tax	小売り売上げ税	*kouri uriage zei*
retail trade	小売業	*kouri gyō*
retained earnings	留保利益	*ryūho rieki*
retaliation	報復	*hōfuku*
retirement (debt)	償還	*shōkan*
retirement (job)	退職	*taishoku*
retroactive (adj)	遡って効力を発する	*sakanobotte kōryoku o hassuru*
return on capital	資本収益	*shihon shūeki*
return on equity	持分利益率	*mochibun rieki ritsu*
return on investment	投資収益率	*tōshi shūeki ritsu*
return on sales	販売利益率	*hanbai rieki ritsu*
return, rate of	収益率	*shūeki ritsu*
returns	収益	*shūeki*
revaluation	再評価	*sai hyōka*
revaluation (government)	貨幣価値回復	*kahei kachi kaifuku*
revenue	収入／収益	*shūnyū/shūeki*
revenue bond	収入担保債	*shūnyū tanpo sai*
reverse stock split	株式併合	*kabushiki heigō*
revocable trust	取消可能信託	*torikeshi kanō shintaku*
revolving credit	回転信用	*kaiten shin-yō*
revolving fund	回転資金	*kaiten shikin*
revolving letter of credit	回転信用状	*kaiten shin-yō jō*

reward	報酬	*hōshū*
rider (contracts)	追加条項	*tsuika jōkō*
right of recourse	償還請求権	*shōkan seikyū ken*
right of way	通行権	*tsūkō ken*
risk	危険	*kiken*
risk analysis	危険分析	*kiken bunseki*
risk assessment	危険査定	*kiken satei*
risk capital	危険負担資本	*kiken futan shihon*
rod	棒	*bō*
roll turning lathe	ロール旋盤	*rōru senban*
rollback	物価引下げ政策	*bukka hikisage seisaku*
rolling mill	圧延工場	*atsuen kōjō*
rolling stock	車両	*sharyō*
rollover	借換え	*karikae*
ROM	読み出し専用メモリ	*yomidashi senyō memori*
rough draft	下書き	*shita gaki*
rough estimate	概算見積り書	*gaisan mitsumori sho*
round lot	一口の取引き単位	*hitokuchi no torihiki tan-i*
routine	決まり仕事	*kimari shigoto*
routine (computer)	ルーチン	*rūchin*
royalty (patent)	特許使用料	*tokkyo shiyōryō*
royalty (publication)	印税	*inzei*
royalty payment (copyright)	印税	*inzei*
royalty payment (patent)	特許権使用料	*tokkyo ken shiyō ryō*
running expenses	運転費	*unten hi*
rush order	大急ぎの注文	*ōisogi no chūmon*

S

saccharin	サッカリン	*sakkarin*
safe deposit box	貸金庫	*kashi kinko*
safeguard	保護	*hogo*
salad bowl	サラダ　ボール	*sarada bōru*
salad plate	サラダの取り皿	*sarada no tori zara*
salary	サラリー	*sararī*
sale and leaseback	リース契約付き売却	*rīsu keiyaku tsuki baikyaku*
sales	販売	*hanbai*
sales analysis	販売分析	*hanbai bunseki*
sales budget	販売予算	*hanbai yosan*
sales estimate	予想売り上げ高	*yosō uriage daka*
sales force	販売員	*hanbai in*
sales forecasts	販売予測	*hanbai yosoku*
sales management	販売管理	*hanbai kanri*
sales promotion	販売促進	*hanbai sokushin*
sales quota	販売割り当て	*hanbai wariate*
sales tax	売り上げ税	*uriage zei*
sales territory	販売地域	*hanbai chiiki*
sales turnover	総売り上げ高	*sō uriage daka*

sales volume	販売料	*hanbai ryō*
salt	塩	*en*
salt shaker	塩振り容器	*shio furi yōki*
salts (pharmaceuticals)	かぎ塩	*kagi shio*
salvage (v)	回収する	*kaishū suru*
salvage charges	海難救助費	*kainan kyūjo hi*
salvage value (accounting)	残存価額	*zanson kagaku*
salvage value (insurance)	海難救助品価額	*kainan kyūjo hin kagaku*
salve	軟膏	*nankō*
sample (v)	見本をとる	*mihon o toru*
sample line	見本種目	*mihon shumoku*
sample size	標本のサイズ	*hyōhon no saizu*
sanction	制裁	*seisai*
saponification	鹸化	*kenka*
saucer	受け皿	*uke zara*
savings	貯蓄	*chochiku*
savings account	貯蓄勘定口座	*chochiku kanjō kōza*
savings bank	貯蓄銀行	*chochiku ginkō*
savings bond	貯蓄債券	*chochiku saiken*
sawing machine	鋸盤	*nokogiri ban*
scalper (securities)	スカルパー	*sukarupā*
scanner	スキャナ	*sukyana*
scarf	スカーフ	*sukāfu*
schedule	予定	*yotei*
scrap (metalworks)	屑鉄	*kuzu tetsu*
screen (computer)	スクリーン	*sukurīn*
screen (printing)	網	*ami*
screening	選別検査	*senbetsu kensa*
screw cutting lathe	ねじ切り旋盤	*nejikiri senban*
script	抄本	*shōhon*
sealed bid	封緘入札	*fūkan nyūsatsu*
seamless steel tube	継ぎ目なし鋼管	*tsugime nashi kōkan*
seasonal (adj)	季節的	*kisetsu-teki*
seat	シート	*shīto*
seatbelt	シートベルト	*shīto beruto*
second mortgage	二番抵当	*niban teitō*
secondary market (securities)	流通市場	*ryūtsū shijo*
secondary offering (securities)	再売出し	*sai uridashi*
secretary	秘書	*hisho*
secured accounts	担保付き勘定	*tanpo tsuki kanjō*
secured liability	担保付き負債	*tanpo tuski fusai*
securities	有価証券	*yūka shōken*
Securities and Exchange Commission	証券取引委員会	*shōken torihiki iinkai*
securities company	証券会社	*shōken gaisha*
securities market	証券市場	*shōken shijō*
security	担保	*tanpo*
security analyst	証券アナリスト	*shōken anarisuto*
sedative	鎮静薬	*chinsei yaku*

S

seizure	差し押さえ	*sashiosae*
self-management	自己管理	*jiko kanri*
self-appraisal	自己評価	*jiko hyōka*
self-employed, be (v)	自営する	*jiei suru*
self-service	セルフ・サービス	*serufu sābisu*
self-timer	セルフ・タイマー	*serufu taimā*
sell (v)	売る	*uru*
sell direct (v)	直接売る	*chokusetsu uru*
sell, hard	ハード・セル	*hādo seru*
sell, soft	穏やかな商法	*odayaka na shōhō*
semi-variable costs	準変動費	*jun hendō hi*
semiconductor	半導体	*handō tai*
semiconductor laser	半導体レーザー	*handōtai rēzā*
senior issue	上位の株式	*jōi no kabushiki*
seniority	先任権	*sennin ken*
seniority system	年功序列制	*nenkō joretsu sei*
sensitometer	感光計	*kankō kei*
sensor	センサー	*sensā*
separation (employment)	離職	*rishoku*
sequence robot	シーケンス・ロボット	*shīkensu robotto*
sequential control	シーケンス制御	*shīkensu seigyo*
serial bonds	連続償還社債	*renzoku shōkan shasai*
serial port	シリアル・ポート	*shiriaru pōto*
serial printer	シリアル・プリンタ	*shiriaru purinta*
serial storage	直列式記憶装置	*chokuretsu shiki kioku sōchi*
serum	血清	*kessei*
server (computer)	サーバー	*sāba*
service (v)	手入れする	*teire suru*
service contract	定期点検契約	*teiki tenken keiyaku*
service, customer	顧客サービス	*kokyaku sābisu*
serving spoon	取り分け用スプーン	*toriwake yō supūn*
set	セット	*setto*
set-up costs	段取り費	*dandori hi*
settlement	決算	*kessan*
settlement, full	総決算	*sō kessan*
severance pay	退職金	*taishoku kin*
sew (v)	縫う	*nuu*
sewn (adj)	とじた	*tojita*
shaft lather	軸旋盤	*jiku senban*
shape-memory alloy	形状記憶合金	*keijō kioku gōkin*
shaping machine	形削り盤	*katakezuri ban*
share (computer)	共用	*kyōyō*
share (securities)	株	*kabu*
share price	株価	*kabuka*
shareholder	株主	*kabu nushi*
shareholder's equity	株主持分	*kabunushi mochibun*
shareholder's meeting	株主総会／株主会	*kabunushi sōkai/kabunushi kai*

shares	株式	*kabushiki*
shearing machine	シャーリング・マシン	*shāringu mashin*
sheet (printing)	枚葉紙	*maiyōshi*
sheet bar	シート・バー	*shīto bā*
sheet pile	鋼矢板	*kōya ban*
shift (labor)	交代時間	*kotai jikan*
shipment	出荷	*shukka*
shipper	荷主	*ni nushi*
shipping agent	船会社代理店	*funagaisha dairi ten*
shipping charges	船積み費	*funazumi hi*
shipping expenses	船積み費	*funazumi hi*
shipping instructions	船積み指図書	*funazumi sashizu sho*
shirt	シャツ	*shatsu*
shock absorber	ショック・アブソーバー	*shokku abusōbā*
shoe	靴	*kutsu*
shopping center	ショッピング・センター	*shoppingu sentā*
short delivery	受渡し高不足	*ukewatashi daka busoku*
short of, to be (v)	不足している	*fusoku shite iru*
short position	売り越し	*uri koshi*
short sale	から売り	*kara uri*
short shipment	積み残し品	*tsumi nokoshi hin*
short sleeves	半袖	*han sode*
short supply	供給薄	*kyōkyū usu*
short-term capital account	短期資本勘定	*tanki shihon kanjō*
short-term debt	短期負債	*tanki fusai*
short-term financing	短期融資	*tanki yūshi*
short-term	短期	*tanki*
shortage	不足	*fusoku*
shoulder pad	ショルダー・パッド	*shorudā paddo*
shrink-wrapping	収縮包装	*shūshuku hōsō*
shutter	シャッター	*shattā*
shutter speed	シャッター・スピード	*shattā supīdo*
sick leave	有給病気休暇	*yūkyū byōki kyūka*
sight draft	一覧払い為替手形	*ichiran barai kawase tegata*
signature	署名	*shomei*
silent partner	業務無担当の出資者	*gyōmu mutantō no shusshisha*
silk	シルク	*shiruku*
silverplate (adj)	銀めっきの	*gin mekki no*
silverware	食卓用銀器	*shokutaku yō ginki*
simple interest	単利	*tanri*
simulate (v)	まねる	*maneru*
single-lens reflex camera	一眼レフ	*ichigan refu*
sinking fund	減債基金	*gensai kikin*
sinus	鼻腔	*bi kō*

size	サイズ	*saizu*
skilled labor	熟練労働	*jukuren rōdō*
skirt	スカート	*sukāto*
sky lens	全天レンズ	*zenten renzu*
slacks	スラックス	*surakkusu*
sleeping pill	催眠薬	*saimin yaku*
slide projector	スライド映写機	*suraido eisha ki*
slide	スライド	*suraido*
sliding scale	スライド制	*suraido sei*
slot	スロット	*surotto*
slotting machine	縦削り盤	*tatekezuri ban*
slump	景気沈滞	*keiki chintai*
small business	小企業	*shō kigyō*
soft currency	軟貨	*nan ka*
soft focus lens	ソフト・フォーカス・レンズ	*sofuto fōkasu renzu*
soft goods	織物類	*orimono rui*
soft loan	ソフト・ローン	*sofuto rōn*
soft sell	おだやかな商法	*odayaka na shōhō*
soft-cover	紙表紙版	*kami byōshi ban*
software	ソフトウェア	*sofutowea*
software broker	ソフトウェア・ブローカー	*sofutowea burōkā*
sole agent	総代理店	*sō dairi ten*
sole proprietor	個人店主	*kojin tenshu*
sole rights	独占権	*dokusen ken*
solid-state laser	固体レーザー	*kotai rēzā*
solubility	溶解度	*yōkai do*
solute	溶質	*yōshitsu*
solution (chemicals)	溶液	*yōeki*
solvency	支払い能力	*shiharai nōryoku*
solvent (chemicals)	溶剤	*yōzai*
soup dish	スープ皿	*sūpu zara*
soupspoon	スープ用スプーン	*sūpū yō supūn*
spark plug	スパーク・プラグ	*supāku puragu*
speaker	スピーカー	*supīkā*
specialist (stock exchange)	スペシャリスト	*supesharisuto*
specialty goods	専門品	*senmon hin*
specific duty	従量税	*jūryō zei*
specification	仕様書	*shiyōsho*
speculative stock	仕手株	*shite kabu*
speculator	仕手／投機家	*shite/tōki ka*
speed up (v)	急がせる	*isogaseru*
speedometer	速度計	*sokudo kei*
spin off (v)	分離新設する	*bunri shinsetsu suru*
spine (publishing)	背	*se*
spiral tube	スパイラル鋼管	*supairaru kōkan*
spline milling machine	溝切りフライス盤	*mizokiri furaisu ban*
spoilage	仕損品	*shison hin*

sponge (metalworks)	海綿鉄	*kaimen tetsu*
sponsor (of fund, partnership)	保証人	*hoshō nin*
spoon	スプーン	*supūn*
sportswear	スポーツ・ウェア	*supōtsu wea*
spot delivery	現場渡し	*genba watashi*
spot market	現物市場	*genbutsu shijō*
spread (finance)	値幅	*nehaba*
spread (securities)	値開き	*nebiraki*
spreadsheet	スプレッド・シート	*supureddo shīto*
staff	職員	*shokuin*
staff and line (adj)	参謀直系式	*sanbō chokkei-shiki*
staff assistant	スタッフ・アシスタント	*sutaffu ashisutanto*
staff organization	スタッフ組織	*sutaffu soshiki*
stagflation	スタグフレーション	*sutagufurēshon*
stainless steel	ステンレス／ステンレス鋼	*sutenresu/sutenresu kō*
stale check	遅延小切手	*chien kogitte*
stand-alone text processor	独立テキスト・プロセッサ	*dokuritsu tekisuto purosessa*
stand-alone workstation	独立ワーク・ステーション	*dokuritsu wākusutēshon*
standard costs	標準原価	*hyōjun genka*
standard deviation	標準偏差	*hyōjun hensa*
standard equipment	標準装備品	*hyōjun sōbi hin*
standard	標準／規格	*hyōjun/kikaku*
standard lens	標準レンズ	*hyōjun renzu*
standard of living	生活水準	*seikatsu suijun*
standard practice	標準慣行	*hyōjun kankō*
standard time	標準時	*hyōjun ji*
standardization	規格化	*kikaku ka*
standing charges	固定費	*kotei hi*
standing costs	固定費	*kotei hi*
standing order	継続指図書	*keizoku sashizu sho*
starch	澱粉	*denpun*
start-up cost	操業開始経費	*sōgyō kaishi keihi*
statement	声明	*seimei*
statement (banking)	計算書	*keisan sho*
statement of account	勘定書	*kanjō sho*
statement, financial	財務諸表	*zaimu shohyō*
statement, pro forma	見積り計算書	*mitsumori keisan sho*
statement, profit and loss	損益計算書	*son-eki keisan sho*
statistics	統計	*tōkei*
statute	法令	*hōrei*
statute of limitations	時効	*jikō*
steel foil	スチール・フォイル	*suchīru foiru*
steel mill	製鉄所	*seitetsu sho*

S

steering wheel	ハンドル	*handoru*
stereo TV	ステレオ・テレビ	*sutereo terebi*
stereophonic (adj)	ステレオ	*sutereo*
stimulant	興奮薬	*kōfun yaku*
stock	株式	*kabushiki*
stock (merchandising)	在庫品	*zaiko hin*
stock (securities)	有価証券	*yūka shōken*
stock certificate	株券	*kabu ken*
stock control	在庫品管理	*zaiko hin kanri*
stock exchange	株式取引所	*kabushiki torihiki sho*
stock index	株価指数	*kabuka shisū*
stock investment	株式投資	*kabushiki tōshi*
stock investment trust	株式投資信託	*kabushiki tōshi shintaku*
stock issue	株式銘柄	*kabushiki meigara*
stock market	株式市場	*kabushiki shijō*
stock option	ストック・オプション	*sutokku opushon*
stock portfolio	株式投資配分表	*kabushiki tōshi haibun hyō*
stock power	株券譲渡委任状	*kabuken jōto inin jō*
stock price index	株価指数	*kabuka shisū*
stock price	株価	*kabuka*
stock purchase plan	従業員持ち株制度	*jūgyō in mochikabu seido*
stock split	株式分割	*kabushiki bunkatsu*
stock turnover (securities)	株式回転率	*kabushiki kaiten ritsu*
stockbroker	株式仲買人	*kabushiki nakagainin*
stockholder	株主	*kabu nushi*
stockholders' equity	株主持分	*kabu nushi mochibun*
stoneware	厚手の陶器	*atsude no tōki*
stop-loss order	逆指値注文	*gyaku sashine chūmon*
stop-payment	支払い停止	*shiharai teishi*
storage	記憶装置	*kioku sōchi*
storage (computer)	ストレージ	*sutorēji*
storage (general)	倉庫保管	*sōko hokan*
store (v)	保管する	*hokan suru*
stowage	積込み荷物	*tsumikomi nimotsu*
stowage charges	船内積付け賃	*sennai tsumitsuke chin*
straddling	両建て	*ryōdate*
strapping	革ひも	*kawa himo*
strategic articles	戦略品	*senryaku hin*
streamline (v)	能率化する	*nōritsu ka suru*
stress management	ストレス管理	*sutoresu kanri*
strike (v)	ストライキをする	*sutoraiki o suru*
strike, wildcat	山猫スト	*yamaneko suto*
strikebreaker (scab)	スト破り	*suto yaburi*
strobe	ストロボ	*sutorobo*
stuffing	詰め物	*tsumemono*
style	スタイル	*sutairu*
styrene monomer	スチレン・モノマー	*suchiren monomā*
subcontract (v)	下請けに出す	*shitauke ni dasu*

S

subcontractor	下請け業者	*shitauke gyōsha*
sublet	転貸	*tentai*
subpoena (v)	喚問する	*kanmonsuru*
subscription price	応募価格／予約金	*ōbo kakaku/yoyaku kin*
subsidiary	子会社	*ko gaisha*
subsidy	補助金	*hojo kin*
substandard	標準以下の	*hyōjun ika no*
sue	訴える	*uttaeru*
suede	スエード	*suēdo*
sugar bowl	砂糖壷	*satō tsubo*
suit	スーツ	*sūtsu*
sulfate	硫酸塩	*ryūsan en*
sulfuric acid	硫酸	*ryūsan*
sulphamide	スルファミド	*surufamido*
sum of the year's digits	級数逓減法	*kyūsū teigen hō*
summary court	簡易裁判所	*kan-i saibansho*
summary order	略式命令	*ryakushiki meirei*
summon (v)	喚問する	*kanmonsuru*
summons (n)	召喚状	*shōkanjō*
super alloys	スーパー・アロイ	*sūpā aroi*
super computer	スーパー・コンピュータ	*sūpā konpyūta*
super lattice	超格子	*chō kōshi*
superconducting ceramics	超伝導セラミックス	*chō dendō seramikkusu*
superconductive coil	超伝導コイル	*chō dendō koiru*
superconductive materials	超伝導材料	*chō dendō zairyō*
superconductive phenomena	超伝導現象	*chō dendō genshō*
superconductor	超伝導体	*chō dendō tai*
supersede (v)	地位を奪う	*chii o ubau*
supervisor	監督者	*kantoku sha*
supplier	供給者	*kyōkyū sha*
supply and demand	供給と需要	*kyōkyū to juyō*
support activities	支援活動	*shien katsudō*
supreme court	最高裁判所	*saikō saibansho*
surcharge	附加金	*fuka kin*
surety company	身元保証会社	*mimoto hoshō gaisha*
surface grinder	平面研削盤	*heimen kensaku ban*
surplus capital	資本剰余金	*shihon jōyo kin*
surplus goods	剰余品	*jōyo hin*
surtax	付加税	*fuka zei*
suspend payment (v)	支払い停止する	*shiharai teishi suru*
suspension	サスペンション	*sasupenshon*
swap	スワップ	*suwappu*
sweater	セーター	*sētā*
switch	スイッチ	*suitchi*
switching charges	転轍輸送料	*tentetsu yusō ryō*
sworn statement	宣誓陳述書	*sensei chinjutsu sho*
syndicate (v)	シンジケートを作る	*shinjikēto o tsukuru*
synthesis	合成	*gōsei*

S

synthetic (adj)	合成の	*gōsei no*
synthetic suede	合成スエード	*gōsei suēdo*
syringe	注射器	*chūsha ki*
systems analysis	システム分析	*shisutemu bunseki*
systems design	システム設計	*shisutemu sekkei*
systems engineering	システム・エンジニアリング	*shisutemu enjiniaringu*
systems management	システム管理	*shisutemu kanri*

T

35 mm camera	35ミリ・カメラ	*sanjū go miri kamera*
table of contents	目次／目録	*mokuji/mokuroku*
tablecloth	テーブル・クロス	*tēburu kurosu*
tablespoon	大匙	*ōsaji*
tablet	錠剤／タブレット	*jōzai/taburetto*
tachometer	タコ・メーター	*tako mētā*
taffeta	タフタ	*tafuta*
tailor	テーラー	*tērā*
take down (v)	取り壊す	*tori kowasu*
take off (sales) (v)	値引きする	*nebiki suru*
take out (v)	取出す	*toridasu*
take-home pay	手取り給料	*tedori kyūryō*
takeover bid	株式買取り公開申し込み	*kabushiki kaitori kōkai mōshikomi*
takeover	乗っ取り	*nottori*
tangible assets	有形資産	*yūkei shisan*
tanker	タンカー	*tankā*
tape recorder	テープ・レコーダー	*tēpu rekōdā*
target price	目標価格	*mokuhyō kakaku*
tariff	関税	*kanzei*
tariff barriers	関税障壁	*kanzei shōheki*
tariff classification	関税等級分類	*kanzei tōkyū bunrui*
tariff commodity	関税商品	*kanzei shōhin*
tariff differential	関税率格差	*kanzei ritsu kakusa*
tariff war	関税戦	*kanzei sen*
task force	タスク・フォース	*tasuku fōsu*
tax	税金	*zeikin*
tax allowance	税控除	*zei kōjo*
tax base	課税基盤	*kazei kiban*
tax burden	租税負担	*sozei futan*
tax collector	収税官	*shūzei kan*
tax deduction	税控除	*zei kōjo*
tax evasion	脱税	*datsu zei*
tax exempt bond	免税債	*menzei sai*
tax haven	軽課税国	*kei kazei koku*
tax law	税法	*zeihō*

tax rate	税率	*zeiritsu*
tax relief	租税軽減	*sozei keigen*
tax shelter	税金避難手段	*zeikin hinan shudan*
taxation	課税	*kazei*
tax, excise	消費税	*shōhi zei*
tax, export	輸出品税	*yushutsu hin zei*
tax, import	輸入品税	*yunyū hin zei*
tax, sales	売上税	*uriage zei*
tax-free income	非課税所得	*hikazei shotoku*
tax-free	免税の	*menzei no*
team, management	マネジメント・チーム	*manejimento chīmu*
teapot	ティー・ポット	*tī potto*
teaspoon	小匙	*kosaji*
telecommunications	テレコミュニケーション	*terekomyunikēshon*
telephone line	電話回線	*denwa kaisen*
telephoto lens	望遠レンズ	*bōen renzu*
teleprocessing	テレプロセシング	*terepuroseshingu*
television	テレビ	*terebi*
telex	テレックス	*terekkusu*
teller	金銭出納係	*kinsen suitō gakari*
tender	入札	*nyūsatsu*
tender offer	株式の公開買付け	*kabushiki no kōkai kaitsuke*
tender, legal	法貨	*hōka*
term bond	定期債	*teiki sai*
term insurance	定期保険	*teiki hoken*
term loan	期限付き借入金	*kigen tsuki kari ire kin*
terminal (computer)	ターミナル	*tāminaru*
terminal (transportation)	終点	*shūten*
terminal	ターミナル／端末	*tāminaru/tanmatsu*
terminate (v)	廃止する	*haishi suru*
terms	条件	*jōken*
terms of sale	販売条件	*hanbai jōken*
terms of trade	交易条件	*kōeki jōken*
territorial waters	領海	*ryōkai*
territory	地域	*chiiki*
testify	証言する	*shōgensuru*
textile	織物	*orimono*
thermostat	サーモスタット	*sāmosutatto*
thin market	手薄な市況	*teusu na shikyō*
third window	第三の窓	*dai san no mado*
through bill of lading	通し船荷証券	*tōshi funani shōken*
throughput	スループット	*surū putto*
ticker	株式相場表示器	*kabushiki sōba hyōji ki*
ticker tape	株式相場表示テープ	*kabushiki sōba hyōji tēpu*
tie	ネクタイ	*nekutai*
tied aid	ひも付き援助	*hīmo tsuki enjo*
tied loan	タイド・ローン	*taido rōn*

tight market	緊縮市況	*kinshuku shikyō*
time and motion study	作業時間作業動作相関研究	*sagyō jikan sagyō dōsa sōkan kenkyū*
time bill (of exchange)	期限付き為替手形	*kigen tsuki kawase tegata*
time deposit	定期預金	*teiki yokin*
time order	時限注文	*jigen chūmon*
time sharing	タイム・シェアリング	*taimu shearingu*
time zone	時間帯	*jikan tai*
time, lead	所要時間	*shoyō jikan*
time, lead (computer)	リード・タイム	*rīdo taimu*
timetable	時間表	*jikan hyō*
tip (inside information)	インサイド・インフォメーション	*insaido infomēshon*
tire	タイヤ	*taiya*
titanium	チタン	*chitan*
titanium metal	チタン金属	*chitan kinzoku*
title (legal right)	権原	*kengen*
title (publishing)	表題	*hyōdai*
title insurance	権原保険	*kengen hoken*
titles (ownership)	所有権	*shoyūken*
Tokyo foreign exchange market	東京外国為替市場	*Tōkyō gaikoku kawase shijō*
Tokyo foreign stock market	東京外国株式市場	*Tōkyō gaikoku kabushiki shijō*
Tokyo Stock Exchange	東京証券取引所／東証	*Tōkyō shōken torihikijo/Tōshō*
toluene	トルエン	*toruen*
tombstone	墓石広告	*boseki kōkoku*
tonnage	容積トン数	*yōseki ton sū*
tools	道具	*dōgu*
top management	最高経営者	*saikō keiei sha*
top price	最高価格	*saikō kakaku*
top quality	最高品質	*saikō hinshitsu*
top up (v)	仕上げをする	*shiage o suru*
torque	トルク	*toruku*
tort	不法行為	*fuhō kōi*
total return	総合利回り	*sōgō rimawari*
toxicology	毒物学	*dokubutsu gaku*
toxin	毒素	*dokuso*
track ball	トラックボール	*torakkubōru*
Trade Representative (U.S.)	通商代表	*tsūshō daihyō*
trade	取引	*torihiki*
trade (v)	取引きする	*torihiki suru*
trade acceptance	貿易引受手形	*bōekī hikiuke tegata*
trade agreement	貿易協定	*bōeki kyōtei*
trade association	産業団体	*sangyō dantai*
trade barrier	貿易障壁	*bōeki shōheki*
trade commission	貿易委員会	*bōeki iinkai*
trade credit	取引先信用	*torihiki saki shin-yō*

T

trade date	取引期日	*torihiki kijitsu*
trade discount	業者割引	*gyōsha waribiki*
trade house	商社	*shōsha*
trade union	労働組合	*rōdō kumiai*
trade, fair	公正貿易	*kōsei bōeki*
trade, unfair	不公正貿易	*fu kōsei bōeki*
trade-off	トレード・オフ	*torēdo ofu*
trademark	商標	*shōhyō*
trader	貿易業者	*bōeki gyōsha*
trading	取引	*torihiki*
trading company	商事会社	*shōji gaisha*
trading floor	立会場	*tachiai jō*
trading limit	取引制限	*torihiki seigen*
trainee	実習生	*jisshū sei*
tranche	トランシュ	*toranshu*
tranquilizer	トランキライザー	*torankiraizā*
transaction	取引	*torihiki*
transfer (computer)	転送	*tensō*
transfer (securities)	譲渡	*jōto*
transfer agent	名義書換え代理人	*meigi kakikae dairi nin*
transfer machine	トランスファーマシン	*toransufā mashin*
transfer slip	振り替え伝票	*furikae denpyō*
transformer	変圧器	*hen-atsu ki*
transit, in	運送中	*unsō chū*
translator	翻訳者	*hon-yaku sha*
transmission	トランスミッション	*toransumisshon*
transmission loss	伝送損失	*densō sonshitsu*
transportation	輸送	*yusō*
traveler's check	旅行小切手	*ryokō kogitte*
tray	盆	*bon*
treasurer	収入役	*shūnyū yaku*
Treasury Bill	財務省短期証券	*zaimushō tanki shōken*
Treasury Bond	財務省長期証券	*zaimushō chōki shōken*
Treasury Note	財務省中期証券	*zaimushō chūki shōken*
treasury stock	金庫株	*kinko kabu*
treaty	条約	*jōyaku*
trend	動向	*dōkō*
trial	裁判	*saiban*
trial balance	試算表	*shisan hyō*
trichloroethane	トリクロルエタン	*torikuroru etan*
trigger price	引き金価格	*hikigane kakaku*
tripod	三脚	*sankyaku*
trivet	三脚台	*sankyaku dai*
troubleshoot (v)	問題をつきとめて解決する	*mondai o tsukitomete kaiketsu suru*
truckload	貸し切り貨物	*kashikiri kamotsu*
trust	信託	*shintaku*
trust bank	信託銀行	*shintaku ginkō*

trust company	信託会社	*shintaku gaisha*
trust fund	信託資金	*shintaku shikin*
trust receipt	手形担保荷物保管預り証	*tegata tanpo nimotsu hokan azukari shō*
trustee	受託者	*jutaku sha*
tuner	チューナー	*chūnā*
tungsten	タングステン	*tangusuten*
turbo-charger	ターボ・チャージャー	*tābo chājā*
tureen	蓋付き深皿	*futa tsuki fuka zara*
turnkey	ターンキー契約	*tān kī keiyaku*
turnover, asset	資産回転率	*shisan kaiten ritsu*
turnover, inventory	棚卸し資産回転率	*tana oroshi shisan kaiten ritsu*
turnover, sales	総売上げ高	*sō uriage daka*
turnover, stock	株式回転率	*kabushiki kaiten ritsu*
turret lathe	タレット旋盤	*taretto senban*
twin lens reflex camera	二眼レフ・カメラ	*nigan refu kamera*
two-name paper	二人署名手形	*futari shomei tegata*

U

U.S. International Trade Commission	米国際貿易委員会	*bei kokusai bōeki iinkai*
ultra vires acts	越権行為	*ekken kōi*
ultrafine powder	超微粒子	*chō biryūshi*
unaccompanied goods	別送荷物	*bessō nimotsu*
uncollectible accounts	焦げ付き勘定	*kogetsuki kanjō*
undercapitalized (adj)	投資不足の	*tōshi busoku no*
undercut (v)	値段を切り下げる	*nedan o kirisageru*
underdeveloped nations	低開発国	*tei kaihatsu koku*
underestimate (v)	過小評価する	*kashō hyōka suru*
underpaid (adj)	支払い不足の	*shiharai busoku no*
undersigned	署名者	*shomei sha*
understanding (agreement)	協定	*kyōtei*
undertake (v)	引き受ける	*hikiukeru*
undervalue (v)	過小評価する	*kashō hyōka suru*
underwater camera	水中カメラ	*suichū kamera*
underwriter (insurance)	保険業者	*hoken gyōsha*
underwriter (securities)	引受け業者	*hikiuke gyōsha*
undeveloped (adj)	未開発の	*mikaihatsu no*
unearned increment	自然増価	*shizen zōka*
unearned revenue	不労収入	*furō shūnyū*
unemployment	失業	*shitsugyō*
unemployment compensation	失業手当て	*shitsugyō teate*
unfair (adj)	不公正な	*fu kōsei na*
unfair competition	不公正競争	*fu kōsei kyōsō*
unfavorable (adj)	不利な	*furi na*
unfeasible (adj)	実行不可能な	*jikkō fukanō na*

T

union contract	労働契約	*rōdō keiyaku*
union label	組合符標	*kumiai fuhyō*
union, labor	労働組合	*rōdō kumiai*
unisex	ユニセックス	*yunisekkusu*
unit cost	単位原価	*tan-i genka*
unit load discount	ユニットロード割引き	*yunitto rōdo waribiki*
unit price	単価	*tanka*
unitary tax	合算課税	*gassan kazei*
universal grinder	万能研削盤	*bannō kensaku ban*
universal milling machine	万能フライス盤	*bannō furaisu ban*
unlisted (adj)	非上場の	*hijōjō no*
unload (securities) (v)	大量処分する	*tairyō shobun suru*
unload (shipping) (v)	荷揚げする	*niage suru*
unsecured	無担保の	*mutanpo no*
unsecured liability	無担保負債	*mu tanpo fusai*
unsecured loan	信用貸し	*shin-yō gashi*
unskilled labor	未熟練労働	*mi jukuren rōdō*
up to our expectations	期待通りに	*kitai dōri ni*
upgrade	グレード・アップ	*gurēdoappu*
upload	アップ・ロード	*appurōdo*
upmarket	上向き市況	*uwamuki shikyō*
upturn	好転	*kōten*
urban renewal	都市再開発	*toshi sai kaihatsu*
urban sprawl	都市の無計画拡大	*toshi no mu keikaku kakudai*
urea	尿素	*nyōso*
urea resin	ユリア樹脂	*yuria jushi*
use tax	使用税	*shiyō zei*
useful life	耐用年数	*taiyō nensū*
user	使用者	*shiyō sha*
user-friendly	ユーザー・フレンドリー	*yūzā furendorī*
usury	高利	*kōri*
utilities (computer)	ユーティリティー	*yūtiritī*
utility	効用	*kōyō*

V

vaccine	ワクチン	*wakuchin*
valid (adj)	有効な	*yūkō na*
validate (v)	有効と認める	*yūkō to mitomeru*
valuation (finance)	評価	*hyōka*
valuation (real estate)	査定	*satei*
value	価値	*kachi*
value date	受渡日	*ukewatashibi*

value engineering	価値工学	*kachi kōgaku*
value for duty	税額査定価格	*zeigaku satei kakaku*
value, asset	資産価格	*shisan kakaku*
value, book	帳簿価格	*chōbo kakaku*
value, face	額面価格	*gakumen kakaku*
value, market	市場価格	*shijō kakaku*
value-added tax	付加価値税	*fuka kachi zei*
valve	バルブ	*barubu*
vanadium	バナジウム	*banajiumu*
variable annuity	変額年金	*hengaku nenkin*
variable costs	変動費	*hendō hi*
variable import levy	変動輸入賦課税	*hendō yunyū fuka zei*
variable margin	変動マージン	*hendō majin*
variable rate	変動利率	*hendō riritsu*
variable rate mortgage	変動金利制住宅抵当貸付け	*hendō kinri sei jūtaku teitō kashitsuke*
variable sequence robot	可変シーケンス・ロボット	*kahen shīkensu robotto*
variance	相違	*sōi*
veil	ベール	*bēru*
velocity of money	通貨の流通速度	*tsūka no ryūtsū sokudo*
vendor	売主	*uri nushi*
vendor's lien	売主保留権	*uri nushi horyū ken*
venture	ベンチャー	*benchā*
venture capital	危険負担資本	*kiken futan shihon*
verification	検証	*kenshō*
vertical boring mill	縦中ぐり盤	*tate nakaguri ban*
vertical integration	垂直統合	*suichoku tōgō*
vertical milling machine	縦フライス盤	*tate furaisu ban*
very large-scale integrated circuit	超大規模集積回路	*chō daikibo shūseki kairo*
vest	ベスト	*besuto*
vested interests	既得利権	*kitoku riken*
vested rights	既得権	*kitoku ken*
veto	拒否権	*kyohi ken*
vice-president	副社長	*fuku shachō*
video cassette camera	ビデオ・カセット・カメラ	*bideo kasetto kamera*
video cassette player	ビデオ・カセット・プレーヤー	*bideo kasetto purēyā*
video cassette recorder	ビデオ・カセット・レコーダー	*bideo kasetto rekōdā*
video disc	ビデオ・ディスク	*bideo disuku*
video RAM (VRAM)	ビデオ・ラム	*bideo ramu*
videotape recorder	テープ録画装置	*tēpu rokuga sōchi*
view finder	ファインダー	*faindā*
vinyl (adj)	ビニール製の	*binīru sei no*
violation	違反	*ihan*

visible balance of trade	商品貿易収支	*shōhin bōeki shūshi*
vitamin	ビタミン	*bitamin*
voice mail	音声メール	*onsei mēru*
voice recognition	音声認識	*onsei ninshiki*
voice-activated (adj)	音声入力の	*onsei nyūryoku no*
void	無効	*mukō*
void (adj)	無効の	*mukō no*
volatile market	気まぐれ市況	*kimagure shikyō*
volume	量	*ryō*
volume (computer)	ボリューム	*boryūmu*
volume (securities)	出来高	*dekidaka*
volume discount	数量割引	*sūryō waribiki*
volume, sales	販売量	*hanbai ryō*
voting right	投票権	*tōhyō ken*
voucher	伝票	*denpyō*

W

wafer	ウエハー	*uehā*
wage	賃金	*chingin*
wage differential	賃金格差	*chingin kakusa*
wage dispute	賃上げ闘争	*chin age tōsō*
wage drift	賃金ドリフト	*chingin dorifuto*
wage earner	賃金所得者	*chingin shotoku sha*
wage freeze	賃金凍結	*chingin tōketsu*
wage level	賃金水準	*chingin suijun*
wage scale	賃金スケール	*chingin sukēru*
wage structure	給与構造	*kyūyo kōzō*
wage-price spiral	物価と賃金の悪循環	*bukka to chingin no aku junkan*
wages	賃金	*chingin*
waiver clause	免責条項	*menseki jōkō*
waiver clause (insurance)	棄権約款	*kiken yakkan*
walkout	ストライキ	*sutoraiki*
want ad	新聞募集広告	*shinbun boshū kōkoku*
warehouse	倉庫	*sōko*
warehouseman	倉庫業者	*sōko gyōsha*
warrant (law)	令状	*rei jō*
warrant (securities)	ワラント／引受権証書	*waranto/hikiukeken shōsho*
warranty	保証	*hoshō*
wasted asset	減耗資産	*genmō shisan*
water-absorbing resin	高吸水性樹脂	*kō kyūsui sei jushi*
waybill	貨物運送状	*kamotsu unsō jō*
wealth	財産	*zaisan*
wear and tear	消耗磨損	*shōmō mason*
weekly return	週益	*shū eki*
weight	重量	*jūryō*
weighted average	加重平均	*kajū heikin*

wharfage charges	埠頭使用料	*futō shiyō ryō*
wheel	車輪	*sharin*
when issued	発行日取引	*hakkō bi torihiki*
white collar worker	ホワイト・カラー	*howaito karā*
wholesale market	卸売り市場	*oroshiuri shijō*
wholesale price	卸売り価格	*oroshiuri kakaku*
wholesale trade	卸売り業	*oroshiuri gyō*
wholesaler	卸売り業者	*oroshiuri gyōsha*
wide angle lens	広角レンズ	*kōkaku renzu*
wildcat strike	山猫スト	*yamaneko suto*
will	遺言	*yuigon*
win a suit	勝訴する	*shōsosuru*
windfall profits	偶発利益	*gūhatsu rieki*
window dressing (increase appeal) (v)	粉飾する	*funshoku suru*
Windows (computers)	ウインドーズ	*windōzu*
windshield	フロント・ガラス	*furonto garasu*
wineglass	ワイン・グラス	*wain gurasu*
wire	針金	*harigane*
wire transfer	電信為替	*denshin gawase*
with average	単独海損担保	*tandoku kaison tanpo*
withdrawal	引き出し	*hikidashi*
withholding tax	源泉課税	*gensen kazei*
witness	証人	*shōnin*
wool	ウール	*ūru*
word processing	ワープロ処理	*wāpuro shori*
word processor	ワード・プロセッサ／ワープロ	*wādo purosessa/wāpuro*
work (v)	働く	*hataraku*
work committee	工場委員会	*kōjō iinkai*
work council	労使協議会	*rōshi kyōgi kai*
work cycle	仕事サイクル	*shigoto saikuru*
work day	就業日	*shūgyō bi*
work in progress	仕掛り品	*shikakari hin*
work load	仕事量	*shigoto ryō*
work on contract	契約による仕事	*keiyaku ni yoru shigoto*
work order	見積指令書	*mitsumori shirei sho*
work station	ワーク・ステーション	*wāku sutēshon*
workforce	労働力	*rōdō ryoku*
working assets	運用資産	*un-yō shisan*
working balance	営業収支	*eigyō shūshi*
working capital	運転資本	*unten shihon*
working class	労働者階級	*rōdō sha kaikyū*
working contract	工事契約	*kōji keiyaku*
working funds	運転資金	*unten shikin*
working hours	労働時間	*rōdō jikan*
working papers	監査調書	*kansa chōsho*
workplace	仕事場	*shigoto ba*

workshop	作業場	*sagyō jō*
World Bank	世界銀行	*sekai ginkō*
worth, net	正味資産	*shōmi shisan*
worthless (adj)	価値の無い	*kachi no nai*
writ	令状	*rei jō*
write off (v)	帳消しにする	*chōkeshi ni suru*
writedown	評価減	*hyōka gen*
written agreement	契約書	*keiyaku sho*
written bid	記入入札	*kinyū nyūsatsu*

X

xylene	キシレン	*kishiren*

Y

yardstick	判断の基準	*handan no kijun*
yarn	ヤーン	*yān*
year	年	*toshi*
year, fiscal	会計年度	*kaikei nendo*
year-end (adj)	年末の	*nenmatsu no*
yield	利回り	*rimawari*
yield to maturity	満期利回り	*manki rimawari*

Z

zeolite	ゼオライト	*zeoraito*
zero coupon bond	ゼロ・クーポン債	*zero kūpon sai*
zinc	亜鉛	*aen*
zip code	郵便番号	*yūbin bangō*
zone	地域	*chiiki*
zoom lens	ズーム・レンズ	*zūmu renzu*

A

JAPANESE/ROMAJI TO ENGLISH

A

a shōsan en	nitrite	亜硝酸塩
adaputa	adaptor	アダプタ
aen	zinc	亜鉛
afutā sābisu	after-sales service	アフターサービス
ahen	opium	アヘン
aionomā jushi	ionomer resin	アイオノマー樹脂
aitai torihiki	arm's length	相対取引き
akaji	deficit	赤字
akaji de	in the red (adv)	赤字で
akaji zaisei	deficit financing	赤字財政
akaunto eguzekutibu	account executive (advertising)	アカウント・エグゼクテイブ
akuriro nitoru	acrylonitrile	アクリロニトル
akuriru amido	acrylamide	アクリルアミド
akuserarēta	accelerator (computer)	アクセラレータ
akuseru	accelerator, gas pedal	アクセル
akusesarī	accessory	アクセサリー
akusesu jikan	access time	アクセス時間
akutibu matorikkusu	active matrix	アクテイブマトリックス
ami	screen (printing)	網
amin	amine	アミン
amorufasu handōtai	amorphous semiconductor	アモルファス半導体
amorufasu shirikon	amorphous silicon	アモルファス・シリコン
anarogu konpūta	analog computer	アナログ・コンピュータ
angora	angora	アンゴラ
anmonia	ammonia	アンモニア
anpu	amplifier	アンプ
antena	antenna	アンテナ
anzen yoyū ritsu	margin of safety	安全余裕率
ao jashin	blueprint	青写真
appurōdo	upload	アップ・ロード
apurikēshon	application (computer)	アプリケーション
arugorizumu	algorithm	アルゴリズム
arugoru	algorithmic language	アルゴル
arukari sei no	alkaline (adj)	アルカリ性の
arukiru benzen	alkylbenzene	アルカリベンゼン
arumina	alumina	アルミナ
aruminyūmu	aluminum	アルミニュウム
asa	linen	麻
asa sei no	linen (adj)	麻性の
asetēto	acetate	アセテート
aseto arudehido	acetaldehyde	アセトアルデヒド
aseton	acetone	アセトン

asupirin	aspirin	アスピリン
atama kin	down payment	頭金
atashe kēsu	attache case	アタシェケース
atatchimento renzu	auxiliary lens	アタッチメントレンズ
ate zuiryō	guesstimate	当て推量
ato ire saki dashi hō	last in-first out	後入先出法
āto shi	coated paper	アート紙
atotsugi tanpo shōken	junior security	後次ぎ担保証券
atsude no tōki	stoneware	厚手の陶器
atsuen kōjō	rolling mill	圧延工場
auto putto	output (computer)	アウトプット

B

baffa memori	buffer memory	バッファ・メモリ
bagu	bug (defect in computer program)	バグ
baibai kakaku sa	margin (difference)	売買価格差
baibai yakutei	bargain (securities)	売買約定
baio konpyūta	bio-computer	バイオ・コンピュータ
baio seramikkusu	bio-ceramics	バイオ・セラミックス
baishō	compensation	賠償
baishū	buyout	買収
baisū	multiples	倍数
baito	byte	バイト
baito	cutting tool	バイト
bakkin	fine (penalty)	罰金
banajiumu	vanadium	バナジウム
bannō furaisu ban	universal milling machine	万能フライス盤
bannō kensaku ban	universal grinder	万能研削盤
banpā	bumper	バンパー
bariki	horsepower	馬力
barubitsūru san kei saimin yaku	barbiturate	バルビツール酸系催眠薬
barubu	valve	バルブ
basuketto	basket	バスケット
batā naifu	butter knife	バターナイフ
batā zara	butter dish	バター皿
batterī	battery	バッテリー
batterī renzoku shiyō jikan	battery life	バッテリー連続使用時間
bei kokusai bōeki iinkai	U.S. International Trade Commission	米国際貿易委員会
benchā	venture	ベンチャー
bengo gawa	the defense	弁護側
bengoshi	attorney, lawyer	弁護士
bengosuru	defend	弁護する
benzen	benzene	ベンゼン

B

bēru	veil	ベール
beruto	belt	ベルト
bēshisu pointo	basis point (1/100%)	ベーシス・ポイント
bessō nimotsu	unaccompanied goods	別送荷物
bēsu rēto	base rate (wage)	ベースレート
besuto	vest	ベスト
betsu kanjō ni suru	earmark (v)	別勘定にする
betsu ni namae no meiki ga nai kagiri	not otherwise indexed by name	別に名前の明記が無い限り
bi kō	sinus	鼻腔
bideo disuku	video disc	ビデオ・ディスク
bideo kasetto kamera	video cassette camera	ビデオ・カセット・カメラ
bideo kasetto purēyā	video cassette player	ビデオ・カセット・プレーヤー
bideo kasetto rekōdā	video cassette recorder	ビデオ・カセット・レコーダー
bideo ramu	video RAM (VRAM)	ビデオ・ラム
bihin	fixtures (on balance sheet)	備品
binīru sei no	vinyl (adj)	ビニール製の
bisu fenōru	bisphenol	ビスフェノール
bitamin	vitamin	ビタミン
bitto	bit	ビット
bō	baud	ボー
bō	bars, rod	棒
bō gurafu	bar chart	棒グラフ
bodī	camera body	ボディー
bōdo	board	ボード
bōeki gai shūshi	invisibles	貿易外収支
bōeki gyōsha	trader	貿易業者
bōeki hikiuke tegata	trade acceptance	貿易引受手形
bōeki iinkai	trade commission	貿易委員会
bōeki kyōtei	trade agreement	貿易協定
bōeki shōheki	trade barrier	貿易障壁
bōeki shūshi	balance of trade	貿易収支
bōen renzu	telephoto lens	望遠レンズ
boikotto suru	boycott (v)	ボイコットする
boirā ban	boilerplate (metal)	ボイラー板
bokei	matrix	母型
boki	bookkeeping	簿記
bon	tray	盆
bōn chaina	bone china	ボーンチャイナ
bōru ban	drilling machine	ボール盤
bōru	bowl	ボール
boryūmu	volume (computer)	ボリューム
boseki kōkoku	tombstone	墓石広告
bosshū	escheat/foreclosure	没収
buai shūnyū	percentage earnings	歩合収入
buhin	parts	部品

buki	armaments	武器
bukka hikisage seisaku	rollback	物価引下げ政策
bukka shisū	price index	物価指数
bukka suraido sei	indexing	物価スライド制
bukka to chingin no aku junkan	wage-price spiral	物価と賃金の悪循環
bumon	department	部門
bungyō	division of labor	分業
bunka zai	cultural property	文化財
bunka zai yushutsu kyoka sho	cultural export permit	文化財輸出許可書
bunkatsu haraikomi	partial payment	分割払い込み
bunkatsu shiharai hōshiki	installment plan	分割支払い方式
bunpai	distribution	分配
bunpai hō	distribution policy	分配法
bunri shinsetsu suru	spin off (v)	分離新設する
bunseki	analysis	分析
bunseki	assay (metalworks)	分析
bunseki sha	analyst	分析者
burando manējā	brand manager	ブランド・マネージャー
buraun kan	Braun tube	ブラウン管
burausu	blouse	ブラウス
burein sutōmingu	brainstorming	ブレインストーミング
burēki	brake	ブレーキ
burezā	blazer	ブレザー
burīfu kēsu	briefcase	ブリーフケース
burōchi ban	broaching machine	ブローチ盤
burū karā rōdō sha	blue-collar worker	ブルーカラー労働者
butanōru	butanol	ブタノール
būtsu	boots	ブーツ

C

chakudatsugata hādodisuku	removable hard disk	着脱型ハード・ディスク
chakusen watashi	ex ship	着船渡し
chawan	cup	茶碗
chēn sutoa	chain store	チェーンストア
chēn sutoa soshiki	chain store group	チェーンストア組織
chien kogitte	stale check	遅延小切手
chihō ginkō	local bank	地方銀行
chihō kōkyō dantai saiken	municipal bond	地方公共団体債券
chihō saibansho	district court	地方裁判所
chihō zei	local taxes	地方税
chihō zeikan	local customs	地方税関
chii o ubau	supersede (v)	地位を奪う
chiiki	territory	地域
chiiki tantō shihai nin	area manager	地域担当支配人
chikō shihyō	lagging indicator	遅行指標
chin age tōsō	wage dispute	賃上げ闘争
chin gari ryō	rent	賃借料

C

chin shigoto	piecework	賃仕事
chingari depāto	leased department	賃借りデパート
chingari nin	lessee	賃借り人
chingari suru	lease (to hold) (v)	賃借りする
chingashi nin	lessor	賃貸し人
chingashi suru	lease (to grant) (v)	賃貸しする
chingin	wages	賃金
chingin baigaku barai	double time	賃金倍額払い
chingin dorifuto	wage drift	賃金ドリフト
chingin kakusa	wage differential	賃金格差
chingin shotoku sha	wage earner	賃金所得者
chingin suijun	wage level	賃金水準
chingin sukēru	wage scale	賃金スケール
chingin tōketsu	wage freeze	賃金凍結
chinjō	lobbying	陳情
chinō robotto	intelligent robot	知能ロボット
chinpu ka	obsolescence	陳腐化
chinsei yaku	sedative	鎮静薬
chintai	downturn	沈滞
chintsū yaku	analgesic	鎮痛薬
chippu	chip	チップ
chippu kondensa	chip condenser	チップ・コンデンサ
chiryō hō	remedies	治療法
chiso	land tax	地租
chisso	nitrogen	窒素
chitan	titanium	チタン
chitan kinzoku	titanium metal	チタン金属
chiteki shoyūken	intellectual property	知的所有権
chīzu no mori zara	cheese tray	チーズの盛皿
chō biryūshi	ultrafine powder	超微粒子
chō daikibo shūseki kairo	very large-scale integrated circuit	超大規模集積回路
chō dendō genshō	superconductive phenomena	超伝導現象
chō dendō koiru	superconductive coil	超伝導コイル
chō dendō seramikkusu	superconducting ceramics	超伝導セラミックス
chō dendō tai	superconductor	超伝導体
chō dendō zairyō	superconductive materials	超伝導材料
chō kōshi	super lattice	超格子
chō nekutai	bow tie	蝶ネクタイ
chō shōten renzu	long-focus lens	長焦点レンズ
chōbo gai no	off-the-books (adj)	帳簿外の
chōbo kakaku	book value	帳簿価格
chōbo tanaoroshi	book inventory	帳簿棚卸し
chochiku	savings	貯蓄
chochiku ginkō	savings bank	貯蓄銀行
chochiku kanjō kōza	savings account	貯蓄勘定口座

chochiku saiken	savings bond	貯蓄債券
chōka juyō	excess demand	超過需要
chōka kinmu	overtime	超過勤務
chōka shishutsu	deficit spending	超過支出
chōkeshi ni suru	write off (v)	帳消しにする
chōki	long-term	長期
chōki kariire kin	long-term debt	長期借入れ金
chōki keikaku	long-range planning	長期計画
chōki sai	funded debt	長期債
chōki shihon kanjō	long-term capital account	長期資本勘定
chōki shin-yō ginkō	long-term credit bank	長期信用銀行
chokkaku zahyō robotto	cartesian coordinates robot	直角座標ロボット
chokuretsu shiki kioku sōchi	serial storage	直列式記憶装置
chokuryū ki	DC machine	直流器
chokusen no	linear (adj)	直線の
chokusetsu akusesu sutorēji	direct access storage	直接アクセス・ストレージ
chokusetsu hanbai	direct selling	直接販売
chokusetsu hi	direct cost	直接費
chokusetsu kawase tegata	direct papers	直接為替手形
chokusetsu keihi	direct expenses	直接経費
chokusetsu rōdō	direct labor	直接労働
chokusetsu seitetsu hō	direct reduction process	直接製鉄法
chokusetsu shusshi	equity investments	直接出資
chokusetsu sōba	direct quotation	直接相場
chokusetsu tōshi	direct investment	直接投資
chokusetsu uru	sell direct (v)	直接売る
chosakuken	copyright	著作権
chosakuken hō	copyright law	著作権法
chōsei kanō na kugizuke sōba	adjustable peg	調整可能な釘づけ相場
chōsei katei	adjustment process	調整過程
chosei kijun ten	adjustment trigger	調整基準点
chōsei ki-nyū	adjusting entry	調整記入
chōsei ritsu	adjusted rate	調整率
chōsei suru	adjust (v)	調整する
chōsei zumi hoken ryō unchin komi nedan	adjusted CIF price	調整済保険料運賃込値段
chōsei zumi kinrō shotoku	adjusted earned income	調整済み勤労所得
chōshū	expropriation	徴収
chōtatsu	procurement	調達
chōtei	mediation	調停
chōteisha	arbitrator	調停者
chozō suru	lay up (v)	貯蔵する
chūi sū	median	中位数
chūjitsu de yūnō na ashisutanto	man (gal) Friday	忠実で有能なアシスタント
chūkai	mediation	仲介
chūkai sha	intermediary	仲介者

chūkan gyōsha	middleman	中間業者
chūkan zai	intermediary goods	中間財
chūki	medium-term	中期
chūki no	medium term (adj)	中期の
chūkō	cast steel	鋳鋼
chūkoku suru	advise (v)	忠告する
chūmon	order	注文
chūmon bangō	order number	注文番号
chūmon kakunin	confirmation of order	注文確認
chūmon shoshiki	order form	注文書式
chūmon suru	order (v)	注文する
chūmon zandaka	backlog	注文残高
chūnā	tuner	チューナー
chūō ginkō	central bank/ government bank	中央銀行
chūō shori sōchi	central processing unit (CPU)	中央処理装置
chūsai	arbitration	仲裁
chūsai kyōtei	arbitration agreement	仲裁協定
chūsainin	arbitrator	仲裁人
chūsei no	neutral (adj)	中性の
chūsha	injection	注射
chūsha ki	syringe	注射器
chūtetsu	cast iron	鋳鉄
chūzō kōjō	foundry	鋳造工場

D

dai go sedai konpyūta	fifth-generation computer	第五世代コンピュータ
dai ichi shiharai junbi kin	primary reserves	第一支払い準備金
dai san no mado	third window	第三の窓
daibutsu bensai	accord and satisfaction	代物弁済
daigae kanō butsu	fungible goods	代替え可能物
daihin sentaku chūmon	alternative order	代品選択注文
daiichi yūsen kabu	first preferred stock	第一優先株
daikasuto	die casting	ダイカスト
daikibo no	large-scale (adj)	大規模の
daikibo shūseki kairo	large-scale integrated circuit	大規模集積回路
daikin hikikae barai	collect on delivery	代金引き替え払い
dainamikku memori	dynamic memory	ダイナミック・メモリ
dainamikku ramu	D-RAM	ダイナミック・ラム
dainamo	dynamo	ダイナモ
daiōdo	diode	ダイオード
dairekuto mēru	direct mail	ダイレクト・メール
dairi	proxy/representative	代理
dairi gyōsha	factor (sales)	代理業者

dairi nin	agent	代理人
dairi ten	agency	代理店
dairi ten tesū ryō	agency fee	代理店手数料
dairiken	proxy (right)	代理権
daishō	consideration (bus. law)	代償
dandori hi	set-up costs	段取り費
dangō	collusion	談合
dankaīteki ni kumiireru	phase in (v)	段階的に組入れる
dankaīteki ni torinozoku	phase out (v)	段階的に取除く
danpingu	dumping (goods in foreign market)	ダンピング
danpingu bōshi kanzei	antidumping duty	ダンピング防止関税
danryoku sei	elasticity (of supply or demand)	弾力性
dantai hoken	group insurance	団体保険
dantai kōshō	collective bargaining	団体交渉
dantai kyōyaku	collective agreement	団体協約
datsu zei	tax evasion	脱税
Dau Jōnzu heikin	Dow Jones Average	ダウ・ジョーンズ平均
daunrōdo	download	ダウンロード
debaggu suru	debug (v)	デバッグする
defurosutā	defroster	デフロスター
dejitaru	digital (adj)	デジタル
dejitaru konpyūta	digital computer	デジタル・コンピュータ
dejitaru ōdio disuku	digital audio disc	デジタル・オーディオ・ディスク
dejitaru ōdio tēpu rekōdā	digital audio tape recorder	デジタル・オーディオテープ・レコーダー
dekantā	decanter	デカンター
dekidaka	volume (securities)	出来高
denbun shōko	hearsay evidence	伝聞証拠
dendō ritsu	conductivity	電導率
dendō sei garasu	electroconductive glass	電導性ガラス
dendō sei gomu	electrically conductive rubber	電導性ゴム
dendō sei kōbunshi	electroconductive polymer	電導性高分子
denji ha shīrudo	electro-magnetic shielding	電磁波シールド
denjishaku	electromagnet	電磁石
denkai hō	electrolytic process	電解法
denki bunkai	electrolysis	電気分解
denki danbō ki	electric heater	電気暖房器
denki kairo	electric circuit	電気回路
denki kamisori	electric shaver	電気剃刀
denki kōgaku	electrical engineering	電気工学
denki kōgu	electric tools	電気工具
denki rendō ki	electric interlocking machine	電気連動器

denki ro	electric furnace	電気炉
denki teikō	electrical resistance	電気抵抗
denkyoku	electrode	電極
denpun	starch	澱粉
denpyō	voucher	伝票
denshi bīmu	electron beam	電子ビーム
denshi gakki	electronic musical instruments	電子楽器
denshi jū	electron gun	電子銃
denshi kamera	EE camera	電子カメラ
denshi keijiban	electronic bulletin board	電子掲示板
denshi kenbikyō	electron microscope	電子顕微鏡
denshi kōgaku	electronics	電子工学
denshi mēru	electronic mail	電子メール
denshi mishin	electronic sewing machine	電子ミシン
denshi orugan	electronic organ	電子オルガン
denshi rejisutā	electronic cash register	電子レジスター
denshi renji	microwave oven	電子レンジ
denshi taipuraitā	electronic typewriter	電子タイプライター
denshin	cable	電信
denshin gawase	wire transfer	電信為替
denshin sōkin	cable transfer	電信送金
densō sonshitsu	transmission loss	伝送損失
dentaku	desk-top calculator	電卓
denwa kaisen	telephone line	電話回線
depāto	department store	デパート
desukugata konpyūta	desktop computer	デスク型コンピュータ
desukutoppu purezentēshon	desktop presentation (DTPR)	デスクトップ・プレゼンテーション
desutoribyūtā	distributor	デストリビューター
dēta asshuku	data compression	データ圧縮
detā banku	data bank	データ・バンク
dēta bēsu	data base	データ・ベース
dēta shori	data processing	データ処理
dēta shūshū	data acquisition	データ収集
dēta tensō	data transmission	データ転送
dēta fairu	data file	データ・ファイル
dezain kōgaku	design engineering	デザイン工学
dezain suru	design (v)	デザインする
dezainā	designer	デザイナー
dezāto zara	dessert plate	デザート皿
dīrā	dealer	ディーラー
disuku	disk	ディスク
disuku burēki	disc brake	ディスク・ブレーキ
disupurei	display	ディスプレイ
disupurei sōchi	display unit	ディスプレイ装置
dīzeru	diesel	ディーゼル

dō	copper	銅
doboku kōgaku	civil engineering	土木工学
dōgu	tools	道具
dōitsu rōdō dōitsu chingin	equal pay for equal work	同一労働同一賃金
dōji kaisetsu shin-yō jō	back-to-back credit	同時開設信用状
dōki chōsa	motivation study	動機調査
dokku uketori shō	dock (ship's receipt)	ドック受取り証
dōkō	trend	動向
dōkō no shina	accompanied goods	同行の品
dokubutsu gaku	toxicology	毒物学
dokuritsu kenka	independent suspension	独立懸架
dokuritsu tekisuto purosessa	stand-alone text processor	独立テキスト・プロセッサ
dokuritsu wākusutēshon	stand-alone work-station	独立ワーク・ステーション
dokusen	monopoly	独占
dokusen ken	sole rights	独占権
dokusen kinshi hō	anti-monopoly law/ antitrust law	独占禁止法
dokuso	toxin	毒素
doraibu	drive	ドライブ
doresu	dress	ドレス
doru heikin hō	dollar cost averaging	ドル平均法
dōryō	colleague	同僚
dōsa	motion	動作
dōsan	chattel/personal property	動産
dōsan teitō	chattel mortgage	動産抵当

E

ē emu	amplitude modulation	エー・エム
ē esu ē kando	ASA speed	ASA感度
echiren	ethylene	エチレン
echiren gurikōru	ethylene glycol	エチレン・グリコール
echiren okisaido	ethylene oxide	エチレン・オキサイド
efu ē kē rēto	freight all kinds	エフ・エー・ケー・レート
efu emu	frequency modulation	エフ・エム
ei ton	long ton	英トン
eigyō hi	operating expenses	営業費
eigyō hinmoku	line of business	営業品目
eigyō ken	goodwill	営業権
eigyō rijun	operating profit	営業利潤
eigyō sho	place of business	営業所
eigyō shūeki	operating income	営業収益
eigyō shūshi	working balance	営業収支

eigyō son-eki keisan sho	operating statement	営業損益計算書
eigyō yosan	operating budget	営業予算
eikyō o ataeru	have an impact on (v)	影響を与える
eisha ki	projector	映写機
ekishō	liquid crystal	液晶
ekishō disupurei	liquid-crystal display (LCD)	液晶ディスプレイ
ekitai heriumu	liquid helium	液体ヘリウム
ekken kōi	ultra vires acts	越権行為
en	salt	塩
en gurafu	pie chart	円グラフ
endo miru	end mill	エンド・ミル
enjin	engine	エンジン
enjiniaringu purasuchikku	engineering plastic	エンジニアリング・プラスチック
enka butsu	chloride	塩化物
enki	base (chemicals)	塩基
enki suru	postpone (v)	延期する
ensan	hydrochloric acid	塩酸
entai	delay	延滞
entō kensaku ban	cylindrical grinder	円筒研削盤
entō zahyō robotto	cylindrical coordinates robot	円筒座標ロボット
enu shī kōsaku kikai	numerical control machine	NC工作機械
enu shī robotto	numerical control robot	NCロボット
erā	error	エラー
eri	collar	衿
esukarētā jōkō	escalator clause	エスカレーター条項
esukurō akaunto	escrow account	エスクロー・アカウント
esupuresso kōhī yō chawan	espresso cup	エスプレッソ・コーヒー用茶碗
etan	ethane	エタン
ēteru	ether	エーテル

F

faburikku	fabric	ファブリック
fain porimā	fine polymer	ファイン・ポリマー
fain seramikkusu	fine ceramics	ファイン・セラミックス
fainansharu rebarejji	financial leverage	ファイナンシャル・レバレッジ
fainansharu sābisu	financial services	ファイナンシャル・サービス
faindā	view finder	ファインダー
fairu	file	ファイル
fakkusu	fax	ファックス
fakushimiri	facsimile	ファクシミリ
fasshon	fashion	ファッション

fendā	fender	フェンダー
fenōru	phenol	フェノール
feraito	ferrite	フェライト
ferokurōmu	ferrochromium	フェロクローム
feromangan	ferromanganese	フェロマンガン
feronikkeru	ferronickel	フェロニッケル
feroshirikon	ferrosilicon	フェロシリコン
fīdo bakku	feedback	フィード・バック
firumu	film	フィルム
firutā	filter	フィルター
fōku	fork	フォーク
fonto	font	フォント
fu kōsei bōeki	unfair trade	不公正貿易
fu kōsei kyōsō	unfair competition	不公正競争
fu kōsei na	unfair (adj)	不公正な
fuantei	instability	不安定
fubarai shin-yō	installment credit	賦払い信用
fūdo purosessa	food processor	フード・プロセッサ
fudō shōsūten yunitto	floating point unit (FPU)	不動小数点ユニット
fudō tanpo	floating charge	浮動担保
fudōsan	real assets	不動産
fudōsan tōshi shintaku	real estate investment trust	不動産投資信託
fuhō kōi	tort	不法行為
fuhō no	illegal (adj)	不法の
fuka kachi zei	value-added tax	付加価値税
fuka kin	surcharge	附加金
fuka kōryoku	act of God	不可抗力
fuka kyūfu	fringe benefits	付加給付
fuka ritsu	load factor	付加率
fuka ryō	load (sales charge)	付加料
fuka zei	surtax	付加税
fūkan nyūsatsu	sealed bid	封緘入札
fukeiki	depression	不景気
fuku gyō	moonlighting	副業
fuku kaichō	deputy chairman	副会長
fuku kōkan shinkei yokusei zai	anticholinergic	副交感神経抑制剤
fuku sanbutsu	by-product	副産物
fuku shachō	vice-president	副社長
fuku shihai nin	assistant manager/ deputy manager	副支配人
fuku sō shihai nin	assistant general manager	副総支配人
fuku zei	multiple taxation	複税
fukugō kigyō	conglomerate	複合企業
fukugō zairyō	composite materials	複合材料
fukumi shisan	hidden assets (securities)	含み資産

F

fukuri	compound interest	複利
fukusen	duopoly	複占
fukushiki boki	double-entry bookkeeping	複式簿記
fukusū kawase sōba	multiple exchange rate	複数為替相場
fukusū tsūka	multicurrency	複数通貨
fukuyō ryō	dose	服用量
fukyō	depression	不況
funagaisha dairi ten	shipping agent	船会社代理店
funani shōken	bill of lading	船荷証券
funani unsō yōsen keiyaku	affreightment	船荷運送傭船契約
funani zei	floating rates (shipping)	船荷税
funazumi hi	shipping charges, shipping expenses	船積み費
funazumi sashizu sho	shipping instructions	船積み指図書
funmatsu jō no	ground (adj)	粉末状の
funmatsu yakin	powder metallurgy	粉末冶金
funshoku suru	window dressing (increase appeal) (v)	粉飾する
furaisu ban	milling machine	フライス盤
furanneru	flannel	フランネル
furasshu barubu	flashbulb	フラッシュ・バルブ
furasshu kyūbu	flashcube	フラッシュ・キューブ
furenchi kafusu	french cuff	フレンチ・カフス
furi na	unfavorable (adj)	不利な
furikae denpyō	transfer slip	振り替え伝票
furīto hoken shōken	fleet policy	フリート保険証券
furō shūnyū	unearned revenue	不労収入
furonto garasu	windshield	フロント・ガラス
furontoendo purosessa	front end processor (FEP)	フロンエンド・プロセッサ
furoppī disuku	floppy disk	フロッピー・ディスク
furōto	float (outstanding checks, stock)	フロート
furyō saiken	bad debt	不良債権
fūsa kanjō	closed account	封鎖勘定
fūsa tsūka	blocked currency	封鎖通貨
fusai	debt/indebtedness	負債
fusen	allonge (of a draft)	附箋
fusoku	shortage	不足
fusoku jitai	contingencies	不測事態
fusoku shite iru	short of, to be (v)	不足している
futa tsuki fuka zara	tureen	蓋付き深皿
futan	encumbrances (liens, liabilities)	負担
futari shomei tegata	two-name paper	二人署名手形
futekisetsu na	inadequate (adj)	不適切な
futō shiyō ryō	wharfage charges	埠頭使用料

F

futō watashi	ex dock	埠頭渡し
futsū hikiuke	general acceptance	普通引受け
futsū kabu	common stock	普通株
futsū sōko	regular warehouse	普通倉庫
futsū yunyū shinkoku	cash entry	普通輸入申告
fuwatari kogitte	dishonored check	不渡り小切手
fuzai jinushi ken	absentee ownership	不在地主権
fuzoku hin	accessory	付属品
fuzui hiyō	ancillary expenses	付随費用

G

gaibu	external	外部
gaichū suru	farm out (v)	外注する
gaido rain	guidelines	ガイドライン
gaiju	foreign demand	外需
gaika	foreign currency	外貨
gaika sai	foreign currency bond	外貨債
gaikoku bōeki	foreign trade	外国貿易
gaikoku dairi ten	foreign agent	外国代理店
gaikoku gaisha	alien corporation, foreign corporation	外国会社
gaikoku kawase	foreign exchange	外国為替
gaikoku kawase kanri	exchange control	外国為替管理
gaikoku kawase shijō	exchange market	外国為替市場
gaikoku kawase sōba	foreign exchange rate	外国為替相場
gaikoku kawase tegata	foreign bill of exchange	外国為替手形
gaikoku saiken	foreign bond	外国債券
gaikoku shōken	foreign securities	外国証券
gaikoku zeigaku kōjo	foreign tax credit	外国税額控除
gaisai	foreign debt	外債
gaisan mitsumori sho	rough estimate	概算見積り書
gakumen ijō- de	above par (adv)	額面以上で
gakumen ijō- no kakaku	above par (n)	額面以上の価格
gakumen ika de	below par (adv)	額面以下で
gakumen ika no kakaku	below par (n)	額面以下の価格
gakumen kabu	par value stock	額面株
gakumen kagaku	par value	額面価額
gakumen kakaku	face value	額面価格
gakushū kyokusen	learning curve	学習曲線
gan yaku	pill	丸薬
gankin	corpus/principal	元金
ganpon	principal	元本
ganpon hoshō	principal guaranteed	元本保証
ganri	principal and interest	元利
ganryō	pigment	顔料
gappei	amalgamation/ consolidation	合併

gappei • baishū	merger and acquisition (M & A)	合併・買収
garami	around (exchange term) (adv)	がらみ
garasu handōtai	glassy semiconductor	ガラス半導体
garasu kyōka semento	glass-reinforced cement	ガラス強化セメント
garasu rēzā	glass laser	ガラス・レーザー
garasu sen-i	glass fiber	ガラス繊維
garasu sen-i kyōka purasuchikku	fiber-reinforced plastics	ガラス繊維強化プラスチック
gasorin	gasoline	ガソリン
gasorin tanku	gasoline tank	ガソリン・タンク
gassan kazei	unitary tax	合算課税
gen zairyō	raw materials	原材料
genba watashi	spot delivery	現場渡し
genbutsu barai	payment in kind	現物払い
genbutsu shijō	spot market	現物市場
genbutsu torihiki suru	barter (v)	現物取引きする
genchi hōjin	overseas affiliated firm	現地法人
genchi nōsanbutsu	native produce	現地農産物
genezō suru	develop (v)	現像する
genjitsu zenson	actual total loss	現実全損
genka	cost	原価
genka bunseki	cost analysis	原価分析
genka haibun	allocation of costs (accounting)	原価配分
genka hikishime	cost-price squeeze	原価引き締め
genka kanri	cost control	原価管理
genka kasan keiyaku	cost-plus contract	原価加算契約
genka keisan	cost accounting	原価計算
genka kirisage	cost reduction	原価切下げ
genka nōritsu	cost effectiveness	原価能率
genka shōkyaku	depreciation (accounting)	減価償却
genka shōkyaku hikiate kin	depreciation allowance	減価償却引当金
genka shōkyaku ruikei gaku	accrued depreciation	減価償却累計額
genka yōso	cost factor	原価要素
genkai hiyō	marginal cost	限界費用
genkai kakaku kettei	marginal pricing	限界価格決定
genkai kanjō	marginal account	限界勘定
genkai seisan sei	marginal productivity	限界生産性
genkai shūnyū	marginal revenue	限界収入
genkin	cash	現金
genkin bēsu	cash basis	現金ベース
genkin haitō	cash dividend	現金配当
genkin hikikae barai	cash on delivery	現金引き替え払い
genkin jikokusen shugi no	cash and carry (trade)	現金自国船主義の

genkin kanka kachi	actual cash value	現金換価価値
genkin ryūnyū	positive cash flow	現金流入
genkin ryūshutsu	negative cash flow	現金流出
genkin shugi	cash basis (accounting)	現金主義
genkin shūshi ichiran hyō	cash flow statement	現金収支一覧表
genkin shūshi waribiki hō	discounted cash flow	現金収支割引法
genkin shūshi yosan	cash budget	現金収支予算
genkin suitō bo	cash book	現金出納簿
genkin tentō watashi no	cash-and-carry (adj)	現金店頭渡しの
genkin waribiki	cash discount	現金割引
genkin zandaka	cash balance	現金残高
genkinbarai shugi	pay-as-you-go basis	現金払い主義
genkō	copy	原稿
genkō buai	going rate (or price)	現行歩合
genkō chōsa	copy testing	原稿調査
genkoku	plaintiff	原告
genmō shisan	wasted asset	減耗資産
gensai kikin	sinking fund	減債基金
gensan koku	country of origin	原産国
gensanchi shōmei sho	certificate of origin	原産地証明書
gensankoku nai shitei chiten	named inland point in country of origin	原産国内指定地点
gensen kazei	withholding tax	源泉課税
genzai rimawari	current yield	現在利回り
genzō suru	develop (v)	現像する
gera zuri	galley proof	ゲラ刷り
gezai	purgative	下剤
gia no nai	gearless	ギアのない
gia tenkan sōchi	gearshift	ギア転換装置
giaringu	gearing	ギアリング
gifuto	gratuity	ギフト
giji shinkō ni kansuru ken	point of order	議事進行に関する件
gijutsu kakushin	innovation	技術革新
gijutsu sekkei bumon	engineering and design department	技術設計部門
gimu	duty	義務
gimu furikō	nonfeasance	義務不履行
gin mekki no	silverplate (adj)	銀めっきの
ginkō	bank	銀行
ginkō hikiuke tegata	bank acceptance	銀行引受手形
ginkō kan no	interbank (adj)	銀行間の
ginkō kanjō hōkoku sho	bank statement	銀行勘定報告書
ginkō kashitsuke	bank loan	銀行貸付
ginkō kawase tegata	bank exchange	銀行為替手形
ginkō ken	bank note	銀行券
ginkō kensa kan	bank examiner	銀行検査官
ginkō kogitte	bank check	銀行小切手
ginkō kyūjitsu	bank holiday	銀行休日
ginkō shin-yō jō	bank letter of credit	銀行信用状

ginkō sōkin tegata	bank money order	銀行送金手形
ginkō tegata	bank bill/bank draft	銀行手形
ginkō tesū ryō	bank charges	銀行手数料
ginkō yokin	bank deposit	銀行預金
ginkō yokin kōza	bank account	銀行預金口座
ginkō yokin zandaka	bank balance	銀行預金残高
gizō	forgery	偽造
gizō hin	counterfeit	偽造品
goban me	grid	碁盤目
gōben	joint venture	合弁
gōi	agreement	合意
gōin ni settoku suru	jawbone (v)	強引に説得する
gokai	misunderstanding	誤解
gokai saseyasui	misleading	誤解させやすい
gōkaku hinshitsu suijun	acceptable quality level	合格品質水準
gokansei	compatibility	互換性
gokei bōeki	reciprocal trade	互恵貿易
gōkin	alloy	合金
gōkin kō	alloy steel	合金鋼
gōkin tetsu	ferroalloys	合金鉄
gokuchō tanpa	microwave	極超短波
gōmei gaisha	general partnership	合名会社
gōsei	synthesis	合成
gōsei no	synthetic (adj)	合成
gōsei sen-i	man-made fibers	合成繊維
gōsei suēdo	synthetic suede	合成スエード
gōshi gaisha	limited partnership	合資会社
gūhatsu rieki	windfall profits	偶発利益
gūhatsu saimu	contingent liability	偶発債務
gūhatsu teki songai	accidental damage	偶発的損害
gurafikku ikoraizā	graphic equalizer	グラフィック・イコライザー
gurafikkusu	graphics	グラフィックス
gurafu	graph	グラフ
gurēdoappu	upgrade	グレード・アップ
gurei māketto	gray market	グレイ・マーケット
gurēsukēru	gray scale	グレー・スケール
gurūpu dainamikkusu	group dynamics	グループ・ダイナミクッス
gurūpu kanjō	group accounts	グループ勘定
gyakkō	back haul	逆航
gyaku sashine chūmon	stop-loss order	逆指値注文
gyakuryū kōka	backwash effect	逆流効果
gyakushin zei	regressive tax	逆進税
gyō	line	行
gyogan renzu	fish-eye lens	魚眼レンズ
gyōkan o soroeru	justify (v)	行間を揃える
gyōmu daikō ginkō	agency bank, agent bank	業務代行銀行
gyōmu kanri	operations management	業務管理

G

gyōmu kansa	operations audit	業務監査
gyōmu mutantō no shusshisha	silent partner	業務無担当の出資者
gyōmu unkō hyō	flow chart	業務運行表
gyōsei shidō	administrative guidance	行政指導
gyōsha waribiki	trade discount	業者割引

H

ha kabu	broken lot, odd lot	端株
ha kabu no burōka	odd lot broker	端株のブローカー
habu	hub	ハブ
hadaka yōsen	bareboat charter	裸傭船
hādo disuku	hard disk	ハード・ディスク
hādo kopī	hard copy (computer)	ハード・コピー
hādo seru	hard sell	ハード・セル
hādo wea	hardware	ハード・ウェア
hagiri ban	gear cutting machine	歯切り盤
haiburiddo konpyūta	hybrid computer	ハイブリッド・コンピュータ
haiburiddo zairyō	hybrid materials	ハイブリッド材料
haichi	placement (personnel)	配置
haifai	high fidelity	ハイファイ
haikyū suru	ration (v)	配給する
haishi suru	terminate (v)	廃止する
haisosuru	lose a suit	敗訴する
haiteku	high technology	ハイテク
haitō	dividend	配当
haitō ochi	ex dividend	配当落ち
haitō rimawari	dividend yield	配当利回り
haitō saitōshi	dividend reinvestment plan	配当再投資
haitō tsuki	cum dividend	配当付き
hakaru	measure (v)	測る
hakkō	issue (stock)	発行
hakkō bi torihiki	when issued	発行日取引
hakkō daiōdo	light-emitting diode	発光ダイオード
hakkō kakaku	issue price	発行価格
hakkō suru	issue (v)	発行する
hakkō zumi kabushiki	issued stocks/ outstanding stock	発行済み株式
hamono rui	cutlery	刃物類
han	edition	版
han sode	short sleeves	半袖
hanbai	sales	販売
hanbai bunseki	sales analysis	販売分析
hanbai chiiki	sales territory	販売地域
hanbai genka	distribution costs (advertising)	販売原価

hanbai in	sales force	販売員
hanbai itaku	consignment	販売委託
hanbai jiten	point of sale	販売時点
hanbai jōken	terms of sale	販売条件
hanbai kanō ryō	market potential	販売可能量
hanbai kanō sei	potential sales	販売可能性
hanbai kanri	sales management	販売管理
hanbai ken	dealership	販売権
hanbai mō o hirogeru	network (v)	販売網を広げる
hanbai moto	distributor	販売元
hanbai rieki ritsu	return on sales	販売利益率
hanbai ryō	sales volume	販売量
hanbai sokushin	sales promotion	販売促進
hanbai wariate	sales quota	販売割り当て
hanbai yosan	sales budget	販売予算
hanbai yosoku	sales forecasts	販売予測
hanbai zōshin saku	merchandising (retailing)	販売増進策
handan no kijun	yardstick	判断の基準
handekyappu	handicap	ハンデキャップ
handobaggu	handbag	ハンドバッグ
handora	handler (computer)	ハンドラ
handoru	steering wheel	ハンドル
handosukyana	hand scanner	ハンド・スキャナ
handōtai	semiconductor	半導体
handōtai rēzā	semiconductor laser	半導体レーザー
hanji	judge	判事
hanken	copyright	版権
hanketsu	adjudication, judicial decision	判決
hanpa nimotsu	part cargo	半端荷物
hanro	outlet	販路
hantai jinmon	cross examination	反対尋問
hantei suru	adjudge (v)	判定する
hantō	rally	反騰
harai modoshi	rebate (sales)/refund/ rollover	払い戻し
harai modosu	reimburse (v)	払い戻す
haraikomi jōyokin	paid-in surplus	払い込み剰余金
haraikomizumi kabu	paid up shares	払い込み済み株
haraikomizumi shihonkin	paid up capital	払い込み済み資本金
haraisugi no	overpaid (adj)	払い過ぎの
haridashi	overhang	張出し
harigane	wire	針金
horyū rieki	retained earnings	保留利益
hasan	bankruptcy	破産
hasan senkoku	declaration of bankruptcy	破産宣告
hashike chin	lighterage	艀賃

hassei shugi hō	accrual method	発生主義法
hassō	dispatch	発送
hataraku	work (v)	働く
hatchū suru	place an order (v)	発注する
hatsuden ki	generator	発電機
heddo rain	headline	ヘッド・ライン
heika	par	平価
heika de	at par (adv)	平価で
heika kirisage	devaluation	平価切り下げ
heika no kokizami chōsei	crawling peg	平価の小刻み調整
heikin	average	平均
heikin genka	average cost	平均原価
heikin hō	averaging	平均法
heikin jumyō	average life	平均寿命
heikin nedan	average price	平均値段
heikin no	mean (average) (adj)	平均の
heikin rimawari	average yield	平均利回り
heikin tan-i genka	average unit cost (accounting)	平均単位原価
heikin tanka	average unit cost	平均単価
heimen kensaku ban	surface grinder	平面研削盤
heiretsu shori	parallel processing	並列処理
hekisakurorofen	hexachlorophene	ヘキサクロロフェン
hen-atsu ki	transformer	変圧器
hendō hi	variable costs	変動費
hendō kawase sōba	floating exchange rate	変動為替相場
hendō kinri sei jūtaku teitō kashitsuke	variable rate mortgage	変動金利制住宅抵当貸付け
hendō mājin	variable margin	変動マージン
hendō riritsu	variable rate	変動利率
hendō yunyū fuka zei	variable import levy	変動輸入賦課税
hengaku nenkin	variable annuity	変額年金
henkan ki	converter	変換器
henkō	alteration	変更
hensai	repayment	返済
hensai suru	repay (v)	返済する
henshū sha	editor	編集者
henshū suru	edit (v)	編集する
heri	hem	縁
herutsu	hertz	ヘルツ
hi dansei juyō/kyōkyū	inelastic demand or supply	非弾性需要／供給
hi eiri no	nonprofit (adj)	非営利の
hi jōto nin	assignee	被譲渡人
hi kaiin	nonmember	非会員
hi kamei ginkō	nonmember bank	非加盟銀行
hi kanzei shōheki	nontariff barrier	非関税障壁
hi kōkai gaisha	closely held corporation	非公開会社

hi kyojū sha	nonresident	非居住者
hi nōritsūteki na	inefficient (adj)	非能率的な
hi ruiseki yūsen kabu	noncumulative preferred stock	非累積優先株
hi taikyū zai	nondurable goods	非耐久財
hi uragaki nin	endorsee	被裏書き人
higai	injury	被害
hijōjō no	unlisted (adj)	非上場の
hikari jiki memori	optical magnetic memory	光磁気メモリ
hikari dendō	photo conductivity	光伝導
hikari dendō busshitsu	photo conductive materials	光伝導物質
hikari denji kōka	photo electromagnetic effect	光電磁効果
hikari densō	optical transmission	光伝送
hikari disuku	optical disc	光ディスク
hikari faibā	optical fiber	光ファイバー
hikari gijutsu	opto-electronics	光技術
hikari handōtai	optical integrated circuit	光半導体
hikari jiki disuku	magnet optical disk (MO)	光磁気ディスク
hikari kēburu	optical cable	光ケーブル
hikari konpyūta	optical computer	光コンピュータ
hikari memori	optical memory	光メモリ
hikari sangyō	opto-electronics industry	光産業
hikari tsūshin	fiber-optic communication	光通信
hikazei shotoku	tax-free income	非課税所得
hikiate kin	allowance (finance)	引当金
hikidashi	withdrawal	引き出し
hikigane kakaku	trigger price	引金価格
hikikae ken	rain check	引換え券
hikinobashi	blowup, enlargement	引伸し
hikinobashi ki	enlarger	引伸し機
hikiorosu	draw down (v)	引下ろす
hikiuke	acceptance	引受け
hikiuke gyōsha	underwriter (securities)	引受業者
hikiuke nin	acceptor	引受人
hikiuke o kyozetsu suru	refuse acceptance (v)	引受けを拒絶する
hikiuke shōdaku sho	acceptance agreement	引受承諾書
hikiuke tegata	acceptance bill	引受手形
hikiukeken shōsho	warrant	引受権証書
hikiukeru	accept (v)/undertake (v)	引受ける
hikiwatashi	delivery	引渡し
hikiwatashi mae no genkin barai	cash before delivery	引渡し前の現金払い

hikiwatashi nedan	delivered price	引渡し値段
hikiwatashi tsūchi sho	delivery notice	引渡し通知書
hikkoshi hiyō	moving expenses	引越し費用
himo tsuki enjo	tied aid	ひも付き援助
hina gata shokan	form letter	ひな形書簡
hindo kyokusen	frequency curve	頻度曲線
hinshitsu kanri	quality control	品質管理
hiradai kasha	flatcar	平台貨車
hiritsu	ratio	比率
hishaku	ladle	柄杓
hisho	secretary	秘書
hitokabu atari no	per share (adj)	一株当りの
hitokabu atari no chōbo kakaku	book value per share	一株当りの帳簿価格
hitokabu atari no rieki	earnings per share	一株当りの利益
hitokuchi	lot	一口
hitokuchi no torihiki tan-i	round lot	一口の取引き単位
hitori atari no	per capita (adj)	一人当りの
hitsuju hin bunseki	needs analysis	必需品分析
hitsuyō jōken	requirements	必要条件
hiyō ben-eki bunseki	cost-benefit analysis	費用便益分析
hiyō ga kakaru	cost (v)	費用がかかる
hiyō kōka bunseki	cost-benefit analysis	費用効果分析
hiyō no tori modoshi	recovery of expenses	費用の取戻し
hizuke go barai ni suru	afterdate (v)	日付後払いにする
hōfuku	retaliation	報復
hōgai na daikin seikyū	overcharge	法外な代金請求
hogo	safeguard	保護
hogo bōeki shugi	protectionism	保護貿易主義
hogo kanzei	protective duties	保護関税
hōhō	method	方法
hōjin setsuritsu	incorporation	法人設立
hōjin zei	corporate income tax, corporate tax	法人税
hojo kin	subsidy	補助金
hōka	legal tender	法貨
hokan suru	store (v)	保管する
hōkatsu hoken keiyaku	floater (insurance policy)	包括保険契約
hoken	insurance	保険
hoken gaisha	insurance company	保険会社
hoken gyōsha	underwriter (insurance)	保険業者
hoken keiri nin	actuary	保険経理人
hoken keiyaku sha	policyholder	保険契約者
hoken nakadachi nin	insurance broker	保険仲立ち人
hoken ryō	insurance premium	保険料
hoken ryō haraikomi	premium payment	保険料払い込み
hoken shōsho	insurance policy	保険証書
hoken tsumitate kin	insurance fund	保険積立金

hōki	abandonment	放棄
hōki suru	abandon (v)	放棄する
hōkoku	report	報告
hōmuekuiti rōn	home equity loan	ホームエクイティ・ローン
hōmushō	Ministry of Justice	法務省
hon	book	本
hon kaigi	plenary meeting	本会議
hon nin	principal (legal)	本人
honbu	headquarters	本部
honsen watashi	free on board (FOB)	本船渡し
honsha	head office	本社
honshitsu kachi	intrinsic value	本質価値
hon-yaku sha	translator	翻訳者
hōrei	statute	法令
hōritsu	law	法律
hōritsu jimusho	law firm	法律事務所
hōritsu no	legal	法律の
horogurafikku memori	holographic memory	ホログラフィック・メモリ
horu	engrave (v)	彫る
horumarin	formaline	ホルマリン
horumon	hormone	ホルモン
horyū chūmon	open order	保留注文
horyū haitō	passed dividend	保留配当
horyū kikan	holding period	保留期間
horyū rieki	retained earnings	保留利益
hōseki rui	jewel	宝石類
hōshin	policy (administration)	方針
hoshō	compensation (business law)	補償
hoshō	guarantee/warranty	保証
hoshō	indemnity	補償
hoshō gaisha	guaranty company	保証会社
hoshō jō	letter of guaranty/ warrant (securities)	保証状
hoshō kin	cover charge (finance)	保証金
hoshō kogitte	certified check	保証小切手
hoshō nin	sponsor (of fund, partnership)	保証人
hoshō sho	guaranty bond	保証書
hoshō yokin	compensating balance	補償預金
hōshū	remuneration, reward, compensation	報酬
hoshu keiyaku	maintenance contract	保守契約
hōsō	packaging	包装
hōsō meisai sho	packing list	包装明細書
hōsō nōryoku	bale capacity	包装能力
hosonagai shanpen gurasu	flute	細長いシャンペン・グラス
hosuto konpyūta	host computer	ホスト・コンピュータ
hōtei	court	法廷

hōtei dokusen	legal monopoly	法定独占
hōtei shihon	legal capital	法定資本
hōtei tsūka	legal tender	法定通貨
hō-teki jittai	legal entity	法的実体
hotsui	addendum	補追
hotto manē	hot money	ホット・マネー
howaito karā	white collar worker	ホワイト・カラー
hozei chiiki	bond areas	保税地域
hozei kamotsu	bonded goods	保税貨物
hozei kamotsu unpan nin	bonded carrier	保税貨物運搬人
hozei sōko	bonded warehouse, licensed warehouse	保税倉庫
hyōdai	title	表題
hyōhon no saizu	sample size	標本のサイズ
hyōji kakaku	list price	表示価格
hyōjun	standard	標準
hyōjun genka	standard costs	標準原価
hyōjun hensa	standard deviation	標準偏差
hyōjun ika no	substandard	標準以下の
hyōjun ji	standard time	標準時
hyōjun jōkō (keiyaku sho ni fukumareru)	boilerplate (contract)	標準条項（契約書に含まれる）
hyōjun kankō	standard practice	標準慣行
hyōjun renzu	standard lens	標準レンズ
hyōjun sōbi hin	standard equipment	標準装備品
hyōka	appraisal, evaluation, valuation (finance)	評価
hyōka gen	writedown	評価減
hyōshi	cover	表紙

I

ichigan refu	single-lens reflex camera	一眼レフ
ichiji kaiko	lay-off	一時解雇
ichiji kariire kin	floating debt	一時借り入れ金
ichinichi atari no	per diem (adj)	一日当りの
ichinin kanjō	discretionary account	一任勘定
ichinin mae no shokutaku yō shokkigu	place setting	一人前の食卓用食器具
ichiran barai de	at sight (adv)	一覧払いで
ichiran barai kawase tegata	sight draft	一覧払い為替手形
idō heikin hō	moving average	移動平均法
ifu	abandonment (insurance)	委付
ifu suru	abandon (insurance) (v)	委付する
ifuku	apparel	衣服
igi o mōshitateru	protest (banking law) (v)	異議を申し立てる

igunisshon	ignition	イグニッション
ihan	violation	違反
ihō no	illegal	違法の
ihō no funazumi	illegal shipments	違法の船積み
iine	asking price	言い値
iji	maintenance	維持
iji shōko kin	maintenance margin (securities)	維持証拠金
ikiwataru	go around (v)	行きわたる
ikizumari	deadlock	行詰まり
ikkatsu shori	batch processing	一括処理
ikkatsu torihiki	package deal	一括取引き
ikoraizā	equalizer	イコライザー
imēji	image	イメージ
inbāta	inverter	インバータ
indasutoriaru enjiniaringu	industrial engineering	インダストリアル・エンジニアリング
infure	inflation	インフレ
infure no	inflationary (adj)	インフレの
ingotto	ingot	インゴット
inin	mandate	委任
inin jō	proxy statement	委任状
inin ken	power of attorney	委任権
injekushon ponpu	injection pump	インジェクション・ポンプ
inku	ink	インク
inputto	input	インプット
insaidā torihiki	insider trading	インサイダー取引き
insaido infomēshon	tip (inside information)	インサイド・インフォメーション
insatsu	printing	印刷
insatsu butsu	printed matter	印刷物
insatsu sho	printing shop	印刷所
inshurin	insulin	インシュリン
intā akutibu	interactive	インターアクティブ
intā fēsu	interface	インターフェース
intabyū	interview	インタビュー
intoku shisan	hidden assets	隠匿資産
inzei	royalty (publication)	印税
(ippan) kanri hi	administrative expense	(一般)管理費
ippan shain	junior partner	一般社員
ippan unchin ritsu	base rate (transportation)	一般運賃率
ippan unsōgyōsha	common carrier	一般運送業者
irainin	client	依頼人
irasuto	illustration	イラスト
iro	color	色
isan	estate (business law)	遺産
isan sōzoku zei	estate tax, inheritance tax	遺産相続税

isha	physician	医者
isogaseru	speed up (v)	急がせる
issha kashikiri kamotsu	carload	一車貸切貨物
ita	plate	板
itaku baibai keiyaku	commitment (securities)	委託売買契約
itaku hanbai de	on consignment (adv)	委託販売で
itaku kamotsu unsō jō	consignment note	委託貨物運送状
itaku shōko kin	margin requirements	委託証拠金
itaku sōko gyōmu	field warehousing	委託倉庫業務
itarikku tai	italic	イタリック体
itte dairi ten	exclusive agent	一手代理店
itte hanbai ken	franchise (insurance)	一手販売権
iyaku jōkō	penalty clause	違約条項
iyaku kin soshō	penalty action	違約金訴訟
iyakukin	penalty	違約金
izō	bequest	遺贈
izō zaisan	legacy	違贈財産

J

jakku	jack	ジャック
janku bondo	junk bond	ジャンク・ボンド
jenerētā	generator	ジェネレーター
Jēson jōkō	Jason clause	ジェーソン条項
jetto kondensa	jet condenser	ジェット・コンデンサ
jidan	out-of-court settlement	示談
jidō furikae sābisu	automatic transfer service	自動振替サービス
jidō genzō ki	automatic developing machine	自動現像機
jidō hensoku ki	automatic transmission	自動変速機
jidō kōgu kōkan sōchi	automatic tool changer	自動工具交換装置
jidō makiage	automatic rewinding	自動巻上げ
jidō nejikiri ban	automatic screw machine	自動ねじ切り盤
jidō roshutsu kikō	automatic exposure	自動露出機構
jidō shibori	automatic aperture control device	自動絞り
jidō shōten	automatic focusing	自動焦点
jidō shūkin sābisu	automatic collection service	自動集金サービス
jidō sōnyū ki	insert machine	自動挿入機
jidō sōten	auto-loading	自動装填
jidō teki na	automatic (adj)	自動的な
jidō teki ni	automatically (adv)	自動的に
jidō yokin ukebarai ki	automatic teller machine	自動預金受け払い機

jidōsha	automobile, car	自動車
jidōsha buhin	auto parts	自動車部品
jidōsha denwa	car telephone	自動車電話
jiei suru	to be self-employed	自営する
jigen chūmon	time order	時限注文
jigo hizuke no	postdated (adj)	事後日付の
jigu	jig (production)	ジグ
jigyō keitai	corporate structure	事業形態
jigyōka hoken	key man insurance	事業家保険
jika shōhyō	private label (or brand)	自家商標
jikan gai torihiki	after-hours trading	時間外取引き
jikan hyō	timetable	時間表
jikan shū	hourly earnings	時間収
jikan tai	time zone	時間帯
jiki	china	磁器
jiki baburu memori	magnetic bubble memory	磁気バブルメモリ
jiki disuku sōchi	magnetic disc unit	磁気ディスク装置
jiki memori	magnetic memory	磁気メモリ
jiki tēpu	magnetic tape	磁気テープ
jiki tēpu sōchi	magnetic tape unit	磁気テープ装置
jikkō chōsa	action research	実行調査
jikkō fukanō na	unfeasible (adj)	実行不可能な
jikkō keikaku	action plan	実行計画
jikkō rimawari	effective yield	実効利回り
jikō	statute of limitations	時効
jiko hyōka	self-appraisal	自己評価
jiko kanri	self-management	自己管理
jiko kin-yū	internal finance	自己金融
jiko shihon	equity (capital)	自己資本
jiku senban	shaft lather	軸旋盤
jikyū jisoku	autarky	自給自足
jimu kanri	office management	事務管理
jimu kyokuchō	executive secretary	事務局長
jin-in sakugen	attrition	人員削減
jinji bu	personnel department	人事部
jinji kanri	personnel administration/personnel management	人事管理
jinkō chinō	artificial intelligence	人工知能
jinkō tōkei gaku jō no	demographic (adj)	人口統計学上の
jin-teki shigen	human resources/manpower	人的資源
jinushi	landowner	地主
jinzai sukauto	headhunter	人材スカウト
jisa boke	jet lag	時差ぼけ
jisan nin	bearer	持参人
jisan nin barai	payable to bearer	持参人払い

J

jisei ryūtai	magnetic fluid	磁性流体
jishu teki na	autonomous (adj)	自主的な
jishu teki ni	autonomously (adv)	自主的に
jissai genka	actual costs	実際原価
jissai no	actual (adj)	実際の
jisshitsu chingin	real wages	実質賃金
jisshitsu kakaku	real price	実質価格
jisshitsu kinri	real interest rate	実質金利
jisshitsu rimawari	real yield	実質利回り
jisshitsu saimu	actual liability	実質債務
jisshitsu shijō torihiki daka	actual market volume	実質市場取引き高
jisshitsu shotoku	real income	実質所得
jisshitsu tōshi shūeki ritsu	real investment return	実質投資収益率
jisshū sei	trainee	実習生
jisshūnyū	actual income	実収入
jitai	font	字体
jitchi tanaoroshi	physical inventory	実地棚卸し
jitsubutsu dai no mokei	mock-up	実物大の模型
jitsubutsu tōshi	real investment	実物投資
jitsuyō-teki na	practical (adj)	実用的な
jiyū bōeki	free trade	自由貿易
jiyū bōeki ken	free trade zone	自由貿易圏
jiyū bōeki kō	free port	自由貿易港
jiyū hendō sōba	floating rate	自由変動相場
jiyū jikan	free time	自由時間
jiyū kigyō	free enterprise	自由企業
jiyū sairyō ken	discretion	自由裁量権
jiyū shijō	free market	自由市場
jiyū shijō kigyō	free market industry	自由市場企業
jiyūgyō sha	freelancer	自由業者
jo	introduction (publishing)	序
jōi no kabushiki	senior issue	上位の株式
joi sutikku	joystick	ジョイ・スティック
jōjō kabu	listed stock	上場株
jōjō shōken	listed securities	上場証券
jōken	terms	条件
jōken tsuki baibai keiyaku	conditional sales contract	条件付き売買契約
jōken tsuki hikiuke	conditional acceptance	条件付き引受け
jōken tsuki jōto shōsho	escrow	条件付き譲渡証書
jōki no	above-mentioned (adj)	上記の
jōkoku suru	appeal (v)	上告する
jōmu shikkō iinkai	executive committee	常務執行委員会
jōnai nakagai nin	jobber (securities)	場内仲買人
jōnin riji kai	executive board	常任理事会
jōryū	distillation	蒸留
Josefuson sōchi	Josephson device	ジョセフソン装置
josei keiei sha	administratrix	女性経営者

josei shōsū minzoku sekkyoku koyō	affirmative action	女性、少数民族積極雇用
joshu	assistant	助手
jōshū kekkin	absenteeism	常習欠勤
jōshū tenshoku sha	job hopper	常習転職者
jōsū	multiplier	乗数
jōto	transfer (securities)	譲渡
jōto dekiru	negotiable (adj)	譲渡できる
jōto nin	assignor	譲渡人
jōto suru	assign (v) (business law)	譲渡する
jōyaku	treaty	条約
jōyo hin	surplus goods	剰余品
jōzai	tablet	錠剤
jū kōgyō	heavy industry	重工業
jūdenchi	battery recharger	充電池
jūfuku	overlap	重複
jūgō tai	polymer	重合体
jūgyō in	employee	従業員
jūgyō in kankei	employee relations	従業員関係
jūgyō in mochikabu seido	stock purchase plan	従業員持ち株制度
jūgyō in sōdan seido	employee counseling	従業員相談制度
jūka kanzei	ad valorem duty	従価関税
jukuren rōdō	skilled labor	熟練労働
jun	net (adj)	純
jun eki	net profit	純益
jun hendō hi	semi-variable costs	準変動費
jun kiken	pure risk	純危険
jun kōkyō kigyō tai	quasi-public company	準公共企業体
jun rieki	net margin	純利益
jun shisan	net assets	純資産
jun shisan kachi	net asset value (securities)	純資産価値
jun shotoku	net income	純所得
jun sonshitsu	net loss	純損失
jun tōshi	net investment	純投資
jun tsūka	near money	準通貨
jun unten shihon	net working capital	純運転資本
jun uriage daka	net sales	純売上げ高
junbi kin	reserve	準備金
jūryō	weight	重量
jūryō kamotsu ageni ryō	heavy lift charges	重量貨物揚荷料
jūryō zei	specific duty	従量税
jūtaku mōgēji	home mortgage	住宅モーゲージ
jūtaku rōn	housing loan	住宅ローン
jutaku sha	consignee/fiduciary/trustee	受託者
jutaku sho	depository	受託書
juyō	demand (business)	需要
juyō dokusen	monopsony	需要独占

K

kā kūrā	air conditioner	カー・クーラー
kabā	jacket (publishing)	カバー
kabu ken	stock certificate	株券
kabu kōzō	infrastructure (industry)	下部構造
kabu nushi	stockholder	株主
kabu nushi mochibun	stockholders' equity	株主持分
kabu	share	株
kabuka	share price, stock price	株価
kabuka shisū	stock index	株価指数
kabuka shisū	stock price index	株価指数
kabuka shūeki ritsu	price-earnings ratio	株価収益率
kabuken	stock certificate	株券
kabuken jōto inin jō	stock power	株券譲渡委任状
kabunushi mochibun	shareholder's equity	株主持分
kabunushi	shareholder, stockholder	株主
kabunushi kai	shareholder's meeting	株主会
kabunushi sōkai	general meeting (securities)/shareholder's meeting	株主総会
kabushiki	stock/equity/shares (stock)	株式
kabushiki bunkatsu	stock split	株式分割
kabushiki gaisha	joint stock company	株式会社
kabushiki gaisha ni suru	incorporate (v)	株式会社にする
kabushiki heigō	reverse stock split	株式併合
kabushiki kaiten ritsu	stock turnover (securities)	株式回転率
kabushiki kaitori kōkai mōshikomi	bid/takeover bid	株式買取り公開申し込み
kabushiki kaitsuke sentaku ken	call option	株式買い付け選択権
kabushiki kōkai gaisha	public company (finance)	株式公開会社
kabushiki kōkai suru	go public (v)	株式公開する
kabushiki meigara	stock issue	株式銘柄
kabushiki nakagainin	stockbroker	株式仲買人
kabushiki no kōkai kaitsuke	tender offer	株式の公開買付け
kabushiki shihon kin	capital stock	株式資本金
kabushiki shijō	stock market	株式市場
kabushiki sōba hyōji ki	price ticker, ticker	株式相場表示器
kabushiki sōba hyōji tēpu	ticker tape	株式相場表示テープ
kabushiki torihiki sho	stock exchange	株式取引所
kabushiki tōshi	stock investment	株式投資
kabushiki tōshi haibun hyō	stock portfolio	株式投資配分表
kabushiki tōshi shintaku	stock investment trust	株式投資信託
kabushiki wariate tsūchi sho	allotment letter	株式割当て通知書
kachi	value	価値

kachi geraku	depreciation	価値下落
kachi kōgaku	value engineering	価値工学
kachi no nai	worthless (adj)	価値の無い
kadai hyōka sareta	overvalued (adj)	過大評価された
kadai shihon no	overcapitalized (adj)	過大資本の
kādo	card	カード
kafusu botan	cufflink	カフス・ボタン
kagaku hiryō	chemical fertilizer	化学肥料
kagaku seihin	chemical (n)	化学製品
kagi shio	salts (pharmaceuticals)	かぎ塩
kagō butsu	compounds	化合物
kagō butsu handōtai	compound semiconductor	化合物半導体
kahansū kabushiki mochibun	majority interest	過半数株式持分
kahei kachi kaifuku	revaluation (government)	貨幣価値回復
kahen shīkensu robotto	variable sequence robot	可変シーケンス・ロボット
kai chūmon	purchase order (securities)	買い注文
kai sōba	bull market	買相場
kaifuku	recovery	回復
kaigai fando	offshore fund	海外ファンド
kaigai minkan tōshi gaisha	overseas private investment corporation	海外民間投資会社
kaigai tōshi	foreign investment/ overseas investment	海外投資
kaigi shitsu	boardroom/conference room	会議室
kaigō	meeting	会合
kaihi kanō genka	avoidable costs	回避可能原価
kaiire kakaku	purchase price	買入価格
kaiji keiyaku	maritime contract	海事契約
kaijō hoken gyōsha	marine underwriter	海上保険業者
kaikei bu	accounting department	会計部
kaikei buchō	paymaster	会計部長
kaikei gakari	accountant	会計係り
kaikei hōshiki	accounting method	会計方式
kaikei kansa nin	auditor	会計監査人
kaikei kansa suru	audit (v)	会計監査する
kaikei kansa yaku	comptroller	会計監査役
kaikei kansa yaku	controller	会計監査役
kaikei kikan	account period	会計期間
kaikei kikan	accounting period/ financial period	会計期間
kaikei nendo	financial year, fiscal year	会計年度
kaikei sekinin	accountability (accounting)	会計責任

kaikei shunin	chief accountant	会計主任
kaiki bunseki	regression analysis	回帰分析
kaikikaeru	renew (securities) (v)	書替える
kaiko suru	discharge (personnel) (v)/ fire (v)	解雇する
kaimen tetsu	sponge	海綿鉄
kaimodohi nedan	call price (securities)	買い戻し値段
kaimodosu	buy back (v)	買い戻す
kainan kyūjo hi	salvage charges	海難救助費
kainan kyūjo hin kagaku	salvage value (insurance)	海難救助品価額
kainyū suru	intervene (v)	介入する
kairo shadan ki	circuit breaker	回路遮断機
kairyō o kuwaeru	improve upon (v)	改良を加える
kaisha	company, firm	会社
kaisha kikō zu	organization chart	会社機構図
kaisha setsuritsu kyoka shō	certificate of incorporation	会社設立許可証
kaishū	callback/recovery (insurance)	回収
kaishū kikan	payback period/ payout period	回収期間
kaishū suru	salvage (v)	回収する
kaison	average (shipping)	海損
kaisugiru	overbuy (v)	買いすぎる
kaite	buyer	買い手
kaite gawa sekinin	buyer's responsibility	買い手側責任
kaite no sentaku ken	buyer's option	買い手の選択権
kaite shijō	buyer's market	買い手市場
kaiten shikin	revolving fund	回転資金
kaiten shin-yō	revolving credit	回転信用
kaiten shin-yō jō	revolving letter of credit	回転信用状
kaitoru	negotiate (securities) (v)	買い取る
kaitsunagi	hedge-buying	買いつなぎ
kaiyaku	cancellation	解約
kaiyaku kin	cancellation money	解約金
kaiyaku modoshikin	cash surrender value	解約戻し金
kaizen	improvements	改善
kaizōdo	resolution	解像度
kajū heikin	weighted average	荷重平均
kakaku	price (n)	価格
kakaku danryoku sei	price elasticity	価格弾力性
kakaku hyō	price list	価格表
kakaku kakusa	price differential	価格格差
kakaku shiji	price support	価格支持
kakaku sōsa o suru	fix the price (v)	価格操作をする

kakaku tai	price range	価格帯
kakaku tōki	appreciation	価格騰貴
kake gai nin	credit buyer	掛け買い人
kake tsunagu	hedge (v)	掛けつなぐ
kakekanjō	credit account	掛け勘定
kaketsunagi baibai	hedge	掛けつなぎ売買
kakeuri de	on account (adv)	掛け売りで
kakikaeru	renew (securities)	書替える
kakitome yūbin	registered mail	書留郵便
kakō	downswing	下降
kakō shori suru	process (v)	加工処理する
kakuchō kanō	expandable	拡張可能
kakuchō surotto	expansion slot	拡張スロット
kakudai suru	enlarge (v)	拡大する
kakujitsu na shōken	approved securities	確実な証券
kakusage	demotion	格下げ
kakusen jō no kōmoku	above-the-line item	画線上の項目
kakusen ka no kōmoku	below-the-line item	画線下の項目
kakutei hi	fixed charges (business)	確定費
kakutei jōken	fixed terms	確定条件
kakuyasu hin	bargain	格安品
kamei gaisha	member firm	加盟会社
kamera	camera	カメラ
kami	paper	紙
kami byōshi ban	paperback, soft cover	紙表紙版
kami tēpu	paper tape	紙テープ
kamotsu	freight	貨物
kamotsu kaijō hoken	marine cargo insurance	貨物海上保険
kamotsu unsō gyōsha	freight forwarder	貨物運送業者
kamotsu unsō jō	waybill	貨物運送状
kamushafuto	camshaft	カムシャフト
kan ni	dry cargo	乾荷
kanbu yakuin hōshū	executive compensation	幹部役員報酬
kangen	reduction (chemicals)	還元
kangen hyō	freeboard	乾舷標
kan-i hoken	industrial insurance	簡易保険
kan-i saibansho	summary court	簡易裁判所
kanji tesū ryō	management fee (securities)	幹事手数料
kanjō	account (n)	勘定
kanjō kōza bangō	account number	勘定口座番号
kanjō kessai bi	account day	勘定決済日
kanjō sho	statement of account, account statement	勘定書
kankatsu	jurisdiction	管轄
kankin kanō shōken	marketable securities	換金可能証券
kankō kei	sensitometer	感光計

kanmonsuru	subpoena (v), summon (v)	喚問する
kanren gaisha	associate company	関連会社
kanri hendō sōba sei	managed float	管理変動相場制
kanri kaikei	management accounting	管理会計
kanri kanō hi	controllable costs	管理可能費
kanri katsudō hyō	management chart	管理活動表
kanri keizai	managed economy	管理経済
kanri no	administrative (adj)	管理の
kanri shokuin kai	board of supervisors	管理職員会
kanryō	bureaucrat	官僚
kansa chōsho	working papers	監査調書
kansa shōseki	audit trail	監査証跡
kansa taishaku taishō hyō	auditing balance sheet	監査貸借対照表
kansetsu hi	indirect cost/on cost/ overhead	間接費
kansetsu keihi	indirect expenses	間接経費
kansetsu rōdō	indirect labor	間接労働
kansetsu yōkyū	indirect claim	間接要求
kansetsu zei	indirect tax	間接税
kantoku sha	supervisor	監督者
kanzei	customs duty, tariff	関税
kanzei dōmei	customs union	関税同盟
kanzei ritsu kakusa	tariff differential	関税率格差
kanzei sen	tariff war	関税戦
kanzei shōheki	tariff barriers	関税障壁
kanzei shōhin	tariff commodity	関税商品
kanzei tōkyū bunrui	tariff classification	関税等級分類
kanzen kesshō gijutsu	perfect crystal device technology	完全結晶技術
kappu hanbai	add-on sales	割賦販売
kapuseru	capsule	カプセル
karā	color	カラー
karā bunkai	color separation	カラー分解
karā ekishō	color liquid crystal	カラー液晶
karā firumu	color film	カラーフィルム
karā purinto	color print	カラープリント
karā suraido	color slide	カラースライド
karā terebi	color TV	カラーテレビ
kara uri	short sale	から売り
karani unchin	dead freight	空荷運賃
karauri suru	oversell (securities) (v)	から売りする
kari keisan sho	interim statement	仮計算書
kari keiyaku	binder	仮契約
kari no	interim (adj)	仮りの
kari shui sho	preliminary prospectus	仮趣意書
kari yunyū menkyo	carnet	仮輸入免許
kari yunyū negai	bill of sight	仮輸入願

karigata	debit	借方
karigata hyō	debit note	借方票
karigata kinyū	debit entry	借方記入
karikae	rollover	借り換え
karushūmu	calcium	カルシュウム
karuteru	cartel	カルテル
karuteru o tsukuru	pool (organization) (v)	カルテルを作る
kasen	oligopoly	寡占
kasetto	cassette	カセット
kasha watashi	free on rail	貨車渡し
kashi kinko	safe deposit box	貸金庫
kashi no kiri mori naifu	pastry server	菓子の切り盛りナイフ
kashidashi gendo gaku	credit line	貸出し限度額
kashigata	credit (accounting)	貸方
kashigata hyō	credit note	貸方票
kashigata kanjō	overdraft	貸方勘定
kashigata zandaka	credit balance	貸方残高
kashikiri kamotsu	truckload	貸切り貨物
kashimiya	cashmere	カシミヤ
kashira moji	capital (letter)	頭文字
kashira moji go	acronym	頭文字語
kashitsuke	lending/loan	貸付け
kashō hyōka suru	underestimate (v)/ undervalue (v)	過小評価する
kasoku genka shōkyaku	accelerated depreciation	加速減価償却
kasui bunkai	hydrolysis	加水分解
kata byōshi bon	hardcover	堅表紙本
kata ryō	overage (shipping)	過多量
kata	pattern	型
katakezuri ban	shaping machine	形削り盤
katarogu	catalog	カタログ
kātorijji	cartridge	カートリッジ
katsudō chōsa hyō	activity chart	活動調査表
katsudō fusai	active debt	活動負債
katsudō kanjō	active account	活動勘定
katsuji insatsu	letterpress	活字印刷
katto gurasu	crystal glass	カットグラス
kawa himo	strapping	革ひも
kawase risuku	exchange risk	為替リスク
kawase sason	exchange loss	為替差損
kawase tegata	bill of exchange	為替手形
kawase teiritsu	fixed rate of exchange	為替定率
kawase waribiki	exchange discount	為替割引き
kazei	taxation	課税
kazei hyōjun	tax base	課税標準
kazei suru	levy taxes (v)	課税する
kēburu rerīzu	cable release	ケーブル・レリーズ
kei kazei koku	tax haven	軽課税国

keiei hōshin	business policy	経営方針
keiei kanbu	executive	経営幹部
keiei kanri	administration/management/business management	経営管理
keiei kanri keikaku	business plan	経営管理計画
keiei komon	management consultant	経営顧問
keiei konsarutanto	management consultant	経営コンサルタント
keiei sekinin	accountability (management)	経営責任
keiei senryaku	business strategy	経営戦略
keiei sha	administrator	経営者
keiei suru	manage (v)	経営する
keihi	expenses	経費
keihi no ichiji tatekae	out-of-pocket expenses	経費の一時立て替え
keihi wariate	allocation of costs	経費割り当て
keihō	criminal law	刑法
keiji ban	billboard	掲示版
keiji soshō	criminal action	刑事訴訟
keijō kioku gōkin	shape-memory alloy	形状記憶合金
keika rishi	accrual, accrued interest	経過利子
keikaku	plan/program	計画
keikaku o tateru	program (v)	計画を立てる
keikaku suru	plan (v)	計画する
keikakūteki rōkyū ka	planned obsolescence	計画的老朽化
keiki	business activity	景気
keiki chintai	slump	景気沈滞
keiki junkan	business cycle	景気循環
keiki kōtai	recession	景気後退
Keinzu keizaigaku	Keynesian economics	ケインズ経済学
keiretsu gaisha	affiliate	系列会社
keiryō keizaigaku	econometrics	計量経済学
keisan chigai	miscalculation	計算違い
keisan ki	calculator	計算機
keisan sho	statement (banking)	計算書
keisen suru	lay up (shipping) (v)	係船する
keishō saimu	assumed liability	継承債務
keiyaku	contract	契約
keiyaku furikō	non-performance of contract	契約不履行
keiyaku ihan	breach of contract	契約違反
keiyaku ni yoru shigoto	work on contract	契約による仕事
keiyaku rikō hoshō	performance bond	契約履行保証
keiyaku sho	indenture/written agreement	契約書
keiyaku zuki	contract month	契約月

keizai kansoku shisū	economic barometer	経済観測指数
keizai kiban	infrastructure (economy)	経済基盤
keizai no	economic (adj)	経済の
keizai shihyō	economic indicators	経済指標
keizai teki hatchū ryō	economic order quantity	経済的発注量
keizai teki kinō teki taiyō nen sū	economic life	経済的機能的耐用年数
keizaigaku	economics	経済学
keizoku kigyō kachi	going concern value	継続企業価値
keizoku sashizu sho	standing order	継続指図書
keizoku seizō sashizu sho	blanket order (production)	継続製造指図書
keizoku tanaoroshi	perpetual inventory	継続棚卸し
kekkan ga aru	defective (adj)	欠陥がある
kenchiku kōji no ryūchi ken	mechanics' lien	建築工事の留置権
kenchō na	firm (securities) (adj)	堅調な
kengen	title	権原
kengen hoken	title insurance	権限保険
kengen o ataeru	authorize (v)	権限を与える
ken-i o shoyū suru	to have authority (v)	権威を所有する
kenji	public prosecutor	検事
kenka	saponification	鹸化
kenkyū	research	研究
kenkyū kaihatsu	research and development	研究開発
kennin jūyaku	interlocking directorate	兼任重役
kenri hōki shōsho	quitclaim deed	権利放棄証書
kenri ochi	ex rights	権利落ち
kenri shōmei yōyaku sho	abstract of title	権利証明要約書
kenri shōmetsu jōtai	public domain (patent)	権利消滅状態
kenri sōshitsu	divestment	権利喪失
kensa	inspection	検査
kensa kan	inspector	検査官
kensaku ban	grinder	研削盤
kensatsu tōkyoku	the prosecution	検察当局
kenshō	verification	検証
kessan	settlement	決算
kessan kinyū	closing entry	決算記入
kessei	serum	血清
ketsueki	blood	血液
ketsueki gyōko soshi yaku	anticoagulant	血液凝固阻止薬
ketsugi	resolution (legal document)	決議
ketsugō genka	joint cost	結合原価
kī bōdo	keyboard	キーボード
kī panchā	keypuncher	キーパンチャー

kibishiku saisoku suru	dun (v)	厳しく催促する
kibo no keizai	economy of scale	規模の経済
kigen tsuki kari ire kin	term loan	期限付き借入金
kigen tsuki kawase tegata	time bill (of exchange)	期限付き為替手形
kigen tsuki kawase tegata shinyō jō	acceptance credit	期限付為替手形信用状
kigyō	enterprise	企業
kigyō imēji	corporate image	企業イメージ
kigyō ka	entrepreneur	企業家
kigyō keikaku	corporate planning	企業計画
kigyō ketsugō	combination	企業結合
kigyō kōkoku	institutional advertising	企業広告
kigyō mokuteki	company goal	企業目的
kigyō rengō	cartel	企業連合
kigyō seichō	corporate growth	企業成長
kigyō seisaku	company policy	企業政策
kijun	norm	基準
kijun nedan	base price	基準値段
kijun nenji	base year	基準年次
kijun tsūka	base currency	基準通貨
kikai	machinery	機械
kikai hiyō	opportunity costs	機会費用
kikai kōgaku	mechanical engineering	機械工学
kikaku	project	企画
kikaku	standard	規格
kikaku ka	standardization	規格化
kikaku suru	project (v)	企画する
kikan tōshi ka	institutional investor	機関投資家
kiken	risk	危険
kiken bunseki	risk analysis	危険分析
kiken futan shihon	risk capital, venture capital	危険負担資本
kiken satei	risk assessment	危険査定
kiken shihon	risk capital	危険資本
kiken yakkan	waiver clause (insurance)	棄権約款
kimagure shikyō	volatile market	気まぐれ市況
kimari shigoto	routine	決まり仕事
kimatsu	end of period	期末
kime	grain (printing)	きめ
kimei shōken	registered security	記名証券
kimitsu no	confidential (adj)	機密の
kin junbi	gold reserves	金準備
kin kakaku	gold price	金価格
kin mekki no	goldplated (adj)	金めっきの
kin yakkan	gold clause	金約款
kinbuchi shōken	gilt (Brit. govt. security)	金縁証券

kin-itsu rimawari	flat yield	均一利回り
kin-itsu ryōkin	flat rate	均一料金
kinko kabu	treasury stock	金庫株
kinkyū yō tsumitate kin	contingent fund	緊急用積立金
kinō bunseki	functional analysis	機能分析
kinri	interest rate	金利
kinri heika	interest parity	金利平価
kinri kikan	interest period	金利期間
kinri saitei torihiki	interest arbitrage	金利裁定取引き
kinrō iyoku	morale	勤労意欲
kinsei hin	prohibited goods	禁制品
kinsen suitō gakari	teller	金銭出納係
kinshuku shikyō	tight market	緊縮市況
kin-yū gaisha	finance company	金融会社
kin-yū gyōsha	money broker	金融業者
kinyū nyūsatsu	written bid	記入入札
kin-yū seisaku	monetary policy	金融政策
kin-yū shijō	financial market/ money market	金融市場
kin-yū shōhin	financial instrument, financial product	金融商品
kinzoku	metals	金属
kinzoku sen-i	metallic fiber	金属繊維
kinzoku suiso ka butsu	metal hydride	金属水素化物
kioku sōchi	storage	記憶装置
kiri mori yō naifu	carving knife	切り盛り用ナイフ
kisai suru	float (issue stock) (v)	記載する
kisei fuku	ready-to-wear	既製服
kisetsuteki	seasonal (adj)	季節的
kishiren	xylene	キシレン
kishu zandaka	opening balance	期首残高
kiso kōjo	personal exemption	基礎控除
kisoku	regulation	規則
kison nimotsu hoshō jō	letter of indemnity (transportation)	毀損荷物保証状
kisosuru	prosecute	起訴する
kitai dōri ni	up to our expectations	期待通りに
kitai rēzā	gas laser	気体レーザー
kitai rieki	expected results	期待利益
kitoku ken	acquired rights, vested rights	既得権
kitoku riken	vested interests	既得利権
kizoku shita	imputed (adj)	帰属した
kō enshō yō no	anti-inflammatory (adj)	抗炎症用の
ko gaisha	subsidiary	子会社
kō kaizodo	high resolution	高解像度
kō kyūsui sei jushi	water-absorbing resin	高吸水性樹脂
kō mitsudo	high density	高密度
kō rimawari	high yield	高利回り

kō ro	blast furnace	高炉
kōbai	public sale	公売
kōbai daikin teitō	purchase money mortgage	購買代金抵当
kōbai gakari	purchasing agent	購買係
kōbai ryoku	purchasing power	購買力
kōbai shunin	chief buyer, purchasing manager	購買主任
kobetsu hōmon hanbai	door-to-door (sales)	個別訪問販売
kōbo	public offering	公募
kōchizon	cortisone	コーチゾン
kōchōkai	public hearing	公聴会
kōdō yokusei yōso	disincentive	行動抑制要素
kōdoresu hon	cordless phone	コードレス・ホン
kōeki jigyō	public utilities	公益事業
kōeki jōken	terms of trade	交易条件
kōfun yaku	stimulant	興奮薬
kōgaku	engineering	工学
kōgaku shiki māku yomitori sōchi	optical mark reader	光学式マーク読み取り装置
kōgakushiki moji yomitori sōchi	optical character reader (OCR)	光学式文字読み取り装置
kogetsuki kanjō	uncollectible accounts	焦げ付き勘定
kogitte	check (banking)	小切手
koguchi atsukai tetsudō kamotsu	less-than-carload	小口扱い鉄道貨物
koguchi atsukai torakku kamotsu	less-than-truckload	小口扱いトラック貨物
kōgyō sho watashi	ex mine	鉱業所渡し
kōhī potto	coffeepot	コーヒーポット
koiru	coil	コイル
kōji keiyaku	working contract	工事契約
kojin shotoku	personal income	個人所得
kojin shotoku zei	personal income tax	個人所得税
kojin shotoku zei no kōjo (gaku)	personal deduction	個人所得税の控除(額)
kojin shotoku zeiritsu	personal income tax rate	個人所得税率
kojin songai baishō sekinin	personal liability	個人損害賠償責任
kojin taishoku nenkin kanjō	individual retirement account	個人退職年金勘定
kojin tenshu	sole proprietor	個人店主
kojin tōza kogitte	personal check	個人当座小切手
kōjo	deduction	控除
kōjō	factory	工場
kōjō chō	plant manager	工場長
kōjo dekiru	deductible (adj)	控除できる
kōjō heisa kikan	down period	工場閉鎖期間
kōjō iinkai	work committee	工場委員会
kōjō no ichi	plant location	工場の位置

kōjō seisan nōryoku	plant capacity	工場生産能力
kōjō watashi	ex factory/ex mill/ ex works	工場渡し
kōkai	novation	更改
kōkai shijō	open market	公開市場
kōkai shijō sōsa	open market operations	公開市場操作
kōkaku renzu	wide angle lens	広角レンズ
kōkan buhin	replacement parts	交換部品
kōkan kachi	exchange value	交換価値
kōkan kanō tsūka	hard currency	交換可能通貨
kōkan renzu	interchangeable lens	交換レンズ
kōkan shudan	medium of exchange	交換手段
kōkan suru	exchange (v)	交換する
kōkin	public funds	公金
kokka saimu	national debt	国家債務
kokkyō	border	国境
kokkyō zei chōsei	border tax adjustment	国境税調整
kokō shiki ro	electric arc furnace	弧光式炉
kōkoku	advertising	広告
kōkoku baitai	advertising media	広告媒体
kōkoku buchō	advertising manager	広告部長
kōkoku bun-an	copy (text) (advertising)	広告文案
kōkoku chōsa	advertising research	広告調査
kōkoku dairi ten	advertising agency	広告代理店
kōkoku hi	advertising expenses	広告費
kōkoku hi yosan	advertising budget	広告費予算
kōkoku waritsuke	layout (advertising)	広告割り付け
kokoro nashi kensaku ban	centerless grinder	心無し研削盤
kōkū kamera	aerial photographic camera	航空カメラ
kokumotsu	grain (food)	穀物
kōkū kamotsu yusō	air freight	航空貨物輸送
kōkū sokutatsu bin	air express	航空速達便
kokumin sō seisan	gross national product (GNP)	国民総生産
kokunai funani shōken	inland bill of lading	国内船荷証券
kokunai gaisha	domestic corporation	国内会社
kokunai shijō	home market	国内市場
kokunai shōhi zei	excise tax	国内消費税
kokunai sō seisan	gross domestic product (GDP)	国内総生産
kokunai tegata	domestic bill	国内手形
kokuritsu ginkō	national bank	国立銀行
kokurui	dry goods (grain)	穀類
kokusai	government bonds	国債
kokusai hizuke henkō sen	International Date Line	国際日付け変更線
kokusai shūshi	balance of payments	国際収支
kokusai tōshi shintaku	international investment trust	国際投資信託

kokusaihō	international law	国際法
kokuyū ka	nationalization	国有化
kokyaku	customer	顧客
kokyaku gakari	registered representative	顧客係
kokyaku sābisu	customer service	顧客サービス
kōkyō	boom	好況
kōkyō bumon	public sector	公共部門
kōkyō jigyō	public works	公共事業
kōkyō jūtaku kikan	housing authority	公共住宅機関
kōkyō kigyō tai	public company (government)	公共企業体
kōkyō kikin	public funds	公共基金
kōkyū bi	legal holiday	公休日
komāsharu	commercial (advertisement)	コマーシャル
komi uri no renbai hin	job lot (merchandising)	込売りの廉売品
komoji	lower case	小文字
kōmoku	item	項目
kōmoku betsu kōkoku	classified ad	項目別広告
komon bengoshi	legal adviser	顧問弁護士
komon ryō	advisor's fee	顧問料
kōnai	premises (location)	構内
kondensā	condenser	コンデンサー
konekutā	connector	コネクター
kongō hi	mixed cost	混合費
kōnin kaikeishi	certified public accountant/ chartered accountant	公認会計士
kōnin toriatsukai gyōsha	authorized dealer	公認取扱業者
konpakuto disuku	compact disc	コンパクト・ディスク
konpakuto disuku purēyā	compact disc player	コンパクト・ディスクプレーヤー
konpo	component (stereo)	コンポ
konpyūta	computer	コンピュータ
konpyūta banku	computer bank	コンピュータ・バンク
konpyūta gengo	computer language	コンピュータ言語
konpyūta memori	computer memory	コンピュータ・メモリ
konpyūta naizō sūchi seigyo sōchi	computerized numerical control (CNC)	コンピュータ内蔵数値制御装置
konpyūta nyūryoku	computer input	コンピュータ入力
konpyūta puroguramu	computer program	コンピュータ・プログラム
konpyūta sentā	computer center	コンピュータ・センター
konpyūta shutsuryoku	computer output	コンピュータ出力
konpyūta sutorēji	computer storage	コンピュータ・ストレージ
konpyūta tāminaru	computer terminal	コンピュータ・ターミナル
konsarutanto	consultant	コンサルタント
kontenā	container	コンテナー
kontorōra	controller (computer)	コントローラ

kōnyū sashizu sho	purchase order	購入指図書
kōnyū suru	purchase (v)	購入する
koppu	glass	コップ
koppu shiki	coaster	コップ敷き
kopurosessa	coprocessor	コプロセッサ
korekushon	collections	コレクション
kōri	usury	高利
kōri ire	ice bucket	氷入れ
kōritsu	efficiency	効率
kōru manē	call money	コール・マネー
kōru rēto	call rate	コール・レート
kōru rōn	call loan	コール・ローン
kōru rūru	call rule	コール・ルール
koruresu saki ginkō	foreign correspondent bank	コルレス先銀行
kōryū	alternating current	交流
kōsai jizen karikae	advance refunding	公債事前借り換え
kosaji	teaspoon	小匙
kōsaku kikai	machine tools	工作機械
kōsei	proofreading	校正
kōsei bōeki	fair trade	公正貿易
kōsei busshitsu	antibiotic	抗生物質
kōsei shijō kakaku	fair market value	公正市場価格
kōsei torihiki iinkai	Fair Trade Commission	公正取引き委員会
kōsei yōso	component	構成要素
kōshajiku	rear axle	後車軸
kōshin	renewal	更新
kōshin suru	renew (v)	更新する
kōshō	negotiation	交渉
koshō hiki	pepper mill	胡椒挽
koshō ire	pepper shaker	胡椒入
kōshō ken	bargaining power	交渉権
kōshō suru	negotiate (v)	交渉する
koshō tsuki funani shōken	foul bill of lading	故障付船荷証券
kōshōnin	notary	公証人
kōso	enzyme	酵素
kotaeru	reply (v)	答える
kōtai jikan	shift (labor)	交代時間
kotai rēzā	solid-state laser	固体レーザー
kōtei buai	bank rate/official discount rate	公定歩合
kotei fusai	fixed liability	固定負債
kotei hi	fixed charges/fixed costs/fixed expenses/ standing charges/ standing costs	固定費
kotei kinri	fixed rate	固定金利
kotei saseru	lock in (rate of interest) (v)	固定させる

kotei shihon	fixed capital	固定資本
kotei shihon tōshi	fixed investment	固定資本投資
kotei shīkensu robotto	fixed sequence robot	固定シーケンス・ロボット
kotei shisan	capital asset, fixed assets	固定資産
kotei shisan zei	real estate tax	固定資産税
kotei shishutsu yosan	capital budget	固定支出予算
kotei shōten kamera	fixed focus camera	固定焦点カメラ
kotei teikō ki	fixed resistor	固定抵抗器
kōten	upturn	好転
kōto	coat	コート
kōtō nyūsatsu	oral bid	口頭入札
kōtō saibansho	high court	高等裁判所
kottō hin nintei sho	antique authenticity certificate	骨董品認定書
kouri	retail	小売り
kouri gyō	retail trade	小売業
kouri nedan	retail price	小売り値段
kouri shōhin	retail merchandise	小売り商品
kouri ten	retail outlet	小売店
kouri uriage zei	retail sales tax	小売り売上げ税
kōya ban	sheet pile	鋼矢板
kōyō	utility	効用
kōyū chi	public domain (government)	公有地
kōyū zaisan	public property	公有財産
kōza	account	口座
kōza bangō	account number	口座番号
kozutsumi yūbin	parcel post	小包郵便
kuchi buki gurasu	handblown glass	口吹きグラス
kugizuke kakaku	pegged price	釘付け価格
kugizuke ni suru	peg (v)	釘付けにする
kujō shori tetsuzuki	grievance procedure	苦情処理手続き
kumiai fuhyō	union label	組合符標
kumiban	form (printing)	組版
kumitate	assembly	組み立て
kumitate kōjō	assembly factory	組み立て工場
kumitateru	assemble (v)	組み立てる
kuni betsu shin-yō do	country risk	国別信用度
kurankushafuto	crankshaft	クランクシャフト
kurasuakushon	class action	クラス・アクション
kuratchi	clutch	クラッチ
kurejittokādo	credit card	クレジット・カード
kurikaeshi robotto	repeatable robot	繰返しロボット
kurikoshi	carry-forward/carry-over (accounting)	繰越し
kurikosu	carry forward (accounting) (v)	繰越す
kurimodoshi	carryback	繰戻し

K

kurinobe hiyō	deferred charges	繰延べ費用
kurinobe shisan	deferred assets	繰延べ資産
kurinobe shūeki	deferred income	繰延べ収益
kurinobe tesū ryō	carrying charges (securities)	繰延べ手数料
kurōmu	chromium	クローム
kurorohorumu	chloroform	クロロホルム
kurōzu appu renzu	close-up lens	クローズ・アップ・レンズ
kusuri	drug, medicine	薬
kutsu	shoe	靴
kūyu	air shipment	空輸
kuzu tetsu	scrap (iron)	屑鉄
kyaburetā	carburetor	キャブレター
kyapitaru gein zei	capital gain tax	キャピタルゲイン税
kyōbai	public auction	競売
kyōdō hoken	coinsurance	共同保険
kyōdō kaison sonshitsu	general average loss	共同海損損失
kyōdō kōkoku	cooperative advertising	協同広告
kyōdō kumiai	cooperative	協同組合
kyōdō shijō	common market	共同市場
kyōdō shoyū ken	co-ownership	共同所有権
kyōdō shusshi	pool (funds) (n)	共同出資
kyōdō shusshi suru	pool (funds) (v)	共同出資する
kyōdō tōgi	colloquium	共同討議
kyōdō yokin kōza	joint account	共同預金口座
kyōdō yūshi	participation loan	共同融資
kyōgi jikō	agenda	協議事項
kyōgō sha bunseki	competitor analysis	競合者分析
kyōgyō kyōyaku	cooperation agreement	協業協約
kyōhaku	duress	強迫
kyohi ken	veto	拒否権
kyōjutsu sho	affidavit	供述書
kyoka	permit	許可
kyoku zahyō robotto	polar coordinates robot	極座標ロボット
kyōkyū kajō	glut/overage/ oversupply	供給過剰
kyōkyū sha	supplier	供給者
kyōkyū to juyō	supply and demand	供給と需要
kyōkyū usu	short supply	供給薄
kyori kei	rangefinder	距離計
kyōsei meirei	injunction	強制命令
kyōsō	competition	競争
kyōsō aite	competitor	競争相手
kyōsō jō no riten	competitive advantage	競争上の利点
kyōsō jō no yūetsu sei	competitive edge	競争上の優越性
kyōsō nedan	competitive price	競争値段
kyōsō senryaku	competitive strategy	競争戦略

kyōtaku kin	deposit (securities)	供託金
kyōtei	understanding (agreement)	協定
kyōyō	share	共用
kyōyū sha	joint owner	共有者
kyōyū zaisan	joint estate	共有財産
kyūka	leave of absence	休暇
kyūkei jikan	coffee break	休憩時間
kyūpora	cupola	キューポラ
kyūryō futan	payload (administration)	給料負担
kyūryō shiharai bo	payroll	給料支払い簿
kyūsai tetsuzuki	remedy (law)	救済手続き
kyūshō bō-eki	compensation trade	求償貿易
kyūshū gappei	merger	吸収合併
kyūshū suru	absorb (v)	吸収する
kyūsoku kanka shisan	quick assets (finance)	急速換価資産
kyūsū teigen hō	sum of the year's digits	級数逓減法
kyūyo kōzō	wage structure	給与構造
kyūyo zei	payroll tax	給与税

M

mae barai	advance payments, cash in advance	前払い
mae barai suru	advance (v)	前払いする
mae barai unchin	advance freight	前払い運賃
mae hizuke ni suru	back date (v)	前日付けにする
maebarai	prepayment	前払い
maebarai hiyō	prepaid expenses (balance sheet)	前払い費用
maebarai suru	prepay (v)	前払いする
maegaki	preface	前書き
maegashikin	advance	前借し金
maewatashi kin	down payment	前渡金
magu kappu	mug	マグカップ
maikuro chippu	microchip	マイクロ・チップ
maikuro firumu	microfilm	マイクロ・フィルム
maikuro fisshu	microfiche	マイクロ・フィッシュ
maikuro kamera	micro camera	マイクロ・カメラ
maikuro kasetto rekōdā	micro cassette recorder	マイクロ・カセット レコーダー
maikuro konpyūta	micro computer	マイクロ・コンピュータ
maikuro purosessa	micro processor	マイクロ・プロセッサ
mainen no	annual (adj)	毎年の
mainichi	daily (adv)	毎日
mainichi no	daily (adj)	毎日の

maiyōshi	sheet (printing)	枚葉紙
māketingu	marketing	マーケティング
māketingu keikaku	marketing plan	マーケティング計画
māketingu konseputo	marketing concept	マーケティング・コンセプト
makuro keizai gaku	macroeconomics	マクロ経済学
manē shoppu	money shop	マネーショップ
manējido kosuto	managed costs	マネージド・コスト
manejimento chīmu	management team	マネジメント・チーム
manejimento gurūpu	management group	マネジメント・グループ
maneru	simulate (v)	まねる
mangan kō	manganese ore	マンガン鉱
mangan kō	manganese steel	マンガン鋼
manipyurēta	manipulator	マニピュレータ
manki	maturity	満期
manki rimawari	yield to maturity	満期利回り
manki shiharai daka	amount due	満期支払高
mankibi	due date	満期日
maruchi puroguramingu	multiprogramming	マルチ・プログラミング
maruchi shōhō	pyramid selling	マルチ商法
maruchimedia	multimedia	マルチメディア
maruchitasuku operēshon	multitask operation	マルチタスク・オペレーション
masatsu puresu	friction press	摩擦プレス
mashiningu sentā	machining center	マシニング・センター
masshō kogitte	cancelled check	抹消小切手
masui yaku	narcotic, anesthetic	麻酔薬
masukomi	mass communications	マスコミ
masumedia	mass media	マスメディア
matehan robotto	material handling robot	マテハン・ロボット
matorikkusu manejimento	matrix management	マトリックス・マネジメント
mausu	mouse	マウス
mazābōdo	motherboard	マザーボード
medama shōhin	loss leader	目玉商品
megabaito	megabyte (MB)	メガバイト
megaherutsu	megahertz (MHz)	メガヘルツ
meigara	brand	銘柄
meigara chūjitsu sei	brand loyalty	銘柄忠実性
meigara imēji	brand image	銘柄イメージ
meigara ninshiki	brand recognition	銘柄認識
meigara shōnin	brand acceptance	銘柄承認
meigi kakikae dairi nin	transfer agent	名義書換え代理人
meigi kakikae shōsho	deed of transfer	名義書換証書
meimoku kakaku	nominal price	名目価格
meimoku rimawari	nominal yield	名目利回り
mein furēmu	mainframe	メインフレーム
mein furēmu konpyūta	mainframe computer	メインフレーム・コンピュータ
meisai hōkoku suru	account for (v)	明細報告する
meisai seisan sho	itemized account	明細生産書

meisaika suru	itemize (v)	明細化する
meishi	business card	名刺
meiyo kison	libel	名誉毀損
mekanikaru puresu	mechanical press	メカニカル・プレス
memori	memory	メモリ
men	cotton	綿
menjo	exempt, exemption	免除
menkyo	license	免許
menkyo zei	excise license	免許税
menseki buai	franchise (insurance)	免責歩合
menseki jōkō	escape clause/waiver clause	免責条項
menzei hin mokuroku	free list (commodities without duty)	免税品目録
menzei no	duty-free (adj)/tax-free	免税の
menzei sai	tax exempt bond	免税債
mēru ōdā	mail order	メール・オーダー
metan	methane	メタン
metanōru	methanol	メタノール
mētoru hō ni kansan	metrication	メートル法に換算
mi chōtatsu chūmon	back order	未調達注文
mi jukuren rōdō	unskilled labor	未熟練労働
midoru manejimento	middle management	ミドル・マネジメント
miharai hiyō	accrued expenses	未払い費用
miharai saimu	outstanding debt	未払い債務
miharai zeikin	accrued taxes	未払い税金
mihon o toru	sample (v)	見本をとる
mihon shumoku	sample line	見本種目
mikaeri tanpo	collateral	見返り担保
mikaihatsu no	undeveloped (adj)	未開発の
mikan no keiyaku	outstanding contract	未完の契約
mikomi kyaku	potential buyer	見込み客
mikoshi shisan	accrued assets	見越し資産
mimoto hoshō gaisha	surety company	身元保証会社
mimoto hoshō hoken	fidelity insurance	身元保証保険
minarai	apprentice	見習い
mini konpo	mini component system	ミニコンポ
mini konpyūta	minicomputer	ミニ・コンピュータ
minji soshō	civil action, civil suit	民事訴訟
minpō	civil law	民法
mishū shūeki	accrued revenue	未収収益
mitomeru	acknowledge (v)	認める
mitōshi	outlook	見通し
mitsumori	estimate	見積り
mitsumori kakaku	estimated price	見積り価格
mitsumori keisan sho	pro forma statement	見積り計算書
mitsumori okurijō	pro forma invoice	見積り送り状
mitsumori shirei sho	work order	見積り指令書
mitsumori sho	pro forma statement	見積り書

mitsumoru	estimate (v)	見積る
mizokiri furaisu ban	spline milling machine	溝切りフライス盤
mizu sashi	pitcher	水差し
mizusaki annai ryō	pilotage	水先案内料
moare	moire	モアレ
mochibun	equity	持ち分
mochibun pūringu	pooling of interests	持分プーリング
mochibun rieki ritsu	return on equity	持分利益率
mochidaka seigen	position limit	持高制限
mochikabu gaisha	holding company	持株会社
mochikabu hiritsu no teika	dilution of equity	持株比率の低下
modemu	modem	モデム
moderu	model	モデル
mōdo	mode	モード
modoshi zei	drawback	戻し税
mōgeji	mortgage	モーゲジ
mojurā seisan	modular production	モジュラー生産
moku daku	implied agreement	黙諾
mokuhyō kakaku	target price	目標価格
mokuhyō kanri	management by objectives	目標管理
mokuji	table of contents	目次
mokuroku	table of contents	目録
mokuroku ni kinyū suru	list (v)	目録に記入する
mondai	problem	問題
mondai bunseki	problem analysis	問題分析
mondai kaiketsu	problem solving	問題解決
mondai nashi	no problem	問題無し
mondai o tsukitomete kaiketsu suru	troubleshoot (v)	問題をつきとめて解決する
monitā	monitor	モニター
monko kaihō seisaku	open door policy	門戸開放政策
monokurōmu	monochrome	モノクローム
Monte Karuro hō	Monte Carlo technique	モンテカルロ法
moribuden	molybdenum	モリブデン
moruhine	morphine	モルヒネ
mōshikomi	proposal	申し込み
mōshikomi chōka no	oversubscribed (adj)	申し込み超過の
mosurin	muslin	モスリン
mōtā doraibu	motor drive	モータードライブ
motochō	ledger	元帳
motochō kanjō	ledger account	元帳勘定
motochō ki-nyū	ledger entry	元帳記入
mottomo yūri na nedan de	at best (adv)	最も有利な値段で
mottomo yūri na nedan de kau	buy at best (v)	最も有利な値段で買う
mozō hin	imitation	模造品
moyō	pattern	模様
mu giketsu ken kabushiki	nonvoting stock	無議決権株式
mu hoshō hin	as is goods	無保証品

mu tanpo fusai	unsecured liability	無担保負債
mu yuigon shibō sha	intestate (n)	無遺言死亡者
mugakumen no	no par value (adj)	無額面の
mukanshō shugi	laissez-faire	無干渉主義
mukei shisan	intangible assets	無形資産
mukimei kabu	bearer stock	無記名株
mukimei saiken	bearer bond	無記名債券
mukimei shōken	bearer security	無記名証券
mukō	void	無効
mukō na	null and void (adj)	無効な
mukō ni suru	invalidate (v)	無効にする
mukō no	void (adj)	無効の
murisoku kōsai	flat bond	無利息公債
musakui chūshutsu mihon	random sample	無作為抽出見本
mushō tochi haraisage	land grant	無償土地払い下げ
mutanpo fusai	unsecured liability	無担保負債
mutanpo no	unsecured	無担保の
muzai	innocence, not guilty	無罪
myūchuaru fando	mutual fund	ミューチュアル・ファンド

N

nafusa	naptha	ナフサ
naga sode	long sleeves	長袖
nagare sagyō	production line	流れ作業
nagare sagyō retsu	assembly line	流れ作業列
naibu	internal	内部
naibu kansa	internal audit	内部監査
naibu no	internal (adj)	内部の
naibu shūeki ritsu	internal rate of return	内部収益率
naifu	knife	ナイフ
naikoku shūnyū zei	internal revenue tax	内国収入税
naimen kensaku ban	internal grinder	内面研削盤
nairon	nylon	ナイロン
naizō	built-in	内蔵
nakagai nin	broker	仲買人
nakaguri ban	boring machine	中刳盤
nan ka	soft currency	軟貨
nankō	ointment, salve	軟膏
nanpin baibai	averaging (securities)	なんぴん売買
napukin	napkin	ナプキン
nariyuki chūmon	discretionary order	成り行き注文
nariyuki chūmon de	at the market (adv)	成り行き注文で
nashonarizumu	nationalism	ナショナリズム
ne sage	price cutting	値下げ
ne sage kyōsō	price war	値下げ競争
ne zaya	gross spread	値ざや
neage	markup	値上げ

nebiki suru	take off (sales) (v)	値引きする
nebiraki	spread (securities)	値開き
nedan ni ōjiru	meet the price (v)	値段に応じる
nedan o kirisageru	undercut (v)	値段を切り下げる
nedan o tsukeru	price (v)	値段を付ける
nega	negative (photography)	ネガ
nehaba	spread (finance)	値幅
nejikiri daisu	die	ねじ切りダイス
nejikiri senban	screw cutting lathe	ねじ切り旋盤
nekkan atsuen	hot rolling	熱間圧延
nekutai	tie	ネクタイ
nenji eigyō hōkoku	annual report	年次営業報告
nenji kaikei kensa	annual audit	年次会計検査
nenji kessan hōkoku	annual accounts	年次決算報告
nenkin	annuity	年金
nenkin kikin	pension fund	年金基金
nenkin uketori nin	annuitant	年金受取人
nenkō joretsu sei	seniority system	年功序列制
nenmatsu no	year-end (adj)	年末の
nenpu shōkan	amortization	年賦償還
nenri	per annum rate	年利
nenryō funsha sōchi	fuel injection system	燃料噴射装置
nenryō shōhi ryō	fuel consumption	燃料消費量
nensho	letter of indemnity	念書
nesage suru	mark down (v)	値下げする
netsuen hirohaba obikō	hot strip coil	熱延広幅帯鋼
netto kyasshu furō	net cash flow	ネット・キャッシュ・フロー
ni enka echiren	ethylene dichloride	二塩化エチレン
ni kanshite wa	regarding (with regard to)	に関しては
ni nushi	shipper	荷主
ni shiki	dunnage	荷敷き
niage suru	unload (shipping) (v)	荷揚げする
niban teitō	second mortgage	二番抵当
Nichibenren (Nippon bengoshi rengōkai)	Japan Federation of Bar Associations	日弁連（日本弁護士連合会）
nigan refu kamera	twin lens reflex camera	二眼レフ・カメラ
niji teki shijō	fringe market	二次的市場
nijū kakaku	double pricing	二重価格
nijū kazei	double taxation	二重課税
nikkado denchi	nickel-cadmium battery	ニッカド電池
Nikkei Dau	Nikkei Dow Jones Average	日経ダウ
Nikkei heikin kabuka	Nikkei Stock Average	日経平均株価
niku jū sōsu ire	gravy boat	肉汁ソース入れ
nikubuto katsuji	boldface	肉太活字
nikutai rōdō sha	manual workers	肉体労働者

nimotsu hikitori hoshō jō	letter of guaranty (transportation)	荷物引取り保証状
ningen kōgaku	ergonomics	人間工学
ninka	approval, permission	認可
ninka suru	approve (v)	認可する
ninka zumi hikiwatashi shisetsu	approved delivery facility	認可済み引渡し施設
ninmei	appointment	任命
ninshō	certification	認証
nintei kabu	authorized shares	認定株
nishin hō	binary notation	二進法
nittei	order of the day	日程
niuke nin	consignee (shipping)	荷受け人
no kotae to shite	reply (in . . . to)	の答えとして
nō sanbutsu	agricultural products	農産物
no uketori o mitomeru	acknowledge receipt of (v)	の受取りを認める
nobe jikan	man hours	延べ時間
nobe watashi	deferred delivery	延べ渡し
nōchi kaikaku	land reform	農地改革
nōdo	density	濃度
nōgyō	agriculture	農業
nōgyōshōken	agricultural paper	農業証券
nōki	delivery date	納期
nokogiri ban	sawing machine	鋸盤
nōritsu ka suru	streamline (v)	能率化する
nōrōdō fando	no-load fund	ノーロード・ファンド
nōryoku	capacity	能力
nōtobukku konpyūta	notebook computer	ノートブック・コンピュータ
notto	knot (nautical)	ノット
nottori	takeover	乗っ取り
nou hau	know-how	ノウハウ
nukini	pilferage	抜荷
nuu	sew (v)	縫う
nyōso	urea	尿素
nyū seramikkusu	new ceramics	ニューセラミックス
nyūkō zei	harbor dues	入港税
nyūsatsu	bid, tender	入札
nyūsatsu kanyū	invitation to bid	入札勧誘
nyūsatsu kōkoku	advertisement (request) for bid	入札広告
nyūsatsu seikyū	request for bid	入札請求
nyūsatsu suru	put in a bid (v)	入札する
nyūshoku ritsu	accession rate	入職率
nyūshu kanō sei o jōken to shite	subject to availability	入手可能性を条件として
Nyūyōku shōken torihiki jo	New York Stock Exchange	ニューヨーク証券取引所

O

ōbānaito torihiki	overnight transaction	オーバーナイト取引き
ōbike de kau	buy on close (v)	大引けで買う
ōbike nedan	closing price	大引け値段
ōbike sōba chūmon de	at the close (adv)	大引け相場注文で
ōbo kakaku	subscription price	応募価格
oboegaki	memorandum	覚書
odayaka na shōhō	soft sell	おだやかな商法
ōdio konpo	audio component system	オーディオコンポ
ofādo rēto	offered rate	オファード・レート
ofisu	office	オフィス
ofu rain	off-line (computer)	オフライン
ofusetto insatsu	offset printing	オフセット印刷
ofushoa kanpanī	offshore company	オフショア・カンパニー
oikake chūmon	follow-up order	追掛け注文
oiru darā	petrodollars	オイル・ダラー
oiru ponpu	oil pump	オイル・ポンプ
ōisogi no chūmon	rush order	大急ぎの注文
okurijō	invoice	送り状
okurijō kingaku	invoice cost	送り状金額
omowaku tōshi	go-go fund	思惑投資
ōmu	ohm	オーム
on rain de	on line (computer) (adv)	オンラインで
onbōdo	onboard	オンボード
onkyō kapura	acoustic coupler	音響カプラ
onrain	online	オンライン
onsei mēru	voice mail	音声メール
onsei ninshiki	voice recognition	音声認識
onsei nyūryoku no	voice-activated (adj)	音声入力の
onsei ōtō sōchi	audio response equipment	音声応答装置
operēta	operator (computer)	オペレータ
ōpun kanjō	open account	オープン勘定
ōpun shoppu	open shop	オープン・ショップ
opushon	option	オプション
opushon buhin	optional equipment	オプション部品
opushon torihiki	option trading	オプション取引き
orimono	dry goods (textile)/ textile	織物
orimono rui	soft goods	織物類
oroshiuri gyō	wholesale trade	卸売り業
oroshiuri gyōsha	wholesaler	卸売り業者
oroshiuri kakaku	wholesale price	卸売り価格
oroshiuri shijō	wholesale market	卸売り市場
oroshiya	jobber (merchandising)	卸し屋

orutanētā	alternator	オルタネーター
ōryō	embezzlement	横領
ōsaji	tablespoon	大匙
ōto chekkā	autochecker	オート・チェッカー
ōto kuratchi	automatic gearshift	オートクラッチ
ōto purinta	automatic printing machine	オート・プリンタ
ōto ribāsu	autoreverse	オート・リバース
ōtomēshon	automation	オートメーション
oya gaisha	parent company	親会社
oyakusho shigoto	red tape	御役所仕事
ōzara	platter	大皿

P

paipu yusō	pipage	パイプ輸送
pan kago	breadbasket	パン篭
panchi kādo	punch card	パンチ・カード
panchi puresu	punch press	パンチ・プレス
panfuretto	pamphlet	パンフレット
parareru pōto	parallel port	パラレル・ポート
paretto	pallet	パレット
paretto chenjā	automatic pallet changer	パレット・チェンジャー
paretto yusō	palletized freight	パレット輸送
paritī kakaku	parity price	パリティー価格
paritī shūnyū hiritsu	parity income ratio	パリティー収入比率
parusu	pulse	パルス
pasokon	personal computer	パソコン
pāsonaru kasetto purēyā	personal cassette player	パーソナル・カセット プレーヤー
pāsonaru konpyūta	personal computer	パーソナル・コンピュータ
pāsonaru sutereo rajio	personal stereo radio	パーソナル・ステレオ ラジオ
pāsonaru terebi	personal TV	パーソナル・テレビ
patān ninshiki	pattern recognition	パターン認識
pātonā	partner	パートナー
pawā sutearingu	power steering	パワー・ステアリング
pēji	page	ページ
pēji kumi	page makeup	ページ組
pēji zuke	pagination	ページ付け
penī kabu	penny stock	ペニー株
penishirin	penicillin	ペニシリン
penta erisuritōru	pentaerythritol	ペンタエリスリトール
peretto	pellet	ペレット
pī āru	public relations	ピーアール
pigī bakku sābisu	piggyback service	ピギーバック・サービス
piketto rain	picket line	ピケット・ライン
pīku rōdo	peak load	ピーク・ロード

pikuseru	pixel	ピクセル
pinion	pinion	ピニオン
pisuton	piston	ピストン
pointo	point (percentage, mortgage term)	ポイント
poketto terebi	pocket-size TV	ポケット・テレビ
pokettogata konpyūta	palm-size computer	ポケット型コンピュータ
popurin	poplin	ポプリン
poriesuteru	polyester	ポリエステル
porisuchiren	polystyrene	ポリスチレン
poriuretan	polyurethane	ポリウレタン
pōtaburu terebi	portable TV	ポータブル・テレビ
pōto	port	ポート
puraibēto furīto	private fleet	プライベート・フリート
puraimurēto	prime rate	プライム・レート
puranto yushutsu	plant export	プラント輸出
purazuma etchingu	plasma etching	プラズマ・エッチング
purazuma setsudan sōchi	plasma cutting machine	プラズマ切断装置
purehabu	prefabrication	プレハブ
pureibakku robotto	playback robot	プレイバック・ロボット
purēto	plate	プレート
purinta	printer	プリンタ
purinto	print	プリント
purinto auto	printout	プリントアウト
purītsu	pleat	プリーツ
purofairā	profiler	プロファイラー
puroguramingu	programming	プログラミング
puroguramu o kumu	program (computer) (v)	プログラムを組む
puroguramu	program (computer)	プログラム
purojekuto puranningu	project planning	プロジェクト・プランニング
puropiren	propylene	プロピレン
purosessa	processor	プロセッサ
purūdento man rūru	prudent man rule	プルーデント・マン・ルール

R

rain bumon kanbu shokuin	line executive	ライン部門幹部職員
rain bumon kanri	line management	ライン部門管理
rain purinta	line printer	ライン・プリンタ
raisensu	license	ライセンス
rajiaru bōru ban	radial drilling machine	ラジアル・ボール盤
rajiaru taiya	radial tire	ラジアル・タイヤ
rajietā	radiator	ラジエター
rajikase	radio cassette player	ラジカセ
rajio	radio	ラジオ
rakku jobā	rack jobber	ラック・ジョバー
rakuda	camel's hair	駱駝
rakunō seihin	dairy products	酪農製品

randamu akusesu memori	random-access memory (RAM)	ランダム・アクセス・メモリ
rappu ban	lapping machine	ラップ盤
rappugata konpyūta	laptop computer	ラップ型コンピュータ
ratekkusu	latex	ラテックス
rēdā	radar	レーダー
refurekkusu kamera	reflex camera	リフレックス・カメラ
rei auto	layout (computer)	レイアウト
rei jō	warrant (law)/writ	令状
reikan atsuen	cold rolling	冷間圧延
reinkōto	raincoat	レインコート
rejisutā	register (printing)	レジスター
rejisutādo chekku	registered check	レジスタード・チェック
rekōdo purēyā	record player	レコード・プレーヤー
ren	ream	連
renketsu zaimu shohyō	consolidated financial statement	連結財務諸表
renraku	liaison	連絡
rensetsu bō	connecting rod	連接棒
rentai sekinin	joint liability	連帯責任
renza	implication	連座
renzoku chūzō	continuous caster	連続鋳造
renzoku seisan	batch production	連続生産
renzoku shōkan shasai	serial bonds	連続償還社債
renzu	lens	レンズ
rēsu	lace	レース
rēyon	rayon	レーヨン
rēzā	laser	レーザー
rēzā bīmu purinta	laser beam printer	レーザー・ビーム プリンタ
rēzā kakō	laser processing	レーザー加工
rēzā kaku yūgō	laser fusion	レーザー核融合
rēzā purinta	laser printer	レーザー・プリンタ
ri mawari	yield	利回り
ri zaya	margin, profit	利ざや
riaru taimu	real time	リアル・タイム
ribēto	kickback	リベート
rīdo onri memori	read-only memory (ROM)	リード・オンリ・メモリ
rīdo taimu	lead time (computer)	リード・タイム
rieki haitō	earnings/bonus (premium)	利益配当
rieki haitō yūsen kabu	participating preferred stock	利益配当優先株
rieki kakutoku gyōseki	earnings performance	利益獲得業績
rieki ritsu	percentage of profits	利益率
rieki yōso	profit factor	利益要素
rieki yosoku	profit projection	利益予測
rifainansu	refinancing	リファイナンス

rifuda	coupon (bond interest)	利札
rifurēshon	reflation	リフレーション
rigai no shōtotsu	conflict of interest	利害の衝突
rigui	profit taking	利食い
riji kai	executive board	理事会
rijun	profit	利潤
rijun bunpai	profit sharing	利潤分配
rikuage hi	landing charges/ landing costs	陸揚げ費
rikuage hi komi nedan	landed cost	陸揚げ費込み値段
rikuage shōmei sho	landing certificate	陸揚げ証明書
rīma	reamer	リーマ
rimawari	yield	利回り
rimōto kontorōru	remote control	リモート・コントロール
riniā puroguramingu	linear programming	リニアー・プログラミング
rinji hi	incidental expenses	臨時費
rinji shikin	contingent fund	臨時資金
rinji teate	perks	臨時手当て
rinsan en	phosphate	燐酸塩
rinyō yaku	diuretic	利尿薬
rireki sho	résumé (n)	履歴書
riritsu	interest rate	利率
rishi	interest	利子
rishi o shōzuru	accrue (v)	利子を生ずる
rishi shotoku	interest income	利子所得
rishoku	separation	離職
rīsu	lease (n)	リース
rīsu keiyaku tsuki baikyaku	sale and leaseback	リース契約付き売却
risutora	restructuring	リストラ
riyō dekiru yō ni suru	make available (v)	利用できるようにする
riyō nōryoku	utilization capacity	利用能力
rizaya	profit margin	利ざや
rīzu ando ragusu	leads and lags	リーズ・アンド・ラグス
ro	furnace	炉
rōdō	labor	労働
rōdō chōtei	industrial arbitration	労働調停
rōdō hō	labor law	労働法
rōdō idō	labor turnover	労働移動
rōdō jikan	working hours	労働時間
rōdō keiyaku	union contract	労働契約
rōdō kishaku	dilution of labor	労働稀釈
rōdō kiyaku	labor code	労働規約
rōdō kumiai	labor union, trade union	労働組合
rōdō kumiai kanbu	labor leader	労働組合幹部
rōdō ryoku	labor force, workforce	労働力
rōdō ryoku no idō sei	mobility of labor	労働力の移動性
rōdō setsuyaku teki	labor-saving (adj)	労働節約的
rōdō sha	laborer	労働者

rōdō sha kaikyu	working class	労働者階級
rōdō shijō	labor market	労働市場
rōdō shūyaku sangyō	labor-intensive industry	労働集約産業
rōdō sōgi	labor dispute	労働争議
rojisutikkusu	logistics	ロジスティックス
rōkaru eria nettowāku	local area network (LAN)	ローカル・エリア・ネットワーク
rokku auto	lock out	ロック・アウト
rōmu saigai	industrial accident	労務災害
rōn	loan	ローン
ronsō suru	dispute (v)	論争する
rōretto	knurling tool	ローレット
rōru senban	roll turning lathe	ロール旋盤
rōshi kankei	industrial relations, labor relations	労使関係
rōshi kyōgi kai	work council	労使協議会
roshutsu	exposure	露出
roshutsu kei	exposure meter	露出計
rōsoku tate	candlestick	ろうそく立て
rōson	leakage	漏損
rūchin	routine (computer)	ルーチン
ruiseki genka shōkyaku hikiate kin	accumulated depreciation	累積減価償却引当金
ruiseki teki	cumulative (adj)	累積的
ruiseki yūsen kabu	cumulative preferred stock	累積優先株
rusuban denwa	phone answering machine	留守番電話
rutsubo	crucible	るつぼ
ryakushiki meirei	summary order	略式命令
ryō	volume	量
ryō tenbin torihiki	double dealing	両天秤取引き
ryōdate	straddling	両建て
ryohi nittō	per diem	旅費日当
ryōji shōmei okurijō	consular invoice	領事証明送り状
ryōkai	territorial waters	領海
ryōkin	charges (finance)/ rate (finance)	料金
ryokō kogitte	traveler's check	旅行小切手
ryūdō fusai	current liabilities	流動負債
ryūdō hiritsu	current ratio/ liquidity ratio	流動比率
ryūdō sei	liquidity	流動性
ryūdō sei erigonomi	liquidity preference (economics)	流動性選り好み
ryūdō shisan	current assets/floating assets/liquid assets/ quick assets	流動資産

R

ryūho rieki	retained earnings	留保利益
ryūsan	sulfuric acid	硫酸
ryūsan en	sulfate	硫酸塩
ryūtsū	negotiation (securities)	流通
ryūtsū keiro	channel of distribution	流通経路
ryūtsū kosuto	distribution costs	流通コスト
ryūtsū mō	distribution network	流通網
ryūtsū seisaku	distribution policy (merchandising)	流通政策
ryūtsū shijō	secondary market (securities)	流通市場
ryūtsū shite iru	afloat (finance)	流通している

S

sābā	server (computer)	サーバー
sābisu ryō	cover charge	サービス料
sagi	fraud	詐欺
sagi soshō	fraud action	詐欺訴訟
sagyō ichiji chūshi jikan	downtime	作業一時中止時間
sagyō jikan sagyō dōsa sōkan kenkyū	time and motion study	作業時間作業動作相関研究
sagyō jō	workshop	作業場
sai chūmon	repeat order	再注文
sai chūmon suru	reorder (v)	再注文する
sai hensei suru	reorganize (v)	再編成する
sai hoken sha	reinsurer	再保険者
sai hyōka	revaluation	再評価
sai jūden kanō no	rechargeable (adj)	再充電可能の
sai kōchō ki	prime time	最高潮期
sai kōsei suru	restructure (v)	再構成する
sai kōshō suru	renegotiate (v)	再交渉する
sai seisan hi	reproduction costs	再生産費
sai tōshi	reinvestment	再投資
sai uridashi	secondary offering (securities)	再売出し
sai waribiki ritsu	rediscount rate	再割引き率
sai yushutsu	re-export	再輸出
saiban	trial	裁判
saibankan	judge	裁判官
saibansho	court	裁判所
saichō keiro bunseki	critical path analysis	最長経路分析
saidaigen ni katsuyō suru	maximize (v)	最大限に活用する
saidan suru	cut (fashion) (v)	裁断する
saigai hoken	casualty insurance	災害保険
saikei koku	most-favored nation	最恵国
saiken	bond	債券
saiken kakuzuke	bond rating	債券格付け

saiken sha	creditor	債権者
saikō gendo	ceiling	最高限度
saikō hinshitsu	top quality	最高品質
saikō kakaku	top price	最高価格
saikō keiei sekininsha	chief executive	最高経営責任者
saikō keiei sha	top management	最高経営者
saikō nyūsatsu nin	highest bidder	最高入札人
saikō saibansho	supreme court	最高裁判所
saimin yaku	sleeping pill	催眠薬
saimu	liability, obligation	債務
saimu no sokuji hensai jōkō	acceleration clause	債務の即時返済条項
saimu rikō o okotaru	default (v)	債務履行を怠る
saishū ka suru	finalize (v)	最終化する
saishū kigen	deadline	最終期限
saishū seisan butsu	end product	最終生産物
saishū yōto shōmei sho	end-use certificate	最終用途証明書
saisoku suru	remainder (v)	催促する
saitei chingin	minimum wage	最低賃金
saitei junbi seido	minimum reserves	最低準備制度
saitei shōkokin ritsu	minimum margin requirement	最低証拠金率
saitei torihiki	arbitrage	裁定取引き
saitōshi suru	plow back (earnings) (v)	再投資する
saizu	size	サイズ
sakanobotte kōryoku o hassuru	retroactive (adj)	遡って効力を発する
saki ire saki dashi hō	first in-first out	先入先出法
saki tsumidashi	forward shipment	先積出し
sakidori tokken	lien (securities)	先取り特権
sakimono kaitsuke	forward purchase	先物買い付け
sakimono keiyaku	forward contract, futures (securities)	先物契約
sakimono mājin	forward margin	先物マージン
sakimono opushon	futures option (securities)	先物オプション
sakimono shijō	forward market	先物市場
sakimono torihiki	futures	先物取引き
sakkarin	saccharin	サッカリン
sakugen	cutback	削減
sakusan	acetic acid	酢酸
sakuzuke menseki wariate	acreage allotment	作付け面積割当て
sāmetto	cermet	サーメット
sāmosutatto	thermostat	サーモスタット
san arai	pickling	酸洗い
san sei no	acid (adj)	酸性の
sanbō chokkeishiki	staff and line (adj)	参謀直系式
sangyō	industry	産業
sangyō betsu rōdō kumiai	industrial union	産業別労働組合
sangyō dantai	trade association	産業団体

sangyō keikaku	industrial planning	産業計画
sangyō robotto	industrial robot	産業ロボット
sangyō zentai no	industrywide (adj)	産業全体の
sanjū go miri kamera	35 mm camera	35ミリ・カメラ
sanka	oxidation	酸化
sanka ryō	participation fee	参加料
sankyaku	tripod	三脚
sankyaku dai	trivet	三脚台
sanshutsu gaku	outturn	産出額
sara	dish, plate	皿
sarada bōru	salad bowl	サラダ・ボール
sarada no tori zara	salad plate	サラダの取り皿
sararī	salary	サラリー
sashi osaeru	impound (v)	差押える
sashihiku	allow (v)	差引く
sashine	price limit	指値
sashine chūmon	limit order (stock market)	指値注文
sashine mata wa sore yori yoi kakaku de	at or better (adv)	指値又はそれより良い価格で
sashiosae	attachment, seizure, garnishment	差押え
sashiosae ken	lien	差押え権
sashisematta henka	impending changes	差迫った変化
sashizu nin barai	payable to order	指図人払い
sashizu suru	instruct (v)	指図する
sasupenshon	suspension	サスペンション
satei	assessment/valuation	査定
satei kakaku	assessed valuation	査定価格
satei suru	assess (v)	査定する
satō tsubo	sugar bowl	砂糖壷
sayatori	arbitrage (securities)	鞘取り
se	spine (publishing)	背
sei kagaku	biochemistry	生化学
seichō	growth	成長
seichō kabu	growth stock	成長株
seichō no kanōsei	growth potential	成長の可能性
seichō ritsu	growth rate	成長率
seichō sangyō	growth industry	成長産業
seichō shisū	growth index	成長指数
seifu	government	政府
seifu kikan	government agency	政府機関
seifu shōken	government securities	政府証券
seifun	milling	製粉
seigen-teki rōdō kanshū	restrictive labor practices	制限的労働慣習
seihin	product	製品
seihin bunseki	product analysis	製品分析
seihin gurūpu	product group	製品グループ

seihin jumyō	life cycle of a product/ product life	製品寿命
seihin kaihatsu	product development	製品開発
seihin kanri	product management	製品管理
seihin no shūeki sei	product profitability	製品の収益性
seihin sekkei	product design	製品設計
seihin shumoku	product line	製品種目
seikaku kensa	personality test	性格検査
seikatsu hi	cost of living	生活費
seikatsu suijun	standard of living	生活水準
seikyū	demand (finance)	請求
seikyū sho	bill (sales)	請求書
seikyū sho no bunkatsu hakkō	cycle billing	請求書の分割発行
seimei	statement	声明
seimei hoken shōken	life insurance policy	生命保険証券
seimitsu kikai	precision machinery	精密機械
seiryū ki	rectifier	整流器
seisai	sanction	制裁
seisan	liquidation	精算
seisan	production	生産
seisan daka	output (manufacturing)	生産高
seisan hi	production costs	生産費
seisan kachi	liquidation value	精算価値
seisan kanri	production control	生産管理
seisan kōtei	production process	生産工程
seisan kōtei junjo ichiran hyō	flow chart (production)	生産行程順序一覧表
seisan sei	productivity	生産性
seisan sei kōjō undō	productivity campaign	生産性向上運動
seisan sha chokusō	drop shipment	生産者直送
seisan shisan	active assets	生産資産
seisan shizai	industrial goods	生産資材
seisan yaku	antacid	制酸薬
seishiki no shomei	authorized signature	正式の署名
seitetsu sho	steel mill	製鉄所
seitō na shoji nin	holder in due course	正当な所持人
seiyaku	covenant	誓約
seizō gyōsha	manufacturer	製造業者
seizō gyōsha dairi ten	manufacturer's agent, manufacturer's representative	製造業者代理店
seizō kanri	manufacturing control	製造管理
seizō kansetsu hi	factory overhead	製造間接費
seizō kansetsu hi haifu ritsu	burden rate (production)	製造間接費配布率
seizō nōryoku	manufacturing capacity	製造能力
seizō shihon	instrumental capital	製造資本
seizō yotei hyō	production schedule	製造予定表
seizon shintaku	living trust	生存信託
sekai ginkō	World Bank	世界銀行

seki dome doroppu	cough drop	咳止めドロップ
seki dome shiroppu	cough syrup	咳止めシロップ
sekigai shashin firumu	infrared film	赤外写真フィルム
sekinin buntan	allocation of responsibilities	責任分担
sekinin hoken	liability insurance	責任保険
sekinin kaijo suru	discharge (business law)	責任解除する
sekitan	coal	石炭
sekitan san	phenol	石炭酸
sekiyu	petroleum	石油
sekiyu kagaku seihin	petrochemical	石油化学製品
sekkai gan	limestone	石灰岩
sekkei bumon	engineering and design department	設計部門
sekkyoku shintaku	active trust	積極信託
senban	lathe	旋盤
senbetsu kensa	screening	選別検査
senchō mata wa sen-in no fuhō kōi	barratry (transportation)	船長又は船員の不法行為
senden	publicity	宣伝
senden katsudō	advertising campaign	宣伝活動
senden kōkoku hi	advertising budget	宣伝広告費
senden urikomi	advertising drive	宣伝売り込み
senga	line drawing	線画
senkei suitei	linear estimation	線型推定
senkō kikan	lead time	先行期間
senkō shihyō	leading indicator	先行指標
senkyo kamotsu toriatsukai hi	dock handling charges	船渠貨物取扱い費
senmei mishō hoken keiyaku	floater (maritime insurance)	船名未詳保険契約
senmon hin	specialty goods	専門品
senmon shoku	profession	専門職
senmu torishimari yaku	executive director	専務取締役
sennai ninpu chin senshu futan	berth terms	船内人夫賃船主負担
sennai tsumitsuke chin	stowage charges	船内積付け賃
sennin ken	seniority	先任権
senryaku hin	strategic articles	戦略品
sensā	sensor	センサー
sensei chinjutsu sho	sworn statement	宣誓陳述書
sensei kyōjutsusho	deposition, affidavit	宣誓供述書
sensoku ni	alongside (adv)	船側に
sensoku watashi	free alongside ship	船側渡し
sentaku jiyū no	optional (adj)	選択自由の
sentan gijutsu	advanced technology	先端技術
sentetsu	pig iron	銑鉄
sentoraru rēto	central rate	セントラル・レート
seramikku enjin	ceramic engine	セラミック・エンジン
seramikku faibā	ceramic fiber	セラミック・ファイバー

seramikku firutā	ceramic filter	セラミック・フィルター
seramikku kondensa	ceramic condenser	セラミック・コンデンサ
seramikku sensā	ceramic sensor	セラミック・センサー
seriotosu	outbid (v)	競り落とす
serufu sābisu	self-service	セルフ・サービス
serufu taimā	self-timer	セルフ・タイマー
sessha renzu	macro lens	接写レンズ
sētā	sweater	セーター
setsubi	equipment/facilities	設備
setsubi hin no rīsu	equipment leasing	設備品のリース
setsuzoku kēburu	connector cable	接続ケーブル
settai hi	expense account	接待費
setten	contact	接点
setto	bundle (computer)/set	セット
shachō	president	社長
shadan hōjin	corporation	社団法人
shain	member of firm	社員
shajiku	axle	車軸
shakkan dan	consortium	借款団
shakkin suru	borrow (v)	借金する
shakunyū kosuto	borrowing cost	借入コスト
shakuyō shōsho	IOU	借用証書
shanpen gurasu	champagne glass	シャンペン・グラス
sharin	wheel	車輪
shāringu mashin	shearing machine	シャーリング・マシン
sharyō	rolling stock	車両
shasai	corporate bonds, debentures	社債
shasai hakkō	bond issue	社債発行
shāshī	chassis	シャーシー
shashi zei	luxury tax	奢侈税
shashutsu seikei ki	injection molding machine	射出成形機
shatai	body	車体
shatsu	shirt	シャツ
shattā	shutter	シャッター
shattā supīdo	shutter speed	シャッター・スピード
shiage o suru	top up (v)	仕上げをする
shi saiken	municipal bond	市債券
shibo	private placement (finance)	私募
shibori	aperture	絞り
shichū ginkō	commercial bank	市中銀行
shīdīromu disuku	CD-ROM disk	シーディーロム・ディスク
shīdīromu doraibu	CD-ROM drive	シーディーロム・ドライブ
shidō sha	leader	指導者
shien katsudō	support activities	支援活動
shigachi no	liable to (adj)	しがちの
shigen haibun	resources allocation	資源配分

shigoto	job	仕事
shigoto ba	workplace	仕事場
shigoto no hoshō	job security	仕事の保障
shigoto ryō	work load	仕事量
shigoto saikuru	work cycle	仕事サイクル
shihai ken	controlling interest	支配権
shihai nin	manager	支配人
shihanki	quarter	四半期
shiharai	disbursement/payment	支払い
shiharai bi	payoff (administration)	支払い日
shiharai busoku no	underpaid (adj)	支払い不足の
shiharai entai kanjō	delinquent account	支払い延滞勘定
shiharai funō	default	支払い不能
shiharai funō no	insolvent (adj)	支払い不能の
shiharai funō sha	insolvent	支払い不能者
shiharai hoshō kogitte	certified check	支払い保証小切手
shiharai jōken	payment terms	支払い条件
shiharai jūtō kin	appropriation	支払い充当金
shiharai kanjō	accounts payable	支払い勘定
shiharai kigen ga sugita	overdue (adj)	支払い期限が過ぎた
shiharai kigen keika	past due	支払い期限経過
shiharai kijitsu	maturity date	支払い期日
shiharai kyozetsu	payment refused	支払い拒絶
shiharai nin	payer	支払い人
shiharai nōryoku	solvency	支払い能力
shiharai nōryoku gainen	ability-to-pay concept	支払い能力概念
shiharai o kyozetsu suru	refuse payment (v)	支払いを拒絶する
shiharai risoku	interest expenses	支払い利息
shiharai seikyū	claim (insurance)	支払い請求
shiharai teishi	moratorium/ stop-payment	支払い停止
shiharai teishi suru	suspend payment (v)	支払い停止する
shiharai yūyo kikan	grace period	支払い猶予期間
shiharau	pay (v)	支払う
shihei	bill *(*banknote)	紙幣
shiharainin	payer	支払い人
shihon	capital	資本
shihon hikiate	capital allowance	資本引当
shihon jōyo kin	capital surplus/ surplus capital	資本剰余金
shihon ka	capitalization	資本化
shihon kanjō	capital account	資本勘定
shihon keisei	capital formation	資本形成
shihō ken	jurisdiction	司法権
shihon kōsei	capital structure	資本構成
shihon kosuto	cost of capital	資本コスト
shihon rieki ritsu	return on capital	資本利益率
shihon ritoku oyobi sonshitsu	capital gain/loss	資本利得及び損失
shihon saikōsei	recapitalization	資本再構成

S

shihon sanshutsu ryō hiritsu	capital-output ratio	資本産出量比率
shihon shijō	capital market	資本市場
shihon shishutsu	capital expenditure, capital spending	資本支出
shihon shishutsu satei	capital expenditure appraisal	資本支出査定
shihon shugi	capitalism	資本主義
shihon shūyaku no	capital-intensive (adj)	資本集約の
shihon yushutsu	capital exports	資本輸出
shihon zai	capital goods	資本財
shihon zōka	capital increase	資本増加
shihōshō	Department of Justice (U.S.)	司法省
shihyō	indicator	指標
shihyō meigara	bellwether issue	指標銘柄
shiire kakaku	purchase price	仕入れ価格
shijō	market (n)/marketplace	市場
shijō chōsa	market research, market survey	市場調査
shijō dōkō	market trends	市場動向
shijō e no sekkin	market access	市場への接近
shijō hōwa	market saturation	市場飽和
shijō hyōka	market appraisal	市場評価
shijō kaitaku hi	marketing budget	市場開拓費
shijō kakaku	market price/market value	市場価格
shijō kakuzuke	market rating	市場格付け
shijō kanri	market management	市場管理
shijō keikaku	market plan	市場計画
shijō mitōshi	market forecast	市場見通し
shijō ni dasu	market (v)	市場に出す
shijō no jissei	market forces	市場の実勢
shijō rieki	paper profit	紙上利益
shijō satei	market appraisal	市場査定
shijō sen-yū ritsu	market share	市場占有率
shijō shintō	market penetration	市場浸透
shijō shisū	market index	市場指数
shijō shūchū	market concentration	市場集中
shika	market price	市価
shikakari hin	work in progress	仕掛り品
shikaku	qualifications	資格
shīkensu robotto	sequence robot	シーケンス・ロボット
shīkensu seigyo	sequential control	シーケンス制御
shiki keitō	chain of command	指揮系統
shikin	fund	資金
shikin chōtatsu	funding/raising capital	資金調達
shikin fūsa	blockage of funds	資金封鎖
shikin kanri	cash management	資金管理
shikinguri	cash flow	資金繰り

shikkō	execution	執行
shikkō	invalidation	失効
shikkō yūyo	probation	執行猶予
shikyō	market position	市況
shikyō hōkoku	market report	市況報告
shimedaka	footing (accounting)	締め高
shimin rajio	CB	市民ラジオ
shimon kaigi	advisory council	諮問会議
shin seihin kaihatsu	new product development	新製品開発
shin sozai	new materials	新素材
shin tsūka	new money	新通貨
shinboru māku	logo	シンボル・マーク
shinbun boshū kōkoku	want ad	新聞募集広告
shinbun yō shi	newsprint	新聞用紙
shingai	infringement	侵害
shinjikēto o tsukuru	syndicate (v)	シンジケートを作る
shinjikēto sosei hi	front-end fee	シンジケート組成費
shinkabu hikiuke ken	preemptive right	新株引受け権
shinki hakkō saiken	new issue	新規発行債券
shinki kōbo	initial public offering	新規公募
shinpan gaisha	consumer credit company	信販会社
shinpin torikae hi	replacement cost	新品取替え費
shinrai suji	reliable source	信頼筋
shinsei	application	申請
shinsei sho	application form	申請書
shinshi kyōtei	gentleman's agreement	紳士協定
shinshuku kanzei	flexible tariff	伸縮関税
shintaku	trust	信託
shintaku gaisha	trust company	信託会社
shintaku ginkō	trust bank	信託銀行
shintaku shikin	trust fund	信託資金
shintaku shōsho	deed of trust	信託証書
shin-yō	credit (finance)	信用
shin-yō chōsa	credit check	信用調査
shin-yō gashi	unsecured loan	信用貸し
shin-yō gendo gaku	credit line	信用限度額
shin-yō ginkō	credit bank	信用銀行
shin-yō hakkō	fiduciary issue	信用発行
shin-yō hoken	credit insurance	信用保険
shin-yō hoken seigen daka	coverage (insurance)	信用保険制限高
shin-yō jō	letter of credit	信用状
shin-yō kakuzuke	credit rating	信用格付け
shin-yō kashitsuke	fiduciary loan	信用貸付
shin-yō kumiai	credit union	信用組合
shin-yō shiharai jōken	credit terms	信用支払条件
shin-yō shōkai	credit reference	信用紹介
shin-yō suru	credit (v)	信用する

shin-yō torihiki	margin trading	信用取引き
shin-yō tōsei	credit control	信用統制
shio furi yōki	salt shaker	塩振り容器
shippai	failure	失敗
shippai suru	fail (v)	失敗する
shiriaru pōto	serial port	シリアル・ポート
shiriaru purinta	serial printer	シリアル・プリンタ
shirindā	cylinder	シリンダー
shirindā nakaguri ban	cylinder boring machine	シリンダー中刳盤
shiro kuro firumu	black and white film	白黒フィルム
shiro kuro terebi	black and white TV	白黒テレビ
shiruku	silk	シルク
shiryō	data	資料
shisan	asset/estate	資産
shisan baibai eki	capital gain	資産売買益
shisan hyō	trial balance	試算表
shisan kaiten ritsu	asset turnover	資産回転率
shisan kakaku	asset value	資産価格
shisan sentaku no riron	portfolio theory	資産選択の理論
shisan shotoku	earnings on assets	資産所得
shishutsu	expenditure/outlay	支出
shison hin	spoilage	仕損品
shisū	index (indicator)	指数
shisutemu bunseki	systems analysis	システム分析
shisutemu enjiniaringu	systems engineering	システム・エンジニアリング
shisutemu kanri	systems management	システム管理
shisutemu sekkei	systems design	システム設計
shita gaki	draft (document)/ rough draft	下書き
shitauke gyōsha	subcontractor	下請け業者
shitauke ni dasu	subcontract (v)	下請けに出す
shite kabu	speculative stock	仕手株
shite	speculator	仕手
shitei gensan chiten	named point of origin	指定原産地点
shitei shimukai chiten	named point of destination	指定仕向い地点
shitei suru	assign (v)	指定する
shitei tsumidashi kō	named port of shipment	指定積出し港
shitei yuigon shikkō sha	executor	指定遺言執行者
shitei yunyū kō	named port of importation	指定輸入港
shitei yushutsu chiten	named point of exportation	指定輸出地点
shiten	branch, branch office	支店
shīto	seat	シート
shīto bā	sheet bar	シート・バー
shīto beruto	seatbelt	シート・ベルト

shitsugyō	unemployment	失業
shitsugyō teate	unemployment compensation	失業手当て
shiwake chō	journal (accounting)	仕分け帳
shiyō sha	user	使用者
shiyō zei	use tax	使用税
shiyōsho	specification	仕様書
shizen zōka	accretion	自然増加
shizen zōka	unearned increment	自然増価
shō	chapter	章
shō	department (U.S. Government)	省
shō kankō	business practice	商慣行
shō kigyō	small business	小企業
sho kinyū	original entry	初記入
shō kōhen	billets	小鋼片
shobun kanō shotoku	disposable income	処分可能所得
shōdan	negotiation	商談
shōdan ni yoru hanbai	negotiated sale	商談による販売
shōdō gai	impulse buying	衝動買い
shōdoku zai	antiseptic	消毒剤
shogakari	carrying charges/ charges (sales)	諸掛かり
shogakari komi nedan	gross price	諸掛かり込み値段
shogakari komi no	overhead (adj)	諸掛かり込みの
shōgensuru	testify	証言する
shōgō bangō	reference number	照合番号
shōgō hyō	checklist	照合表
shōgyō ginkō	commercial bank, merchant bank	商業銀行
shōgyō kakuzuke	commercial grade	商業格付け
shōgyō kōshin sho	credit bureau/ mercantile agency	商業興信所
shōgyō no	mercantile (adj)	商業の
shōgyō okurijō	commercial invoice	商業送り状
shōhi sha	consumer	消費者
shōhi sha bukka shisū	consumer price index	消費者物価指数
shōhi sha chōsa	consumer research	消費者調査
shōhi sha manzoku	consumer satisfaction	消費者満足
shōhi sha shin-yō	consumer credit	消費者信用
shōhi sha shōnin	consumer acceptance	消費者承認
shōhi zai	consumer goods	消費財
shōhi zei	excise duty	消費税
shōhin	commodity/goods/ merchandise	商品
shōhin bōeki shūshi	visible balance of trade	商品貿易収支
shōhin ka keikaku	merchandising (manufacturing)	商品化計画
shōhin no deiri	movement of goods	商品の出入り

shōhin shijō	commodity market	商品市場
shōhin torihikisho	commodity exchange	商品取引き書
shōhin torimodoshi	repossession	商品取戻し
shōhisha rōn	consumer loan	消費者ローン
shōhō	commercial law, mercantile law	商法
shohō sen	prescription	処方箋
shōhon	script	抄本
shōhyō	trademark	商標
shōji gaisha	trading company	商事会社
shoji nin	holder (negotiable instruments)	所持人
shōkai jō	letter of introduction	紹介状
shōkan	redemption/retirement (debt)	償還
shōkan kikan	maturity	償還期間
shōkan seikyū ken	recourse, right of recourse	償還請求権
shōkan tsumitate kin	redemption fund	償還積立て金
shōkanjō	summons (n)	召喚状
shōkei kyokusen	bell-shaped curve	鐘形曲線
shōken	certificate (securities)	証券
shōken anarisuto	security analyst	証券アナリスト
shōken gaisha	securities company	証券会社
shōken gaisha eigyō buin	account executive (securities)	証券会社営業部員
shōken shijō	securities market	証券市場
shōken torihiki iinkai	Securities and Exchange Commission	証券取引委員会
shokkō	journeyman	職工
shokku abusōbā	shock absorber	ショック・アブソーバー
shōko	evidence	証拠
shōkō kaigisho	chamber of commerce	商工会議所
shōkokin	margin (money)	証拠金
shoku chō	foreman	職長
shokuba kunren	on-the-job training	職場訓練
shokubai	catalyst	触媒
shokubutsu sei yakuhin	botanic	植物性薬品
shokugyō	occupation	職業
shokugyō jō no kiken	occupational hazard	職業上の危険
shokugyō shōkai sho	employment agency	職業紹介所
shokuin	staff	職員
shokumu bunseki	job analysis	職務分析
shokumu hyōtei	job evaluation	職務評定
shokumu kijutsu sho	job description	職務記述書
shokumu suikō	job performance	職務遂行
shokuryō	foodstuffs	食料
shokutaku yō ginki	silverware	食卓用銀器

S

shōkyo kanō yomidashi senyō memori	EP-ROM	消去可能読み出し専用メモリ
shomei	signature	署名
shomei no ninshō	attestation	署名の認証
shomei sha	undersigned (n)	署名者
shōmei sho	certificate	証明書
shōmi genzai kachi	net present value	正味現在価値
shōmi kariire junbi kin	net borrowed reserves	正味借り入れ準備金
shōmi mochibun shisan	net equity assets	正味持分資産
shōmi rieki	net margin	正味利益
shōmi shisan	net worth	正味資産
shomi shisan kachi	net asset worth	正味資産価値
shōmō mason	wear and tear	消耗摩損
shōmushō	Department of Commerce (U.S.)	商務省
shōnin	merchant	商人
shōnin	witness	証人
shōnin girudo	merchant guild	商人ギルド
shoppingu sentā	shopping center	ショッピング・センター
shori katei de no gosa	processing error	処理過程での誤差
shorudā paddo	shoulder pad	ショルダー・パッド
shorui	document, paper (document)	書類
shōryaku suru	omit (v)	省略する
shōsan	nitric acid	硝酸
shōsan en	nitrate	亜硝酸塩
shōsha	trade house	商社
shōshin	promotion (personnel)	昇進
shōsho	deed/instrument/letter (certificate)	証書
shōsosuru	win a suit	勝訴する
shōsū kabunushi mochibun	minority interest	少数株主持分
shōsū kōbai dokusen	oligopsony	少数購買独占
shōten	focus	焦点
shotoku	income	所得
shotoku kaisō	income bracket	所得階層
shotoku keisan sho	income statement	所得計算書
shotoku shinkoku	income return	所得申告
shotoku zeiritsu	income tax rate	所得税率
shoyō jikan	lead time	所要時間
shoyū ken	ownership/titles	所有権
shoyū nushi no	proprietary (adj)	所有主の
shoyū sha	owner, proprietor	所有者
shoyū sha mochibun	owner's equity	所有者持分
shoyū yūka shōken	portfolio	所有有価証券
shū eki	weekly return	週益
shū kan tsūshō	interstate commerce	州間通商
shūchū ka	centralization	集中化
shūdan kunren	group training	集団訓練

S

shūdan rikigaku	group dynamics	集団力学
shudō kabu	market-leader (securities)	主導株
shūeki	earnings, returns/ revenue	収益
shūeki hōkoku	earnings report	収益報告
shūeki kabuka ritsu	earnings/price ratio	収益株価率
shūeki rimawari	earnings yield, income yield	収益利回り
shūeki ritsu	rate of return/profit margin	収益率
shūeki ritsu bunseki	profitability analysis	収益率分析
shūeki saiken	income bonds	収益債券
shūeki sei	profitability	収益性
shūeki teigen no hōsoku	law of diminishing returns	収益逓減の法則
shūgyō bi	work day	就業日
shūhai sābisu	pickup and delivery	集配サービス
shūhen kiki	peripheral equipment	周辺機器
shūhen sōchi	peripherals	周辺装置
shui sho	prospectus	趣意書
shukka	shipment	出荷
shukketsu suru	bleed (v)	出血する
shukkin jikan sū	attended time	出勤時間数
shūkō renzu	condenser lens	集光レンズ
shūnyū	revenue/income	収入
shūnyū kanjō	income account	収入勘定
shūnyū tanpo sai	revenue bond	収入担保債
shūnyū yaku	treasurer	収入役
shuppan sha	publisher	出版社
shuppatsu yotei jikoku	estimated time of departure	出発予定時刻
shūsei	amendment	修正
shūsei suru	amend (v)	修正する
shūseki kairo	integrated circuit	集積回路
shūshi hiritsu	balance ratios	収支比率
shūshin kaiin	life member	終身会員
shūshin koyō	lifetime employment	終身雇用
shūshuku hōsō	shrink-wrapping	収縮包装
shussan kyūka	maternity leave	出産休暇
shūten	terminal (transportation)	終点
shutoku	acquisition	取得
shutoku genka	acquisition cost/ original cost	取得原価
shutoku suru	acquire (v)	取得する
shūwai	graft	収賄
shuyō hiyō	prime cost (economics)	主要費用

S

shuyō shijō	primary market	主要市場
shuyō yushutsu hin	key exports	主要輸出品
shūzei kan	tax collector	収税官
sō dairi ten	sole agent	総代理店
sō genka	all in cost	総原価
sō jūryō	gross weight	総重量
sō juyō	aggregate demand	総需要
sō kessan	full settlement	総決算
sō kyōkyū	aggregate supply	総供給
sō rieki	gross margin/gross profit	総利益
sō rimawari	gross yield	総利回り
sō risuku	aggregate risk	総リスク
sō shihai nin	general manager	総支配人
sō shotoku	gross income	総所得
sō sonshitsu	gross loss	総損失
sō tōshi	gross investment	総投資
sō uriage daka	gross sales/sales turnover	総売り上げ高
sōba	quotation	相場
sōba shi	operator (securities)	相場師
soejō	cover letter	添状
sofuto fōkasu renzu	soft focus lens	ソフト・フォーカス・レンズ
sofuto rōn	soft loan	ソフト・ローン
sofutowea	software	ソフトウェア
sofutowea burōkā	software broker	ソフトウェア・ブローカー
sōgaku	amount/lump sum	総額
sōgi	dispute (n)	争議
sōgo chochiku ginkō	mutual savings bank	相互貯蓄銀行
sōgo haitateki kaikyū	mutually exclusive classes	相互排他的階級
sōgō rimawari	total return	総合利回り
sōgo sayō suru	interact (v)	相互作用する
sōgō shisū	composite index	総合指数
sōgyō kaishi keihi	start-up cost	操業開始経費
sōi	variance	相違
soka	prime cost (manufacturing)	素価
sōkai	general meeting	総会
sōkan ki	correlator	相関器
sōkatsu chūmon	blanket order	総括注文
sōkatsu teitō ken tsuki saiken	blanket bond	総括抵当権付債券
sōkin kogitte	remittance check	送金小切手
sokkin barai	ready cash	即金払い
sōko	godown/warehouse	倉庫
sōko gyōsha	warehouseman	倉庫業者
sōko hokan	storage (general)	倉庫保管
sōkō kyori kei	odometer	走行距離計
sōkō mairu sū	mileage	走行マイル数

sōko watashi	ex warehouse	倉庫渡し
sokudo kei	speedometer	速度計
sokushin	promotion (retailing)	促進
sokuza no	prompt (adj)	即座の
sokyū kazei	back taxes	遡及課税
son-eki bunki ten	break-even point	損益分岐点
son-eki bunki ten bunseki	break-even analysis	損益分岐点分析
son-eki keisan sho	profit and loss statement	損益計算書
son-eki nashi ni yaru	break even (v)	損益無しにやる
songai	damage	損害
songai baishō seikyū	claim (business law)	損害賠償請求
songai shōmei sho	proof of loss	損害証明書
sono chi ni oite	at and from (adv)	その地において
sonshitsu	loss	損失
sonshitsu atsukai ni suru	charge off (v)	損失扱いにする
sonshitsu o kyūshū suru	absorb the loss (v)	損失を吸収する
sōnyū	insert	挿入
sōsai kanzei	countervailing duty	相殺関税
soshiki	organization	組織
soshō	lawsuit, litigation, penalty action	訴訟
soshō kyōsa	barratry (business law)	訴訟教唆
sozei futan	tax burden	租税負担
sozei keigen	tax relief	租税軽減
sūchi enzan kopurosessa	math coprocessor	数値演算コプロセッサ
sūchi seigyo	numerical control	数値制御
suchiren monomā	styrene monomer	スチレン・モノマー
suchīru foiru	steel foil	スチール・フォイル
suēdo	suede	スエード
sueoki fusai	deferred liabilities	据え置き負債
sueoki nenkin	deferred annuities	据え置き年金
sueoki zei	deferred tax	据え置き税
sūgakuteki moderu	mathematical model	数学的モデル
sugu ni	as soon as possible	すぐに
suichoku tōgō	vertical integration	垂直統合
suichū kamera	underwater camera	水中カメラ
suiso kyūzō gōkin	metal alloys for hydrogen storage	水素吸蔵合金
suitchi	switch	スイッチ
sukāfu	scarf	スカーフ
sukarupā	scalper (securities)	スカルパー
sukāto	skirt	スカート
sukurīn	screen	スクリーン
sukyana	scanner	スキャナ
sūpā aroi	super alloys	スーパー・アロイ
sūpā konpyūta	super computer	スーパー・コンピュータ
supairaru kōkan	spiral tube	スパイラル鋼管
supāku puragu	spark plug	スパーク・プラグ

supesharisuto	specialist (stock exchange)	スペシャリスト
supīkā	speaker	スピーカー
supōtsu wea	sportswear	スポーツ・ウェア
sūpu yō supūn	soupspoon	スープ用スプーン
sūpu zara	soup dish	スープ皿
supūn	spoon	スプーン
supureddo shīto	spreadsheet	スプレッド・シート
suraido	slide	スライド
suraido eisha ki	slide projector	スライド映写機
suraido sei	sliding scale	スライド制
surakkusu	slacks	スラックス
surotto	slot	スロット
surū putto	throughput	スループット
surufamido	sulphamide	スルファミド
sūryō	quantity	数量
sūryō waribiki	quantity discount/ volume discount	数量割引き
susumeru	carry forward (v)	進める
sutaffu ashisutanto	staff assistant	スタッフ・アシスタント
sutaffu soshiki	staff organization	スタッフ組織
sutagufurēshon	stagflation	スタグフレーション
sutairu	style	スタイル
sutenresu, sutenresu kō	stainless steel	ステンレス、ステンレス鋼
sutereo	stereophonic (adj)	ステレオ
sutereo terebi	stereo TV	ステレオ・テレビ
suto yaburi	strikebreaker (scab)	スト破り
sutokku opushon	stock option	ストック・オプション
sutoraiki	walkout	ストライキ
sutoraiki o suru	strike (v)	ストライキをする
sutorēji	storage (computer)	ストレージ
sutoresu kanri	stress management	ストレス管理
sutorobo	strobe	ストロボ
sūtsu	suit	スーツ
suwappu	swap	スワップ

T

ta no shisan (oyobi fusai)	other assets (and liabilities)	他の資産(及び負債)
tābo chājā	turbo-charger	ターボ・チャージャー
taburetto	tablet	タブレット
tachiai jō	boardroom (securities), floor (of exchange), trading floor	立会場
tachiai jō gai no	off board (stock market) (adj)	立会場外の
tachikiri	bleed (printing)	断ち切り

tafuta	taffeta	タフタ
taibutsu renzu	objective lens	対物レンズ
taido rōn	tied loan	タイド・ローン
taika renga	refractories	耐火煉瓦
taikyū zai	durable goods	耐久財
taiman na	negligent (adj)	怠慢な
taimu shearingu	time sharing	タイム・シェアリング
tainetsu seramikkusu	heat-resistant ceramics	耐熱セラミックス
tainō kin	arrears	滞納金
tairyō māketingu	mass marketing	大量マーケティング
tairyō seisan	mass production	大量生産
tairyō shobun suru	unload (securities) (v)	大量処分する
taishaku taishō hyō	balance sheet	貸借対照表
Taishō	Osaka Stock Exchange	大証
taishoku	retirement (job)	退職
taishoku kin	severance pay	退職金
taiya	tire	タイヤ
taiyō nensū	useful life	耐用年数
taizō suru	hoard (v)	退蔵する
tajiku bōru ban	multispindle drilling machine	多軸ボール盤
tajin senban	multicut lathe	多刃旋盤
takaku bōeki	multilateral trade	多角貿易
takaku keiei ka	diversification (business)	多角経営化
takaku tōshi	diversification (securities)	多角投資
takansetsu robotto	articulated robot	多関節ロボット
take	length	丈
takesshō shirikon	poly-crystal silicon	多結晶シリコン
tako mētā	tachometer	タコ・メーター
takoku kan kyōtei	multilateral agreement	多国間協定
takokuseki kigyō	multinational corporation	多国籍企業
takuhai bin	courier service	宅配便
takujō denshi keisan ki	electronic desk calculator	卓上電子計算機
takujō denshi shuppan	desktop publishing	卓上電子出版
tāminaru	terminal (computer)	ターミナル
tāminaru	terminal	ターミナル
tān kī keiyaku	turnkey	ターンキー契約
tana oroshi shisan kaiten ritsu	inventory turnover	棚卸し資産回転率
tandoku kaison futanpo	free of particular average	単独海損不担保
tandoku kaison sonshitsu	particular average loss	単独海損損失
tandoku kaison tanpo	with average	単独海損担保
tangansuru	plead	嘆願する
tangusuten	tungsten	タングステン
tan-i	lot (securities)	単位

tan-i genka	unit cost	単位原価
tanjun sanjutsu heikin	arithmetic mean	単純算術平均
tankā	tanker	タンカー
tanka	unit price	単価
tanka suiso	hydrocarbon	炭化水素
tanki	short-term	短期
tanki fusai	short-term debt	短期負債
tanki kin-yū kōza	money market account	短期金融口座
tanki kin-yū shōhin tōshi shintaku	money market fund	短期金融商品投資信託
tanki kōsai	floating debt (government)	短期公債
tanki shihon kanjō	short-term capital account	短期資本勘定
tanki yūshi	short-term financing	短期融資
tanki yūshi de	at call (adv)	短期融資で
tanmatsu	terminal	端末
tanpo	security, collateral	担保
tanpo gashi ginkō	mortgage bank	担保貸し銀行
tanpo keiyaku	hypothecation	担保契約
tanpo tsuki fusai	secured liability	担保付き負債
tanpo tsuki kanjō	secured accounts	担保付き勘定
tanpo tsuki saiken	mortgage bond	担保付き債券
tanpo tsuki shasai ken	mortgage debenture	担保付き社債券
tanri	simple interest	単利
tansan gasu rēzā	carbon dioxide laser	炭酸ガス・レーザー
tansan kō	carbon steel	炭酸鋼
tanshoku no	black and white (adj)	単色の
tanso sen-i	carbon fiber	炭素繊維
taretto senban	turret lathe	タレット旋盤
tasuku fōsu	task force	タスク・フォース
tate furaisu ban	vertical milling machine	縦フライス盤
tate nakaguri ban	vertical boring mill	縦中ぐり盤
tatekezuri ban	slotting machine	縦削り盤
tawara kamotsu	bale cargo	俵貨物
teami no	hand-knit (adj)	手編みの
tēburu kurosu	tablecloth	テーブル・クロス
tēburu matto	place mat	テーブル・マット
tedori kyūryō	take-home pay	手取り給料
tegata	draft/paper (securities)	手形
tegata furidashi	draft (banking)	手形振出し
tegata furidashi nin	drawer/maker (of a check, draft, etc.)	手形振出し人
tegata hikiuke gyōsha	acceptance house	手形引受け業者
tegata kaitori saishū bi	expiry date (securities)	手形買い取り最終日
tegata kōkansho	clearinghouse	手形交換所
tegata naate nin	drawee	手形名当人

T

tegata nakagai nin	bill broker	手形仲買人
tegata seigen hikiuke uragaki	qualified acceptance endorsement	手形制限引受け裏書き
tegata tanpo nimotsu hokan azukari shō	trust receipt	手形担保荷物保管預り証
tegata waribiki buai	discount rate (securities)	手形割引き歩合
tei kaihatsu koku	underdeveloped nations	低開発国
tei kinri rōn	low-interest loans	低金利ローン
tei rimawari saiken	low-yield bonds	低利回り債券
tei shotoku	low income	低所得
teihaku kikan	laydays, lay time	碇泊期間
teihaku ryō	anchorage (dues)	碇泊料
teiji shōkan	mandatory redemption	定時償還
teika	fixed price	定価
teikan	bylaws	定款
teikei	affiliation	提携
teiki	fixed term	定期
teiki hoken	term insurance	定期保険
teiki sai	term bond	定期債
teiki tanaoroshi	periodic inventory	定期棚卸し
teiki tenken keiyaku	service contract	定期点検契約
teiki yokin	time deposit	定期預金
teikyō suru	offer (v)	提供する
teire suru	service (v)	手入れする
teisai	format	体裁
teisai mihon	dummy (publishing)	体裁見本
teisū	quorum	定数
teitai ryō	demurrage	停滞料
teitō	pledge	抵当
teitō ginkō	mortgage bank	抵当銀行
teitō ken	mortgage	抵当権
teitō shōken	mortgage certificate	抵当証券
tekihō ukewatashi	good delivery (securities)	適法受け渡し
tekisei rieki	fair return	適正利益
tekkō	iron ore	鉄鉱
tenbai	resale	転売
tenkan shasai	convertible bond, convertible debentures, loan stock	転換社債
tenkan shōken	convertible securities	転換証券
tenkan yūsen kabu	convertible preferred stock	転換優先株
tenki suru	post (bookkeeping) (v)	転記する
tennen shigen	natural resources	天然資源
tenpu suru	attach (v)	添付する
tensō	transfer (computer)	転送

T

tentai	sublet	転貸
tenteki yaku	drop (pharmaceuticals)	点滴薬
tentetsu yusō ryō	switching charges	転轍輸送料
tentō torihiki sōba	over-the-counter quotation	店頭取引き相場
tenui no	hand-sewn (adj)	手縫いの
tenuri no	handpainted (adj)	手塗りの
teori no	handwoven (adj)	手織りの
tēpu rekōdā	tape recorder	テープ・レコーダー
tēpu rokuga sōchi	videotape recorder	テープ録画装置
tērā	tailor	テーラー
terebi	television	テレビ
terekkusu	telex	テレックス
terekomyunikēshon	telecommunications	テレコミュニケーション
terepuroseshingu	teleprocessing	テレプロセシング
testudō yusō	rail shipment	鉄道輸送
tesūryō	commission, fee	手数料
tetsu zai	iron (pharmaceuticals)	鉄剤
tetsuke kin	earnest money	手付け金
teusu na shikyō	thin market	手薄な市況
tezukuri no	handmade (adj)	手作りの
tī potto	teapot	ティー・ポット
tōchaku yotei jikoku	estimated time of arrival	到着予定時刻
tochi	land	土地
tōgō-teki keiei kanri hōshiki	integrated management system	統合的経営管理方式
tōhyō ken	voting right	投票権
tojita	sewn (adj)	とじた
tōjitsu kagiri kashitsuke	day loan	当日限り貸付
tōjitsu kagiri yūkō chūmon	day order	当日限り有効注文
tōjitsu kessai torihiki	cash delivery	当日決済取引き
tōka	parity	等価
tōka shihon	invested capital	投下資本
tōkei	statistics	統計
tōketsu shisan	frozen assets	凍結資産
tōki	earthenware	陶器
tōki ka	speculator	投機家
tōki rui	pottery	陶器類
tokkei kanzei	preferred tariff	特恵関税
tokken tsuki baibai	put and call	特権付き売買
tokkyo	patent	特許
tokkyo hō	patent law	特許法
tokkyo ken	patent right	特許権
tokkyo ken kōkan	cross-licensing	特許権交換
tokkyo ken no sonzoku kikan	life of a patent	特許権の存続期間
tokkyo ken o motsu seisan hōhō	patented process	特許権を持つ生産方法

T

tokkyo ken shinsei	patent application	特許権申請
tokkyo ken shiyō ryō	license fees, patent royalty, royalty payment (patent)	特許権使用料
tokkyo shiyōryō	royalty (patent)	特許使用料
tokkyo shutsugan chū	patent pending	特許出願中
tokubetsu haitō kin	extra dividend	特別配当金
tokudai hin	outsized articles	特大品
tokui saki kanri	credit management	得意先管理
Tōkyō gaikoku kabushiki shijō	Tokyo foreign stock market	東京外国株式市場
Tōkyō gaikoku kawase shijō	Tokyo foreign exchange market	東京外国為替市場
Tōkyō shōken torihikijo	Tokyo Stock Exchange	東京証券取引所
tōmorokoshi	maize (grain)	とうもろこし
tōnyō byō	diabetes	糖尿病
tōnyū sanshutsu bunseki	input-output analysis	投入算出分析
toppu manejimento	top management	トップ・マネジメント
torakkubōru	track ball	トラックボール
torankiraizā	tranquilizer	トランキライザー
toranshu	tranche	トランシュ
toransufā mashin	transfer machine	トランスファーマシン
toransumisshon	transmission	トランスミッション
torēdo ofu	trade-off	トレード・オフ
tori kowasu	take down (v)	取壊す
toridasu	take out (v)	取出す
torihiki	deal/trade/trading/ transaction	取引き
torihiki kanjō zandaka	account balance	取引き勘定残高
torihiki kijitsu	trade date	取引き期日
torihiki saki ginkō	correspondent bank	取引き先銀行
torihiki saki shin-yō	trade credit	取引き先信用
torihiki seigen	trading limit	取引き制限
torihiki sho	exchange (stock, commodity)	取引所
torihiki suru	trade (v)	取引きする
torikae genka	replacement cost	取替え原価
torikeshi kanō shintaku	revocable trust	取消可能信託
torikesu	cancel (v)/nullify (v)	取消す
torikuroru etan	trichloroethane	トリクロルエタン
torishimari yaku	director	取締役
torishimariyaku kai	board of directors	取締役会
torishimariyaku kaichō	chairman of the board	取締役会長
torishimariyaku kaigi	board meeting	取締役会議
toritate kikan	collection period	取立て期間
toritsugi	commission (agency)	取次
toriwake yō supūn	serving spoon	取分け用スプーン
tōroku kijitsu	record date	登録期日
tōroku shōhyō	registered trademark	登録商標

toruen	toluene	トルエン
toruku	torque	トルク
tōsan	failure (business)	倒産
tōsan suru	fail (business) (v)	倒産する
tōshi	investment	投資
toshi	year	年
tōshi bunseki	investment analysis	投資分析
tōshi busoku no	undercapitalized (adj)	投資不足の
tōshi funani shōken	through bill of lading	通し船荷証券
tōshi ginkō	investment bank	投資銀行
tōshi kanri	portfolio management	投資管理
tōshi keikaku	investment program	投資計画
tōshi kijun	investment criteria	投資基準
tōshi komon	investment adviser	投資顧問
tōshi komon gaisha	investment management company	投資顧問会社
toshi no mu keikaku kakudai	urban sprawl	都市の無計画拡大
tōshi rimawari	return on investment	投資利回り
toshi sai kaihatsu	urban renewal	都市再開発
tōshi satei	investment appraisal	投資査定
tōshi seisaku	investment policy	投資政策
tōshi senryaku	investment strategy	投資戦略
tōshi shintaku	investment trust	投資信託
tōshi shintaku gaisha	investment company	投資信託会社
tōshi shintaku ginkō	investment trust bank	投資信託銀行
tōshi shin-yō	investment credit	投資信用
tōshi shūeki ritsu	return on investment	投資収益率
tōshi suru	invest (v)	投資する
tōshi yosan	investment budget	投資予算
Tōshō	Tokyo Stock Exchange	東証
tosō	paint	塗装
tōza kanjō	current account	当座勘定
tōza karikoshi o mitomeru	grant an overdraft (v)	当座借越しを認める
tōza kashi koshi	overdraft	当座貸越し
tōza shinogi no	makeshift (adj)	当座しのぎの
tōza shinogi no shudan	makeshift (n)	当座しのぎの手段
tōza yokin kōza	checking account	当座預金口座
tōzen no chūi	reasonable care	当然の注意
tsūchi jō	advice note	通知状
tsūchi no tōri	as per advice	通知の通り
tsūchō chokin kōza	passbook savings account	通帳貯金口座
tsugime nashi kōkan	seamless steel tube	継ぎ目なし鋼管
tsuika jōkō	codicil/rider (contracts)	追加条項
tsuika shōko kin	margin call	追加証拠金
tsuika tokuyaku	addendum (insurance)	追加特約
tsuiseki chōsa suru	follow up (v)	追跡調査する
tsūka	currency/money	通貨
tsūka kirikae	currency conversion	通貨切り替え

T

tsūka kyōkyū ryō	money supply	通貨供給量
tsūka no ryūtsū sokudo	velocity of money	通貨の流通速度
tsūka shūshuku	deflation	通貨収縮
tsūka tai	currency band	通貨帯
tsūka teiraku	depreciation of currency	通貨低落
tsūka yakkan	currency clause	通貨約款
tsūkan kisei	customs regulations	通関規制
tsūkan menkyo	entry permit	通関免許
tsūkō ken	right of way	通行権
tsukuru ka kau ka no kettei	make-or-buy decision	作るか買うかの決定
tsumemono	stuffing	詰め物
tsumi ni	cargo	積荷
tsumi nokoshi hin	short shipment	積残し品
tsumikomi nimotsu	stowage	積込み荷物
tsumini kajū	overcharge (shipping)	積荷過重
tsumini mokuroku	manifest	積荷目録
tsumini shūsen ryō	address commission	積荷周旋料
tsūsanshō	Ministry of International Trade and Industry (MITI)	通産省
tsūshin	correspondence	通信
tsūshō	commerce	通商
tsūshō daihyō	Trade Representative (U.S.)	通商代表
tsūshō sangyō shō	Ministry of International Trade and Industry (MITI)	通商産業省
tsūshō teishi	embargo	通商停止
tsuya dashi no	glossy (adj)	つや出しの
tsuya keshi no	matt (adj)	つや消しの
tsuyoki	long interest (securities)	強気

U

uehā	wafer	ウエハー
uke zara	saucer	受け皿
ukeire kensa	acceptance test	受入れ検査
ukeire mihon nukitori kensa	acceptance sampling	受入れ見本抜取検査
ukeoi unsō gyōsha	contract carrier	請負運送業者
uketori kanjō	accounts receivable	受取勘定
uketori nin	beneficiary/payee	受取り人
uketori shō	receipt	受取り書
uketori yakusoku tegata	notes receivable	受取り約束手形
ukewatashi basho	delivery points	受渡し場所
ukewatashi bi	date of delivery	受渡し日
ukewatashi daka busoku	short delivery	受渡し高不足
ukewatashi hyōjun nedan	delivery price (securities)	受渡し標準値段

ukewatashi yūyo	backwardation	受渡し猶予
ukewatashibi	value date	受渡日
umeni	broken stowage	埋荷
unchin komi	freight included	運賃込み
unchin komi nedan	cost and freight, delivery price (shipping)	運賃込み値段
unchin mae barai	freight prepaid	運賃前払い
unchin tatekae barai kyōyaku	freight allowed	運賃立替払い協約
unchin tōchaku chi barai	freight collect	運賃到着地払い
un-ei honbu	operations headquarters	運営本部
unpan chin	drayage	運搬賃
unsōchū	in transit (adv)	運送中
unsō gyōsha	carrier, forwarding agent	運送業者
unsō gyōsha kiken tanpo	carrier's risk	運送業者危険担保
unten hi	running expenses	運転費
unten shihon	working capital	運転資本
unten shikin	working funds	運転資金
un-yō jisseki	performance	運用実績
un-yō shisan	working assets	運用資産
uragaki	endorsement	裏書き
uragaki kamotsu uketori shō	backed note (shipping)	裏書き貨物受取証
uragaki nin	endorser	裏書き人
uraji	lining	裏地
uri koshi	short position	売り越し
uri ni dasu	offer for sale (v)	売りに出す
uri nushi	vendor	売主
uri nushi horyū ken	vendor's lien	売主保留権
uri opushon	put option	売りオプション
uri sōba	bear market	売相場
uriage daka	proceeds	売上高
uriage genka	cost of goods sold	売り上げ原価
uriage zei	sales tax	売り上げ税
urigake kin kanjō	charge account	売掛け金勘定
urisugiru	oversell (v)	売りすぎる
uritsunagi	hedge-selling	売りつなぎ
uriwatashi shōsho	bill of sale/deed of sale	売渡し証書
uru	sell (v)	売る
ūru	wool	ウール
uttaeru	sue	訴える
uwamuki shikyō	upmarket	上向き市況

W

wādo purosessa	word processor	ワード・プロセッサ
wain gurasu	wineglass	ワイン・グラス
wakai	amicable settlement, reconciliation	和解

wāku sutēshon	work station	ワーク・ステーション
wakuchin	vaccine	ワクチン
wāpuro	word processor	ワープロ
wāpuro shori	word processing	ワープロ処理
waranto	warrant	ワラント
wari modoshi	rebate (finance)	割戻し
wariai	rate	割合
wariate	allotment	割当て
wariate gaku	quota	割当て額
wariate sei	quota system	割当て制
wariateru	allot (v)	割当てる
waribiki	allowance (sales)/ discount (n)	割引き
waribiki saiken	discount securities	割引き債券
waribiki suru	discount (v)	割引きする
warimashi kin tsuki shōkan	redemption with a premium	割増し金付き償還
warimodoshi	abatement	割戻し
waritsuke	layout	割付け
waritsuke yō daishi	mechanical	割付け用台紙
windōzu	Windows	ウィンドーズ

Y

yakan yokin hokan sho	night depository	夜間預金保管所
yaki namashi	annealing	焼なまし
yakiire suru	quench (v)	焼き入れする
yakitsuke	printing	焼き付け
yakubutsu chiryō	medication	薬物治療
yakuhin	pharmaceutical	薬品
yakusoku tegata	promissory note	約束手形
yakutei	commitment	約定
yakutei sho	deed of contract	約定書
yakuzai shi	pharmacist	薬剤師
yamagata furaisu	angular cutter	山形フライス
yamaneko suto	wildcat strike	山猫スト
yami ichiba	black market	闇市場
yān	yarn	ヤーン
yasui	cheap (adj)	安い
yobi mizu seisaku	pump priming	呼び水政策
yobine	bid and asked, offered price	呼び値
yobō hozen	preventive maintenance	予防保全
yōchi sangyō	infant industry	幼稚産業
yōdo	iodine	ヨード
yōeki	solution (chemicals)	溶液
yōga	positive (photography)	陽画
yohaku o kiriotosu	crop (v)	余白を切り落とす

yoi goshi no	overnight (adj)	宵越しの
yōkai do	solubility	溶解度
yokin	deposit	預金
yokin hikidashi hyō	counter check	預金引出票
yokin kanjō	deposit account	預金勘定
yokin shōsho	certificate of deposit	預金証書
yokin tsūchō	passbook	預金通帳
yokobai ni naru	level out (v)	横ばいになる
yokoku	advance notice	予告
yokujitsu mono	overnight (securities) (n)	翌日物
yōkyū barai	payable on demand	要求払い
yōkyū barai de	on demand (adv)	要求払いで
yōkyū barai yokin	demand deposit	要求払い預金
yōkyū suru	demand (v)	要求する
yomidashi senyō memori	ROM	読み出し専用メモリ
yonrin kudō	four-wheel drive	四輪駆動
yonshoku zuri	four colors	四色刷り
yoritsuki de kau	buy on opening (v)	寄付きで買う
yoritsuki nedan	opening price	寄付き値段
yoritsuki sōba chūmon de	at the opening (adv)	寄付き相場注文で
yoron chōsa	public opinion poll	世論調査
yōryō	content (pharmaceuticals)	容量
yosan	budget	予算
yosan mitsumori	budget forecast	予算見積り
yosan wariate	budget appropriation	予算割当て
yosan yosoku	budget forecast	予算予測
yōseki ton sū	tonnage	容積トン数
yōsen	charter (shipping)	傭船
yōsen keiyaku dairiten	charterparty agent	傭船契約代理店
yōshitsu	solute	溶質
yōso	factor	要素
yōso bunseki	factor analysis	要素分析
yosō uriage daka	sales estimate	予想売り上げ高
yosoku	forecast (n)	予測
yosoku suru	forecast (v)	予測する
yotei	schedule	予定
yoyaku kin	subscription price	予約金
yotei hoken	open cover	予定保険
yōzai	solvent	溶剤
yūbin bangō	zip code	郵便番号
yūbin gawase	money order	郵便為替
yūbin saki meibo	mailing list	郵便先名簿
yude tamago tate	egg cup	ゆで卵立て
yūdō ro	induction furnace	誘導炉
yūgen sekinin	limited liability	有限責任
yuigon	will	遺言
yuigon kennin ken	probate	遺言検認権

yuigon no nai	intestate (adj)	遺言のない
yūin	incentive	誘因
yūka shōken	negotiable securities/ securities/stock (securities)	有価証券
yūka shōken meisai sho	portfolio	有価証券明細書
yūkei shisan	tangible assets	有形資産
yūkō na	valid (adj)	有効な
yūkō to mitomeru	validate (v)	有効と認める
yūkyū byōki kyūka	sick leave	有給病気休暇
yūkyū kyūka	paid holiday	有給休暇
yūkyū setsubi	idle capacity	遊休設備
yunisekkusu	unisex	ユニセックス
yunitto rōdo waribiki	unit load discount	ユニット・ロード割引き
yunyū	import (n)	輸入
yunyū chōka	adverse balance	輸入超過
yunyū hin zei	import tax	輸入品税
yunyū kachōkin	import surcharge	輸入加徴金
yunyū kanzei	import duty	輸入関税
yunyū kisei	import regulation	輸入規制
yunyū kisoku	import regulation	輸入規則
yunyū kyoka	import license	輸入許可
yunyū seigen	import restriction	輸入制限
yunyū shinkoku	import declaration	輸入申告
yunyū suru	import (v)	輸入する
yunyū tanpo	import deposits	輸入担保
yunyū tetsuzuki	import entry	輸入手続き
yunyū wariate	import quota	輸入割当て
yunyū zei	import tax	輸入税
yunyū zeiritsu	import tariff	輸入税率
yuria jushi	urea resin	ユリア樹脂
yūro bondo	Eurobond	ユーロ・ボンド
yūro darā	Eurodollar	ユーロ・ダラー
yūro tsūka	Eurocurrency	ユーロ通貨
yūryō hin	quality goods	優良品
yūryō kabu	blue chip stock	優良株
yūryō kajū	payload (transportation)	有料荷重
yūsei haguruma sōchi	planetary gear train	遊星歯車装置
yūsen kabu	preferred stock	優先株
yūsen ken	priority	優先権
yūsen saimu	preferential debts	優先債務
yūshi	loan	融資
yūshi suru	finance (v)	融資する
yushutsu burōkā	export middleman	輸出ブローカー
yushutsu dairi ten	export agent	輸出代理店
yushutsu gyōsha	export house	輸出業者
yushutsu hanbai keiyaku	export sales contract	輸出販売契約
yushutsu hin zei	export tax	輸出品税
yushutsu kachō	export manager	輸出課長

yushutsu kanzei	export duty	輸出関税
yushutsu kinshi	export ban	輸出禁止
yushutsu kisei	export regulations	輸出規制
yushutsu kyoka	export permit	輸出許可
yushutsu seigen	restrictions on export	輸出制限
yushutsu shinkoku sho	export entry	輸出申告書
yushutsu shin-yō jō	export credit	輸出信用状
yushutsu suru	export (v)	輸出する
yushutsu wariate	export quota	輸出割当て
yushutsu yō	for export	輸出用
yushutsu zei	export duty	輸出税
yushutsunyū ginkō	export-import bank	輸出入銀行
yusō	transportation	輸送
yusō yō hōsō bako	packing case	輸送用包装箱
yūtiritī	utilities (computer)	ユーティリティー
yūyo kikan	grace period	猶予期間
yūzā furendorī	user-friendly	ユーザー・フレンドリー
yūzai	guilty	有罪
yūzū tegata	accommodation bill/ accommodation paper	融通手形
yūzū tegata no furidashi	kiting (banking)	融通手形の振出し
yūzū tegata no uragaki	accommodation endorsement	融通手形の裏書
yūzū tegata shinyō jō	accommodation credit	融通手形信用状
yūzū tegata tōji sha	accommodation party	融通手形当事者

Z

zaijū shiire nin	resident buyer	在住仕入れ人
zaiko hin	inventory, stock (merchandising)	在庫品
zaiko hin kanri	inventory control, stock control	在庫品管理
zaiko kajō	overstock	在庫過剰
zaiko seihin mokuroku	finished goods inventory	在庫製品目録
zaimu bunseki	financial analysis	財務分析
zaimu dairi ten	fiscal agent	財務代理店
zaimu kanri	financial management	財務管理
zaimu kanri sha	financial director	財務管理者
zaimu keikaku	financial planning	財務計画
zaimu sai jūyō ten	financial highlights	財務最重要点
zaimu satei	financial appraisal	財務査定
zaimu shohyō	financial statement	財務諸表
zaimu tōsei	financial control	財務統制
zaimu yūin	financial incentive	財務誘因
zaimushō chōki shōken	Treasury Bond	財務省長期証券

zaimushō chūki shōken	Treasury Note	財務省中期証券
zaimushō tanki shōken	Treasury Bill	財務省短期証券
zairyō	materials	材料
zaisan	property/wealth	財産
zaisan kanri nin	estate agent	財産管理人
zaisan kizō	endowment	財産寄贈
zaisei kiban	monetary base	財政基盤
zandaka	balance	残高
zangaku kijitsu ikkatsu hensai	balloon (payment)	残額期日一括返済
zanpin	carryover (merchandising)	残品
zanson kagaku	salvage value (accounting)	残存価額
zantei yosan	interim budget	暫定予算
zatta na	miscellaneous (adj)	雑多な
zei biki rieki ritsu	after-tax real rate of return	税引き利益率
zei kōjo	tax allowance/ tax deduction	税控除
zei menjo	remission of a tax	税免除
zeigaku satei kakaku	value for duty	税額査定価格
zeihō	tax law	税法
zeikan	customs	税関
zeikan chō	collector of customs	税関長
zeikan kamotsu toriatsukai nin	customs broker	税関貨物取扱人
zeikan okuri jō	customs invoice	税関送り状
zeikan tetsuzuki	customs entry	税関手続き
zeikin	tax	税金
zeikin hinan shudan	tax shelter	税金避難手段
zeikin shiharai no gimu ga aru	liable for tax	税金支払いの義務がある
zeiritsu	tax rate	税率
zeitaku hin	luxury goods	贅沢品
zen kiken tanpo de	against all risks (insurance)	全危険担保で
zen tenkō kamera	all-weather camera	全天候カメラ
zenbu genka keisan	absorption costing (accounting)	全部原価計算
zenbu hikiuke ichibu fuka	all or none	全部引受一部不可
zenesuto	general strike	ゼネスト
zengaku shiharai	payment in full	全額支払い
zengaku shiharaizumi	paid in full	全額支払い済み
zengaku shiharau	pay up (v)	全額支払う
zenjitsu hi	net change	前日比
zenmen teki kanzei kōshō	across-the-board tariff negotiation	全面的関税交渉
zenmen teki ketchaku	across-the-board settlement	全面的決着
zenmen teki na	down-the-line (adj)	全面的な
zenmen teki ni	down the line (adv)	全面的に

zenrin kudō	front-wheel drive	前輪駆動
zenten renzu	sky lens	全天レンズ
zeoraito	zeolite	ゼオライト
zero kūpon sai	zero coupon bond	ゼロ・クーポン債
zettai ondo	absolute temperature	絶対温度
zōbun genka	incremental costs	増分原価
zōfuku ki	amplifier	増幅器
zōhei kyoku	mint	造幣局
zōka	increase (n)	増加
zōka hiyō	increased costs	増加費用
zōka kyasshu furō	incremental cash flow	増加キャッシュ・フロー
zōka ritsu	rate of increase	増加率
zōka suru	increase (v)	増加する
zōkei ki	molding machine	造形機
zōshi	new stock issue	増資
zōshoku shisan	accrued assets	増殖資産
zōtei bon	complimentary copy	贈呈本
zōwai	payoff (illegal finance)	贈賄
zuiji kakikomi yomidashi memori	RAM	随時書き込み読み出しメモリ
zuiji shōkan kōsai	redeemable bonds	随時償還公債
zūmu renzu	zoom lens	ズーム・レンズ

Z

KEY WORDS FOR KEY INDUSTRIES

The dictionary that forms the centerpiece of *Japanese for the Business Traveler* is a compendium of some 3000 words that you are likely to use or encounter as you do business abroad. It will greatly facilitate fact-finding about the business possibilities that interest you, and will help guide you through negotiations as well as reading documents. To supplement the dictionary, we have added a special feature—groupings of key terms about 15 industries. As you explore any of these industries, you'll want to have *Japanese for the Business Traveler* at your fingertips to help make sure you don't misunderstand or overlook an aspect that could have a material effect on the outcome of your business decision. The industries covered in the vocabulary lists are the following:

- *advanced technology*
- *banking and finance*
- *chemicals*
- *chinaware and tableware*
- *computers*
- *electricity and electronics*
- *fashion and textiles*
- *legal matters*
- *machine tools*
- *metalworks*
- *motor vehicles*
- *pharmaceuticals*
- *photography*
- *printing and publishing*
- *securities*

ADVANCED TECHNOLOGY

English to Japanese

advanced technology	先端技術	*sentan gijutsu*
absolute temperature	絶対温度	*zettai ondo*
amorphous semiconductor	アモルファス半導体	*amorufasu handōtai*
amorphous silicon	アモルファス・シリコン	*amorufasu shirikon*
artificial intelligence	人口知能	*jinkō chinō*
bio-ceramics	バイオセラミックス	*baio seramikkusu*
bio-computer	バイオコンピュータ	*baio konpyūta*
carbon dioxide laser	炭酸ガス・レーザー	*tansan gasu rēzā*
carbon fiber	炭素繊維	*tanso sen-i*
ceramic engine	セラミックエンジン	*seramikku enjin*
ceramic fiber	セラミックファイバー	*seramikku faibā*
ceramic filter	セラミックフィルター	*seramikku firutā*
ceramic sensor	セラミックセンサー	*seramikku sensā*
composite materials	複合材料	*fukugō zairyō*
compound semiconductor	化合物半導体	*kagō butsu handōtai*
electrical resistance	電気抵抗	*denki teikō*
electrically conductive rubber	電導性ゴム	*dendō sei gomu*
electroconductive glass	電導性ガラス	*dendō sei garasu*
electroconductive polymer	電導性高分子	*dendō sei kōbunshi*
electro-magnetic shielding	電磁波シールド	*denji ha shīrudo*
engineering plastic	エンジニアリングプラスチック	*enjiniaringu purasuchikku*
fiber-optic communication	光通信	*hikari tsūshin*
fiber-reinforced plastics	ガラス繊維強化プラスチック	*garasu sen-i kyōka purasuchikku*
fifth-generation computer	第五世代コンピュータ	*dai go sedai konpyūta*
fine ceramics	ファインセラミックス	*fain seramikkusu*
fine polymer	ファインポリマー	*fain porimā*
gas laser	気体レーザー	*kitai rēzā*
glass fiber	ガラス繊維	*garasu sen-i*
glass laser	ガラスレーザー	*garasu rēzā*
glass-reinforced cement	ガラス強化セメント	*garasu kyōka semento*
glassy semiconductor	ガラス半導体	*garasu handōtai*
heat-resistant ceramics	耐熱セラミックス	*tainetsu seramikkusu*
holographic memory	ホログラフィックメモリ	*horogurafikku memori*
hybrid materials	ハイブリッド材料	*haiburiddo zairyō*
intelligent robot	知能ロボット	*chinō robotto*
Josephson device	ジョセフソン素子	*Josefuson soshi*
laser	レーザー	*rēzā*
laser fusion	レーザー核融合	*rēzā kaku yūgō*

laser processing	レーザー加工	*rēzā kakō*
light-emitting diode	発光ダイオード	*hakkō daiōdo*
liquid crystal	液晶	*ekishō*
liquid helium	液体ヘリウム	*ekitai heriumu*
magnetic fluid	磁性液体	*jisei ekitai*
new ceramics	ニューセラミックス	*nyū seramikkusu*
new materials	新素材	*shin sozai*
optical cable	光ケーブル	*hikari kētburu*
optical computer	光コンピュータ	*hikari konpyūta*
optical disc	光ディスク	*hikari disuku*
optical fiber	光ファイバー	*hikari faibā*
optical integrated circuit	光半導体	*hikari handōtai*
optical magnetic memory	光磁気メモリ	*hikari jiki memori*
optical memory	光メモリ	*hikari memori*
optical transmission	光伝送	*hikari densō*
opto-electronics	光技術	*hikari gijutsu*
opto-electronics industry	光産業	*hikari sangyō*
pattern recognition	パターン認識	*patān ninshiki*
perfect crystal device technology	完全結晶技術	*kanzen kesshō gijutsu*
photo conductive materials	光電導物質	*hikari dendō busshitsu*
photo conductivity	光電導	*hikari dendō*
photo electromagnetic effect	光電磁効果	*hikari denji kōka*
pulse	パルス	*parusu*
semiconductor laser	半導体レーザー	*handōtai rēzā*
solid-state laser	固体レーザー	*kotai rēzā*
superconducting ceramics	超電導セラミックス	*chō dendō seramikkusu*
superconductive coil	超電導コイル	*chō dendō koiru*
superconductive materials	超電導材料	*chō dendō zairyō*
superconductive phenomena	超電導現象	*chō dendō genshō*
superconductor	超電導体	*chō dendō tai*
super lattice	超格子	*chō kōshi*
transmission loss	伝送損失	*densō sonshitsu*

Japanese to English

amorufasu handōtai	amorphous semiconductor	アモルファス半導体
amorufasu shirikon	amorphous silicon	アモルファス・シリコン
baio konpyūta	bio-computer	バイオコンピュータ
baio seramikkusu	bio-ceramics	バイオセラミックス
chinō robotto	intelligent robot	知能ロボット
chō dendō genshō	superconductive phenomena	超電導現象
chō dendō koiru	superconductive coil	超電導コイル
chō dendō seramikkusu	superconducting ceramics	超電導セラミックス
chō dendō tai	superconductor	超電導体
chō dendō zairyō	superconductive materials	超電導材料

chō kōshi	super lattice	超格子
dai go sedai konpyūta	fifth-generation computer	第五世代コンピュータ
dendō sei garasu	electroconductive glass	電導性ガラス
dendō sei gomu	electrically conductive rubber	電導性ゴム
dendō sei kōbunshi	electroconductive polymer	電導性高分子
denji ha shīrudo	electro-magnetic shielding	電磁波シールド
denki teikō	electrical resistance	電気抵抗
densō sonshitsu	transmission loss	伝送損失
ekishō	liquid crystal	液晶
ekitai heriumu	liquid helium	液体ヘリウム
enjiniaringu purasuchikku	engineering plastic	エンジニアリングプラスチック
fain porimā	fine polymer	ファインポリマー
fain seramikkusu	fine ceramics	ファインセラミックス
fukugō zairyō	composite materials	複合材料
garasu handōtai	glassy semiconductor	ガラス半導体
garasu kyōka semento	glass-reinforced cement	ガラス強化セメント
garasu rēzā	glass laser	ガラスレーザー
garasu sen-i	glass fiber	ガラス繊維
garasu sen-i kyōka purasuchikku	fiber-reinforced plastics	ガラス繊維強化プラスチック
haiburuddo zairyō	hybrid materials	ハイブリッド材料
hakkō daiōdo	light-emitting diode	発光ダイオード
handōtai rēzā	semiconductor laser	半導体レーザー
hikari dendō	photo conductivity	光電導
hikari dendō busshitsu	photo conductive materials	光電導物質
hikari denji kōka	photo electromagnetic effect	光電磁効果
hikari densō	optical transmission	光伝送
hikari disuku	optical disc	光ディスク
hikari faibā	optical fiber	光ファイバー
hikari gijutsu	opto-electronics	光技術
hikari handōtai	optical integrated circuit	光半導体
hikari jiki memori	optical magnetic memory	光磁気メモリ
hikari kēburu	optical cable	光ケーブル
hikari konpyūta	optical computer	光コンピュータ
hikari memori	optical memory	光メモリ
hikari sangyō	opto-electronics industry	光産業
hikari tsūshin	fiber-optic communication	光通信

horogurafikku memori	holographic memory	ホログラフィックメモリ
jinkō chinō	artificial intelligence	人口知能
jisei ekitai	magnetic fluid	磁性液体
Josefuson soshi	Josephson device	ジョセフソン素子
kagō butsu handōtai	compound semiconductor	化合物半導体
kanzen kesshō gijutsu	perfect crystal device technology	完全結晶技術
kitai rēzā	gas laser	気体レーザー
kotai rēzā	solid-state laser	固体レーザー
nyū seramikkusu	new ceramics	ニューセラミックス
parusu	pulse	パルス
patān ninshiki	pattern recognition	パターン認識
rēzā	laser	レーザー
rēzā kakō	laser processing	レーザー加工
rēzā kaku yūgō	laser fusion	レーザー核融合
sentan gijutsu	advanced technology	先端技術
seramikku enjin	ceramic engine	セラミックエンジン
seramikku faibā	ceramic fiber	セラミックファイバー
seramikku firutā	ceramic filter	セラミックフィルター
seramikku sensā	ceramic sensor	セラミックセンサー
shin sozai	new materials	新素材
tainetsu seramikkusu	heat-resistant ceramics	耐熱セラミックス
tansan gasu rēzā	carbon dioxide laser	炭酸ガス・レーザー
tanso sen-i	carbon fiber	炭素繊維
zettai ondo	absolute temperature	絶対温度

BANKING AND FINANCE

English to Japanese

account	口座	*kōza*
account number	口座番号	*kōza bangō*
account statement	勘定書	*kanjōsho*
advance	前貸金	*maegashikin*
assets	資産	*shisan*
automatic collection service	自動集金サービス	*jidō shūkin sābisu*
automatic teller machine	自動預金受払機	*jidō yokin ukebarai ki*
automatic transfer service	自動振替サービス	*jidō furikae sābisu*
average yield	平均利回り	*heikin rimawari*
balance	残高	*zandaka*
bank	銀行	*ginkō*
bank bill	銀行手形	*ginkō tegata*
bank note	銀行券	*ginkō ken*
borrowing cost	借入コスト	*shakunyū kosuto*
branch	支店	*shiten*
cable transfer	電信送金	*denshin sōkin*
cancellation	解約	*kaiyaku*
carry-forward	繰越	*kurikoshi*
cash	現金	*genkin*
cashier's check	銀行小切手	*ginkō kogitte*
certificate of deposit	預金証書	*yokinshōsho*
certified check	支払保証小切手	*shiharai hoshō kogitte*
check (n)	小切手	*kogitte*
checking account	当座預金口座	*tōza yokin kōza*
collateral	担保	*tanpo*
commercial bank	商業銀行	*shōgyō ginkō*
compound interest	複利	*fukuri*
consumer credit company	信販会社	*shinpan gaisha*
consumer loan	消費者ローン	*shōhisha rōn*
contract	契約	*keiyaku*
credit	信用	*shin-yō*
credit account	掛勘定	*kakekanjō*
credit card	クレジットカード	*kurejittokādo*
credit check	信用調査	*shin-yō chōsa*
credit line	貸出限度額	*kashidashi gendo gaku*
credit rating	信用格付け	*shin-yō kakuzuke*
credit reference	信用照会	*shin-yō shōkai*
creditor	債権者	*saikensha*
debit	負債	*fusai*
debt	負債	*fusai*
deduction	控除	*kōjo*
default	支払不能	*shiharai funō*
deposit	預金	*yokin*
dishonored check	不渡小切手	*fuwatari kogitte*
down payment	頭金／前渡金	*atamakin/maewatashikin*
draft	手形	*tegata*

due date	満期日	*mankibi*
endorsement	裏書き	*uragaki*
fixed rate	固定金利	*kotei kinri*
fund	資金	*shikin*
funding	資金調達	*shikin chōtatsu*
grace period	支払猶予期間	*shiharai yūyo kikan*
guarantee	保証	*hoshō*
home equity loan	ホームエクイティ・ローン	*hōmuekuiti rōn*
home mortgage	住宅モーゲージ	*jūtaku mōgēji*
housing loan	住宅ローン	*jūtaku rōn*
IOU	借用証書	*shakuyō shōsho*
income	収入／所得	*shūnyū/shotoku*
income return	所得申告	*shotoku shinkoku*
income tax rate	所得税率	*shotoku zeiritsu*
individual retirement account	個人退職年金勘定	*kojin taishoku nenkin kanjō*
interest	利子	*rishi*
interest rate	金利	*kinri*
investment	投資	*tōshi*
investment bank	投資銀行	*tōshi ginkō*
investment management company	投資顧問会社	*tōshi komon gaisha*
investment trust bank	投資信託銀行	*tōshi shintaku ginkō*
lending	貸付	*kashitsuke*
liability	債務	*saimu*
loan	融資／貸付	*yūshi/kashitsuke*
local bank	地方銀行	*chihō ginkō*
long-term credit bank	長期信用銀行	*chōki shin-yō ginkō*
maturity	満期	*manki*
money market account	短期金融口座	*tanki kin-yū kōza*
mortgage	モーゲージ／抵当権	*mōgēji/teitō ken*
mortgage bank	抵当銀行	*teitō ginkō*
net profit	純益	*jun-eki*
official discount rate	公定歩合	*kōtei buai*
overdraft	借方勘定／当座貸越し	*kashigata kanjō/tōza kashikoshi*
passbook savings account	通帳貯金口座	*tsūchō chokin kōza*
payee	受取人	*uketorinin*
payer	支払人	*shiharainin*
payment terms	支払条件	*shiharai jōken*
penalty	違約金	*iyakukin*
per annum rate	年利	*nenri*
personal check	個人当座小切手	*kojin tōza kogitte*
personal income	個人所得	*kojin shotoku*
personal income tax	個人所得税	*kojin shotoku zei*
personal income tax rate	個人所得税率	*kojin shotoku zeiritsu*
prepayment	前払い	*maebarai*
prime rate	プライムレート	*puraimurēto*
principal	元金	*gankin*

principal and interest	元利	*ganri*
promissory note	約束手形	*yakusoku tegata*
real estate	不動産	*fudōsan*
real estate tax	固定資産税	*kotei shisan zei*
real interest rate	実質金利	*jisshitsu kinri*
real yield	実質利回り	*jisshitsu rimawari*
remittance check	送金小切手	*sōkin kogitte*
renewal	更新	*kōshin*
repayment	返済	*hensai*
revenue	収入	*shūnyū*
revolving credit	回転信用	*kaiten shin-yō*
safe deposit box	貸金庫	*kashi kinko*
savings bank	貯蓄銀行	*chochiku ginkō*
simple interest	単利	*tanri*
stop-payment	支払停止	*shiharai teishi*
tax	税金	*zeikin*
tax rate	税率	*zeiritsu*
time deposit	定期預金	*teiki yokin*
transfer slip	振替伝票	*furikae denpyō*
trust	信託	*shintaku*
trust bank	信託銀行	*shintaku ginkō*
trust company	信託会社	*shintaku gaisha*
unsecured	無担保の	*mutanpo no*
value date	受渡日	*ukewatashibi*
variable rate	変動利率	*hendō riritsu*
void	無効	*mukō*
withdrawal	引き出し	*hikidashi*
yield	利回り	*rimawari*

Japanese to English

atamakin	down payment	頭金
chihō ginkō	local bank	地方銀行
chochiku ginkō	savings bank	貯蓄銀行
chōki shin-yō ginkō	long-term credit bank	長期信用銀行
denshin sōkin	cable transfer	電信送金
fudōsan	real estate	不動産
fukuri	compound interest	複利
furikae denpyō	transfer slip	振替伝票
fusai	debit/debt	負債
fuwatari kogitte	dishonored check	不渡小切手
gankin	principal	元金
ganri	principal and interest	元利
genkin	cash	現金
ginkō	bank	銀行
ginkō ken	bank note	銀行券
ginkō kogitte	cashier's check	銀行小切手
ginkō tegata	bank bill	銀行手形
heikin rimawari	average yield	平均利回り
hendō riritsu	variable rate	変動利率

hensai	repayment	返済
hikidashi	withdrawal	引き出し
hōmuekuiti rōn	home equity loan	ホームエクイティ・ローン
hoshō	guarantee	保証
iyakukin	penalty	違約金
jidō furikae sābisu	automatic transfer service	自動振替サービス
jidō shūkin sābisu	automatic collection service	自動集金サービス
jidō yokin ukebarai ki	automatic teller machine	自動預金受払機
jisshitsu kinri	real interest rate	実質金利
jisshitsu rimawari	real yield	実質利回り
jun-eki	net profit	純益
jūtaku mōgēji	home mortgage	住宅モーゲージ
jūtaku rōn	housing loan	住宅ローン
kaiten shin-yō	revolving credit	回転信用
kaiyaku	cancellation	解約
kakekanjō	credit account	掛勘定
kanjōsho	account statement	勘定書
kashidashi gendo gaku	credit line	貸出限度額
kashigata kanjō	overdraft	借方勘定
kashi kinko	safe deposit box	貸金庫
kashitsuke	lending/loan	貸付
keiyaku	contract	契約
kinri	interest rate	金利
kogitte	check (n)	小切手
kojin shotoku	personal income	個人所得
kojin shotoku zei	personal income tax	個人所得税
kojin shotoku zeiritsu	personal income tax rate	個人所得税率
kojin taishoku nenkin kanjō	individual retirement account	個人退職年金勘定
kojin tōza kogitte	personal check	個人当座小切手
kōjo	deduction	控除
kōshin	renewal	更新
kōtei buai	official discount rate	公定歩合
kotei kinri	fixed rate	固定金利
kotei shisan zei	real estate tax	固定資産税
kōza	account	口座
kōza bangō	account number	口座番号
kurejittokādo	credit card	クレジットカード
kurikoshi	carry-forward	繰越
maebarai	prepayment	前払い
maegashikin	advance	前貸金
maewatashikin	down payment	前渡金
manki	maturity	満期
mankibi	due date	満期日
mōgēji	mortgage	モーゲージ

mukō	void	無効
mutanpo no	unsecured	無担保の
nenri	per annum rate	年利
puraimurēto	prime rate	プライムレート
rimawari	yield	利回り
rishi	interest	利子
saikensha	creditor	債権者
saimu	liability	債務
shakunyū kosuto	borrowing cost	借入コスト
shakuyō shōsho	IOU	借用証書
shiharai funō	default	支払不能
shiharai hoshō kogitte	certified check	支払保証小切手
shiharai jōken	payment terms	支払条件
shiharai teishi	stop-payment	支払停止
shiharai yūyo kikan	grace period	支払猶予期間
shiharainin	payer	支払人
shikin	fund	資金
shikin chōtatsu	funding	資金調達
shinpan gaisha	consumer credit company	信販会社
shintaku	trust	信託
shintaku gaisha	trust company	信託会社
shintaku ginkō	trust bank	信託銀行
shin-yō	credit	信用
shin-yō chōsa	credit check	信用調査
shin-yō kakuzuke	credit rating	信用格付け
shin-yō shōkai	credit reference	信用照会
shisan	assets	資産
shiten	branch	支店
shōgyō ginkō	commercial bank	商業銀行
shōhisha rōn	consumer loan	消費者ローン
shotoku	income	所得
shotoku shinkoku	income return	所得申告
shotoku zeiritsu	income tax rate	所得税率
shūnyū	revenue/income	収入
sōkin kogitte	remittance check	送金小切手
tanki kin-yū kōza	money market account	短期金融口座
tanpo	collateral	担保
tanri	simple interest	単利
tegata	draft	手形
teiki yokin	time deposit	定期預金
teitō ginkō	mortgage bank	抵当銀行
teitō ken	mortgage	抵当権
tōshi	investment	投資
tōshi ginkō	investment bank	投資銀行
tōshi komon gaisha	investment management company	投資顧問会社
tōshi shintaku ginkō	investment trust bank	投資信託銀行
tōza kashikoshi	overdraft	当座貸越し

tōza yokin kōza	checking account	当座預金口座
tsūchō chokin kōza	passbook savings account	通帳貯金口座
uketorinin	payee	受取人
ukewatashibi	value date	受渡日
uragaki	endorsement	裏書き
yakusoku tegata	promissory note	約束手形
yokin	deposit	預金
yokinshōsho	certificate of deposit	預金証書
yūshi	loan	融資
zandaka	balance	残高
zeikin	tax	税金
zeiritsu	tax rate	税率

CHEMICALS

English to Japanese

acetaldehyde	アセトアルデヒド	*aseto arudehido*
acetate	アセテート	*asetēto*
acetic acid	酢酸	*sakusan*
acetone	アセトン	*aseton*
acid (adj)	酸性の	*san sei no*
acrylamide	アクリルアミド	*akuriru amido*
acrylonitrile	アクリロニトル	*akuriro nitoru*
alkaline (adj)	アルカリ性の	*arukari sei no*
alkylbenzene	アルキルベンゼン	*arukiru benzen*
amine	アミン	*amin*
ammonia	アンモニア	*anmonia*
base	塩基	*enki*
benzene	ベンゼン	*benzen*
biochemistry	生化学	*sei kagaku*
bisphenol	ビスフェノール	*bisu fenōru*
butanol	ブタノール	*butanōru*
catalyst	触媒	*shokubai*
chemical fertilizer	化学肥料	*kagaku hiryō*
chloride	塩化物	*enka butsu*
chloroform	クロロホルム	*kurorohorumu*
compound	化合物	*kagō butsu*
distillation	蒸留	*jōryū*
electrolysis	電気分解	*denki bunkai*
enzyme	酵素	*kōso*
ethane	エタン	*etan*
ether	エーテル	*ēteru*
ethylene	エチレン	*echiren*
ethylene dichloride	二塩化エチレン	*ni enka echiren*
ethylene glycol	エチレングリコール	*echiren gurikōru*
ethylene oxide	エチレンオキサイド	*echiren okisaido*
formaline	ホルマリン	*horumarin*
hydrocarbon	炭化水素	*tanka suiso*
hydrochloric acid	塩酸	*ensan*
hydrolysis	加水分解	*kasui bunkai*
ionomer resin	アイオノマー樹脂	*aionomā jushi*
latex	ラテックス	*ratekkusu*
methane	メタン	*metan*
methanol	メタノール	*metanōru*
naphtha	ナフサ	*nafusa*
neutral (adj)	中性の	*chūsei no*
nitrate	硝酸塩	*shōsan en*
nitric acid	硝酸	*shōsan*
nitrite	亜硝酸塩	*a shōsan en*
oxidation	酸化	*sanka*
pentaerythritol	ペンタエリスリトール	*penta erisuritōru*

petrochemicals	石油化学製品	*sekiyu kagaku seihin*
petroleum	石油	*sekiyu*
phenol	フェノール	*fenōru*
phosphate	燐酸塩	*rinsan en*
polymer	重合体	*jūgō tai*
polystyrene	ポリスチレン	*porisuchiren*
polyurethane	ポリウレタン	*poriuretan*
propylene	プロピレン	*puropiren*
reduction	還元	*kangen*
salt	塩	*en*
saponification	鹸化	*kenka*
solubility	溶解度	*yōkai do*
solute	溶質	*yōshitsu*
solution	溶液	*yōeki*
solvent	溶剤	*yōzai*
styrene monomer	スチレンモノマー	*suchiren monomā*
sulfate	硫酸塩	*ryūsan en*
sulfuric acid	硫酸	*ryūsan*
toluene	トルエン	*toruen*
trichloroethane	トリクロルエタン	*torikuroru etan*
urea	尿素	*nyōso*
urea resin	ユリア樹脂	*yuria jushi*
water-absorbing resin	高吸水性樹脂	*kō kyūsui sei jushi*
xylene	キシレン	*kishiren*
zeolite	ゼオライト	*zeoraito*

Japanese to English

aionomā jushi	ionomer resin	アイオノマー樹脂
akuriro nitoru	acrylonitrile	アクリロニトル
akuriru amido	acrylamide	アクリルアミド
amin	amine	アミン
anmonia	ammonia	アンモニア
arukari sei no	alkaline (adj)	アルカリ性の
arukiru benzen	alkylbenzene	アルキルベンゼン
asetēto	acetate	アセテート
aseto arudehido	acetaldehyde	アセトアルデヒド
aseton	acetone	アセトン
a shōsan en	nitrite	亜硝酸塩
benzen	benzene	ベンゼン
bisu fenōru	bisphenol	ビスフェノール
butanōru	butanol	ブタノール
chūsei no	neutral (adj)	中性の
denki bunkai	electrolysis	電気分解
echiren	ethylene	エチレン
echiren gurikōru	ethylene glycol	エチレングリコール
echiren okisaido	ethylene oxide	エチレンオキサイド
en	salt	塩
enka butsu	chloride	塩化物

enki	base	塩基
ensan	hydrochloric acid	塩酸
etan	ethane	エタン
ēteru	ether	エーテル
fenōru	phenol	フェノール
horumarin	formaline	ホルマリン
jōryū	distillation	蒸留
jūgō tai	polymer	重合体
kagaku hiryō	chemical fertilizer	化学肥料
kagō butsu	compound	化合物
kangen	reduction	還元
kasui bunkai	hydrolysis	加水分解
kenka	saponification	鹸化
kishiren	xylene	キシレン
kō kyūsui sei jushi	water-absorbing resin	高吸水性樹脂
kōso	enzyme	酵素
kurorokorumu	chloroform	クロロホルム
metan	methane	メタン
metanōru	methanol	メタノール
nafusa	naphtha	ナフサ
ni enka echiren	ethylene dichloride	二塩化エチレン
nyōso	urea	尿素
penta erisuritōru	pentaerythritol	ペンタエリスリトール
porisuchiren	polystyrene	ポリスチレン
poriuretan	polyurethane	ポリウレタン
puropiren	propylene	プロピレン
ratekkusu	latex	ラテックス
rinsan en	phosphate	燐酸塩
ryūsan	sulfuric acid	硫酸
ryūsan en	sulfate	硫酸塩
sakusan	acetic acid	酢酸
sanka	oxidation	酸化
san sei no	acid (adj)	酸性の
sei kagaku	biochemistry	生化学
sekiyu	petroleum	石油
sekiyu kagaku seihin	petrochemicals	石油化学製品
shokubai	catalyst	触媒
shōsan	nitric acid	硝酸
shōsan en	nitrate	硝酸塩
suchiren monomā	styrene monomer	スチレンモノマー
tanka suiso	hydrocarbon	炭化水素
torikuroru etan	trichloroethane	トリクロルエタン
toruen	toluene	トルエン
yōeki	solution	溶液
yōkai do	solubility	溶解度
yōshitsu	solute	溶質
yōzai	solvent	溶剤
yuria jushi	urea resin	ユリア樹脂
zeoraito	zeolite	ゼオライト

CHINAWARE AND TABLEWARE

English to Japanese

basket	バスケット	*basuketto*
bone china	ボーンチャイナ	*bōn chaina*
bowl	ボール	*bōru*
breadbasket	パンかご	*pan kago*
butter dish	バター皿	*batā zara*
butter knife	バターナイフ	*batā naifu*
candlestick	ろうそく立て	*rōsoku tate*
carving knife	切り盛り用ナイフ	*kiri mori yō naifu*
champagne glass	シャンペン・グラス	*shanpen gurasu*
cheese tray	チーズの盛り皿	*chīzu no mori zara*
china	磁器	*jiki*
coaster	コップ敷き	*koppu shiki*
coffeepot	コーヒーポット	*kōhī potto*
crystal glass	カットグラス	*katto gurasu*
cup	茶わん	*chawan*
cutlery	刃物類	*hamono rui*
decanter	デカンター	*dekantā*
dessert plate	デザート皿	*dezāto zara*
dish	皿	*sara*
earthenware	陶器	*tōki*
egg cup	ゆで卵立て	*yude tamago tate*
espresso cup	エスプレッソコーヒー用茶わん	*esupuresso kōhī yō chawan*
flute	細長いシャンペン・グラス	*hosonagai shanpen gurasu*
fork	フォーク	*fōku*
glass	コップ	*koppu*
goldplated (adj)	金めっきの	*kin mekki no*
gravy boat	肉汁ソース入れ	*niku jū sōsu ire*
handblown glass	口吹きグラス	*kuchi buki gurasu*
handmade (adj)	手作りの	*tezukuri no*
handpainted (adj)	手塗りの	*tenuri no*
ice bucket	氷入れ	*kōri ire*
knife	ナイフ	*naifu*
lace	レース	*rēsu*
ladle	ひしゃく	*hishaku*
linen (adj)	麻性の	*asa sei no*
mug	マグカップ	*magu kappu*
napkin	ナプキン	*napukin*
pastry server	菓子の切り盛りナイフ	*kashi no kiri mori naifu*
pattern	模様	*moyō*
pepper mill	こしょうひき	*koshō hiki*
pepper shaker	こしょう入れ	*koshō ire*
pitcher	水差し	*mizu sashi*
place mat	テーブルマット	*tēburu matto*

place setting	一人前の食卓用食器具	*ichinin mae no shokutaku yō shokkigu*
plate	皿	*sara*
platter	大皿	*ōzara*
pottery	陶器類	*tōki rui*
salad bowl	サラダボール	*sarada bōru*
salad plate	サラダの取り皿	*sarada no tori zara*
salt shaker	塩振り容器	*shio furi yōki*
saucer	受け皿	*uke zara*
serving spoon	取り分け用スプーン	*toriwake yō supūn*
set	セット	*setto*
silverplated (adj)	銀めっきの	*gin mekki no*
silverware	食卓用銀器	*shokutaku yō ginki*
soup dish	スープ皿	*sūpu zara*
soupspoon	スープ用スプーン	*sūpū yō supūn*
spoon	スプーン	*supūn*
stainless steel	ステンレス	*sutenresu*
stoneware	厚手の陶器	*atsude no tōki*
sugar bowl	砂糖壷	*satō tsubo*
tablecloth	テーブルクロス	*tēburu kurosu*
tablespoon	大さじ	*ōsaji*
teapot	ティーポット	*tī potto*
teaspoon	小さじ	*kosaji*
tray	盆	*bon*
trivet	三脚台	*sankyaku dai*
tureen	ふた付き深皿	*futa tsuki fuka zara*
vinyl (adj)	ビニール製の	*binīru sei no*
wineglass	ワイングラス	*wain gurasu*

Japanese to English

asa sei no	linen (adj)	麻製の
atsude no tōki	stoneware	厚手の陶器
basuketto	basket	バスケット
batā naifu	butter knife	バターナイフ
batā zara	butter dish	バター皿
binīru sei no	vinyl (adj)	ビニール製の
bon	tray	盆
bōn chaina	bone china	ボーンチャイナ
bōru	bowl	ボール
chawan	cup	茶わん
chīzu no mori zara	cheese tray	チーズの盛り皿
dekantā	decanter	デカンター
dezāto zara	dessert plate	デザート皿
esupuresso kōhī yō chawan	espresso cup	エスプレッソコーヒー用茶わん
fōku	fork	フォーク
futa tsuki fuka zara	tureen	ふた付き深皿
gin mekki no	silverplated (adj)	銀めっきの

hamono rui	cutlery	刃物類
hishaku	ladle	ひしゃく
hosonagai shanpen gurasu	flute	細長いシャンペン・グラス
ichinin mae no shokutaku yō shokkigu	place setting	一人前の食卓用食器具
jiki	china	磁器
kashi no kiri mori naifu	pastry server	菓子の切り盛りナイフ
katto gurasu	crystal glass	カットグラス
kin mekki no	goldplated (adj)	金めっきの
kiri mori yō naifu	carving knife	切り盛り用ナイフ
kōhī potto	coffeepot	コーヒーポット
koppu	glass	コップ
koppu shiki	coaster	コップ敷き
kōri ire	ice bucket	氷入れ
kosaji	teaspoon	小さじ
koshō hiki	pepper mill	こしょうひき
koshō ire	pepper shaker	こしょう入れ
kuchi buki gurasu	handblown glass	口吹きグラス
magu kappu	mug	マグカップ
mizu sashi	pitcher	水差し
moyō	pattern	模様
naifu	knife	ナイフ
napukin	napkin	ナプキン
niku jū sōsu ire	gravy boat	肉汁ソース入れ
ōsaji	tablespoon	大さじ
ōzara	platter	大皿
pan kago	breadbasket	パンかご
rēsu	lace	レース
rōsoku tate	candlestick	ろうそく立て
sankyaku dai	trivet	三脚台
sara	dish/plate	皿
sarada bōru	salad bowl	サラダボール
sarada no tori zara	salad plate	サラダの取り皿
satō tsubo	sugar bowl	砂糖壷
setto	set	セット
shanpen gurasu	champagne glass	シャンペン・グラス
shio furi yōki	salt shaker	塩振り容器
shokutaku yō ginki	silverware	食卓用銀器
supūn	spoon	スプーン
sūpu yō supūn	soupspoon	スープ用スプーン
sūpu zara	soup dish	スープ皿
sutenress	stainless steel	ステンレス
tēburu kurosu	tablecloth	テーブルクロス
tēburu matto	place mat	テーブルマット
tenuri no	handpainted (adj)	手塗りの
tezukuri no	handmade (adj)	手作りの
tī potto	teapot	ティーポット
tōki	earthenware	陶器
tōki rui	pottery	陶器類

toriwake yō supūn	serving spoon	取り分け用スプーン
uke zara	saucer	受け皿
wain gurasu	wineglass	ワイングラス
yude tamago tate	egg cup	ゆで卵立て

COMPUTERS

English to Japanese

accelerator	アクセラレータ	*akuserarēta*
access time	アクセス時間	*akusesu jikan*
active matrix	アクティブマトリックス	*akutibu matorikkusu*
adaptor	アダプタ	*adaputa*
application	アプリケーション	*apurikēshon*
battery life	バッテリ連続使用時間	*batteri renzoku shiyō jikan*
battery recharger	充電地	*jūdenchi*
bit	ビット	*bitto*
board	ボード	*bōdo*
built-in	内蔵	*naizō*
bundle	セット	*setto*
byte	バイト	*baito*
card	カード	*kādo*
CD-ROM disk	シーディーロムディスク	*shīdīromu disuku*
CD-ROM drive	シーディーロムドライブ	*shīdīromu doraibu*
central processing unit (CPU)	中央処理装置	*chūō shori sōchi*
color	カラー	*karā*
compatibility	互換性	*gokansei*
connector cable	接続ケーブル	*setsuzoku kēburu*
controller	コントローラ	*kontorōra*
coprocessor	コプロセッサ	*kopurosessa*
data base	データベース	*dētabēsu*
data compression	データ圧縮	*dēta asshuku*
data file	データファイル	*dēta fairu*
data processing	データ処理	*dēta shori*
data transmission	データ転送	*dēta tensō*
desktop computer	デスク型コンピュータ	*desukugata konpyūta*
desktop presentation (DTPR)	デスクトップ・プレゼンテーション	*desukutoppu purezentēshon*
desktop publishing	卓上電子出版	*takujō denshi shuppan*
display	ディスプレイ	*disupurei*
download	ダウンロード	*daunrōdo*
drive	ドライブ	*doraibu*
electronic bulletin board	電子掲示板	*denshi keijiban*
electronic mail	電子メール	*denshi mēru*
expandable	拡張可能	*kakuchō kanō*
expansion slot	拡張スロット	*kakuchō surotto*
external	外部	*gaibu*
fax	ファックス	*fakkusu*
floating point unit (FPU)	浮動小数点ユニット	*fudō shōsūten yunitto*
floppy disk	フロッピーディスク	*furoppī disuku*

font	フォント／字体	*fonto/jitai*
front end processor (FEP)	フロントエンド・プロセッサ	*furontoendo purosessa*
graphics	グラフィックス	*gurafikkusu*
gray scale	グレースケール	*gurēsukēru*
hand scanner	ハンドスキャナ	*handosukyana*
hard disk	ハードディスク	*hādo disuku*
hardware	ハードウェア	*hādowea*
high density	高密度	*kō mitsudo*
high resolution	高解像度	*kō kaizōdo*
host computer	ホストコンピュータ	*hosuto konpyūta*
hub	ハブ	*habu*
image	イメージ	*imēji*
interactive	インターアクティブ	*intā akutibu*
interface	インターフェース	*intāfēsu*
internal	内部	*naibu*
jack	ジャック	*jakku*
keyboard	キーボード	*kībōdo*
laptop computer	ラップ型コンピューター	*rappugata konpyūta*
laser printer	レーザープリンタ	*rēzā purinta*
liquid-crystal display (LCD)	液晶ディスプレイ	*ekishō disupurei*
local area network (LAN)	ローカル・エリア・ネットワーク	*rōkaru eria nettowāku*
magnet optical disk (MO)	光磁気ディスク	*hikari jiki disuku*
mainframe	メインフレーム	*meinfurēmu*
math coprocessor	数值演算コプロセッサ	*sūchi enzan kopurosessa*
megabyte (MB)	メガバイト	*megabaito*
megahertz (MHz)	メガヘルツ	*megaherutsu*
memory	メモリ	*memori*
modem	モデム	*modemu*
monitor	モニタ	*monita*
monochrome	モノクローム	*monokurōmu*
motherboard	マザーボード	*mazābōdo*
mouse	マウス	*mausu*
multimedia	マルチメディア	*maruchimedia*
multitask operation	マルチタスクオペレーション	*maruchitasuku operēshon*
notebook computer	ノートブックコンピュータ	*nōtobukku konpyūta*
onboard	オンボード	*onbōdo*
online	オンライン	*onrain*
optical character reader (OCR)	光学式文字読み取り装置	*kōgakushiki moji yomitori sōchi*
option	オプション	*opushon*
palm-size computer	ポケット型コンピュータ	*pokettogata konpyūta*
parallel port	パラレルポート	*parareru pōto*

parallel processing	並列処理	*heiretsu shori*
peripherals	周辺機器	*shūhen kiki*
personal computer	パーソナルコンピュータ	*pāsonaru konpyūta*
pixel	ピクセル	*pikuseru*
port	ポート	*pōto*
printer	プリンタ	*purinta*
processor	プロセッサ	*purosessa*
programming	プログラミング	*puroguramingu*
random-access memory (RAM)	ランダム・アクセス・メモリ	*randamu akusesu memori*
read-only memory (ROM)	リード・オンリ・メモリ	*rīdo onri memori*
realtime	リアルタイム	*riarutaimu*
removable hard disk	着脱型ハードディスク	*chakudatsugata hādodisuku*
resolution	解像度	*kaizōdo*
scanner	スキャナ	*sukyana*
screen	スクリーン	*sukurīn*
serial port	シリアルポート	*shiriaru pōto*
server	サーバ	*sāba*
share	共用	*kyōyō*
slot	スロット	*surotto*
software	ソフトウェア	*sofutowea*
stand-alone workstation	独立ワークステーション	*dokuritsu wākusutēshon*
standard	標準	*hyōjun*
storage	記憶装置	*kioku sōchi*
super computer	スーパーコンピュータ	*sūpā konpyūta*
tablet	タブレット	*taburetto*
telephone line	電話回線	*denwa kaisen*
terminal	ターミナル／端末	*tāminaru/tanmatsu*
track ball	トラックボール	*torakkubōru*
upgrade	グレードアップ	*gurēdoappu*
upload	アップロード	*appurōdo*
utilities	ユーティリティー	*yūtiritī*
video RAM (VRAM)	ビデオラム	*bideo ramu*
voice mail	音声メール	*onsei mēru*
voice recognition	音声認識	*onsei ninshiki*
Windows	ウィンドウズ	*windōzu*
word processing	ワープロ処理	*wāpuro shori*
word processor	ワープロ	*wāpuro*

Japanese to English

adaputa	adaptor	アダプタ
akuserarēta	accelerator	アクセラレータ
akusesu jikan	access time	アクセス時間

akutibu matorikkusu	active matrix	アクティブマトリックス
appurōdo	upload	アップロード
apurikēshon	application	アプリケーション
baito	byte	バイト
batteri renzoku shiyō jikan	battery life	バッテリ連続使用時間
bideo ramu	video RAM (VRAM)	ビデオラム
bitto	bit	ビット
bōdo	board	ボード
chakudatsugata hādodisuku	removable hard disk	着脱型ハードディスク
chūō shori sōchi	central processing unit (CPU)	中央処理装置
daunrōdo	download	ダウンロード
denshi keijiban	electronic bulletin board	電子掲示板
denshi mēru	electronic mail	電子メール
denwa kaisen	telephone line	電話回線
desukugata konpyūta	desktop computer	デスク型コンピュータ
desukutoppu purezentēshon	desktop presentation (DTPR)	デスクトップ・プレゼンテーション
deta asshuku	data compression	データ圧縮
dētabēsu	data base	データベース
dēta fairu	data file	データファイル
dēta shori	data processing	データ処理
dēta tensō	data transmission	データ転送
disupurei	display	ディスプレイ
dokuritsu wākusutēshon	stand-alone workstation	独立ワークステーション
doraibu	drive	ドライブ
ekishō disupurei	liquid-crystal display (LCD)	液晶ディスプレイ
fakkusu	fax	ファックス
fonto	font	フォント
fudō shōsūten yunitto	floating point unit (FPU)	浮動小数点ユニット
furontoendo purosessa	front end processor (FEP)	フロントエンド・プロセッサ
furoppī disuku	floppy disk	フロッピーディスク
gaibu	external	外部
gokansei	compatibility	互換性
gurafikkusu	graphics	グラフィックス
gurēdoappu	upgrade	グレードアップ
gurēsukēru	gray scale	グレースケール
habu	hub	ハブ
hādo disuku	hard disk	ハードディスク
hādowea	hardware	ハードウェア
handosukyana	hand scanner	ハンドスキャナ
heiretsu shori	parallel processing	並列処理
hikari jiki disuku	magnet optical disk (MO)	光磁気ディスク

hosuto konpyūta	host computer	ホストコンピュータ
hyōjun	standard	標準
imēji	image	イメージ
intā akutibu	interactive	インターアクティブ
intāfēsu	interface	インターフェース
jakku	jack	ジャック
jitai	font	字体
jūdenchi	battery recharger	充電地
kādo	card	カード
kaizōdo	resolution	解像度
kakuchō kanō	expandable	拡張可能
kakuchō surotto	expansion slot	拡張スロット
karā	color	カラー
kībōdo	keyboard	キーボード
kioku sōchi	storage	記憶装置
kōgakushiki moji yomitori sōchi	optical character reader (OCR)	光学式文字読み取り装置
kō kaizōdo	high resolution	高解像度
ko mitsudo	high density	高密度
kontorōra	controller	コントローラ
kopurosessa	coprocessor	コプロセッサ
kyōyō	share	共用
maruchimedia	multimedia	マルチメディア
maruchitasuku operēshon	multitask operation	マルチタスクオペレーション
mausu	mouse	マウス
mazābōdo	motherboard	マザーボード
megabaito	megabyte (MB)	メガバイト
megaherutsu	megahertz (MHz)	メガヘルツ
meinfurēmu	mainframe	メインフレーム
memori	memory	メモリ
modemu	modem	モデム
monita	monitor	モニタ
monokurōmu	monochrome	モノクローム
naibu	internal	内部
naizō	built-in	内蔵
nōtobukku konpyūta	notebook computer	ノートブックコンピュータ
onbōdo	onboard	オンボード
onrain	online	オンライン
onsei mēru	voice mail	音声メール
onsei ninshiki	voice recognition	音声認識
opushon	option	オプション
parareru pōto	parallel port	パラレルポート
pāsonaru konpyūta	personal computer	パーソナルコンピュータ
pikuseru	pixel	ピクセル
pokettogata konpyūta	palm-size computer	ポケット型コンピュータ
pōto	port	ポート
purinta	printer	プリンタ
puroguramingu	programming	プログラミング
purosessa	processor	プロセッサ

randamu akusesu memori	random-access memory (RAM)	ランダム・アクセス・メモリ
rappugata konpyūta	laptop computer	ラップ型コンピュータ
rēzā purinta	laser printer	レーザープリンタ
riarutaimu	realtime	リアルタイム
rīdo onri memori	read-only memory (ROM)	リード・オンリ・メモリ
rōkaru eria nettowāku	local area network (LAN)	ローカル・エリア・ネットワーク
sāba	server	サーバ
setsuzoku kēburu	connector cable	接続ケーブル
setto	bundle	セット
shīdīromu disuku	CD-ROM disk	シーディーロム　ディスク
shīdīromu doraibu	CD-ROM drive	シーディーロム　ドライブ
shiriaru pōto	serial port	シリアルポート
shūhen kiki	peripherals	周辺機器
sofutowea	software	ソフトウェア
sūchi enzan kopurosessa	math coprocessor	数値演算コプロセッサ
sukurīn	screen	スクリーン
sukyana	scanner	スキャナ
sūpā konpyūta	super computer	スーパーコンピュータ
surotto	slot	スロット
taburetto	tablet	タブレット
takujō denshi shuppan	desktop publishing	卓上電子出版
tāminaru	terminal	ターミナル
tanmatsu	terminal	端末
torakkubōru	track ball	トラックボール
wāpuro	word processor	ワープロ
wāpuro shori	word processing	ワープロ処理
windōzu	Windows	ウィンドウズ
yūtiritī	utilities	ユーティリティー

ELECTRICITY AND ELECTRONICS

English to Japanese

alternating current	交流	*kōryū*
amplifier	増幅器／アンプ	*zōfuku ki/anpu*
amplitude modulation	エーエム	*ē emu*
antenna	アンテナ	*antena*
audio component system	オーディオ・コンポ	*ōdio konpo*
audio response equipment	音声応答装置	*onsei ōtō sōchi*
autoreverse	オート・リバース	*ōto ribāsu*
BIT	ビット	*bitto*
black and white TV	白黒テレビ	*shiro kuro terebi*
Braun tube	ブラウン管	*buraun kan*
buffer memory	バッファ・メモリ	*baffa memori*
calculator	計算器	*keisan ki*
car telephone	自動車電話	*jidōsha denwa*
cash register	レジスター	*rejisutā*
cassette	カセット	*kasetto*
CB	市民ラジオ	*shimin rajio*
ceramic condenser	セラミック・コンデンサ	*seramikku kondensa*
chip condenser	チップ・コンデンサ	*chippu kondensa*
circuit breaker	回路遮断器	*kairo shadan ki*
color liquid crystal	カラー液晶	*karā ekishō*
color TV	カラーテレビ	*karā terebi*
compact disc	コンパクト・ディスク	*konpakuto disuku*
compact disc player	コンパクト・ディスク・プレーヤー	*konpakuto disuku purēyā*
component	コンポ	*konpo*
computer	コンピュータ	*konpyūta*
condenser	コンデンサ	*kondensa*
conductivity	電導率	*dendō ritsu*
connector	コネクター	*konekutā*
contact	接点	*setten*
converter	変換機	*henkan ki*
cordless phone	コードレスホン	*kōdoresu hon*
correlator	相関器	*sōkan ki*
DC machine	直流機	*chokuryū ki*
desk-top calculator	電卓	*dentaku*
digital (adj)	デジタル	*dejitaru*
digital audio disc	デジタル・オーディオ・ディスク	*dejitaru ōdio disuku*
digital audio tape recorder	デジタル・オーディオ・テープレコーダー	*dejitaru ōdio tēpu rekōdā*
diode	ダイオード	*daiōdo*
display unit	ディスプレイ装置	*disupurei sōchi*
D-RAM	ダイナミック・ラム	*dainamikku ramu*

dynamic memory	ダイナミック・メモリ	*dainamikku memori*
dynamo	ダイナモ	*dainamo*
electric circuit	電気回路	*denki kairo*
electric furnace	電気炉	*denki ro*
electric heater	電気暖房器	*denki danbō ki*
electric interlocking machine	電気連動機	*denki rendō ki*
electric resistance	電気抵抗	*denki teikō*
electric shaver	電気かみそり	*denki kamisori*
electric tools	電気工具	*denki kōgu*
electrode	電極	*denkyoku*
electromagnet	電磁石	*denjishaku*
electron beam	電子ビーム	*denshi bīmu*
electron gun	電子銃	*denshi jū*
electronic cash register	電子レジスター	*denshi rejisutā*
electronic desk calculator	卓上電子計算器	*takujō denshi keisan ki*
electronic musical instruments	電子楽器	*denshi gakki*
electronic organ	電子オルガン	*denshi orugan*
electronics	電子工学	*denshi kōgaku*
electronic sewing machine	電子ミシン	*denshi mishin*
electronic typewriter	電子タイプライター	*denshi taipuraitā*
electron microscope	電子顕微鏡	*denshi kenbikyō*
EP-ROM	消去可能読み出し専用メモリ	*shōkyo kanō yomidashi senyō memori*
equalizer	イコライザー	*ikoraizā*
facsimile	ファクシミリ	*fakushimiri*
fixed resistor	固定抵抗器	*kotei teikō ki*
food processor	フード・プロセッサ	*fūdo purosessa*
frequency modulation	エフエム	*efu emu*
generator	発電機	*hatsuden ki*
graphic equalizer	グラフィック・イコライザー	*gurafikku ikoraizā*
hertz	ヘルツ	*herutsu*
high fidelity	ハイファイ	*haifai*
industrial robot	産業ロボット	*sangyō robotto*
integrated circuit	集積回路	*shūseki kairo*
inverter	インバータ	*inbāta*
keyboard	キーボード	*kī bōdo*
large-scale integrated circuit	大規模集積回路	*daikibo shūseki kairo*
laser beam printer	レーザー・ビーム・プリンタ	*rēzā bīmu purinta*
light emitting diode	発光ダイオード	*hakkō daiōdo*
line printer	ライン・プリンタ	*rain purinta*
liquid crystal	液晶	*ekishō*
machine tools	工作機械	*kōsaku kikai*
magnetic bubble memory	磁気バブルメモリ	*jiki baburu memori*
magnetic disc unit	磁気ディスク装置	*jiki disuku sōchi*
magnetic tape unit	磁気テープ装置	*jiki tēpu sōchi*
micro cassette recorder	マイクロ・カセット・レコーダー	*maikuro kasetto rekōdā*

micro computer	マイクロ・コンピュータ	*maikuro konpyūta*
micro processor	マイクロ・プロセッサ	*maikuro purosessa*
microwave	極超短波	*gokuchō tanpa*
microwave oven	電子レンジ	*denshi renji*
mini component system	ミニコンポ	*mini konpo*
ohm	オーム	*ōmu*
optical character reader	光学式文字読み取り装置	*kōgaku shiki moji yomitori sōchi*
optical mark reader	光学式マーク読み取り装置	*kōgaku shiki māku yomitori sōchi*
opto-electronics	光技術	*hikari gijutsu*
peripheral equipment	周辺機器	*shūhen kiki*
personal cassette player	パーソナル・カセット・プレーヤー	*pāsonaru kasetto purēyā*
personal computer	パソコン	*pasokon*
personal stereo radio	パーソナル・ステレオ・ラジオ	*pāsonaru sutereo rajio*
personal TV	パーソナル・テレビ	*pāsonaru terebi*
phone answering machine	留守番電話	*rusuban denwa*
plasma etching	プラズマ・エッチング	*purazuma etchingu*
pocket-size TV	ポケット・テレビ	*poketto terebi*
poly-crystal silicon	多結晶シリコン	*takesshō shirikon*
portable TV	ポータブル・テレビ	*pōtaburu terebi*
precision machinery	精密機械	*seimitsu kikai*
printer	プリンタ	*purinta*
radar	レーダー	*rēdā*
radio	ラジオ	*rajio*
radio cassette player	ラジカセ	*rajikase*
RAM	随時書込み読み出しメモリ	*zuiji kakikomi yomidashi memori*
rechargeable (adj)	再充電可能の	*sai jūden kanō no*
record player	レコード・プレーヤー	*rekōdo purēyā*
rectifier	整流器	*seiryū ki*
remote control	リモート・コントロール	*rimōto kontorōru*
ROM	読み出し専用メモリ	*yomidashi senyō memori*
semiconductor	半導体	*handō tai*
sensor	センサー	*sensā*
serial printer	シリアル・プリンタ	*shiriaru purinta*
speaker	スピーカー	*supīkā*
stereophonic (adj)	ステレオ	*sutereo*
stereo TV	ステレオ・テレビ	*sutereo terebi*
switch	スイッチ	*suitchi*
tape recorder	テープ・レコーダー	*tēpu rekōdā*
television	テレビ	*terebi*

telex	テレックス	*terekkusu*
terminal	ターミナル	*tāminaru*
thermostat	サーモスタット	*sāmosutatto*
transformer	変圧器	*hen-atsu ki*
tuner	チューナー	*chūnā*
very large-scale integrated circuit	超大規模集積回路	*chō daikibo shūseki kairo*
video cassette camera	ビデオ・カセット・カメラ	*bideo kasetto kamera*
video cassette player	ビデオ・カセット・プレーヤー	*bideo kasetto purēyā*
video cassette recorder	ビデオ・カセット・レコーダー	*bideo kasetto rekōdā*
video disc	ビデオ・ディスク	*bideo disuku*
videotape recorder	テープ録画装置	*tēpu rokuga sōchi*
wafer	ウェハー	*uehā*
word processor	ワード・プロセッサ	*wādo purosessa*

Japanese to English

anpu	amplifier	アンプ
antena	antenna	アンテナ
baffa memori	buffer memory	バッファ・メモリ
bideo disuku	video disc	ビデオ・ディスク
bideo kasetto kamera	video cassette camera	ビデオ・カセット・カメラ
bideo kasetto purēyā	video cassette player	ビデオ・カセット・プレーヤー
bideo kasetto rekōdā	video cassette recorder	ビデオ・カセット・レコーダー
bitto	BIT	ビット
buraun kan	Braun tube	ブラウン管
chippu kondensa	chip condenser	チップ・コンデンサ
chō daikibo shūseki kairo	very large-scale integrated circuit	超大規模集積回路
chokuryū ki	DC machine	直流機
chūnā	tuner	チューナー
daikibo shūseki kairo	large-scale integrated circuit	大規模集積回路
dainamikku memori	dynamic memory	ダイナミック・メモリ
dainamikku ramu	D-RAM	ダイナミック・ラム
dainamo	dynamo	ダイナモ
daiōdo	diode	ダイオード
dejitaru	digital (adj)	デジタル
dejitaru ōdio disuku	digital audio disc	デジタル・オーディオ・ディスク
dejitaru ōdio tēpu rekōdā	digital audio tape recorder	デジタル・オーディオ・テープレコーダー
dendō ritsu	conductivity	電導率

denjishaku	electromagnet	電磁石
denki danbō ki	electric heater	電気暖房器
denki kairo	electric circuit	電気回路
denki kamisori	electric shaver	電気かみそり
denki kōgu	electric tools	電気工具
denki rendō ki	electric interlocking machine	電気連動機
denki ro	electric furnace	電気炉
denki teikō	electric resistance	電気抵抗
denkyoku	electrode	電極
denshi bīmu	electron beam	電子ビーム
denshi gakki	electronic musical instruments	電子楽器
denshi jū	electron gun	電子銃
denshi kenbikyō	electron microscope	電子顕微鏡
denshi kōgaku	electronics	電子工学
denshi mishin	electronic sewing machine	電子ミシン
denshi orugan	electronic organ	電子オルガン
denshi rejisutā	electronic cash register	電子レジスター
denshi renji	microwave oven	電子レンジ
denshi taipuraitā	electronic typewriter	電子タイプライター
dentaku	desk-top calculator	電卓
disupurei sōchi	display unit	ディスプレイ装置
ē emu	amplitude modulation	エーエム
efu emu	frequency modulation	エフエム
ekishō	liquid crystal	液晶
fakushimiri	facsimile	ファクシミリ
fūdo purosessa	food processor	フード・プロセッサ
gokuchō tanpa	microwave	極超短波
gurafikku ikoraizā	graphic equalizer	グラフィック・イコライザー
haifai	high fidelity	ハイファイ
hakkō daiōdo	light emitting diode	発光ダイオード
handō tai	semiconductor	半導体
hatsuden ki	generator	発電機
hen-atsu ki	transformer	変圧器
henkan ki	converter	変換機
herutsu	hertz	ヘルツ
hikari gijutsu	opto-electronics	光技術
ikoraizā	equalizer	イコライザー
inbāta	inverter	インバータ
jidōsha denwa	car telephone	自動車電話
jiki baburu memori	magnetic bubble memory	磁気バブルメモリ
jiki disuku sōchi	magnetic disc unit	磁気ディスク装置
jiki tēpu sōchi	magnetic tape unit	磁気テープ装置
kairo shadan ki	circuit breaker	回路遮断器
karā ekishō	color liquid crystal	カラー液晶
karā terebi	color TV	カラーテレビ

kasetto	cassette	カセット
keisan ki	calculator	計算器
kī bōdo	keyboard	キーボード
kōdoresu hon	cordless phone	コードレスホン
kōgaku shiki māku yomitori sōchi	optical mark reader	光学式マーク読み取り装置
kōgaku shiki moji yomitori sōchi	optical character reader	光学式文字読み取り装置
kondensa	condenser	コンデンサ
konekutā	connector	コネクター
konpakuto disuku	compact disc	コンパクト・ディスク
konpakuto disuku purēyā	compact disc player	コンパクト・ディスク・プレーヤー
konpo	component	コンポ
konpyūta	computer	コンピュータ
kōryu	alternating current	交流
kōsaku kikai	machine tools	工作機械
kotei teikō ki	fixed resistor	固定抵抗器
maikuro kasetto rekōdā	micro cassette recorder	マイクロ・カセット・レコーダー
maikuro konpyūta	micro computer	マイクロ・コンピュータ
maikuro purosessa	micro processor	マイクロ・プロセッサ
mini konpo	mini component system	ミニコンポ
ōdio konpo	audio component system	オーディオ・コンポ
ōmu	ohm	オーム
onsei ōtō sōchi	audio response equipment	音声応答装置
ōto ribāsu	autoreverse	オート・リバース
pasokon	personal computer	パソコン
pāsonaru kasetto purēyā	personal cassette player	パーソナル・カセット・プレーヤー
pāsonaru sutereo rajio	personal stereo radio	パーソナル・ステレオ・ラジオ
pāsonaru terebi	personal TV	パーソナル・テレビ
poketto terebi	pocket-size TV	ポケット・テレビ
pōtaburu terebi	portable TV	ポータブル・テレビ
purazuma etchingu	plasma etching	プラズマ・エッチング
purinta	printer	プリンタ
rain purinta	line printer	ライン・プリンタ
rajikase	radio cassette player	ラジカセ
rajio	radio	ラジオ
rēdā	radar	レーダー
rejisutā	cash register	レジスター
rekōdo purēyā	record player	レコード・プレーヤー
rēzā bīmu purinta	laser beam printer	レーザー・ビーム・プリンタ
rimōto kontorōru	remote control	リモート・コントロール
rusuban denwa	phone answering machine	留守番電話

sai jūden kanō no	rechargeable (adj)	再充電可能の
sāmosutatto	thermostat	サーモスタット
sangyō robotto	industrial robot	産業ロボット
seimitsū kikai	precision machinery	精密機械
seiryū ki	rectifier	整流器
sensā	sensor	センサー
seramikku kondensa	ceramic condenser	セラミック・コンデンサ
setten	contact	接点
shimin rajio	CB	市民ラジオ
shiriaru purinta	serial printer	シリアル・プリンタ
shiro kuro terebi	black and white TV	白黒テレビ
shōkyo kanō yomidashi senyō memori	EP-ROM	消去可能読み出し専用メモリ
shūhen kiki	peripheral equipment	周辺機器
shūseki kairo	integrated circuit	集積回路
sōkan ki	correlator	相関器
suitchi	switch	スイッチ
supīkā	speaker	スピーカー
sutereo	stereophonic (adj)	ステレオ
sutereo terebi	stereo TV	ステレオ・テレビ
takesshō shirikon	poly-crystal silicon	多結晶シリコン
takujō denshi keisan ki	electronic desk calculator	卓上電子計算器
tāminaru	terminal	ターミナル
tēpu rekōdā	tape recorder	テープ・レコーダー
tēpu rokuga sōchi	videotape recorder	テープ録画装置
terebi	television	テレビ
terekkusu	telex	テレックス
uehā	wafer	ウェハー
wādo purosessa	word proccssor	ワード・プロセッサ
yomidashi senyō memori	ROM	読み出し専用メモリ
zōfuku ki	amplifier	増幅器
zuiji kakikomi yomidashi memori	RAM	随時書込み読み出しメモリ

FASHION AND TEXTILES

English to Japanese

accessory	アクセサリー	*akusesarī*
angora	アンゴラ	*angora*
belt	ベルト	*beruto*
blazer	ブレザー	*burezā*
blouse	ブラウス	*burausu*
boots	ブーツ	*būtsu*
bow tie	ちょうネクタイ	*chō nekutai*
camel's hair	ラクダ	*rakuda*
cashmere	カシミヤ	*kashimiya*
coat	コート	*kōto*
collar	えり	*eri*
collections	コレクション	*korekushon*
color	色	*iro*
cotton	綿	*men*
cufflink	カフスボタン	*kafusu botan*
cut (v)	裁断する	*saidan suru*
design (v)	デザインする	*dezain suru*
designer	デザイナー	*dezainā*
dress	ドレス	*doresu*
fabric	ファブリック	*faburikku*
fashion	ファッション	*fasshon*
flannel	フランネル	*furanneru*
french cuff	フレンチカフス	*furenchi kafusu*
handbag	ハンドバッグ	*handobaggu*
hand-knit (adj)	手編みの	*teami no*
hand-sewn (adj)	手縫いの	*te-nui no*
handwoven (adj)	手織りの	*teori no*
hem	へり	*heri*
jewel	宝石類	*hōseki rui*
length	たけ	*take*
linen	麻	*asa*
lining	裏地	*uraji*
long sleeves	長そで	*naga sode*
moire	モアレ	*moare*
muslin	モスリン	*mosurin*
nylon	ナイロン	*nairon*
pattern	型	*kata*
pleat	プリーツ	*purītsu*
polyester	ポリエステル	*poriesuteru*
poplin	ポプリン	*popurin*
print	プリント	*purinto*
raincoat	レインコート	*reinkōto*
rayon	レーヨン	*rēyon*
ready-to-wear	既製服	*kisei fuku*
scarf	スカーフ	*sukāfu*
sew (v)	縫う	*nuu*

shirt	シャツ	*shatsu*
shoe	くつ	*kutsu*
short sleeves	半そで	*han sode*
shoulder pad	ショルダー・パッド	*shorudā paddo*
silk	シルク	*shiruku*
size	サイズ	*saizu*
skirt	スカート	*sukāto*
slacks	スラックス	*surakkusu*
sportswear	スポーツウェア	*supōtsu wea*
style	スタイル	*sutairu*
suede	スエード	*suēdo*
suit	スーツ	*sūtsu*
sweater	セーター	*sētā*
synthetic (adj)	合成の	*gōsei no*
synthetic suede	合成スエード	*gōsei suēdo*
taffeta	タフタ	*tafuta*
tailor	テーラー	*tērā*
textile	織物	*orimono*
tie	ネクタイ	*nekutai*
unisex	ユニセックス	*yunisekkusu*
veil	ベール	*bēru*
vest	ベスト	*besuto*
wool	ウール	*ūru*
yarn	ヤーン	*yān*

Japanese to English

akusesarī	accessory	アクセサリー
angora	angora	アンゴラ
asa	linen	麻
bēru	veil	ベール
beruto	belt	ベルト
besuto	vest	ベスト
burausu	blouse	ブラウス
burezā	blazer	ブレザー
būtsu	boots	ブーツ
chō nekutai	bow tie	ちょうネクタイ
dezainā	designer	デザイナー
dezain suru	design (v)	デザインする
doresu	dress	ドレス
eri	collar	えり
faburikku	fabric	ファブリック
fasshon	fashion	ファッション
furanneru	flannel	フランネル
furenchi kafusu	french cuff	フレンチカフス
gōsei no	synthetic (adj)	合成の
gōsei suēdo	synthetic suede	合成スエード
handobaggu	handbag	ハンドバッグ
han sode	short sleeves	半そで

heri	hem	へり
hōseki rui	jewel	宝石類
iro	color	色
kafusu botan	cufflink	カフスボタン
kashimiya	cashmere	カシミヤ
kata	pattern	型
kisei fuku	ready-to-wear	既製服
korekushon	collections	コレクション
kōto	coat	コート
kutsu	shoe	くつ
men	cotton	綿
moare	moire	モアレ
mosurin	muslin	モスリン
naga sode	long sleeves	長そで
nairon	nylon	ナイロン
nekutai	tie	ネクタイ
nuu	sew (v)	縫う
orimono	textile	織物
popurin	poplin	ポプリン
poriesuteru	polyester	ポリエステル
purinto	print	プリント
purītsu	pleat	プリーツ
rakuda	camel's hair	ラクダ
reinkōto	raincoat	レインコート
rēyon	rayon	レーヨン
saidan suru	cut (v)	裁断する
saizu	size	サイズ
sētā	sweater	セーター
shatsu	shirt	シャツ
shiruku	silk	シルク
shorudā paddo	shoulder pad	ショルダー・パッド
suēdo	suede	スエード
sukāfu	scarf	スカーフ
sukāto	skirt	スカート
supōtsu wea	sportswear	スポーツウェア
surakkusu	slacks	スラックス
sutairu	style	スタイル
sūtsu	suit	スーツ
tafuta	taffeta	タフタ
take	length	たけ
teami no	hand-knit (adj)	手編みの
tenui no	hand-sewn (adj)	手縫いの
teori no	handwoven (adj)	手織りの
tērā	tailor	テーラー
uraji	lining	裏地
ūru	wool	ウール
yān	yarn	ヤーン
yunisekkusu	unisex	ユニセックス

LEGAL MATTERS

English to Japanese

advisor's fee	顧問料	*komon ryō*
affidavit	供述書	*kyōjutsu sho*
amicable settlement	和解	*wakai*
anti-monopoly law	独占禁止法	*dokusen kinshi hō*
appeal (v)	上告する	*jōkoku suru*
application	申請	*shinsei*
arbitration	仲裁／調停	*chūsai/chōtei*
arbitrator	仲裁人／調停者	*chūsainin/chōteisha*
attachment	差し押さえ	*sashiosae*
attorney	弁護士	*bengoshi*
bankruptcy	破産	*hasan*
bid	入札	*nyūsatsu*
breach of contract	契約違反	*keiyaku ihan*
buyout	買収	*baishū*
cartel	カルテル	*karuteru*
certification	認証	*ninshō*
civil law	民法	*minpō*
civil suit	民事訴訟	*minji soshō*
class action	クラスアクション	*kurasuakushon*
client	依頼人	*irainin*
collusion	談合	*dangō*
commercial law	商法	*shōhō*
compensation	賠償	*baishō*
contract	契約	*keiyaku*
copyright	著作権	*chosakuken*
copyright law	著作権法	*chosakuken hō*
corporate tax	法人税	*hōjinzei*
court	裁判所／法廷	*saibansho/hōtei*
criminal action	刑事訴訟	*keiji soshō*
criminal law	刑法	*keihō*
cross examination	反対尋問	*hantai jinmon*
customs	税関	*zeikan*
customs regulations	通関規制	*tsūkan kisei*
damage	損害	*songai*
deed of contract	約定書	*yakutei sho*
declaration of bankruptcy	破産宣告	*hasan senkoku*
defend	弁護する	*bengosuru*
defense, the	弁護側	*bengo gawa*
Department of Commerce (U.S.)	商務省	*shōmushō*
Department of Justice (U.S.)	司法省	*shihōshō*
deposition	宣誓供述書	*sensei kyōjutsusho*
discretion	自由裁量権	*jiyū sairyō ken*
district court	地方裁判所	*chihō saibansho*
dumping	ダンピング	*danpingu*
evidence	証拠	*shōko*

execution	執行	*shikkō*
expenses	経費	*keihi*
Fair Trade Commission	公正取引委員会	*kōsei torihiki iinkai*
fine	罰金	*bakkin*
foreclosure	没収	*bosshū*
guilty	有罪	*yūzai*
hearsay evidence	伝聞証拠	*denbun shōko*
high court	高等裁判所	*kōtō saibansho*
illegal	違法の	*ihō no*
import regulation	輸入規制	*yu-nyū kisei*
import restriction	輸入制限	*yu-nyū seigen*
import surcharge	輸入課徴金	*yu-nyū kachōkin*
incorporation	法人設立	*hōjin setsuritsu*
indemnity	損害賠償	*songai baishō*
infringement	侵害	*shingai*
injury	被害	*higai*
innocence	無罪	*muzai*
inspection	検査	*kensa*
intellectual property	知的所有権	*chiteki shoyūken*
international law	国際法	*kokusaihō*
invalidation	失効	*shikkō*
Japan Federation of Bar Associations	日弁連（日本弁護士連合会）	*Nichibenren (Nippon bengoshi rengōkai)*
joint venture	合弁	*gōben*
judge	裁判官／判事	*saibankan/hanji*
judicial decision	判決	*hanketsu*
jurisdiction	管轄	*kankatsu*
law firm	法律事務所	*hōritsu jimusho*
lawsuit	訴訟	*soshō*
lawyer	弁護士	*bengoshi*
legal	法律の	*hōritsu no*
legal adviser	顧問弁護士	*komon bengoshi*
license	免許	*menkyo*
litigation	訴訟	*soshō*
lose a suit	敗訴する	*haisosuru*
mediation	調停／仲介	*chōtei/chūkai*
merger and acquisition (M & A)	合併・買収	*gappei • baishū*
Ministry of International Trade and Industry (MITI)	通産省	*tsūsanshō*
Ministry of Justice	法務省	*hōmushō*
monopoly	独占	*dokusen*
negotiation	交渉	*kōshō*
non-performance of contract	契約不履行	*keiyaku furikō*
not guilty	無罪	*muzai*
out-of-court settlement	示談	*jidan*
overseas affiliated firm	現地法人	*genchi hōjin*
ownership	所有権	*shoyūken*
patent	特許	*tokkyo*

patent application	特許申請	*tokkyo shinsei*
patent right	特許権	*tokkyoken*
permission	認可	*ninka*
plaintiff	原告	*genkoku*
plead	嘆願する	*tangansuru*
probation	執行猶予	*shikkō yūyo*
prosecute	起訴する	*kisosuru*
prosecution, the	検察当局	*kensatsu tōkyoku*
proxy (right)	代理権	*dairiken*
proxy (document)	委任状	*ininjō*
public hearing	公聴会	*kōchōkai*
public prosecutor	検事	*kenji*
reconciliation	和解	*wakai*
registered trademark	登録商標	*tōroku shōhyō*
royalty (patent)	特許使用料	*tokkyo shiyōryō*
royalty (publication)	印税	*inzei*
Securities and Exchange Commission	証券取引委員会	*shōken torihiki iinkai*
seizure	差し押さえ	*sashiosae*
specification	仕様書	*shiyōsho*
standard	規格	*kikaku*
statute of limitations	時効	*jikō*
subpoena (v)	喚問する	*kanmonsuru*
sue	訴える	*uttaeru*
summary court	簡易裁判所	*kan-i saibansho*
summary order	略式命令	*ryakushiki meirei*
summon (v)	喚問する	*kanmonsuru*
summons (n)	召喚状	*shōkanjō*
supreme court	最高裁判所	*saikō saibansho*
surtax	付加税	*fukazei*
tariff	関税	*kanzei*
tax evasion	脱税	*datsuzei*
tax law	税法	*zeihō*
tender	入札	*nyūsatsu*
terms	条件	*jōken*
testify	証言する	*shōgensuru*
titles	所有権	*shoyūken*
Trade Representative (U.S.)	通商代表	*tsūshō daihyō*
trial	裁判	*saiban*
U.S. International Trade Commission	米国際貿易委員会	*bei kokusai bōeki iinkai*
unitary tax	合算課税	*gassan kazei*
venture	ベンチャー	*benchā*
verification	検証	*kenshō*
violation	違反	*ihan*
void (adj)	無効の	*mukō no*
win a suit	勝訴する	*shōsosuru*
witness	証人	*shōnin*

Japanese to English

baishō	compensation	賠償
baishū	buyout	買収
bakkin	fine	罰金
bei kokusai bōeki iinkai	U.S. International Trade Commission	米国際貿易委員会
benchā	venture	ベンチャー
bengo gawa	the defense	弁護側
bengoshi	lawyer/attorney	弁護士
bengosuru	defend	弁護する
bosshū	foreclosure	没収
chihō saibansho	district court	地方裁判所
chiteki shoyūken	intellectual property	知的所有権
chosakuken	copyright	著作権
chosakuken hō	copyright law	著作権法
chōtei	arbitration/mediation	調停
chōteisha	arbitrator	調停者
chūkai	mediation	仲介
chūsai	arbitration	仲裁
chūsainin	arbitrator	仲裁人
dairiken	proxy (right)	代理権
dangō	collusion	談合
danpingu	dumping	ダンピング
datsuzei	tax evasion	脱税
denbun shōko	hearsay evidence	伝聞証拠
dokusen	monopoly	独占
dokusen kinshi hō	anti-monopoly law	独占禁止法
fukazei	surtax	付加税
gappei • baishū	merger and acquisition (M & A)	合併・買収
gassan kazei	unitary tax	合算課税
genchi hōjin	overseas affiliated firm	現地法人
genkoku	plaintiff	原告
gōben	joint venture	合弁
haisosuru	lose a suit	敗訴する
hanji	judge	判事
hanketsu	judicial decision	判決
hantai jinmon	cross examination	反対尋問
hasan	bankruptcy	破産
hasan senkoku	declaration of bankruptcy	破産宣告
higai	injury	被害
hōjin setsuritsu	incorporation	法人設立
hōjinzei	corporate tax	法人税
hōmushō	Ministry of Justice	法務省
hōritsu jimusho	law firm	法律事務所
hōritsu no	legal	法律の
hōtei	court	法廷
ihan	violation	違反

ihō no	illegal	違法の
ininjō	proxy (document)	委任状
inzei	royalty (publication)	印税
irainin	client	依頼人
jidan	out-of-court settlement	示談
jikō	statute of limitation	時効
jiyū sairyō ken	discretion	自由裁量権
jōken	terms	条件
jōkoku suru	appeal (v)	上告する
kan-i saibansho	summary court	簡易裁判所
kankatsu	jurisdiction	管轄
kanmonsuru	subpoena (v)/ summon (v)	喚問する
kanzei	tariff	関税
karuteru	cartel	カルテル
keihi	expenses	経費
keihō	criminal law	刑法
keiji soshō	criminal action	刑事訴訟
keiyaku	contract	契約
keiyaku furikō	non-performance of contract	契約不履行
keiyaku ihan	breach of contract	契約違反
kenji	public prosecutor	検事
kensa	inspection	検査
kensatsu tōkyoku	the prosecution	検察当局
kenshō	verification	検証
kigyō rengō	cartel	企業連合
kikaku	standard	規格
kisosuru	prosecute	起訴する
kōchōkai	public hearing	公聴会
kokusaiho	international law	国際法
komon bengoshi	legal adviser	顧問弁護士
komon ryō	advisor's fee	顧問料
kōsei torihiki iinkai	Fair Trade Commission	公正取引委員会
kōshō	negotiation	交渉
kōtō saibansho	high court	高等裁判所
kurasuakushon	class action	クラスアクション
kyōjutsu sho	affidavit	供述書
menkyo	license	免許
minji soshō	civil suit	民事訴訟
minpō	civil law	民法
mukō no	void (adj)	無効の
muzai	innocence/not guilty	無罪
Nichibenren (Nippon bengoshi rengōkai)	Japan Federation of Bar Associations	日弁連（日本弁護士連合会）
ninka	permission	認可
ninshō	certification	認証
nyūsatsu	bid/tender	入札
ryakushiki meirei	summary order	略式命令

saiban	trial	裁判
saibankan	judge	裁判官
saibansho	court	裁判所
saikō saibansho	supreme court	最高裁判所
sashiosae	attachment/seizure	差し押さえ
sensei kyōjutsusho	deposition	宣誓供述書
shihōshō	Department of Justice (U.S.)	司法省
shikkō	execution	執行
shikkō	invalidation	失効
shikkō yūyo	probation	執行猶予
shingai	infringement	侵害
shinsei	application	申請
shiyōsho	specification	仕様書
shōgensuru	testify	証言する
shōhō	commercial law	商法
shōkanjō	summons (n)	召喚状
shōken torihiki iinkai	Securities and Exchange Commission	証券取引委員会
shōko	evidence	証拠
shōmushō	Department of Commerce (U.S.)	商務省
shōnin	witness	証人
shōsosuru	win a suit	勝訴する
shoyūken	ownership/titles	所有権
songai	damage	損害
songai baishō	indemnity	損害賠償
soshō	lawsuit/litigation	訴訟
tangansuru	plead	嘆願する
tokkyo	patent	特許
tokkyoken	patent right	特許権
tokkyo shinsei	patent application	特許申請
tokkyo shiyōryō	royalty (patent)	特許使用料
tōroku shōhyō	registered trademark	登録商標
tsūkan kisei	customs regulations	通関規制
tsūsanshō	Ministry of International Trade and Industry (MITI)	通産省
tsūshō daihyō	Trade Representative (U.S.)	通商代表
uttaeru	sue	訴える
wakai	amicable settlement/ reconciliation	和解
yakutei sho	deed of contract	約定書
yu-nyū kachōkin	import surcharge	輸入課徴金
yu-nyū kisei	import regulation	輸入規制
yu-nyū seigen	import restriction	輸入制限
yūzai	guilty	有罪
zeihō	tax law	税法
zeikan	customs	税関

MACHINE TOOLS

English to Japanese

angular cutter	山形フライス	*yamagata furaisu*
articulated robot	多関節ロボット	*takansetsu robotto*
autochecker	オートチェッカー	*ōto chekkā*
automatic pallet changer	パレット・チェンジャー	*paretto chenjā*
automatic screw machine	自動ねじ切り盤	*jidō nejikiri ban*
automatic tool changer	自動工具交換装置	*jidō kōgu kōkan sōchi*
bit	ビット	*bitto*
boring machine	中ぐり盤	*nakaguri ban*
broaching machine	ブローチ盤	*burōchi ban*
cartesian coordinates robot	直角座標ロボット	*chokkaku zahyō robotto*
centerless grinder	心なし研削盤	*kokoro nashi kensaku ban*
computerized numerical control (CNC)	コンピュータ内蔵数値制御装置	*konpyūta naizō sūchi seigyo sōchi*
cutting tool	バイト	*baito*
cylinder boring machine	シリンダ中ぐり盤	*shirinda nakaguri ban*
cylindrical coordinates robot	円筒座標ロボット	*entō zahyō robotto*
cylindrical grinder	円筒研削盤	*entō kensaku ban*
die	ねじ切りダイス	*nejikiri daisu*
drilling machine	ボール盤	*bōru ban*
end mill	エンド・ミル	*endo miru*
fixed sequence robot	固定シーケンスロボット	*kotei shīkensu robotto*
friction press	摩擦プレス	*masatsu puresu*
gear cutting machine	歯切り盤	*hagiri ban*
grinder	研削盤	*kensaku ban*
injection molding machine	射出成形機	*shashutsu seikei ki*
insert machine	自動挿入機	*jidō sōnyū ki*
internal grinder	内面研削盤	*naimen kensaku ban*
jet condenser	ジェット・コンデンサ	*jetto kondensa*
jig	ジグ	*jigu*
knurling tool	ローレット	*rōretto*
lapping machine	ラップ盤	*rappu ban*
lathe	旋盤	*senban*
machine tools	工作機械	*kōsaku kikai*
machining center	マシニング・センター	*mashiningu sentā*
manipulator	マニピュレータ	*manipyurēta*
material handling robot	マテハン・ロボット	*matehan robotto*
mechanical press	メカニカル・プレス	*mekanikaru puresu*
milling machine	フライス盤	*furaisu ban*
molding machine	造型機	*zōkei ki*
multicut lathe	多刃旋盤	*tajin senban*
multispindle drilling machine	多軸ボール盤	*tajiku bōru ban*
numerical control machine	NC工作機械	*enu shī kōsaku kikai*

numerical control robot	NCロボット	*enu shī robotto*
planetary gear train	遊星歯車装置	*yūsei haguruma sōchi*
plasma cutting machine	プラズマ切断装置	*purazuma setsudan sōchi*
playback robot	プレイバック・ロボット	*pureibakku robotto*
polar coordinates robot	極座標ロボット	*kyoku zahyō robotto*
precision machinery	精密機械	*seimitsu kikai*
profiler	プロファイラー	*purofairā*
punch press	パンチ・プレス	*panchi puresu*
radial drilling machine	ラジアル・ボール盤	*rajiaru bōru ban*
reamer	リーマ	*rīma*
repeatable robot	繰返しロボット	*kurikaeshi robotto*
roll turning lathe	ロール旋盤	*rōru senban*
sawing machine	のこぎり盤	*nokogiri ban*
screw cutting lathe	ねじ切り旋盤	*nejikiri senban*
sequence robot	シーケンス・ロボット	*shīkensu robotto*
sequential control	シーケンス制御	*shīkensu seigyo*
shaft lathe	軸旋盤	*jiku senban*
shaping machine	形削り盤	*katakezuri ban*
shearing machine	シャーリング・マシン	*shāringu mashin*
slotting machine	縦削り盤	*tatekezuri ban*
spline milling machine	みぞ切りフライス盤	*mizokiri furaisu ban*
surface grinder	平面研削盤	*heimen kensaku ban*
transfer machine	トランスファー・マシン	*toransufā mashin*
turret lathe	タレット旋盤	*taretto senban*
universal grinder	万能研削盤	*bannō kensaku ban*
universal milling machine	万能フライス盤	*bannō furaisu ban*
variable sequence robot	可変シーケンス・ロボット	*kahen shīkensu robotto*
vertical boring mill	縦中ぐり盤	*tate nakaguri ban*
vertical milling machine	縦フライス盤	*tate furaisu ban*

Japanese to English

baito	cutting tool	バイト
bannō furaisu ban	universal milling machine	万能フライス盤
bannō kensaku ban	universal grinder	万能研削盤
bitto	bit	ビット
bōru ban	drilling machine	ボール盤
burōchi ban	broaching machine	ブローチ盤
chokkaku zahyō robotto	cartesian coordinates robot	直角座標ロボット
endo miru	end mill	エンド・ミル
entō kensaku ban	cylindrical grinder	円筒研削盤
entō zahyō robotto	cylindrical coordinates robot	円筒座標ロボット

enu shī kōsaku kikai	numerical control machine	NC工作機械
enu shī robotto	numerical control robot	NCロボット
furaisu ban	milling machine	フライス盤
hagiri ban	gear cutting machine	歯切り盤
heimen kensaku ban	surface grinder	平面研削盤
jetto kondensa	jet condenser	ジェット・コンデンサ
jidō kōgu kōkan sōchi	automatic tool changer	自動工具交換装置
jidō nejikiri ban	automatic screw machine	自動ねじ切り盤
jidō sōnyū ki	insert machine	自動挿入機
jigu	jig	ジグ
jiku senban	shaft lathe	軸旋盤
kahen shīkensu robotto	variable sequence robot	可変シーケンス・ロボット
katakezuri ban	shaping machine	形削り盤
kensaku ban	grinder	研削盤
kokoro nashi kensaku ban	centerless grinder	心なし研削盤
konpyūta naizō sūchi seigyo sōchi	computerized numerical control (CNC)	コンピュータ内蔵数値制御装置
kōsaku kikai	machine tools	工作機械
kotei shīkensu robotto	fixed sequence robot	固定シーケンス・ロボット
kurikaeshi robotto	repeatable robot	繰返しロボット
kyoku zahyō robotto	polar coordinates robot	極座標ロボット
manipyurēta	manipulator	マニピュレータ
masatsu puresu	friction press	摩擦プレス
mashiningu sentā	machining center	マシニング・センター
matehan robotto	material handling robot	マテハン・ロボット
mekanikaru puresu	mechanical press	メカニカル・プレス
mizokiri furaisu ban	spline milling machine	みぞ切りフライス盤
naimen kensaku ban	internal grinder	内面研削盤
nakaguri ban	boring machine	中ぐり盤
nejikiri daisu	die	ねじ切りダイス
nejikiri senban	screw cutting lathe	ねじ切り旋盤
nokogiri ban	sawing machine	のこぎり盤
ōto chekkā	autochecker	オートチェッカー
panchi puresu	punch press	パンチ・プレス
paretto chenjā	automatic pallet changer	パレット・チェンジャー
purazuma setsudan sōchi	plasma cutting machine	プラズマ切断装置
pureibakku robotto	playback robot	プレイバック・ロボット
purofairā	profiler	プロファイラー
rajiaru bōru ban	radial drilling machine	ラジアル・ボール盤
rappu ban	lapping machine	ラップ盤
rīma	reamer	リーマ
rōretto	knurling tool	ローレット
rōru senban	roll turning lathe	ロール旋盤
seimitsu kikai	precision machinery	精密機械
senban	lathe	旋盤

shāringu mashin	shearing machine	シャーリング・マシン
shashutsu seikei ki	injection molding machine	射出成形機
shīkensu robotto	sequence robot	シーケンス・ロボット
shīkensu seigyo	sequential control	シーケンス制御
shirinda nakaguri ban	cylinder boring machine	シリンダ中ぐり盤
tajiku bōru ban	multispindle drilling machine	多軸ボール盤
tajin senban	multicut lathe	多刃旋盤
takansetsu robotto	articulated robot	多関節ロボット
taretto senban	turret lathe	タレット旋盤
tate furaisu ban	vertical milling machine	縦フライス盤
tatekezuri ban	slotting machine	縦削り盤
tate nakaguri ban	vertical boring mill	縦中ぐり盤
toransufā mashin	transfer machine	トランスファー・マシン
yamagata furaisu	angular cutter	山形フライス
yūsei haguruma sōchi	planetary gear train	遊星歯車装置
zōkei ki	molding machine	造型機

METALWORKS

English to Japanese

alloy	合金	*gōkin*
alloy steel	合金鋼	*gōkin kō*
alumina	アルミナ	*arumina*
aluminum	アルミニュウム	*aruminyūmu*
annealing	焼なまし	*yaki namashi*
bars	棒	*bō*
billets	小鋼片	*shō kōhen*
blast furnace	高炉	*kō ro*
carbon steel	炭酸鋼	*tansan kō*
cast iron	鋳鉄	*chūtetsu*
cast steel	鋳鋼	*chūkō*
cermet	サーメット	*sāmetto*
chromium	クロム	*kuromu*
coil	コイル	*koiru*
cold rolling	冷間圧延	*reikan atsuen*
continuous caster	連続鋳造	*renzoku chūzō*
copper	銅	*dō*
crucible	るつぼ	*rutsubo*
cupola	キューポラ	*kyūpora*
die casting	ダイカスト	*daikasuto*
direct reduction process	直接製鉄法	*chokusetsu seitetsu hō*
electric arc furnace	弧光式炉	*kokō shiki ro*
electrolytic process	電解法	*denkai hō*
ferrite	フェライト	*feraito*
ferroalloys	合金鉄	*gōkin tetsu*
ferrochromium	フェロクローム	*ferokurōmu*
ferromanganese	フェロマンガン	*feromangan*
ferronickel	フェロニッケル	*feronikkeru*
ferrosilicon	フェロシリコン	*feroshirikon*
foundry	鋳造工場	*chūzō kōjō*
furnace	炉	*ro*
hot rolling	熱間圧延	*nekkan atsuen*
hot strip coil	熱延広幅帯鋼	*netsuen hirohaba obikō*
induction furnace	誘導炉	*yūdō ro*
ingot	インゴット	*ingotto*
iron ore	鉄鉱	*tekkō*
limestone	石灰岩	*sekkai gan*
magnetic fluid	磁性流体	*jisei ryūtai*
manganese ore	マンガン鉱	*mangan kō*
manganese steel	マンガン鋼	*mangan kō*
metal alloys for hydrogen storage	水素吸蔵合金	*suiso kyūzō gōkin*
metal hydride	金属水素化物	*kinzoku suiso ka butsu*
metallic fiber	金属繊維	*kinzoku sen-i*
molybdenum	モリブデン	*moribuden*
nitrogen	窒素	*chisso*

pickling	酸洗い	*san arai*
pig iron	銑鉄	*sentetsu*
plate	板	*ita*
powder metallurgy	粉末冶金	*funmatsu yakin*
quench (v)	焼入れする	*yakiire suru*
refractories	耐火レンガ	*taika renga*
rod	棒	*bō*
rolling mill	圧延工場	*atsuen kōjō*
scrap	くず鉄	*kuzu tetsu*
seamless steel tube	継ぎ目なし鋼管	*tsugime nashi kōkan*
shape-memory alloy	形状記憶合金	*keijō kioku gōkin*
sheet bar	シート・バー	*shīto bā*
sheet pile	鋼矢板	*kōya ban*
spiral tube	スパイラル鋼管	*supairaru kōkan*
sponge	海綿鉄	*kaimen tetsu*
stainless steel	ステンレス鋼	*sutenresu kō*
steel foil	スチール・フォイル	*suchīru foiru*
steel mill	製鉄所	*seitetsu sho*
super alloys	スーパー・アロイ	*sūpā aroi*
titanium	チタン	*chitan*
titanium metal	チタン金属	*chitan kinzoku*
tungsten	タングステン	*tangusuten*
ultrafine powder	超微粒子	*chō biryūshi*
vanadium	バナジウム	*banajiumu*
wire	針金	*harigane*

Japanese to English

arumina	alumina	アルミナ
aruminyūmu	aluminum	アルミニュウム
atsuen kōjō	rolling mill	圧延工場
banajiumu	vanadium	バナジウム
bō	bars, rod	棒
chisso	nitrogen	窒素
chitan	titanium	チタン
chitan kinzoku	titanium metal	チタン金属
chō biryūshi	ultrafine powder	超微粒子
chokusetsu seitetsu hō	direct reduction process	直接製鉄法
chūkō	cast steel	鋳鋼
chūtetsu	cast iron	鋳鉄
chūzō kōjō	foundry	鋳造工場
daikasuto	die casting	ダイカスト
denkai hō	electrolytic process	電解法
dō	copper	銅
feraito	ferrite	フェライト
ferokurōmu	ferrochromium	フェロクローム
feromangan	ferromanganese	フェロマンガン
feronikkeru	ferronickel	フェロニッケル
feroshirikon	ferrosilicon	フェロシリコン

funmatsu yakin	powder metallurgy	粉末冶金
gōkin	alloy	合金
gōkin kō	alloy steel	合金鋼
gōkin tetsu	ferroalloys	合金鉄
harigane	wire	針金
ingotto	ingot	インゴット
ita	plate	板
jisei ryūtai	magnetic fluid	磁性流体
kaimen tetsu	sponge	海綿鉄
keijō kioku gōkin	shape-memory alloy	形状記憶合金
kinzoku sen-i	metallic fiber	金属繊維
kinzoku suiso ka butsu	metal hydride	金属水素化物
koiru	coil	コイル
kokō shiki ro	electric arc furnace	弧光式炉
kō ro	blast furnace	高炉
kōya ban	sheet pile	鋼矢板
kuromu	chromium	クロム
kuzu tetsu	scrap	くず鉄
kyūpora	cupola	キューポラ
mangan kō	manganese ore	マンガン鉱
mangan kō	manganese steel	マンガン鋼
moribuden	molybdenum	モリブデン
nekkan atsuen	hot rolling	熱間圧延
netsuen hirohaba obikō	hot strip coil	熱延広幅帯鋼
reikan atsuen	cold rolling	冷間圧延
renzoku chūzō	continuous caster	連続鋳造
ro	furnace	炉
rutsubo	crucible	るつぼ
sāmetto	cermet	サーメット
san arai	pickling	酸洗い
seitetsu sho	steel mill	製鉄所
sekkai gan	limestone	石灰岩
sentetsu	pig iron	銑鉄
shīto bā	sheet bar	シート・バー
shō kōhen	billets	小鋼片
suchīru foiru	steel foil	スチール・フォイル
suiso kyūzō gōkin	metal alloys for hydrogen storage	水素吸蔵合金
sūpā aroi	super alloys	スーパー・アロイ
supairaru kōkan	spiral tube	スパイラル鋼管
sutenresu kō	stainless steel	ステンレス鋼
taika renga	refractories	耐火レンガ
tangusuten	tungsten	タングステン
tansan kō	carbon steel	炭酸鋼
tekkō	iron ore	鉄鉱
tsugime nashi kōkan	seamless steel tube	継ぎ目なし鋼管
yakiire suru	quench (v)	焼入れする
yaki namashi	annealing	焼きなまし
yūdō ro	induction furnace	誘導炉

MOTOR VEHICLES

English to Japanese

accelerator	アクセル	*akuseru*
air conditioner	カー・クーラー	*kā kūrā*
alternator	オルタネーター	*orutanētā*
assembly factory	組立て工場	*kumitate kōjō*
automatic gearshift	オート・クラッチ	*ōto kuratchi*
automatic transmission	自動変速機	*jidō hensoku ki*
automobile	自動車	*jidōsha*
auto parts	自動車部品	*jidōsha buhin*
axle	車軸	*shajiku*
battery	バッテリー	*batterī*
body	車体	*shatai*
brake	ブレーキ	*burēki*
bumper	バンパー	*banpā*
camshaft	カムシャフト	*kamushafuto*
car	自動車	*jidōsha*
carburetor	キャブレター	*kyaburetā*
chassis	シャーシー	*shāshī*
clutch	クラッチ	*kuratchi*
condenser	コンデンサー	*kondensā*
connecting rod	連接棒	*rensetsu bō*
crankshaft	クランクシャフト	*kurankushafuto*
cylinder	シリンダー	*shirindā*
defroster	デフロスター	*defurosutā*
designer	デザイナー	*dezainā*
diesel	ディーゼル	*dīzeru*
disc brake	ディスク・ブレーキ	*disuku burēki*
distributor	デストリビューター	*desutoribyūtā*
engine	エンジン	*enjin*
fender	フェンダー	*fendā*
four-wheel drive	四輪駆動	*yonrin kudō*
front-wheel drive	前輪駆動	*zenrin kudō*
fuel consumption	燃料消費量	*nenryō shōhi ryō*
fuel injection system	燃料噴射装置	*nenryō funsha sōchi*
gasoline	ガソリン	*gasorin*
gasoline tank	ガソリン・タンク	*gasorin tanku*
gas pedal	アクセル	*akuseru*
gearshift	ギア転換装置	*gia tenkan sōchi*
generator	ジェネレーター	*jenerētā*
horsepower	馬力	*bariki*
ignition	イグニッション	*igunisshon*
independent suspension	独立懸架	*dokuritsu kenka*
injection pump	インジェクション・ポンプ	*injekushon ponpu*
mileage	走行マイル数	*sōkō mairu sū*
model	モデル	*moderu*
odometer	走行距離計	*sōkō kyori kei*

oil pump	オイル・ポンプ	*oiru ponpu*
optional equipment	オプション部品	*opushon buhin*
paint	塗装	*tosō*
pinion	ピニオン	*pinion*
piston	ピストン	*pisuton*
power steering	パワー・ステアリング	*pawā sutearingu*
radial tire	ラジアル・タイア	*rajiaru taiya*
radiator	ラジエーター	*rajiētā*
rear axle	後車軸	*kōshajiku*
seat	シート	*shīto*
seatbelt	シート・ベルト	*shīto beruto*
shock absorber	ショック・アブソーバー	*shokku abusōbā*
spark plug	スパーク・プラグ	*supāku puragu*
speedometer	速度計	*sokudo kei*
standard equipment	標準装備品	*hyōjun sōbi hin*
steering wheel	ハンドル	*handoru*
suspension	サスペンション	*sasupenshon*
tachometer	タコメーター	*tako mētā*
tire	タイヤ	*taiya*
torque	トルク	*toruku*
transmission	トランスミッション	*toransumisshon*
turbo-charger	ターボ・チャージャー	*tābo chājā*
valve	バルブ	*barubu*
wheel	車輪	*sharin*
windshield	フロント・ガラス	*furonto garasu*

Japanese to English

akuseru	accelerator, gas pedal	アクセル
banpā	bumper	バンパー
bariki	horsepower	馬力
barubu	valve	バルブ
batterī	battery	バッテリー
burēki	brake	ブレーキ
defurosutā	defroster	デフロスター
desutoribyūtā	distributor	デストリビューター
dezainā	designer	デザイナー
disuku burēki	disc brake	ディスク・ブレーキ
dīzeru	diesel	ディーゼル
dokuritsu kenka	independent suspension	独立懸架
enjin	engine	エンジン
fendā	fender	フェンダー
furonto garasu	windshield	フロント・ガラス
gasorin	gasoline	ガソリン
gasorin tanku	gasoline tank	ガソリン・タンク
gia tenkan sōchi	gearshift	ギア転換装置

handoru	steering wheel	ハンドル
hyōjun sōbi hin	standard equipment	標準装備品
igunisshon	ignition	イグニッション
injekushon ponpu	injection pump	インジェクション・ポンプ
jenerētā	generator	ジェネレーター
jidō hensoku ki	automatic transmission	自動変速機
jidōsha	automobile, car	自動車
jidōsha buhin	auto parts	自動車部品
kā kūrā	air conditioner	カー・クーラー
kamushafuto	camshaft	カムシャフト
kondensā	condenser	コンデンサー
kōshajiku	rear axle	後車軸
kumitate kōjō	assembly factory	組立て工場
kurankushafuto	crankshaft	クランクシャフト
kuratchi	clutch	クラッチ
kyaburetā	carburetor	キャブレター
moderu	model	モデル
nenryō funsha sōchi	fuel injection system	燃料噴射装置
nenryō shōhi ryō	fuel consumption	燃料消費量
oiru ponpu	oil pump	オイル・ポンプ
opushon buhin	optional equipment	オプション部品
orutanētā	alternator	オルタネーター
ōto kuratchi	automatic gearshift	オート・クラッチ
pawā sutearingu	power steering	パワー・ステアリング
pinion	pinion	ピニオン
pisuton	piston	ピストン
rajiaru taiya	radial tire	ラジアル・タイヤ
rajiētā	radiator	ラジエーター
rensetsu bō	connecting rod	連接棒
sasupenshon	suspension	サスペンション
shajiku	axle	車軸
sharin	wheel	車輪
shāshī	chassis	シャーシー
shatai	body	車体
shirindā	cylinder	シリンダー
shīto	seat	シート
shīto beruto	seatbelt	シート・ベルト
shokku abusōbā	shock absorber	ショック・アブソーバー
sōkō kyori kei	odometer	走行距離計
sōkō mairu sū	mileage	走行マイル数
sokudo kei	speedometer	速度計
supāku puragu	spark plug	スパーク・プラグ
tābo chājā	turbo-charger	ターボ・チャージャー
taiya	tire	タイヤ
tako mētā	tachometer	タコメーター
toransumisshon	transmission	トランスミッション
toruku	torque	トルク
tosō	paint	塗装
yonrin kudō	four-wheel drive	四輪駆動
zenrin kudō	front-wheel drive	前輪駆動

PHARMACEUTICALS

English to Japanese

analgesic	鎮痛薬	*chintsū yaku*
anesthetic	麻酔薬	*masui yaku*
antacid	制酸薬	*seisan yaku*
anti-inflammatory (adj)	抗炎症用の	*kō enshō yō no*
antibiotic	抗生物質	*kōsei busshitsu*
anticholinergic	副交感神経抑制剤	*fuku kōkan shinkei yokusei zai*
anticoagulant	血液凝固阻止薬	*ketsueki gyōko soshi yaku*
antiseptic	消毒剤	*shōdoku zai*
aspirin	アスピリン	*asupirin*
barbiturate	バルビツール酸系催眠薬	*barubitsūru san kei saimin yaku*
bleed (v)	出血する	*shukketsu suru*
blood	血液	*ketsueki*
botanic	植物性薬品	*shokubutsu sei yakuhin*
calcium	カルシュウム	*karushūmu*
capsule	カプセル	*kapuseru*
compounds	化合物	*kagō butsu*
content	容量	*yōryō*
cortisone	コーチゾン	*kōchizon*
cough drop	せき止めドロップ	*seki dome doroppu*
cough syrup	せき止めシロップ	*seki dome shiroppu*
density	濃度	*nōdo*
diabetes	糖尿病	*tōnyō byō*
diuretic	利尿薬	*rinyō yaku*
dose	服用量	*fukuyō ryō*
drop	点滴薬	*tenteki yaku*
drug	薬	*kusuri*
ground (adj)	粉末状の	*funmatsu jō no*
hexachlorophene	ヘキサクロロフェン	*hekisakurorofen*
hormone	ホルモン	*horumon*
injection	注射	*chūsha*
insulin	インシュリン	*inshurin*
iodine	ヨード	*yōdo*
iron	鉄剤	*tetsu zai*
medication	薬物治療	*yakubutsu chiryō*
medicine	薬	*kusuri*
morphine	モルヒネ	*moruhine*
narcotic	麻酔薬	*masui yaku*
nitrate	硝酸塩	*shōsan en*
nitrite	亜硝酸塩	*a shōsan en*
ointment	軟膏	*nankō*
opium	アヘン	*ahen*
pellet	ペレット	*peretto*
penicillin	ペニシリン	*penishirin*
pharmaceutical	薬品	*yakuhin*
pharmacist	薬剤師	*yakuzai shi*

phenol	石炭酸	*sekitan san*
physician	医者	*isha*
pill	丸薬	*gan yaku*
prescription	処方箋	*shohō sen*
purgative	下剤	*gezai*
remedies	治療法	*chiryō hō*
saccharin	サッカリン	*sakkarin*
salts	かぎ塩	*kagi shio*
salve	軟膏	*nankō*
sedative	鎮静薬	*chinsei yaku*
serum	血清	*kessei*
sinus	鼻腔	*bi kō*
sleeping pill	催眠薬	*saimin yaku*
starch	澱粉	*denpun*
stimulant	興奮薬	*kōfun yaku*
sulphamide	スルファミド	*surufamido*
synthesis	合成	*gōsei*
syringe	注射器	*chūsha ki*
tablet	錠剤	*jōzai*
toxicology	毒物学	*dokubutsu gaku*
toxin	毒素	*dokuso*
tranquilizer	トランキライザー	*torankiraizā*
vaccine	ワクチン	*wakuchin*
vitamin	ビタミン	*bitamin*
zinc	亜鉛	*aen*

Japanese to English

aen	zinc	亜鉛
ahen	opium	アヘン
a shōsan en	nitrite	亜硝酸塩
asupirin	aspirin	アスピリン
barubitsūru san kei saimin yaku	barbiturate	バルビツール酸系催眠薬
bi kō	sinus	鼻腔
bitamin	vitamin	ビタミン
chinsei yaku	sedative	鎮静薬
chintsū yaku	analgesic	鎮痛薬
chiryō hō	remedies	治療法
chūsha	injection	注射
chūsha ki	syringe	注射器
denpun	starch	澱粉
dokubutsu gaku	toxicology	毒物学
dokuso	toxin	毒素
fuku kōkan shinkei yokusei zai	anticholinergic	副交感神経抑制剤
fukuyō ryō	dose	服用量
funmatsu jō no	ground (adj)	粉末状の
gan yaku	pill	丸薬
gezai	purgative	下剤

gōsei	synthesis	合成
hekisakurorofen	hexachlorophene	ヘキサクロロフェン
horumon	hormone	ホルモン
inshurin	insulin	インシュリン
isha	physician	医者
jōzai	tablet	錠剤
kagi shio	salts	かぎ塩
kagō butsu	compounds	化合物
kapuseru	capsule	カプセル
karushūmu	calcium	カルシュウム
kessei	serum	血清
ketsueki	blood	血液
ketsueki gyōko soshi yaku	anticoagulant	血液凝固阻止薬
kōchizon	cortisone	コーチゾン
kō enshō yō no	anti-inflammatory (adj)	抗炎症用の
kōfun yaku	stimulant	興奮薬
kōsei busshitsu	antibiotic	抗生物質
kusuri	drug	薬
masui yaku	narcotic, anesthetic	麻酔薬
moruhine	morphine	モルヒネ
nankō	ointment, salve	軟膏
nōdo	density	濃度
penishirin	penicillin	ペニシリン
peretto	pellet	ペレット
rinyō yaku	diuretic	利尿薬
saimin yaku	sleeping pill	催眠薬
sakkarin	saccharin	サッカリン
seisan yaku	antacid	制酸薬
seki dome doroppu	cough drop	せき止めドロップ
seki dome shiroppu	cough syrup	せき止めシロップ
sekitan san	phenol	石炭酸
shōdoku zai	antiseptic	消毒剤
shohō sen	prescription	処方箋
shokubutsu sei yakuhin	botanic	植物性薬品
shōsan en	nitrate	硝酸塩
shukketsu suru	bleed (v)	出血する
suruphamido	sulphamide	スルファミド
tenteki yaku	drop	点滴薬
tetsu zai	iron	鉄剤
tōnyō byō	diabetes	糖尿病
torankiraizā	tranquilizer	トランキライザー
wakuchin	vaccine	ワクチン
yakubutsu chiryō	medication	薬物治療
yakuhin	pharmaceutical	薬品
yakuzai shi	pharmacist	薬剤師
yōdo	iodine	ヨード
yōryō	content	容量

PHOTOGRAPHY

English to Japanese

accessory	付属品	*fuzoku hin*
aerial photographic camera	航空カメラ	*kōkū kamera*
all-weather camera	全天候カメラ	*zen tenkō kamera*
aperture	絞り	*shibori*
ASA speed	ASA感度	*ē esu ē kando*
auto-loading	自動装填	*jidō sōten*
automatic aperture control device	自動絞り	*jidō shibori*
automatic developing machine	自動現像機	*jidō genzō ki*
automatic exposure	自動露出機構	*jidō roshutsu kikō*
automatic focusing	自動焦点	*jidō shōten*
automatic printing machine	オート・プリンター	*ōto purintā*
automatic rewinding	自動巻上げ	*jidō makiage*
auxiliary lens	アタッチメント・レンズ	*atatchimento renzu*
black and white film	白黒フィルム	*shiro kuro firumu*
cable release	ケーブル・レリーズ	*kēburu rerīzu*
camera	カメラ	*kamera*
camera body	ボディー	*bodī*
cartridge	カートリッジ	*kātorijji*
close-up lens	クローズ・アップ・レンズ	*kurōzu appu renzu*
color film	カラー・フィルム	*karā firumu*
color print	カラー・プリント	*karā purinto*
color slide	カラー・スライド	*karā suraido*
condenser lens	集光レンズ	*shūkō renzu*
develop (v)	現像する	*genzō suru*
EE camera	電子カメラ	*denshi kamera*
enlargement	引伸ばし	*hikinobashi*
enlarger	引伸ばし機	*hikinobashi ki*
exposure	露出	*roshutsu*
exposure meter	露出計	*roshutsu kei*
film	フィルム	*firumu*
filter	フィルター	*firutā*
fish-eye lens	魚眼レンズ	*gyogan renzu*
fixed focus camera	固定焦点カメラ	*kotei shōten kamera*
flashbulb	フラッシュ・バルブ	*furasshu barubu*
flashcube	フラッシュ・キューブ	*furasshu kyūbu*
focus	焦点	*shōten*
infrared film	赤外写真フィルム	*sekigai shashin firumu*
interchangeable lens	交換レンズ	*kōkan renzu*
lens	レンズ	*renzu*
long-focus lens	長焦点レンズ	*chō shōten renzu*
macro lens	接写レンズ	*sessha renzu*
micro camera	マイクロ・カメラ	*maikuro kamera*

microfilm	マイクロ・フィルム	*maikuro firumu*
motor drive	モーター・ドライブ	*mōtā doraibu*
nickel-cadmium battery	ニッカド電池	*nikkado denchi*
objective lens	対物レンズ	*taibutsu renzu*
printing	焼付け	*yakitsuke*
projector	映写機	*eisha ki*
rangefinder	距離計	*kyori kei*
reflex camera	レフレックス・カメラ	*refurekkusu kamera*
screen	スクリーン	*sukurīn*
self-timer	セルフタイマー	*serufu taimā*
sensitometer	感光計	*kankō kei*
shutter	シャッター	*shattā*
shutter speed	シャッター・スピード	*shattā supīdo*
single-lens reflex camera	一眼レフ	*ichigan refu*
sky lens	全天レンズ	*zenten renzu*
slide	スライド	*suraido*
slide projector	スライド映写機	*suraido eisha ki*
soft focus lens	ソフトフォーカス・レンズ	*sofuto fōkasu renzu*
standard lens	標準レンズ	*hyōjun renzu*
strobe	ストロボ	*sutorobo*
telephoto lens	望遠レンズ	*bōen renzu*
35 mm camera	35ミリ・カメラ	*sanjū go miri kamera*
tripod	三脚	*sankyaku*
twin lens reflex camera	二眼レフカメラ	*nigan refu kamera*
underwater camera	水中カメラ	*suichū kamera*
view finder	ファインダー	*faindā*
wide angle lens	広角レンズ	*kōkaku renzu*
zoom lens	ズーム・レンズ	*zūmu renzu*

Japanese to English

atatchimento renzu	auxiliary lens	アタッチメント・レンズ
bodī	camera body	ボディー
bōen renzu	telephoto lens	望遠レンズ
chō shōten renzu	long-focus lens	長焦点レンズ
denshi kamera	EE camera	電子カメラ
ē esu ē kando	ASA speed	ASA感度
eisha ki	projector	映写機
faindā	view finder	ファインダー
firumu	film	フィルム
firutā	filter	フィルター
furasshu barubu	flashbulb	フラッシュ・バルブ
furasshu kyūbu	flashcube	フラッシュ・キューブ
fuzoku hin	accessory	付属品
genezō suru	develop (v)	現像する
gyogan renzu	fish-eye lens	魚眼レンズ

hikinobashi	enlargement	引伸し
hikinobashi ki	enlarger	引伸し機
hyōjun renzu	standard lens	標準レンズ
ichigan refu	single-lens reflex camera	一眼レフ
jidō genzō ki	automatic developing machine	自動現像機
jidō makiage	automatic rewinding	自動巻上げ
jidō roshutsu kikō	automatic exposure	自動露出機構
jidō shibori	automatic aperture control device	自動絞り
jidō shōten	automatic focusing	自動焦点
jidō sōten	auto-loading	自動装填
kamera	camera	カメラ
kankō kei	sensitometer	感光計
karā firumu	color film	カラー・フィルム
karā purinto	color print	カラー・プリント
karā suraido	color slide	カラー・スライド
kātorijji	cartridge	カートリッジ
kēburu rerīzu	cable release	ケーブル・レリーズ
kōkaku renzu	wide angle lens	広角レンズ
kōkan renzu	interchangeable lens	交換レンズ
kōkū kamera	aerial photographic camera	航空カメラ
kotei shōten kamera	fixed focus camera	固定焦点カメラ
kurōzu appu renzu	close-up lens	クローズアップ・レンズ
kyori kei	rangefinder	距離計
maikuro firumu	microfilm	マイクロ・フィルム
maikuro kamera	micro camera	マイクロ・カメラ
mōtā doraibu	motor drive	モーター・ドライブ
nigan refu kamera	twin lens reflex camera	二眼レフカメラ
nikkado denchi	nickel-cadmium battery	ニッカド電池
ōto purintā	automatic printing machine	オート・プリンター
refurekkusu kamera	reflex camera	レフレックス・カメラ
renzu	lens	レンズ
roshutsu	exposure	露出
roshutsu kei	exposure meter	露出計
sanjū go miri kamera	35 mm camera	35ミリ・カメラ
sankyaku	tripod	三脚
sekigai shashin firumu	infrared film	赤外写真フィルム
serufu taimā	self-timer	セルフタイマー
sessha renzu	macro lens	接写レンズ
shattā	shutter	シャッター
shattā supīdo	shutter speed	シャッター・スピード
shibori	aperture	絞り
shiro kuro firumu	black and white film	白黒フィルム

shōten	focus	焦点
shūkō renzu	condenser lens	集光レンズ
sofuto fōkasu renzu	soft focus lens	ソフトフォーカス・レンズ
suichū kamera	underwater camera	水中カメラ
sukurīn	screen	スクリーン
suraido	slide	スライド
suraido eisha ki	slide projector	スライド映写機
sutorobo	strobe	ストロボ
taibutsu renzu	objective lens	対物レンズ
yakitsuke	printing	焼付け
zen tenkō kamera	all-weather camera	全天候カメラ
zenten renzu	sky lens	全天レンズ
zūmu renzu	zoom lens	ズーム・レンズ

PRINTING AND PUBLISHING

English to Japanese

black and white (adj)	単色の	*tanshoku no*
bleed	裁ち切り	*tachikiri*
blowup	引伸し	*hikinobashi*
boldface	肉太活字	*nikubuto katsuji*
book	本	*hon*
capital	頭文字	*kashira moji*
chapter	章	*shō*
coated paper	アート紙	*āto shi*
color separation	カラー分解	*karā bunkai*
copy	原稿	*genkō*
copyright	版権	*hanken*
cover	表紙	*hyōshi*
crop (v)	余白を切落とす	*yohaku o kiriotosu*
dummy	体裁見本	*teisai mihon*
edit (v)	編集する	*henshū suru*
edition	版	*han*
editor	編集者	*henshū sha*
engrave (v)	彫る	*horu*
font	フォント	*fonto*
form	組版	*kumiban*
format	体裁	*teisai*
four colors	四色刷り	*yonshoku zuri*
galley proof	ゲラ刷り	*gera zuri*
glossy (adj)	つやだしの	*tsuya dashi no*
grain	きめ	*kime*
grid	ごばん目	*goban me*
hardcover	堅表紙本	*kata byōshi bon*
headline	ヘッドライン	*heddo rain*
illustration	イラスト	*irasuto*
ink	インク	*inku*
insert	挿入	*sōnyū*
introduction	序	*jo*
italic	イタリック体	*itarikku tai*
jacket	カバー	*kabā*
justify (v)	行間をそろえる	*gyōkan o soroeru*
layout	割付け	*waritsuke*
letterpress	活字印刷	*katsuji insatsu*
line	行	*gyō*
line drawing	線画	*senga*
lower case	小文字	*komoji*
matrix	母型	*bokei*
matt (adj)	つや消しの	*tsuya keshi no*
mechanical	割付け用台紙	*waritsuke yō daishi*
negative	ネガ	*nega*
newsprint	新聞用紙	*shinbun yō shi*
page	ページ	*pēji*

page makeup	ページ組み	*pēji kumi*
pagination	ページ付け	*pēji zuke*
pamphlet	パンフレット	*panfuretto*
paper	紙	*kami*
paperback	紙表紙版	*kami byōshi ban*
pigment	顔料	*ganryō*
plate	プレート	*purēto*
point	ポイント	*pointo*
positive	陽画	*yōga*
preface	前書き	*maegaki*
printing	印刷	*insatsu*
printing shop	印刷所	*insatsu sho*
proofreading	校正	*kōsei*
publisher	出版社	*shuppan sha*
ream	連	*ren*
register	レジスター	*rejisutā*
scanner	スキャナ	*sukyana*
screen	網	*ami*
sewn (adj)	とじた	*tojita*
sheet	枚葉紙	*maiyōshi*
size	サイズ	*saizu*
soft-cover	紙表紙版	*kami byōshi ban*
spine	背	*se*
table of contents	目次	*mokuji*
title	標題	*hyōdai*

Japanese to English

ami	screen	網
āto shi	coated paper	アート紙
bokei	matrix	母型
fonto	font	フォント
ganryō	pigment	顔料
genkō	copy	原稿
gera zuri	galley proof	ゲラ刷り
goban me	grid	ごばん目
gyō	line	行
gyōkan o soroeru	justify (v)	行間をそろえる
han	edition	版
hanken	copyright	版権
heddo rain	headline	ヘッドライン
henshū sha	editor	編集者
henshū suru	edit (v)	編集する
hikinobashi	blowup	引伸し
hon	book	本
horu	engrave (v)	彫る
hyōdai	title	標題
hyōshi	cover	表紙
inku	ink	インク

insatsu	printing	印刷
insatsu sho	printing shop	印刷所
irasuto	illustration	イラスト
itarikku tai	italic	イタリック体
jo	introduction	序
kabā	jacket	カバー
kami	paper	紙
kami byōshi ban	paperback, softcover	紙表紙版
karā bunkai	color separation	カラー分解
kashira moji	capital	頭文字
kata byōshi bon	hardcover	堅表紙本
katsuji insatsu	letterpress	活字印刷
kime	grain	きめ
komoji	lower case	小文字
kōsei	proofreading	校正
kumiban	form	組版
maegaki	preface	前書き
maiyōshi	sheet	枚葉紙
mokuji	table of contents	目次
nega	negative	ネガ
nikubuto katsuji	boldface	肉太活字
panfuretto	pamphlet	パンフレット
pēji	page	ページ
pēji kumi	page makeup	ページ組み
pēji zuke	pagination	ページ付け
pointo	point	ポイント
purēto	plate	プレート
rejisutā	register	レジスター
ren	ream	連
saizu	size	サイズ
se	spine	背
senga	line drawing	線画
shinbun yō shi	newsprint	新聞用紙
shō	chapter	章
shuppan sha	publisher	出版社
sōnyū	insert	挿入
sukyana	scanner	スキャナ
tachikiri	bleed	裁ち切り
tanshoku no	black and white (adj)	単色の
teisai	format	体裁
teisai mihon	dummy	体裁見本
tojita	sewn (adj)	とじた
tsuya dashi no	glossy (adj)	つやだしの
tsuya keshi no	matt (adj)	つや消しの
waritsuke	layout	割付け
waritsuke yō daishi	mechanical	割付け用台紙
yōga	positive	陽画
yohaku o kiriotosu	crop (v)	余白を切落とす
yonshoku zuri	four colors	四色刷り

SECURITIES

English to Japanese

bearer bond	無記名債券	*mukimei saiken*
bearer stock	無記名株	*mukimei kabu*
bellwether issue	指標銘柄	*shihyō meigara*
blue chip stock	優良株	*yūryō kabu*
bond credit rating	債券格付	*saiken kakuzuke*
cancellation money	解約金	*kaiyaku kin*
capital gain	資産売買益	*shisan baibai eki*
capital gain tax	キャピタルゲイン税	*kyapitaru gein zei*
commission	手数料	*tesūryō*
commodity market	商品市場	*shōhin shijō*
convertible bond	転換社債	*tenkan shasai*
convertible securities	転換証券	*tenkan shōken*
corporate bonds	社債	*shasai*
current yield	現在利回り	*genzai rimawari*
dealer	ディーラー	*dīrā*
distribution	分配	*bunpai*
dividend	配当	*haitō*
dividend reinvestment plan	配当再投資	*haitō saitōshi*
Dow Jones Average	ダウ・ジョーンズ平均	*Dau Jōnzu heikin*
earnings	収益	*shūeki*
equity (stock)	株式	*kabushiki*
equity (capital)	自己資本	*jiko shihon*
exempt	免除	*menjo*
face value	額面価格	*gakumen kakaku*
fee	手数料	*tesūryō*
financial instrument	金融商品	*kin-yū shōhin*
financial market	金融市場	*kin-yū shijō*
financial product	金融商品	*kin-yū shōhin*
foreign bond	外国債券	*gaikoku saiken*
foreign currency bond	外貨債	*gaika sai*
foreign exchange	外国為替	*gaikoku kawase*
foreign exchange rate	外国為替相場	*gaikoku kawase sōba*
futures	先物契約	*sakimono keiyaku*
futures option	先物オプション	*sakimono opushon*
government bond	国債	*kokusai*
government securities	政府証券	*seifu shōken*
growth stock	成長株	*seichō kabu*
hedge	掛けつなぎ売買	*kaketsunagi baibai*
hedge-buying	買いつなぎ	*kaitsunagi*
hedge-selling	売りつなぎ	*uritsunagi*
high yield	高利回り	*kō rimawari*
income	収入	*shū-nyū*
index	指数	*shisū*
indicator	指標	*shihyō*
initial public offering	新規公募	*shinki kōbo*

insider trading	インサイダー取引	*insaidā torihiki*
international investment trust	国際投資信託	*kokusai tōshi shintaku*
investment adviser	投資顧問	*tōshi komon*
investment trust	投資信託	*tōshi shintaku*
junk bond	ジャンク・ボンド	*janku bondo*
listed stock	上場株	*jōjō kabu*
long-term	長期	*chōki*
margin (money)	証拠金	*shōkokin*
margin (difference)	売買価格差	*baibai kakaku sa*
margin trading	信用取引	*shin-yō torihiki*
maturity	償還期間	*shōkan kikan*
medium-term	中期	*chūki*
minimum margin requirement	最低証拠金率	*saitei shōkokin ritsu*
money market fund	短期金融商品投資信託	*tanki kin-yū shōhin tōshi shintaku*
municipal bond	地方公共団体債券	*chihō kōkyō dantai saiken*
mutual fund	ミューチュアル・ファンド	*myūchuaru fando*
New York Stock Exchange	ニューヨーク証券取引所	*Nyūyōku shōken torihiki jo*
new stock issue	増資	*zōshi*
Nikkei Dow Jones Average	日経ダウ	*Nikkei Dau*
Nikkei Stock Average	日経平均株価	*Nikkei heikin kabuka*
offshore fund	海外ファンド	*kaigai fando*
option trading	オプション取引	*opushon torihiki*
Osaka Stock Exchange	大証	*Taishō*
overnight transaction	オーバーナイト取引	*ōbānaito torihiki*
overseas investment	海外投資	*kaigai tōshi*
par value stock	額面株	*gakumen kabu*
penalty	違約金	*iyaku kin*
performance	運用実績	*un-yō jisseki*
portfolio	所有有価証券／金融資産	*shoyū yūka shōken/kin-yū shisan*
price earnings ratio	株価収益率	*kabuka shūeki ritsu*
principal	元本	*ganpon*
principal guaranteed	元本保証	*ganpon hoshō*
profit margin	収益率	*shūeki ritsu*
prospectus	趣意書	*shui sho*
purchase price	買入価格	*kaiire kakaku*
quarter	四半期	*shihanki*
quotation	相場	*sōba*
real estate investment trust	不動産投資信託	*fudōsan tōshi shintaku*
real investment return	実質投資収益率	*jisshitsu tōshi shūeki ritsu*
redemption	償還	*shōkan*
reinvestment	再投資	*sai tōshi*
returns	収益	*shūeki*
savings bond	貯蓄債券	*chochiku saiken*
securities	有価証券	*yūka shōken*
securities company	証券会社	*shōken gaisha*

securities market	証券市場	*shōken shijō*
security analyst	証券アナリスト	*shōken anarisuto*
share	株	*kabu*
shareholder's meeting	株主総会	*kabunushi sōkai*
share price	株価	*kabuka*
short-term	短期	*tanki*
speculative stock	仕手株	*shite kabu*
speculator	仕手	*shite*
stock	株式	*kabushiki*
stockbroker	株式仲買人	*kabushiki nakagainin*
stockholder	株主	*kabunushi*
stock investment	株式投資	*kabushiki tōshi*
stock investment trust	株式投資信託	*kabushiki tōshi shintaku*
stock issue	株式銘柄	*kabushiki meigara*
stock market	株式市場	*kabushiki shijō*
stock price	株価	*kabuka*
stock price index	株価指数	*kabuka shisū*
subscription price	応募価格	*ōbo kakaku*
swap	スワップ	*suwappu*
tax-free	免税の	*menzei no*
tax exempt bond	免税債	*menzei sai*
Tokyo foreign exchange market	東京外国為替市場	*Tōkyō gaikoku kawase shijō*
Tokyo foreign stock market	東京外国株式市場	*Tōkyō gaikoku kabushiki shijō*
Tokyo Stock Exchange	東京証券取引所／東証	*Tōkyō shōken torihikijo/Tōshō*
total return	総合利回り	*sōgō rimawari*
trading	取引	*torihiki*
Treasury Bill	財務省短期証券	*zaimushō tanki shōken*
Treasury Bond	財務省長期証券	*zaimushō chōki shōken*
Treasury Note	財務省中期証券	*zaimushō chūki shōken*
volume	出来高	*dekidaka*
warrant	ワラント／引受権証書	*waranto/hikiukeken shōsho*
zero-coupon bond	ゼロクーポン債	*zerokūpon sai*

Japanese to English

baibai kakaku sa	margin (difference)	売買価格差
bunpai	distribution	分配
chihō kōkyō dantai saiken	municipal bond	地方公共団体債券
chochiku saiken	savings bond	貯蓄債券
chōki	long-term	長期
chūki	medium-term	中期
Dau Jōnzu heikin	Dow Jones Average	ダウ・ジョーンズ平均
dekidaka	volume	出来高
dīrā	dealer	ディーラー
fudōsan tōshi shintaku	real estate investment trust	不動産投資信託
gaika sai	foreign currency bond	外貨債

gaikoku kawase	foreign exchange	外国為替
gaikoku kawase sōba	foreign exchange rate	外国為替相場
gaikoku saiken	foreign bond	外国債券
gakumen kabu	par value stock	額面株
gakumen kakaku	face value	額面価格
ganpon	principal	元本
ganpon hoshō	principal guaranteed	元本保証
genzai rimawari	current yield	現在利回り
haitō	dividend	配当
haitō saitōshi	dividend reinvestment plan	配当再投資
hikiukeken shōsho	warrant	引受権証書
insaidā torihiki	insider trading	インサイダー取引
iyaku kin	penalty	違約金
janku bondo	junk bond	ジャンク・ボンド
jiko shihon	equity (capital)	自己資本
jisshitsu tōshi shūeki ritsu	real investment return	実質投資収益率
jōjō kabu	listed stock	上場株
kabu	share	株
kabuka	stock price/share price	株価
kabuka shisū	stock price index	株価指数
kabuka shūeki ritsu	price earnings ratio	株価収益率
kabunushi	stockholder	株主
kabunushi sōkai	shareholder's meeting	株主総会
kabushiki	stock/equity	株式
kabushiki meigara	stock issue	株式銘柄
kabushiki nakagainin	stockbroker	株式仲買人
kabushiki shijō	stock market	株式市場
kabushiki tōshi	stock investment	株式投資
kabushiki tōshi shintaku	stock investment trust	株式投資信託
kaigai fando	offshore fund	海外ファンド
kaigai tōshi	overseas investment	海外投資
kaiire kakaku	purchase price	買入価格
kaitsunagi	hedge-buying	買いつなぎ
kaiyaku kin	cancellation money	解約金
kaketsunagi baibai	hedge	掛けつなぎ売買
kin-yū shijō	financial market	金融市場
kin-yū shisan	portfolio	金融資産
kin-yū shōhin	financial instrument/ financial product	金融商品
kokusai	government bond	国債
kokusai tōshi shintaku	international investment trust	国際投資信託
kō rimawari	high yield	高利回り
kyapitaru gein zei	capital gain tax	キャピタルゲイン税
menjo	exempt	免除
menzei no	tax-free	免税の
menzei sai	tax exempt bond	免税債
mukimei kabu	bearer stock	無記名株

mukimei saiken	bearer bond	無記名債券
myūchuaru fando	mutual fund	ミューチュアル・ファンド
Nikkei Dau	Nikkei Dow Jones Average	日経ダウ
Nikkei heikin kabuka	Nikkei Stock Average	日経平均株価
Nyūyōku shōken torihiki jo	New York Stock Exchange	ニューヨーク証券取引所
ōbānaito torihiki	overnight transaction	オーバーナイト取引
ōbo kakaku	subscription price	応募価格
opushon torihiki	option trading	オプション取引
saiken kakuzuke	bond credit rating	債券格付
sai tōshi	reinvestment	再投資
saitei shōkokin ritsu	minimum margin requirement	最低証拠金率
sakimono keiyaku	futures	先物契約
sakimono opushon	futures option	先物オプション
seichō kabu	growth stock	成長株
seifu shōken	government securities	政府証券
shasai	corporate bonds	社債
shihanki	quarter	四半期
shihyō	indicator	指標
shihyō meigara	bellwether issue	指標銘柄
shinki kōbo	initial public offering	新規公募
shin-yō torihiki	margin trading	信用取引
shisan baibai eki	capital gain	資産売買益
shisū	index	指数
shite	speculator	仕手
shite kabu	speculative stock	仕手株
shōhin shijō	commodity market	商品市場
shōkan	redemption	償還
shōkan kikan	maturity	償還期間
shōken anarisuto	security analyst	証券アナリスト
shōken gaisha	securities company	証券会社
shōken shijō	securities market	証券市場
shōkokin	margin (money)	証拠金
shoyū yūka shōken	portfolio	所有有価証券
shūeki	earnings/returns	収益
shūeki ritsu	profit margin	収益率
shui sho	prospectus	趣意書
shū-nyū	income	収入
sōba	quotation	相場
sōgō rimawari	total return	総合利回り
suwappu	swap	スワップ
Taishō	Osaka Stock Exchange	大証
tanki	short-term	短期
tanki kin-yū shōhin tōshi shintaku	money market fund	短期金融商品投資信託
tenkan shasai	convertible bond	転換社債
tenkan shōken	convertible securities	転換証券

tesūryō	commission/fee	手数料
Tōkyō gaikoku kabushiki shijō	Tokyo foreign stock market	東京外国株式市場
Tōkyō gaikoku kawase shijō	Tokyo foreign exchange market	東京外国為替市場
Tōkyō shōken torihikijo	Tokyo Stock Exchange	東京証券取引所
torihiki	trading	取引
tōshi komon	investment adviser	投資顧問
tōshi shintaku	investment trust	投資信託
Tōshō	Tokyo Stock Exchange	東証
un-yō jisseki	performance	運用実績
uritsunagi	hedge-selling	売りつなぎ
waranto	warrant	ワラント
yūka shōken	securities	有価証券
yūryō kabu	blue chip stock	優良株
zaimushō chōki shōken	Treasury Bond	財務省長期証券
zaimushō chūki shōken	Treasury Note	財務省中期証券
zaimushō tanki shōken	Treasury Bill	財務省短期証券
zerokūpon sai	zero-coupon bond	ゼロクーポン債
zōshi	new stock issue	増資

V. GENERAL INFORMATION

ABBREVIATIONS

a.a. always afloat
a.a.r. against all risks
a/c account
A/C account current
acct. account
a.c.v. actual cash value
a.d. after date
a.f.b. air freight bill
agcy. agency
agt. agent
a.m.t. air mail transfer
a/o account of
A.P. accounts payable
A/P authority to pay
approx. approximately
A.R. accounts receivable
a/r all risks
A/S, A.S. account sales
a/s at sight
at. wt. atomic weight
av. average
avdp. avoirdupois
a/w actual weight
a.w.b. air waybill
bal. balance
bar. barrel
bbl. barrel
b/d brought down
B/E, b/e bill of exchange
b/f brought forward
B.H. bill of health
bk. bank
bkge. brokerage
B/L bill of lading
b/o brought over
B.P. bills payable
b.p. by procuration
B.R. bills receivable
B/S balance sheet
b.t. berth terms
bu. bushel
B/V book value
ca. circa; centaire
C.A. chartered accountant
c.a. current account

C.A.D. cash against documents
C.B. cash book
C.B.D. cash before delivery
c.c. carbon copy
c/d carried down
c.d. cum dividend
c/f carried forward
cf. compare
c & f cost and freight
C/H clearing house
C.H. custom house
ch. fwd. charges forward
ch. pd. charges paid
ch. ppd. charges prepaid
chq. check, cheque
c.i.f. cost, insurance, freight
c.i.f. & c. cost, insurance, freight, and commission
c.i.f. & e. cost, insurance, freight, and exchange
c.i.f. & i. cost, insurance, freight, and interest
c.l. car load
C/m call of more
C/N credit note
c/o care of
co. company
C.O.D. cash on delivery
comm. commission
corp. corporation
C.O.S. cash on shipment
C.P. carriage paid
C/P charter party
c.p.d. charters pay duties
cpn. corporation
cr. credit; creditor
C/T cable transfer
c.t.l. constructive total loss
c.t.l.o. construction total loss only
cum. cumulative
cum div. cum dividend
cum. pref. cumulative preference
c/w commercial weight
C.W.O. cash with order
cwt. hundredweight
D/A documents against acceptance; deposit account
D.A.P. documents against payment
db. debenture
DCF discounted cash flow
d/d days after date; delivered
deb. debenture
def. deferred

dept. department
d.f. dead freight
dft. draft
dft/a. draft attached
dft/c. clean draft
disc. discount
div. dividend
DL dayletter
DLT daily letter telegram
D/N debit note
D/O delivery order
do. ditto
doz. dozen
D/P documents against payment
dr. debtor
Dr. doctor
d/s, d.s. days after sight
d.w. deadweight
D/W dock warrant
dwt. pennyweight
dz. dozen
ECU European Currency Unit
E.E.T. East European Time
e.g. for example
encl. enclosure
end. endorsement
E. & O.E. errors and omissions excepted
e.o.m. end of month
e.o.h.p. except otherwise herein provided
esp. especially
Esq. Esquire
est. established
ex out
ex cp. ex coupon
ex div. ex dividend
ex int. ex interest
ex n. ex new (shares)
ex stre. ex store
ex whf. ex wharf
f.a.a. free of all average
f.a.c. fast as can
f.a.k. freight all kinds
f.a.q. fair average quality; free alongside quay
f.a.s. free alongside ship
f/c for cash
f c. & s. free of capture and seizure
f.c.s.r. & c.c. free of capture, seizure, riots, and civil commotion
F.D. free delivery to dock
f.d. free discharge

ff. following; folios
f.g.a. free of general average
f.i.b. free in bunker
f.i.o. free in and out
f.i.t. free in truck
f.o.b. free on board
f.o.c. free of charge
f.o.d. free of damage
fol. following; folio
f.o.q. free on quay
f.o.r. free on rail
f.o.s. free on steamer
f.o.t. free on truck(s)
f.o.w. free on wagons; free on wharf
F.P. floating policy
f.p. fully paid
f.p.a. free of particular average
frt. freight
frt. pd. freight paid
frt. ppd. freight prepaid
frt. fwd. freight forward
ft. foot
fwd. forward
f.x. foreign exchange
g.a. general average
g.b.o. goods in bad order
g.m.b. good merchantable brand
g.m.q. good merchantable quality
G.M.T. Greenwich Mean Time
GDP gross domestic product
GNP gross national product
g.o.b. good ordinary brand
gr. gross
GRT gross register ton
gr. wt. gross weight
GT gross tonnage
h.c. home consumption
hgt. height
hhd. hogshead
H.O. head office
H.P. hire purchase
HP horsepower
ht. height
IDP integrated data processing
i.e. that is
I/F insufficient funds
i.h.p. indicated horsepower
imp. import
Inc. incorporated

incl. inclusive
ins. insurance
int. interest
inv. invoice
I.O.U. I owe you
J/A, j.a. joint account
Jr. Junior
KV kilovolt
KW kilowatt
KWh kilowatt hour
L/C, l.c. letter of credit
LCD telegram in the language of the country of destination
LCO telegram in the language of the country of origin
ldg. landing; loading
L.t. long ton
Ltd. limited
l. tn. long ton
m. month
m/a my account
max. maximum
M.D. memorandum of deposit
M/D, m.d. months after date
memo. memorandum
Messrs. plural of Mr.
mfr. manufacturer
min. minimum
MLR minimum lending rate
M.O. money order
m.o. my order
mortg. mortgage
M/P, m.p. months after payment
M/R mate's receipt
M/S, m.s. months' sight
M.T. mail transfer
M/U making-up price
n. name; nominal
n/a no account
N/A no advice
n.c.v. no commercial value
n.d. no date
n.e.s. not elsewhere specified
N/F no funds
NL night letter
N/N no noting
N/O no orders
no. number
n.o.e. not otherwise enumerated
n.o.s. not otherwise stated
nos. numbers

NPV no par value
nr. number
n.r.t. net register ton
N/S not sufficient funds
NSF not sufficient funds
n. wt. net weight
o/a on account
OCP overseas common point
O/D, o/d on demand; overdraft
o.e. omissions excepted
o/h overhead
ono. or nearest offer
O/o order of
O.P. open policy
o.p. out of print; overproof
O/R, o.r. owner's risk
ord. order; ordinary
O.S., o/s out of stock
OT overtime
p. page; per; premium
P.A., p.a. particular average; per annum
P/A power of attorney; private account
PAL phase alternation line
pat. pend. patent pending
P.A.Y.E. pay as you earn
p/c petty cash
p.c. percent; price current
pcl. parcel
pd. paid
pf. preferred
pfd. preferred
pkg. package
P/L profit and loss
p.l. partial loss
P/N promissory note
P.O. post office; postal order
P.O.B. post office box
P.O.O. post office order
p.o.r. pay on return
pp. pages
p & p postage and packing
p. pro per procuration
ppd. prepaid
ppt. prompt
pref. preference
prox. proximo
P.S. postscript
pt. payment
P.T.O., p.t.o. please turn over

ptly. pd. partly paid
p.v. par value
qlty. quality
qty. quantity
r. & c.c. riot and civil commotions
R/D refer to drawer
R.D.C. running down clause
re. in regard to
rec. received; receipt
recd. received
red. redeemable
ref. reference
reg. registered
retd. returned
rev. revenue
R.O.D. refused on delivery
R.P. reply paid
r.p.s. revolutions per second
R.S.V.P. please reply
R.S.W.C. right side up with care
Ry. railway
s.a.e. stamped addressed envelope
S.A.V. stock at valuation
S/D sea damaged
S/D, s.d. sight draft
s.d. without date
SDR special drawing rights
sgd. signed
s. & h. ex Sundays and holidays excepted
shipt. shipment
sig. signature
S/LC, s. & l.c. sue and labor clause
S/N shipping note
s.o. seller's option
s.o.p. standard operating procedure
spt. spot
Sr. Senior
S.S., s.s. steamship
s.t. short ton
ster. sterling
St. Ex. stock exchange
stg. sterling
s.v. sub voce
T.A. telegraphic address
T.B. trial balance
tel. telephone
temp. temporary secretary
T.L., t.l. total loss
T.L.O. total loss only

TM multiple telegram
T.O. turn over
TR telegram to be called for
TR, T/R trust receipt
tr. transfer
TT, T.T. telegraphic transfer (cable)
TX Telex
UGT urgent
u.s.c. under separate cover
U/ws underwriters
v. volt
val. value
v.a.t. value-added tax
v.g. very good
VHF very high frequency
v.h.r. very highly recommended
w. watt
W.A. with average
W.B. way bill
w.c. without charge
W.E.T. West European Time
wg. weight guaranteed
whse. warehouse
w.o.g. with other goods
W.P. weather permitting; without prejudice
w.p.a. with particular average
W.R. war risk
W/R, wr. warehouse receipt
W.W.D. weather working day
wt. weight
x.c. ex coupon
x.d. ex dividend
x.i. ex interest
x.n. ex new shares
y. year
yd. yard
yr. year
yrly. yearly

WEIGHTS AND MEASURES

U.S. UNIT	METRIC EQUIVALENT
mile	1.609 kilometers
yard	0.914 meters
foot	30.480 centimeters
inch	2.540 centimeters
square mile	2.590 square kilometers
acre	0.405 hectares
square yard	0.836 square meters
square foot	0.093 square meters
square inch	6.451 square centimeters
cubic yard	0.765 cubic meters
cubic foot	0.028 cubic meters
cubic inch	16.387 cubic centimeters
short ton	0.907 metric tons
long ton	1.016 metric tons
short hundredweight	45.359 kilograms
long hundredweight	50.802 kilograms
pound	0.453 kilograms
ounce	28.349 grams
gallon	3.785 liters
quart	0.946 liters
pint	0.473 liters
fluid ounce	29.573 milliliters
bushel	35.238 liters
peck	8.809 liters
quart	1.101 liters
pint	0.550 liters

TEMPERATURE AND CLIMATE

Temperature Conversion Chart

DEGREES CELSIUS	DEGREES FAHRENHEIT
–5	23
0	32
5	41
10	50
15	59
20	68
25	77
30	86
35	95
40	104

Average daily mean temperatures for major cities

MAJOR CITIES FROM NORTH TO SOUTH	JAN. °C	JAN. °F	APRIL °C	APRIL °F	JULY °C	JULY °F	OCT. °C	OCT. °F
Sapporo	–5.1	22.8	6.1	43.0	20.0	68.4	10.3	50.7
Sendai	0.6	33.1	9.5	49.3	21.9	71.8	13.9	57.2
Tokyo	4.1	39.4	13.4	56.3	25.0	77.4	16.7	62.4
Nagoya	3.2	37.8	13.0	55.6	25.5	78.3	16.4	61.9
Kyoto	3.5	38.3	13.0	55.6	25.9	79.0	16.6	62.2
Hiroshima	4.1	39.4	12.9	55.4	25.2	77.9	16.6	62.2
Takamatsu	4.3	39.9	12.6	54.5	25.9	79.0	16.6	62.1
Fukuoka	5.2	41.5	13.8	57.0	26.2	79.7	17.1	63.1
Kagoshima	6.7	41.1	15.5	60.1	26.6	80.4	18.9	66.4
Naha	15.8	60.8	20.6	69.4	27.9	82.8	23.9	75.4

Weather and Climate Terms

spring	春	*haru*
summer	夏	*natsu*
autumn	秋	*aki*
winter	冬	*fuyu*
hot	暑い	*atsui*
hot and humid	蒸し暑い	*mushiatsui*
sunny	日が照っている	*hi ga tette iru*
warm	暖かい	*atatakai*
cool	涼しい	*suzushii*
windy	風の強い	*kaze no tsuyoi*
foggy	霧のかかった	*kiri no kakatta*
snowing	雪が降っている	*yuki ga futte iru*
raining	雨が降っている	*ame ga futte iru*
earthquake	地震	*jishin*

COMMUNICATIONS

Telephone

telephone — 電話
denwa

public phone — 公衆電話
kōshū denwa

telephone directory — 電話帳
denwa chō

local call — 市内電話
shinai denwa

long-distance call	長距離電話 *chō kyori denwa*
person-to-person call	パーソナル・コール *pāsonaru kōru*
collect call	料金先方払いの電話 *ryōkin senpō barai no denwa*
international call	国際電話 *kokusai denwa*
telephone card	テレフォンカード *terefon kādo*

Using Public Phones

A three-minute local call costs 10 yen. You lift the receiver, deposit your coins, wait for a dial tone, then dial the number. If you're going to speak for more than three minutes, insert the coins at the beginning, or you may be cut off abruptly. If you do hear a warning tone, insert more coins immediately. Any unused coins will be returned at the end of your call.

The easiest way to use a public phone is to first buy a prepaid telephone card: a 500-yen card will buy 50 3-minute calls, and a 1000-yen card will buy 105 3-minute calls. You insert the card into a slot on the phone, and you can talk without interruption. The amount will be deducted from the card. You can buy them everywhere: kiosks at train stations, convenience stores, supermarkets, bookstores—even in some phone booths! These cards are quite popular: you may even receive some as gifts!

Most public phones are green or gray. Both take telephone cards; most take coins as well, although some green ones don't. The gray phones are the newest; they have monitor screens with simple instructions for use in English, as well as information about your call.

To make a direct dial international call from a public phone (you'll need a lot of coins or several telephone cards), look for one that says "International & Domestic Card/Coin Telephone" on the front. Dial the access number 001, then the international country code and the number. [Note: 001 is the access number for Kokusai Denshin Denwa (KDD); other companies also provide international service: International Telecom Japan Inc. (ITJ), access number 0041; and International Digital Communications, Inc. (IDC), access number 0061. The areas served by these companies vary, as do the rates.]

To make an operator-assisted call (person-to-person, collect, or credit card call), dial 0051 from almost any pay phone.

International Country Codes

Algeria	213	Denmark	45
Argentina	54	Finland	358
Australia	61	France	33
Austria	43	Germany	49
Belgium	32	Gibraltar	350
Brazil	55	Greece	30
Canada	1	Hong Kong	852
Chile	56	Hungary	36
China	86	Iceland	354
Colombia	57	India	91

Ireland	353	Saudi Arabia	966
Israel	972	Singapore	65
Italy	39	South Africa	27
Japan	81	South Korea	82
Kuwait	965	Spain	34
Luxembourg	352	Sri Lanka	94
Malta	356	Sweden	46
Mexico	52	Switzerland	41
Morocco	212	Taiwan	886
Netherlands	31	Thailand	66
New Zealand	64	Tunisia	216
Norway	47	Turkey	90
Philippines	63	United Kingdom	44
Poland	48	USA	1
Portugal	351	Venezuela	58
Russia	7		

Area Codes within Japan

Fukuoka	092	Narita	0476
Hiroshima	082	Okayama	086
Kagoshima	0992	Osaka	06
Kobe	078	Sapporo	011
Kyoto	075	Sendai	022
Nagasaki	0958	Tokyo	03
Nagoya	052	Yokohama	045

Faxes, Computer Networking, Telegrams

Most hotels have fax machines, and many have business service centers where computers are also available. Ask at the front desk. Many hotel phones, and also the new gray public phones, can be used for computer network access.

For sending an international fax or telegram, you can also contact the KDD information center (Tel: 0057).

POSTAL SERVICES

The easiest way to send your mail is to request help from your hotel front desk staff. Either they will mail things for you, or they can direct you to the nearest mailbox or post office. Post offices are identified by a symbol that looks like a red capital "T" with a horizontal bar over the top. Mailboxes on the street have this symbol too; the mailboxes are red. You can also buy stamps at shops and kiosks that display the red symbol. Local post offices are open from 9:00 AM–5:00 PM weekdays. District post offices (the main post office of each ward in a city) keep longer hours and are open on Saturdays. Check the business hours with the individual branch. Each large city and town has a central post office, usually located near the main train station. In Tokyo, the Central Post Office, open around the clock daily, is located on Tokyo Station Plaza, Marunouchi side. Tokyo also has an International Post Office, located in Otemachi.

For mailing a large package overseas, if you can't get help from your hotel staff, you have to go to a district, central, or international post office. The local ones don't handle large parcels.

Postal rates within Japan are 80 yen up to 25 grams; 90 yen up to 50 grams for envelopes between 9–12 cm. x 14–23.5 cm. Mail that does not fit within those measurements costs 130 yen up to 50 grams, and 190 yen up to 100 grams. Postcards cost 50 yen.

Overseas Airmail Rates

	ASIA, NORTH PACIFIC	OCEANA, NEAR & MIDDLE EAST, NORTH AMERICA, CENTRAL AMERICA, EUROPE, FORMER USSR	AFRICA, SOUTH AMERICA
Postcards	70 yen	70 yen	70 yen
Aerograms	90 yen	90 yen	90 yen
Letters			
(up to 10 grams)	90 yen	110 yen	130 yen
(each extra 10 grams)	60 yen	80 yen	100 yen

MAJOR HOLIDAYS

January 1	New Year's Day	元旦 *gantan*
January 15	Adulthood Day	成人の日 *seijin no hi*
February 11	National Foundation Day	建国記念日 *kenkoku kinen bi*
March 20 or 21	Vernal Equinox Day	春分の日 *shunbun no hi*
April 29	Greenery Day	緑の日 *midori no hi*
May 3	Constitution Day	憲法記念日 *kenpō kinen bi*
May 5	Children's Day	子供の日 *kodomo no hi*
September 15	Respect for the Aged Day	敬老の日 *keirō no hi*
September 23 or 24	Autumnal Equinox Day	秋分の日 *shūbun no hi*
October 10	Health-Sports Day	体育の日 *taiiku no hi*
November 3	Culture Day	文化の日 *bunka no hi*
November 23	Labor Thanksgiving Day	勤労感謝の日 *kinrō kansha no hi*
December 23	Emperor's Birthday	天皇誕生日 *tennō tanjō bi*

TIME ZONES

Use the following table to know the time difference between where you are and other major cities. Note, however, that during April through September, you will also have to take Daylight Savings Time into account. Since there are four time zones for the United States, eleven zones for the former U.S.S.R., and three for Australia, we've listed major cities for these countries. All of Japan is in the same zone.

–8 HOURS	–5 HOURS	GREENWICH MEAN TIME	+1 HOUR	+7 HOURS
Anchorage Los Angeles San Francisco	Boston New York Washington, D.C.	Great Britain Iceland Ireland Portugal	Austria Belgium Denmark France Germany Hungary Italy Luxembourg Malta Monaco Netherlands Norway Poland Spain Sweden Switzerland	Bangkok Jakarta **+8 HOURS** Hong Kong Kuala Lumpur Manila Shanghai Singapore **+9 HOURS** Beijing Japan Seoul
–10 HOURS	**–6 HOURS**		**+2 HOURS**	**+10 HOURS**
Honolulu	Chicago Dallas Houston		Finland Greece Romania South Africa **+3 HOURS** Turkey Moscow	Sydney **+12 HOURS** New Zealand

CURRENCY INFORMATION

Major Currencies of the World

Argentina	Argentinian Peso
Australia	Australian Dollar
Austria	Schilling

Belgium	Belgian Franc
Brazil	Cruzeiro
China (PRC)	Yuan
Colombia	Colombian Peso
Finland	Finnmark
France	Franc
Germany	Mark (DM)
Greece	Drachma
Hong Kong	Hong Kong Dollar
Iceland	Krone
India	Rupee
Indonesia	Rupian
Ireland	Punt
Italy	Lira
Japan	Yen
Korea (South)	Won
Malaysia	Ringgit
Mexico	Mexican Peso
Netherlands	Guilder
New Zealand	New Zealand Dollar
Norway	Norwegian Krone
Philippines	Peso
Portugal	Escudo
Russia	Ruble
Singapore	Singapore Dollar
Spain	Peseta
Sweeden	Swedish Krone
Switzerland	Swiss Franc
Thailand	Baht
Turkey	Lira
United Kingdom	Pound Sterling
Venezuela	Bolivar

Major Commercial Banks

Note: Japanese names are in parentheses.

Bank of Tokyo, Ltd. (Tokyo Ginko)
3-2 Nihonbashi Hongoku-cho 1-chome
Chuo-ku, Tokyo 103
Tel: (03) 3245-1111

Dai-ichi Kangyo Bank, Ltd. (Daiichi Kangyo Ginko)
1-5 Uchisaiwai-cho 1-chome
Chiyoda-ku, Tokyo 100
Tel: (03) 3596-1111

Fuji Bank, Ltd. (Fuji Ginko)
5-5 Otemachi 1-chome
Chiyoda-ku, Tokyo 100
Tel: (03) 3216-2211

Industrial Bank of Japan, Ltd. (Nihon Kogyo Ginko)
3-3 Marunouchi 1-chome
Chiyoda-ku, Tokyo 100
Tel: (03) 3214-1111
Fax: (03) 3201-7643

Long-Term Credit Bank of Japan, Ltd.
(Nihon Choki Shinyo Ginko)
2-4 Otemachi 1-chome
Chiyoda-ku, Tokyo 100
Tel: (03) 3211-5111

Mitsubishi Bank, Ltd. (Mitsubishi Ginko)
7-1 Marunouchi 2-chome
Chiyoda-ku, Tokyo 100
Tel: (03) 3240-1111

Mitsubishi Trust & Banking Corporation
(Mitsubishi Shintaku Ginko)
4-5 Marunouchi 1-chome
Chiyoda-ku, Tokyo 100
Tel: (03) 3212-1211
Fax: (03) 3288-4095

Sakura Bank, Ltd. (Sakura Ginko)
3-1 Kudan Minami 1-chome
Chiyoda-ku, Tokyo 100-91
Tel: (03) 3230-3111

Sanwa Bank, Ltd. (Sanwa Ginko)
5-6 Fushimimachi 3-chome
Chuo-ku, Osaka, Osaka 541
Tel: (06) 202-2281
Fax: (06) 231-4244

Sumitomo Bank, Ltd. (Sumitomo Ginko)
6-5 Kitahama 4-chome
Chuo-ku, Osaka, Osaka 541
Tel: (06) 227-2111
Fax: (06) 229-1083

Sumitomo Trust & Banking Co., Ltd.
(Sumitomo Shintaku Ginko)
5-33 Kitahama 4-chome
Chuo-ku, Osaka, Osaka 541
Tel: (06) 220-2121

Tokai Bank, Ltd. (Tokai Ginko)
21-24 Nishiki 3-chome
Naka-ku, Nagoya, Aichi 460
Tel: (052) 211-1111

MAJOR PERIODICALS

Japanese language	**English language**
	Business and Economy
Nihon Keizai Shimbun	The Japan Economic Journal (weekly)
	Newspapers
Yomiuri Shimbun	The Japan Times
Asahi Shimbun	Asahi Evening News
Mainichi Shimbun	Mainichi Daily News
Chunichi Shimbun	The Daily Yomiuri
Sankei Shimbun	

Note: Newsstands at major tourist hotels carry the *Far Eastern Economic Review*, the *International Herald Tribune*, *Time*, *Newsweek*, *U.S. News & World Report*, and the *Asian Wall Street Journal*.

ANNUAL TRADE FAIRS

This is a partial list of annual events. Changes may occur from year to year, as well as during the year. It is advisable to consult the Japan Convention Bureau of the Japan National Tourist Organization (JNTO), both in Japan and abroad, for up-to-date information.

Tokyo

January	Tokyo Auto Salon/Tokyo Racing Car Show
February	MACWORLD Expo/Tokyo
March	FOODEX Japan JAPAN SHOP Store Automation Show
April	Communications Tokyo Tokyo International Trade Fair*
April–May	Tokyo International Good Living Show
May	International Food Machinery Exhibition Business Show Tokyo High-Tech Materials Exhibition* High-Tech Tokyo
June	Japan Printed Circuit Association Show (JPCA) Tokyo Toy Show
July	Cold Type Offset Printing Fair Tokyo
August	PRINTEK TOKYO
September	Database Tokyo Data Show IGAS International Graphic Arts Show*
October	Japan Electronics Show
October–November	Tokyo Motor Show*
November	Scientific Instrument Show Japan* Automatic Machines and Technology Exhibition
December	World Travel Fair*

Kita Kyushu

March	West Japan Total Living Show

*held every other year

May	West Japan Machine Tool Fair West Japan Import Fair
September	West Japan China Ware Fair
October	West Japan Foods Fair

Nagoya

January	Nagoya International Automobile Show
March–April	Photo & Video Accessory Show
June	Business Machine Show
October	Mechatronics Technology Japan*
November	Nagoya Motor Show

Osaka

March	Machinery of Bakery and Confectionery Show (MOBAC)* Japan Print: Printing Machinery and Equipment
April–May	Osaka International Trade Fair*
May	Osaka Mechatronics Fair
June	Business Show Osaka*
September	Osaka Wood Technology Fair*
October—November	Japan International Machine Tool Fair (held every 2 years, alternate years in Tokyo)

For additional information, contact the Japan Convention Bureau, Japan National Tourist Organization.

Head Office:	2-10-1 Yurakucho, Chiyoda-ku Tokyo 100, Japan Tel: (03) 3216-2905 Fax: (03) 3214-7680
New York Office:	Rockefeller Plaza 630 Fifth Avenue New York, NY 10011 Tel: (212) 757-5640 Fax: (212) 307-6754

*held every other year

TRAVEL TIMES

Air Travel

Most international flights to Japan arrive at New Tokyo International Airport at Narita (Narita Airport), which is 60 kilometers from downtown Tokyo. Airport limousine buses go nonstop to the Tokyo City Air Terminal (TCAT, pronounced tee-cat). The ride takes one hour. Most leading Tokyo hotels are about a 3,000-yen taxi ride from TCAT. Some limousine buses go to the hotels, either directly or via TCAT. Information on these schedules, other bus schedules, and train transportation from Narita to Tokyo is available in the airport arrival lobby.

Haneda Airport is used for domestic flights to and from the Tokyo area. There are three major domestic airlines: Japan Air Lines (JAL), All Nippon Airways (ANA), and Nippon Air System (JAS). Their phone numbers in Tokyo are as follows:

	INTERNATIONAL	DOMESTIC
ANA	(03) 3272-1212	(03) 5489-8800
JAL	(03) 5259-3777	(03) 5489-2111
JAS	(03) 3438-1155	(03) 3432-6111

Kansai International Airport, which opened in 1994, is an option for travelers with business in the Osaka area or western Japan.

Approximate Flying Time to Japan

Bangkok–Tokyo	5 hours, 50 minutes
Beijing–Tokyo	3 hours, 50 minutes
Hong Kong–Tokyo	3 hours, 55 minutes
London–Tokyo	11 hours, 40 minutes
Los Angeles–Tokyo	11 hours, 15 minutes
New Delhi–Tokyo (via Bangkok)	9 hours, 30 minutes
New York–Tokyo	13 hours, 45 minutes
Seoul–Tokyo	2 hours, 5 minutes
Singapore–Tokyo	6 hours, 40 minutes
Sydney–Tokyo	9 hours, 30 minutes

Average Flying Time Between Major Japanese Cities

Fukuoka–Tokyo	1 hour, 45 minutes
Hiroshima–Tokyo	1 hour, 30 minutes
Kagoshima–Tokyo	1 hour, 55 minutes
Nagasaki–Tokyo	1 hour, 55 minutes
Nagoya–Tokyo	1 hour
Okinawa–Tokyo	2 hours, 45 minutes
Osaka–Tokyo	1 hour
Sapporo–Tokyo	1 hour, 25 minutes
Takamatsu–Tokyo	1 hour, 20 minutes

Rail Travel

Japan has an efficient rail system. Visitors find the Shinkansen, popularly known as the bullet train, operated by Japan Railways (JR), a convenient way to travel between cities. There are many other types of passenger trains as well.

Note: There are few porters available in Japanese train stations and there are many staircases to climb. You'll do well to travel light!

Trains

Super Express or Bullet Trains
Shinkansen

There are three Shinkansen lines; each line has different kinds of trains—faster ones make fewer stops and slower ones make more stops. The different trains have special names for each line, as you can see on the chart. You specify the one you want when buying your ticket.

TOKAIDO-SANYO SHINKANSEN	
Route	Tokyo Station, Tokyo–Hakata
Fewest stops	Nozomi trains
More stops	Hikari trains
Most stops	Kodama trains
TOHOKU-YAMAGATA SHINKANSEN	
Route	Tokyo Station, Tokyo–Morioka
Few stops	Yamabiko trains
More stops	Aoba trains
Route	Tokyo Station, Tokyo–Yamagata
	Tsubasa trains
JOETSU SHINKANSEN	
Route	Tokyo Station, Tokyo–Niigata
Fewer stops	Asahi trains
More stops	Toki trains

Other Types of Trains

Limited express	特急 *tokkyū*
Ordinary express	急行 *kyūkō*
Local trains	普通 *futsū*

Fares and Classes

You need a basic fare ticket for all train travel. And if you travel by Shinkansen, limited express, or ordinary express, you pay a supplementary fare as well. There are three classes of seats on these trains: Green Car (first class), reserved seats, and unreserved seats. Green Car and reserved seats also cost extra.

When traveling on intercity trains in Japan, you should buy your tickets in advance. Trains are popular and choice seats fill up fast. Check with a travel agency, and get the train and class you want. You can, of course, buy tickets at the station as well.

Before you depart for Japan, you might want to inquire at a Japan National Tourist Office or a Japan Airlines office about the money-saving Japan Rail Pass.

Green Car	グリーン車 *gurīn sha*
reserved seats	指定席 *shitei seki*
unreserved seats	自由席 *jiyū seki*

Rail Travel Time Between Tokyo and Major Cities

CITY	**NO. OF HOURS**
Kamakura	1
Hakone	$1\frac{1}{2}$
Nikko	$1\frac{3}{4}$
Nagoya	2
Gifu	$2\frac{1}{4}$
Kyoto	$2\frac{3}{4}$
Osaka	3
Kobe	$3\frac{1}{4}$
Toba	$3\frac{1}{2}$
Nara	$3\frac{1}{4}$
Sendai	$1\frac{3}{4}$
Okayama	$3\frac{3}{4}$
Takamatsu	5
Hiroshima	$4\frac{3}{4}$
Kanazawa	$5\frac{1}{4}$
Hakata (Fukuoka)	6
Beppu	7
Nagasaki	8
Kagoshima	10
Sapporo	$12\frac{1}{2}$

Subways and Commuter Trains

Most major Japanese cities have fast, clean, and efficient subway and commuter train systems. The latter are not quite the Western equivalent of commuter trains. They're actually a complex system of public and private trains crisscrossing and encircling the urban areas, and linking with the subways. In Tokyo, the Yamanote-sen is the line that encircles, or loops around, the city's downtown area; in Osaka, the loop line is called the Kanjo-sen.

Subway entrances are marked by these symbols:

You can use the subways and commuter trains easily if you have a map or guide, and there are many available. The station signs are in Roman letters, or *romaji* so you'll be able to read them. The only difficulty you might have will be with the ticket machines at the entrance. Figuring out the cost of the ride can be complicated. But you can just buy the cheapest ticket in order to get in. Keep it until the end of your ride. Hand it to the ticket taker at the exit; you'll be told how much you owe, and you can pay then.

Taxis

Cruising taxis are plentiful in cities and large towns; there are also taxi stands at train stations, near hotels, and in certain downtown districts. Meters show the fare in digits; there's a 20 percent surcharge added from 11:00 pm until 5:00 am; you don't tip unless the driver does something special for you, like carrying luggage or waiting while you make a stop. Don't open or close the door—the driver operates it automatically.

Japanese taxis don't always take you right to your destination. The drivers may not know exactly where it is, and if they do, they're not expected to venture far from a main road unless they choose to. If you're going someplace well known, like a hotel or train station, there's no problem. Otherwise, tell the driver the main intersection or landmark near your destination (ask someone to write it in Japanese beforehand). Some drivers will help you from there; others will expect you to get out and find your own way from the main road.

TRAVEL TIPS

On the Plane

1. Be aware that the engine noise is less noticeable in the front part of the plane. Try to sleep. Some frequent travelers bring along earplugs, eyeshades, and slippers.
2. Wear comfortable, loose-fitting clothing.
3. Walk up and down the aisles, when permitted, at least five minutes every hour to maintain body circulation.
4. Limit alcohol intake—altitude heightens the intoxicating effect.
5. Avoid heavy foods and caffeine, which dehydrate the body.
6. Drink plenty of liquids and eat foods rich in potassium. Pressurized cabins cause dehydration.
7. Take it easy when you arrive. When possible, schedule your first important meeting according to your "at home" peak period.

Jet Lag

Disruption of the body's natural cycles can put a lingering damper on your trip; so take the following precautions:

1. *Avoid loss of sleep* by taking a flight that will get you to your destination early in the evening, if at all possible. Get a good night's sleep at home the night before your departure.
2. *Rearrange your daily routine* and sleeping schedule to harmonize with a normal body clock at your destination.
3. *Avoid stress and last-minute rush.* You're going to need all your strength.

4. *Rearrange your eating habits*. Start four days early—begin a diet of alternate days of feasting and fasting. "Feast" features high-protein breakfasts and lunches (to increase energy level and wakefulness) and high-carbohydrate dinners (to help induce sleep).

Driving

Foreigners driving in Japan must contend with certain realities: The steering wheel is on the right side of the car, and you drive on the left side of the road; most expressway signs are in Japanese; nonexpress roads may be narrow and usually have no sidewalks. Speedometers are only in kilometers, streets are crowded with pedestrians, bicycles, vendors, and cars, and penalties for accidents are high. In short, for the visitor to Japan, driving is *not* recommended. Do you still want to? If so, you'll need an International Driving Permit. You'll also need to be familiar with Japanese road signs and traffic signs. The Japan Automobile Federation in Tokyo has a useful booklet called "Rules of the Road," which you might want to read if you're planning on driving. One final note: There are road checkpoints for drivers under the influence of alcohol, and penalties can be severe.

Shopping

Most Japanese department stores are open daily from 10:00 AM to 7:00 PM. Each department store is closed once a week. Other stores are open from 10:00 AM to 7:00 PM. Many stay open on Sundays.

Japanese department stores carry all the things you would expect, and a lot more as well. The folkware or *mingei* sections have crafts from all over Japan: handmade dolls, toys, pottery, paper crafts, bamboo baskets, lacquer trays, bowls, chopsticks, handmade and dyed fabrics, and more. You'll also find typical Japanese craft items in the housewares section—in a range from everyday pottery to expensive lacquerware. Such items usually come in sets of five, not six or eight as in Western countries.

Don't miss the food section: the entire basement floor is devoted to fresh and packaged foods, both Japanese and Western style.

Clothing Sizes

You should try on Japanese clothing before you buy it. Although you can find a good fit in most items, some may be short-waisted for Westerners, and some sleeves may also be short. For women, dress sizes run in odd numbers 7, 9, 13, and so forth, and are not too different from American sizes. Men's suit sizes are roughly the centimeter equivalent of American suit sizes (multiplying the inches by 2.5 instead of the usual 2.54 centimeters).

Drugstores

Japanese-style pharmacies are quite different from American drugstores. Most have Japanese medicines and personal care products and little else. You can find Western cosmetics, toiletries, and medicines in drugstores in major hotel arcades. In Tokyo, the American Pharmacy [Hibiya Park Building, 8-1, Yurakucho 1-chome, Chiyoda-ku, 100, Tel. (03) 3271-4034] carries many Western products.

Electricity

Japan's electrical current is 100 volts A.C. Eastern Japan, including Tokyo, is on 50 cycles, and Western Japan, including Osaka and Kyoto, is on 60 cycles. This is close enough to the American current of 110 volts and 60 cycles that small appliances like electric shavers and hair dryers can be used safely.

Film

Film is available throughout Japan. The brands and numbers are just like the ones you use at home if you're from the U.S. If you're from elsewhere and the numbers seem unfamiliar, the shopkeeper can help you select the kind you need.

Tipping

On the whole, Japan is a country where you don't need to tip. Most people in service occupations, like cabdrivers, waiters, and waitresses, for example, don't expect tips. There are a few exceptions to this general guideline. One is at major tourist hotels. There the bellhops have become used to tips for carrying baggage. And some hair styling salons in these hotels have signs which indicate that tipping is expected. Ten percent would be appropriate. At Japanese-style inns, or ryokan, you might want to tip the room-maid. Put the money (2,000 yen will cover several days' stay) in an envelope or wrap it in a piece of paper before presenting it to her.

MAJOR HOTELS

Note: Major hotels such as the ones listed here are similar in quality and service to those in Western cities. Another category is the business hotel, also Western-style, but inexpensive, with small rooms and no-frills service. Then there are the Japanese inns, or ryokan, where accommodations and service are traditional Japanese-style. Most major tourist hotels accept credit cards. Some business hotels and ryokan accept them, but you should check on this beforehand. Credit cards are still not as widely used in Japan as in the West, especially outside the large cities.

Tokyo (Area Code: 03)

Akasaka Prince Hotel
1-2 Kioicho, Chiyoda-ku 102
Tel: 3234-1111
Fax: 3262-5163

Akasaka Tokyu Hotel
2-14-3 Nagatacho
Chiyoda-ku 100
Tel: 3580-2311
Fax: 3580-6066

ANA Hotel Tokyo
1-12-33 Akasaka
Minato-ku 107
Tel: 3505-1111
Fax: 3505-1155

Capital Tokyu Hotel
2-10-3 Nagatacho
Chiyoda-ku 100
Tel: 3581-4511
Fax: 3581-5822

Century Hyatt Tokyo
2-7-2 Nishi-Shinjuku
Shinjuku-ku 160
Tel: 3349-0111
Fax: 3349-5575

Dai-ichi Hotel Tokyo
1-2-6 Shinbashi
Minato-ku 105
Tel: 3501-4411
Fax: 3595-2634

Ginza Dai-ichi Hotel
8-13-1 Ginza
Chuo-ku 104
Tel: 3542-5311
Fax: 3542-3030

Ginza Tokyu Hotel
5-15-9 Ginza
Chuo-ku 104
Tel: 3541-2411
Fax: 3541-6622

Haneda Tokyu Hotel
2-8-6 Haneda Kuko
Ota-ku 144
Tel: 3747-0311
Fax: 3747-0366

Holiday Inn Tokyo
1-13-7 Hatchobori
Chuo-ku 104
Tel: 3553-6161
Fax: 3553-6040

Hotel Grand Palace
1-1-1 Iidabashi
Chiyoda-ku 102
Tel: 3264-1111
Fax: 3230-4985

Hotel New Otani
4-1 Kioicho
Chiyoda-ku 102
Tel: 3265-1111
Fax: 3221-2619

Hotel Okura
2-10-4 Toranomon
Minato-ku 105
Tel: 3582-0111
Fax: 3582-3707

Hotel Pacific Meridien
3-13-3 Takanawa
Minato-ku 108
Tel: 3445-6711
Fax: 3445-5733

Imperial Hotel
1-1-1 Uchisaiwaicho
Chiyoda-ku 100
Tel: 3504-1111
Fax: 3581-9146

Keio Plaza Inter-Continental Hotel
2-2-1 Nishi-Shinjuku
Shinjuku-ku 160
Tel: 3344-0111
Fax: 3345-8269

Miyako Hotel Tokyo
1-1-50 Shiroganedai
Minato-ku 108
Tel: 3447-3111
Fax: 3447-3133

New Takanawa Prince Hotel
3-13-1 Takanawa
Minato-ku 108
Tel: 3442-1111
Fax: 3444-1234

Palace Hotel
1-1-1 Marunouchi
Chiyoda-ku 100
Tel: 3211-5211
Fax: 3211-6987

Shiba Park Hotel
1-5-10 Shibakoen
Minato-ku 105
Tel: 3433-4141
Fax: 5470-7519

Takanawa Prince Hotel
3-13-1 Takanawa
Minato-ku 108
Tel: 3447-1111
Fax: 3446-0849

Tokyo Hilton
6-6-2 Nishi-Shinjuku
Shinjuku-ku 160
Tel: 3344-5111
Fax: 3342-6094

Tokyo Marunouchi Hotel
1-6-3 Marunouchi
Chiyoda-ku 100
Tel: 3215-2151
Fax: 3215-8036

Tokyo Prince Hotel
3-3-1 Shiba Park
Minato-ku 105
Tel: 3432-1111
Fax: 3434-5551

Kyoto (Area Code: 075)

ANA Hotel Kyoto
Nijojomae, Horikawadori
Nakagyo-ku 604
Tel: 231-1155
Fax: 231-5333

Holiday Inn Kyoto
36 Nishihirakicho, Takano
Sakyo-ku 606
Tel: 721-3131
Fax: 781-6178

Hotel New Hankyu Kyoto
Shiokoji-shinmachi
Shimogyo-ku 600
Tel: 343-5300
Fax: 343-5324

International Hotel Kyoto
284 Nijo-Aburanokoji
Nakagyo-ku 604
Tel: 222-1111
Fax: 231-9381

Kyoto Century Hotel
680 Higashi-shiokoji shichijo-sagaru
Higashi-no-Toin-dori
Shimogyo-ku 600
Tel: 351-0111
Fax: 343-3721

Kyoto Grand Hotel
Higashi-Horikawa-Shiokoji
Shimogyo-ku 600
Tel: 341-2311
Fax: 341-3073

Kyoto Royal Hotel
Kawaramachi, Sanjo
Nakagyo-ku 604
Tel: 223-1234
Fax: 223-1702

Miyako Hotel
Sanjo-dori Keage
Higashiyama-ku 605
Tel: 771-7111
Fax: 751-2490

New Miyako Hotel
Nishi-Kujoincho
Minami-ku 601
Tel: 661-7111
Fax: 661-7135

Nagoya (Area Code: 052)

International Hotel Nagoya
3-23-3 Nishiki
Naka-ku 460
Tel: 961-3111
Fax: 962-5937

Hotel Nagoya Castle
3-19 Hinokuchicho
Nishi-ku 451
Tel: 521-2121
Fax: 531-3313

Nagoya Kanko Hotel
1-19-30 Nishiki
Naka-ku 460
Tel: 231-7711
Fax: 442-7413

Osaka (Area Code: 06)

Holiday Inn Nankai
2-5-15 Shinsaibashisuji
Chuo-ku 542
Tel: 213-8281
Fax: 213-8640

Plaza Hotel
2-2-49 Oyodo-Minami
Kita-ku 532
Tel: 453-1111
Fax: 454-0169

Royal Hotel
5-3-68 Nakanoshima
Kita-ku 530
Tel: 448-1121
Fax: 448-4414

Toyo Hotel
3-16-19 Toyosaki
Kita-ku 531
Tel: 372-8181
Fax: 372-8101

MAJOR RESTAURANTS

Japanese cuisine features many styles of cooking and types of food. Many leading restaurants specialize in one category of Japanese food. Some are listed here. Many of those on this list have several branches, usually of equal quality, including some in the major hotels. Most accept major credit cards, but to be sure, you should check beforehand.

Tokyo

Edogin—sushi
4-5-1 Tsukiji, Chuo-ku
Tel: 3543-4401

Inakaya—robatayaki
3-12-7 Akasaka, Minato-ku
Tel: 3586-3054

Kirakuzushi—sushi
3-16-12 Tsukiji, Chuo-ku
Tel: 3541-0908

Kitcho—kaiseki
Imperial Hotel
1-1-1 Uchisaiwaicho
Chiyoda-ku
Tel: 3504-0777

Seryna—sukiyaki, steak
3-12-2 Roppongi
Minato-ku
Tel: 3403-6211

Suehiro—sukiyaki, steak
6-11-2 Ginza, Chuo-ku
Tel: 3571-9271

Ten-ichi—tempura
6-6-5 Ginza, Chuo-ku
Tel: 3571-1949

Torigin—yakitori
5-5-7 Ginza, Chuo-ku
Tel: 3571-3333

Yamazato—Osaka-style food
Hotel Okura
2-10-4 Toranomon
Minato-ku
Tel: 3505-6070

Zakuro—shabu-shabu, sukiyaki
5-3-3 Akasaka
Minato-ku
Tel: 3582-6841

Kyoto

Hyotei—kaiseki
35 Kusakacho, Nanzenji, Sakyo-ku
Tel: 771-4166

Jubei—sushi
Shinbashi-agaru, Nawate-dori
Higashiyama-ku
Tel: 561-2698

Junidanya—shabu-shabu, sukiyaki
570-128 Minamigawa Gion Hanamikoji
Higashiyama-ku
Tel: 561-0213

Minokichi—kaiseki, sukiyaki
65 Awataguchi, Toriicho
Sanjo-agaru, Dobutsuenmae
Sakyo-ku
Tel: 771-4185

Suehiro Kyoto—sukiyaki, shabu-shabu
382 Komeyacho, Shijo-agaru
Kawaramachi-dori
Nakagyo-ku
Tel: 221-7188

Tsuruya—kaiseki
30 Higashi Tennocho
Okazaki, Sakyo-ku
Tel: 761-0171

Osaka

Aji-Kitcho—kaiseki
Daimaru Department Store, 8th floor
Shinsaibashi, Minami-ku
Tel: 251-1436

Honfukuzushi—sushi
1-12 Shinsaibashisuji
Minami-ku
Tel: 271-3344

Kagairo—kaiseki
Holiday Inn Nankai
28-1 Kyuzaemoncho
Minami-ku
Tel: 213-8422

Kani Doraku—crab
1-6-18 Dotonbori
Minami-ku
Tel: 211-8975

Kitamura—sukiyaki, steak
46 Higashi-Shimizumachi
Minami-ku
Tel: 245-4129

Matsubaya—udon
3-8-1 Minami-Semba
Minami-ku
Tel: 251-3339

Nadaman—kaiseki
Osaka Royal Hotel
5-3-68 Nakanoshima
Kita-ku
Tel: 443-7101
and
Osaka Tokyu Hotel
7-20 Chayamachi, Kita-ku
Tel: 376-0518

Suehiro Asahi—sukiyaki, steak
1-5-2 Sonezaki Shinchi
Kita-ku
Tel: 341-1760

USEFUL ADDRESSES

Ministry of International Trade and Industry (MITI)
1-3-1 Kasumigaseki
Chiyoda-ku
Tokyo 100
Tel: 03-3501-1511

Federation of Economic Organizations
Keidanren Kaikan
1-9-4 Otemachi, Chiyoda-ku
Tokyo 100
Tel: 03-3279-1411
Fax: 03-5225-6250

Japan External Trade Organization (JETRO)
2-2-5 Toranomon, Minato-ku
Tokyo 105
Tel: 03-3582-5511

American Chamber of Commerce in Japan
Fukide Building No. 2, 7th floor
4-1-21 Toranomon
Minato-ku

Tokyo 105
Tel: 03-3433-5381
Fax: 03-3436-1446

Kiwanis Club of Tokyo, Inc.
Sankei Building, 7th floor
1-7-2 Otemachi, Chiyoda-ku
Tokyo 100
Tel: 03-3242-0637
Fax: 03-3242-0637

Lions Clubs International
TOC Building, 10th floor
7-22-17 Nishi Gotanda, Shinagawa-ku
Tokyo 141
Tel: 03-3494-2931
Fax: 03-3494-2933

Rotary Club of Tokyo
Marunouchi Building, Room 660
2-4-1 Marunouchi, Chiyoda-ku
Tokyo 100
Tel: 03-3201-3888
Fax: 03-3201-3413

American Embassy
1-10-5 Akasaka, Minato-ku
Tokyo 107
Tel: 03-3224-5000

American Consulate General
2-11-5 Nishi Tenma, Kita-ku
Osaka 530
Tel: 06-315-5900

Japan National Tourist Organization (JNTO)

2-10-1 Yurakucho
Chiyoda-ku
Tokyo 100
Tel: 03-3216-1902
Fax: 03-3214-9680

Overseas Offices:

Rockefeller Plaza
630 Fifth Ave.
New York, NY 10111
Tel: 212-757-5640
Fax: 212-307-6754

401 North Michigan Ave., Suite 770,
Chicago, IL 60611
Tel: 312-222-0874
Fax: 312-222-0876

One Wilshire Bldg., Suite 2640
624 South Grand Avenue
Los Angeles, CA 90017
Tel: 213-623-1952
Fax: 213-623-6301

Tourist Information Centers (TIC)

Tokyo TIC
Kotani Bldg., 1-6-6
Yurakucho, Chiyoda-ku
Tokyo
Tel: 03-3502-1461

Narita TIC
Airport Terminal Bldg.,
Narita, Chiba Pref.
Tel: 0476-32-8711

Kyoto TIC
Kyoto Tower Bldg.
Higashi-Shiokojicho,
Shimogyo-ku
Kyoto
Tel: 075-371-5649

Guide Signs

Emergency Telephone

Parking

National Highway

Prefectural Highway

Entrance to Expressway

Service Area

Toll Gate

Next Exit

Exit

Detour

Caution Signs

Caution

Slippery

Regulation Signs

Road Closed

No Vehicles

No Entry

No Entry for Vehicles

No Entry for Vehicles or Motorcycles

No Right Turn

No U Turn

No Passing

No Parking, No Standing

No Parking

No Parking Over 60 Minutes

Maximum Speed

Minimum Speed

Cars Only

Bicycles Only

Pedestrians and Bicycles Only

Pedestrians Only

One Way

This Lane for Motorcycles and Lightweight Cars

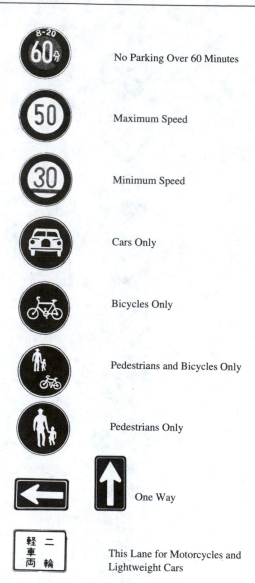

Stop

Slow Down

Sound Horn

End of Speed Limit Restriction

Indication Signs

Parking Permitted

Standing Permitted

Two Way Traffic Dividing Line

Traffic Island

Auxiliary Signs

Caution

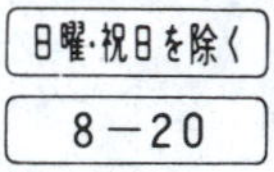

Except Sundays and Holidays

No Passing

End of Restriction

Soft Shoulder

Indication Board

Left Turn Permitted

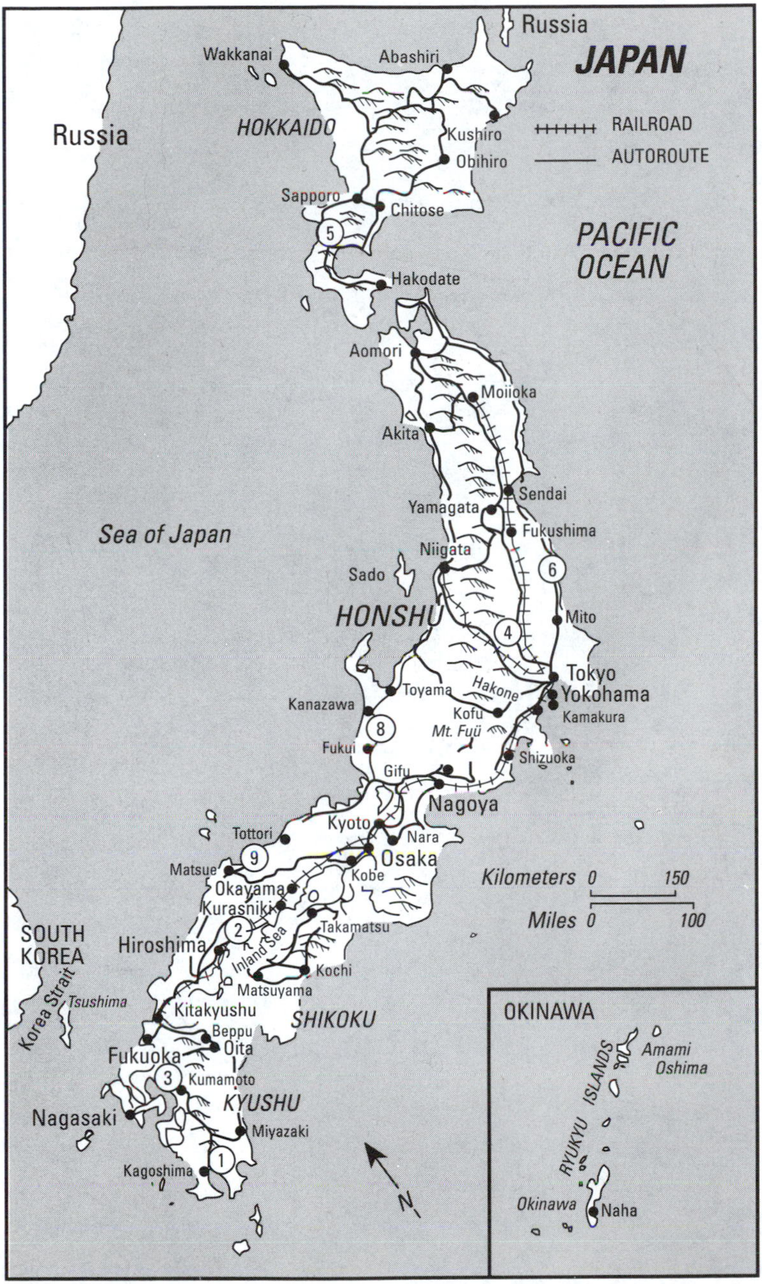
JAPAN
Russia
Russia
RAILROAD
AUTOROUTE
PACIFIC OCEAN
Sea of Japan
HOKKAIDO
HONSHU
SHIKOKU
KYUSHU
Wakkanai
Abashiri
Kushiro
Obihiro
Sapporo
Chitose
Hakodate
Aomori
Moiioka
Akita
Sendai
Yamagata
Fukushima
Niigata
Sado
Mito
Tokyo
Yokohama
Kamakura
Hakone
Toyama
Kanazawa
Kofu
Mt. Fuji
Fukui
Shizuoka
Gifu
Nagoya
Kyoto
Nara
Osaka
Kobe
Tottori
Matsue
Okayama
Kurashiki
Hiroshima
Inland Sea
Takamatsu
Kochi
Matsuyama
Kitakyushu
Beppu
Oita
Fukuoka
Kumamoto
Nagasaki
Miyazaki
Kagoshima
SOUTH KOREA
Korea Strait
Tsushima
Kilometers 0 150
Miles 0 100
N
1
2
3
4
5
6
8
9
OKINAWA
RYUKYU ISLANDS
Amami Oshima
Okinawa
Naha

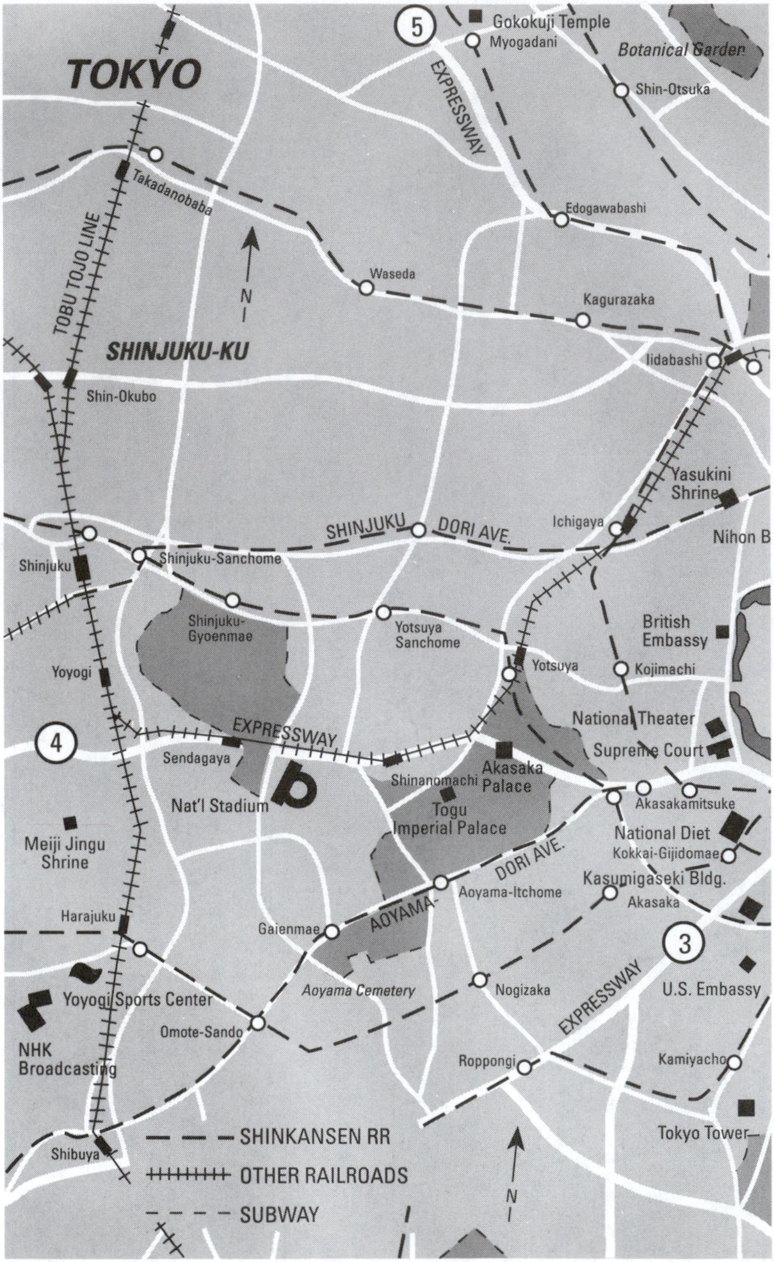
TOKYO
SHINJUKU-KU
TOBU TOJO LINE
5
Gokokuji Temple
Myogadani
Botanical Garden
EXPRESSWAY
Shin-Otsuka
Takadanobaba
Edogawabashi
N
Waseda
Kagurazaka
Iidabashi
Shin-Okubo
Yasukini Shrine
SHINJUKU DORI AVE.
Ichigaya
Nihon B
Shinjuku
Shinjuku-Sanchome
Shinjuku-Gyoenmae
Yotsuya Sanchome
British Embassy
Yoyogi
Yotsuya
Kojimachi
National Theater
4
EXPRESSWAY
Supreme Court
Sendagaya
Akasaka Palace
Shinanomachi
Nat'l Stadium
Togu Imperial Palace
Akasakamitsuke
National Diet
Meiji Jingu Shrine
Kokkai-Gijidomae
DORI AVE.
Kasumigaseki Bldg.
Aoyama-Itchome
Akasaka
AOYAMA-
Harajuku
Gaienmae
3
Aoyama Cemetery
Nogizaka
EXPRESSWAY
U.S. Embassy
Yoyogi Sports Center
Omote-Sando
NHK Broadcasting
Roppongi
Kamiyacho
SHINKANSEN RR
Tokyo Tower
Shibuya
OTHER RAILROADS
SUBWAY
N

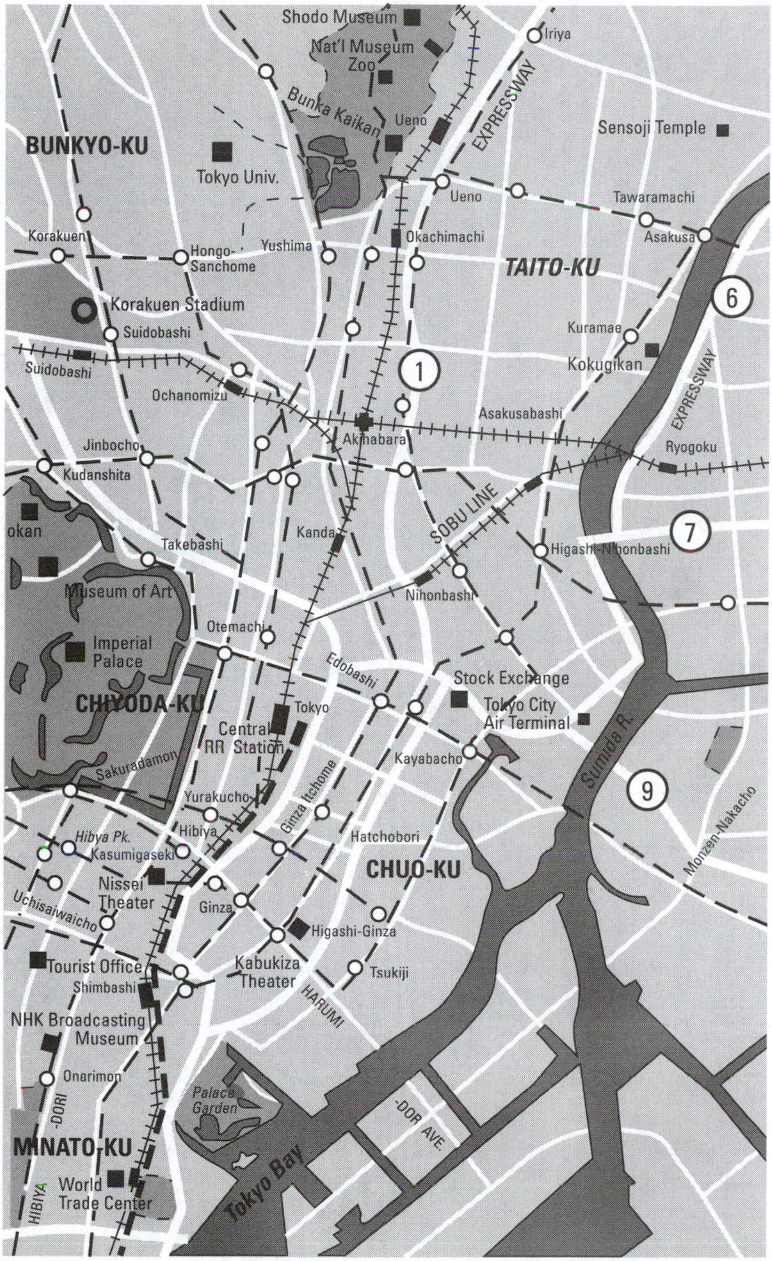
Shodo Museum
Nat'l Museum
Zoo
Iriya
Bunka Kaikan
Ueno
EXPRESSWAY
Sensoji Temple
BUNKYO-KU
Tokyo Univ.
Ueno
Tawaramachi
Korakuen
Hongo-Sanchome
Yushima
Okachimachi
Asakusa
TAITO-KU
Korakuen Stadium
6
Suidobashi
Kuramae
Kokugikan
Suidobashi
1
EXPRESSWAY
Ochanomizu
Asakusabashi
Akihabara
Jinbocho
Ryogoku
Kudanshita
SOBU LINE
okan
Kanda
7
Takebashi
Higashi-Nihonbashi
Museum of Art
Nihonbashi
Otemachi
Imperial Palace
Edobashi
Stock Exchange
CHIYODA-KU
Tokyo
Tokyo City Air Terminal
Central RR Station
Kayabacho
Sumida R.
Sakuradamon
9
Ginza Itchome
Yurakucho
Monzen-Nakacho
Hibiya
Hatchobori
Hibiya Pk.
Kasumigaseki
CHUO-KU
Nissei Theater
Uchisaiwaicho
Ginza
Higashi-Ginza
Tourist Office
Kabukiza Theater
Tsukiji
Shimbashi
HARUMI
NHK Broadcasting Museum
Onarimon
Palace Garden
-DOR AVE.
HIBIYA -DORI
MINATO-KU
World Trade Center
Tokyo Bay

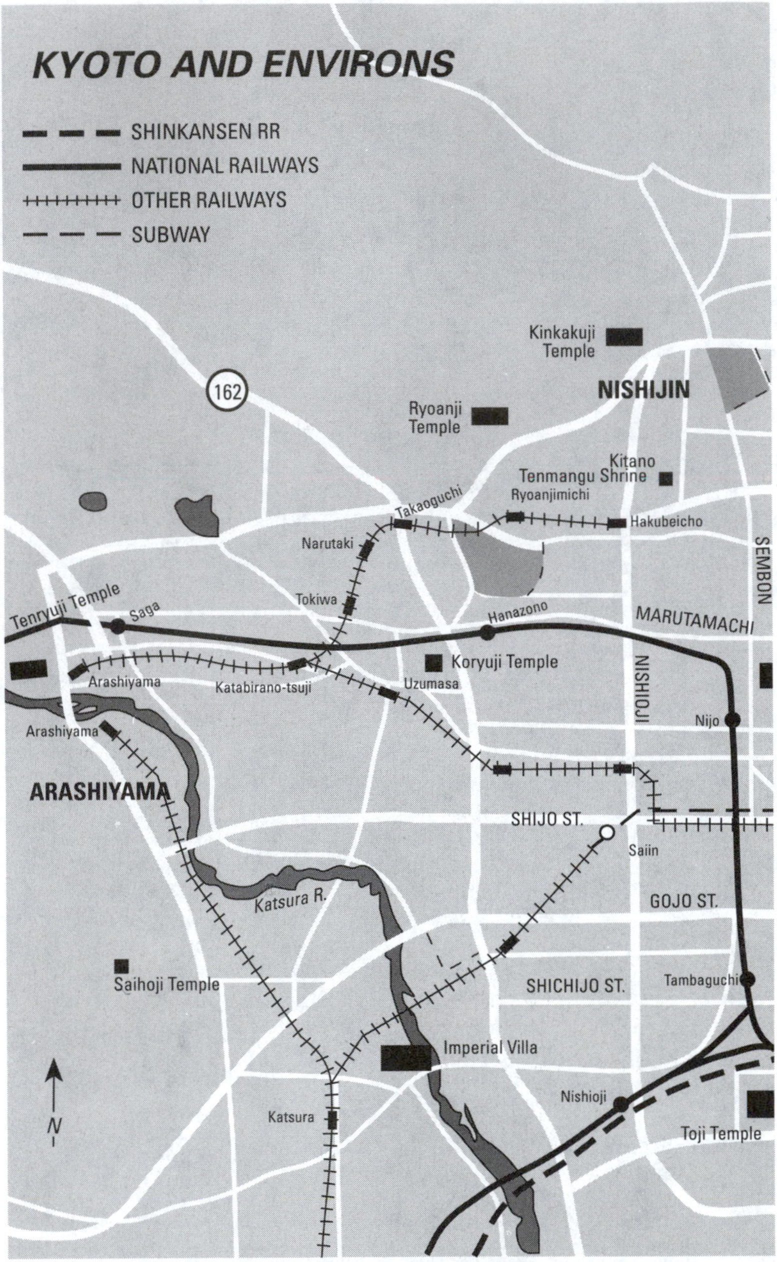
KYOTO AND ENVIRONS
SHINKANSEN RR
NATIONAL RAILWAYS
OTHER RAILWAYS
SUBWAY
Kinkakuji Temple
NISHIJIN
162
Ryoanji Temple
Kitano Tenmangu Shrine
Ryoanjimichi
Takaoguchi
Hakubeicho
Narutaki
SEMBON
Tokiwa
Tenryuji Temple
Saga
Hanazono
MARUTAMACHI
Koryuji Temple
Arashiyama
Katabirano-tsuji
Uzumasa
NISHIOJI
Nijo
Arashiyama
ARASHIYAMA
SHIJO ST.
Saiin
Katsura R.
GOJO ST.
Saihoji Temple
SHICHIJO ST.
Tambaguchi
Imperial Villa
N
Nishioji
Katsura
Toji Temple

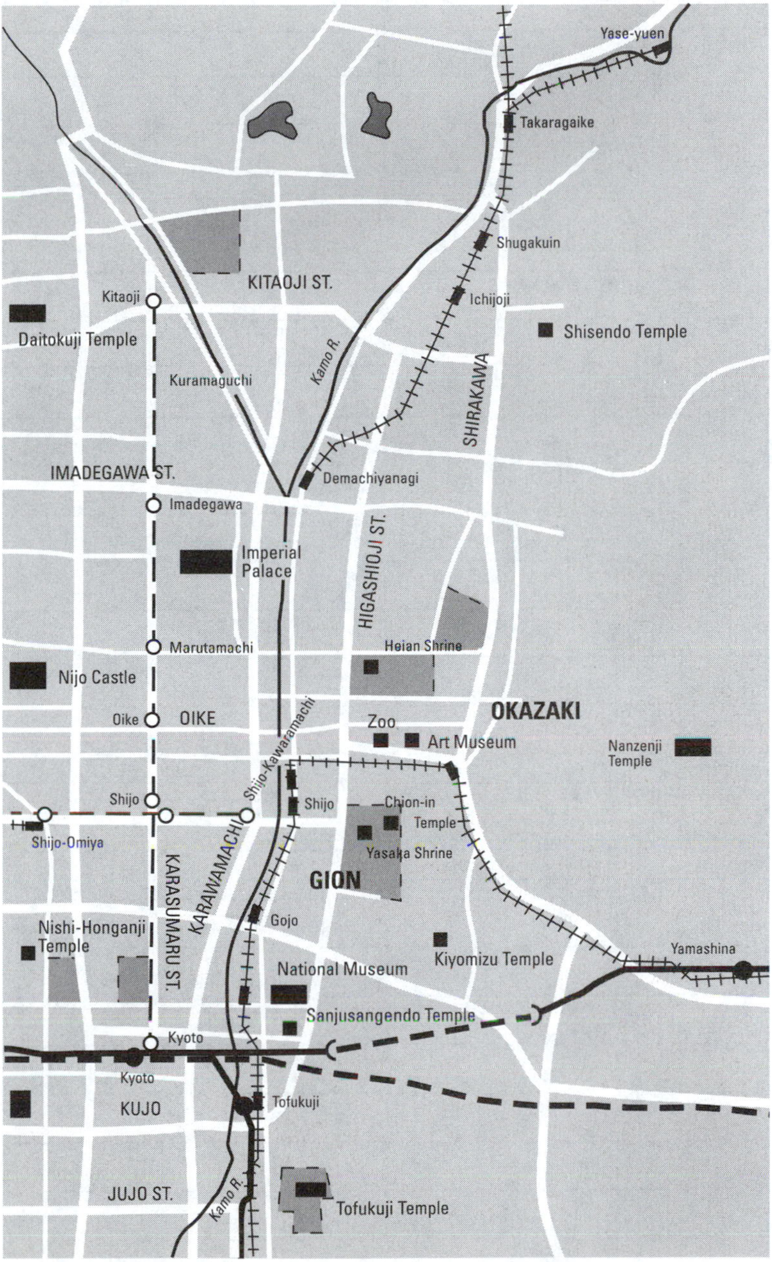
Yase-yuen
Takaragaike
Shugakuin
Ichijoji
Shisendo Temple
KITAOJI ST.
Kitaoji
Daitokuji Temple
Kuramaguchi
Kamo R.
SHIRAKAWA
IMADEGAWA ST.
Demachiyanagi
Imadegawa
Imperial
Palace
HIGASHIOJI ST.
Marutamachi
Heian Shrine
Nijo Castle
Shijo-Kawaramachi
Oike
OIKE
OKAZAKI
Zoo
Art Museum
Nanzenji
Temple
Shijo
Shijo
Chion-in
Temple
Shijo-Omiya
Yasaka Shrine
KARASUMARU ST.
KARAWAMACHI
GION
Gojo
Nishi-Honganji
Temple
Kiyomizu Temple
Yamashina
National Museum
Sanjusangendo Temple
Kyoto
Kyoto
KUJO
Tofukuji
JUJO ST.
Kamo R.
Tofukuji Temple

DAILY DIARY

Date: ____________ Place: ____________

Weather: ____________

Hotel: ____________

Restaurants/Cafes: ____________

Interesting Places: ____________

Names & Addresses: ____________

EXPENSE RECORD

Currency Exchanged ____________

Your Currency ____________

Foreign Currency ____________

Rate ____________

Fee (if any) ____________

Expenses

Hotel: ____________

Food: ____________

Breakfast ____________

Lunch ____________

Dinner ____________

Drinks/Snacks ____________

Gifts/Purchases ____________

____

____

____

Sightseeing/Transportation ____________

____

____

____

Miscellaneous ____________

____

____

____

____

DAILY DIARY

Date: ____________________ Place: ____

Weather: ____

Hotel: ____

Restaurants/Cafes: ____

____

____

Interesting Places: ____

____

____

____

____

____

____

____

____

Names & Addresses: ____

____

____

____

____

____

____

____

____

____

EXPENSE RECORD

Currency Exchanged ______________________

Your Currency ______________________

Foreign Currency ______________________

Rate ______________________

Fee (if any) ______________________

Expenses

Hotel: ______________________

Food: ______________________

Breakfast ______________________

Lunch ______________________

Dinner ______________________

Drinks/Snacks ______________________

Gifts/Purchases ______________________

____

____

____

Sightseeing/Transportation ______________________

____

____

____

Miscellaneous ______________________

____

____

____

____